The Origins of the A

The interwar period marked a transition from a Gulf society characterized by symbiosis and interdependency to a subregion characterized by national divisions, sectarian suspicions, rivalries, and political tension. In this study, Chelsi Mueller tells the story of a formative period in the Gulf, examining the triangular relationship between Iran, Britain, and the Gulf Arab shaykhdoms. By doing so, Mueller reveals how the revival of Iranian national ambitions in the Gulf had a significant effect on the dense web of Arab-Iranian relations during the interwar period. Shedding new light on our current understanding of the present-day Arab-Iranian conflict, this study, which pays particular attention to Bahrain and the Trucial States (United Arab Emirates), fills a significant gap in the literature on the history of Arab-Iranian relations in the Gulf and Iran's Persian Gulf policy during the Reza Shah period.

CHELSI MUELLER is a research fellow at the Moshe Dayan Center for Middle Eastern and African Studies at Tel Aviv University.

The Origins of the Arab-Iranian Conflict

Nationalism and Sovereignty in the Gulf between the World Wars

CHELSI MUELLER
Tel Aviv University

CAMBRIDGE
UNIVERSITY PRESS

CAMBRIDGE
UNIVERSITY PRESS

University Printing House, Cambridge CB2 8BS, United Kingdom

One Liberty Plaza, 20th Floor, New York, NY 10006, USA

477 Williamstown Road, Port Melbourne, VIC 3207, Australia

314-321, 3rd Floor, Plot 3, Splendor Forum, Jasola District Centre, New Delhi - 110025, India

103 Penang Road, #05-06/07, Visioncrest Commercial, Singapore 238467

Cambridge University Press is part of the University of Cambridge.

It furthers the University's mission by disseminating knowledge in the pursuit of education, learning and research at the highest international levels of excellence.

www.cambridge.org
Information on this title: www.cambridge.org/9781108733410
DOI: 10.1017/9781108773881

First published 2020
First paperback edition 2022

A catalogue record for this publication is available from the British Library

Library of Congress Cataloging in Publication data
Names: Mueller, Chelsi, 1978– author.
Title: The origins of the Arab-Iranian conflict : nationalism and sovereignty in the Gulf between the World Wars / Chelsi Mueller.
Description: Cambridge, United Kingdom ; New York, NY : Cambridge University Press, 2020. | Includes bibliographical references and index.
Identifiers: LCCN 2019037795 (print) | LCCN 2019037796 (ebook) | ISBN 9781108489089 (hardback) | ISBN 9781108733410 (paperback) | ISBN 9781108773881 (epub)
Subjects: LCSH: Nationalism–Iran–History–20th century. | Iran–Foreign relations–Persian Gulf States. | Persian Gulf States–Foreign relations–Iran.
Classification: LCC DS274.2.P35 M84 2020 (print) | LCC DS274.2.P35 (ebook) | DDC 953.05/2–dc23
LC record available at https://lccn.loc.gov/2019037795
LC ebook record available at https://lccn.loc.gov/2019037796

ISBN 978-1-108-48908-9 Hardback
ISBN 978-1-108-73341-0 Paperback

Contents

Maps and Figures

Maps

Figures

Acknowledgments

This book is based on a doctoral dissertation supervised by David Menashri and Uzi Rabi at Tel Aviv University. David has been a constant pillar of support and encouragement and for his kindness I am truly grateful. Uzi took me under his wing and helped me through each stage in the process. I could not have done this without him.

This book would not have been possible without the support of numerous institutions and individuals. It was supported by generous scholarships and fellowships from Tel Aviv University, the Lester and Sally Entin Faculty of Humanities, the Zvi Yavetz Graduate School of History, the Alliance Center for Iranian Studies, the Maccabim Foundation, the Moshe Dayan Center for Middle Eastern and African Studies, and the Joseph Kostiner Arabian Peninsula and Persian Gulf Program.

I also want to acknowledge the contributions of the Department of Middle Eastern and African History, especially Meir Litvak, Ami Ayalon, and Joseph Kostiner. Meir Litvak was very supportive: he encouraged my participation in conferences, pushed me to publish, and provided invaluable comments and invaluable advice during the process. Ami Ayalon directed the doctoral seminar during which time I received valuable and constructive comments on a draft of my first chapter from him and from my graduate cohort. I was also fortunate enough to have the opportunity to study under the late Joseph (Yossi) Kostiner. He offered me the opportunity to become his research assistant and shared with me his insights on tribal politics in the Arabian Peninsula. It was under his tutelage that I developed an interest in states and tribes in the Persian Gulf. The graduate students who worked with him are well aware of what a gracious gift he gave us.

I want to acknowledge the kindness and support I received from the staff at the libraries and archives I worked in, including the British Library, the British National Archives, and the SOAS Library at the University of London. Special thanks go to Marion Gliksberg and

Rakefet Cohen, the dedicated staff of the Moshe Dayan Center library, who put up with my constant requests to look at the Cambridge Archive Editions, which are housed there.

I also owe a debt of gratitude to the external reviewers of my dissertation, Christopher Davidson and James Onley. Their reviews were encouraging and their suggestions were very insightful. James went above and beyond the role of an external reader. He meticulously read my work and addressed a number of issues great and small. His generosity and involvement contributed significantly to helping me revise the manuscript. I want to thank Homa Katouzian for reading my work with interest and for the very valuable suggestions he offered. And I also want to thank the two blind reviewers who carefully read this manuscript and wrote immensely valuable critiques and suggestions that helped me to revise and polish the final manuscript. Needless to say, any errors that remain are my own.

I owe a great deal of thanks to my colleague Nir Boms who has energetically supported me and advocated for me. I owe special thanks to Eline Rosenhart, who held my hand throughout the writing of this book. And finally, I want to thank all of my family, the Mueller's, Zimmerman's, Taylor's, Tollen's, Sisler's, Lattimore's, and Cashman's, who encouraged me during my many years as a graduate student.

Transliteration, Terms, and Conventions

Arabic and Persian

As this work includes names and terms from both Arabic and Persian and cites sources in Arabic and Persian, it makes use of two different transliteration schemes. Arabic names, terms and references follow the *International Journal of Middle East Studies* (IJMES) scheme, while Persian follows the scheme prescribed by *Iranian Studies*. While diacritical marks have been omitted, *'Ayn* and *hamza* are preserved as ' and ' in the text, except for the initial *hamza*, which is dropped. The word "the" is retained along with the definite article "*al-*."

The plural of transliterated terms that appear frequently is formed with an –s (*Kargozars*, e.g.). Words found in Merriam-Webster's are spelled as they are in that dictionary and not italicized (e.g., shah, mudir, and nakhoda). Place names are spelled in accordance with the most common contemporary English usage (thus Shariqah is Sharjah, Ra's al-Khaima is Ras al-Khaimah, al-Manama is Manama, and Bandar-e Bushehr is Bushehr). For names of places in Iran preference is given to the Persian rendering (hence Henjam is Hengam).

In the official correspondence of the period Arabic and Persian names are often transliterated erratically, hence Easa, Isa, and Esa could all refer to the same person. The original forms are preserved in quotations but their transliterations have been standardized in the footnotes. Personal names are spelled in accordance with the transliteration scheme of either IJMES or *Iranian Studies* but without diacritics (thus, e.g., "Muhammad" in Arabic and "Mohammad" in Persian). Names are spelled in accordance with an individual or family's preferred use, whenever documentary evidence of a clear preference exists (e.g., business correspondences from the interwar period indicate a clear preference for the spelling of the family name "Bushiri" over "Bushehri" and "Farook" over "Faruk").

Iran and Persia

Since ancient times – and in the Persian documents cited in this work – Persian speakers have referred to the country as *Iran*. In the Western world – and in British archival documents – the country was referred to as *Persia* until 1935 when Reza Shah asked foreign diplomats to refer to the country as *Iran*. This work makes use of the name *Iran* throughout, except where direct quotes – especially from British official documents – refer to the country as *Persia*. The term *Persian* is used in the cultural sense (i.e., Persian shop) or as a referent to the language, also known as Farsi.

Iranians and Persians

Issues of identity, such as Arab or Persian, and the various gradations between the two, form the subject of much debate between scholars. When such distinctions are made in this book, it is an effort to represent, as accurately as possible, the perceptions and self-perceptions of the actors in the story.

With a few notable exceptions, immigrants and children of immigrants, arriving to the Arab shaykhdoms from places in Iran, whether Sunni or Shiʿi, are identified in this study as *Iranian* in preference to the alternatives – Persian or *ʿAjam*. In the Persian language sources from this period, the prevalent term used by Iranian immigrants to describe themselves is *Irani* – Iranian. Some Iranians also referred to themselves as *ʿAjam*. *ʿAjam* was a name given them by Arabs, a pejorative word used to refer to someone who could not speak Arabic properly.

One exception to this rule includes the use of the term *Baluch* to describe the tribal inhabitants of Baluchistan, part of which lies in southeastern Iran (also called Makran). The other notable exception applies to a distinct group of people who identify as *Hawala*. This group is composed of Sunnis of southern Iranian origin, who depicted their transfer to the Arab shaykhdoms of the southern littoral as a "return" to the land of their forebears after a long sojourn in southern Iran. There is ample debate from within the community as well as from outside, as to whether it can be said that *Hawala* are ethnically Arab. It is also important to stress that not all Sunnis who immigrated to the Arab port towns from Iran claimed Arab ancestry or defined themselves as *Hawala*, although the term *Hawala* is elastic. Some Sunni immigrants from Iran depicted themselves as ethnic Persians. This book does not take a stand on the ethnic issue, but rather endeavors to portray the actors in the story as they portray themselves.

Persian Titles and Adopted Names

Iranian elites active in politics before and after the passage of the 1925 Law of Identity and Status, are introduced upon the first mention by both their title and their adopted family name. Thereafter each individual is referred to by the name that he is most recognized by in the historical literature. Thus, the statesman, Mohammad 'Ali Forughi Zoka' al-Molk, is introduced by his name and title and thereafter he is referred to as Mohammad 'Ali Forughi.

The Arabian Littoral

The Arabian littoral of the Persian Gulf is a geographical designation, referring to the eastern coastline of the Arabian Peninsula, without respect to the ethno-linguistic characteristics of its inhabitants. The Arabian littoral is also variously referred to as the Arabian coast or the southern littoral of the Persian Gulf.

The term "Arab shaykhdoms" refers to the small Persian Gulf societies centered around port towns along the southern littoral and ruled by Arab tribal shaykhs, including Kuwait, Bahrain, Qatar, and the Trucial States. Abu Dhabi, Dubai, Sharjah, Ajman, Umm al-Quwain, Ras al-Khaimah, and Fujairah were known collectively as the "Trucial States" until 1971 and the United Arab Emirates thereafter. Other names for the Trucial States include "Trucial Oman," the "Trucial Coast," and the "Trucial Shaykhdoms."

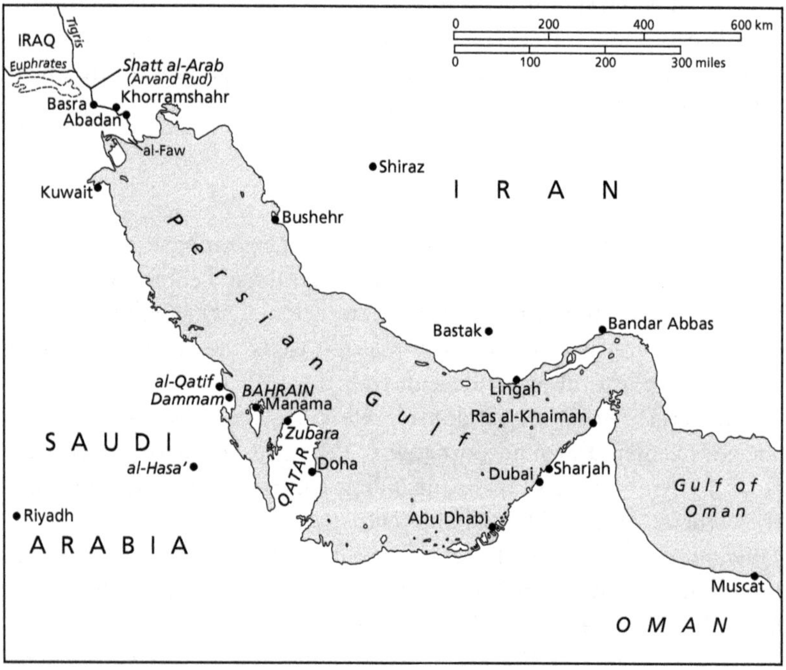

Map 1 The Persian Gulf.

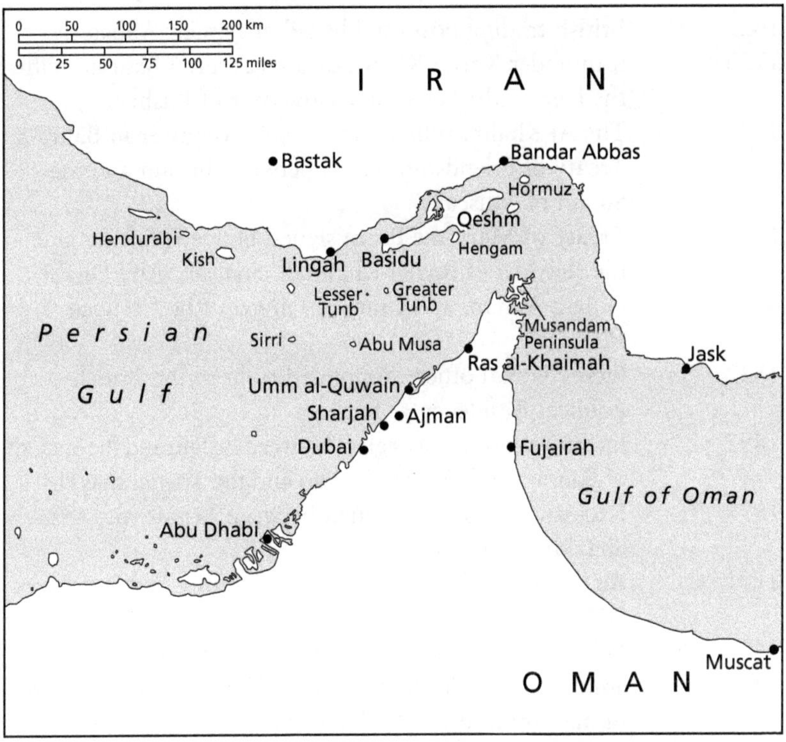

Map 2 The Strait of Hormuz.

Chronology of Major Events

1622	British trading post established at Bandar Abbas
1753	Iran under Karim Khan Zand recaptured Bahrain with the help of the hereditary Governor of Bushehr
1783	The Al Khalifa ruling family came to power in Bahrain
1798	Treaty of Friendship signed between Britain and the Sultan of Muscat
1820	Treaty of Maritime Peace signed between Britain and the shaykhs of Ras al-Khaimah, Sharjah, Abu Dhabi, Dubai, Ajman, and Umm al-Quwain (the "Trucial shaykhs")
1822	First colonial officer appointed to head the British Political Residency at Bushehr
1892	Exclusive agreements signed between Britain and the Shaykh of Bahrain and between Britain and the Trucial shaykhs
1899	Exclusive agreement signed between Britain and the Shaykh of Kuwait
1901	An oil concession obtained from Iran by William Knox D'Arcy
1900–1904	Belgian advisers set up an efficient customs administration in the Persian Gulf Ports spurring waves of migration to the Arabian littoral
1905–1911	Constitutional Revolution in Iran
1907	The Anglo-Russian Convention is signed partitioning Iran into British and Russian spheres of influence and a neutral zone
1909	Anglo-Persian Oil Company formed and D'Arcy concession acquired
1916	Exclusive agreement signed between Britain and the Emir of Qatar
1919	Anglo-Iranian Treaty signed but not ratified
1919	Iranian delegation denied a seat at the Congress of Versailles

1921	Anglo-Iranian Treaty nullified by the Majles
1921	Military coup carried out in Iran by Reza Khan and Sayyed Zia' al-Din Tabataba'i
1921	Russo-Iranian Treaty of Friendship signed
1922	Uprising of the Baharna (Arab Shi'a) in Bahrain
1923	Instructions issued to Iran's port officials to treat Bahrainis as Iranian citizens
1923	Outbreak of sectarian violence involving Iranian nationals in Bahrain
1925	Abolition of the Qajar dynasty
1925	Instructions issued to Iran's port officials to treat all travelers from the southern littoral as Iranian citizens
1925	Shaykh Khaz'al subdued and Arabistan brought under central authority; the older name "Khuzestan" replaced the name "Arabistan"
1926	Coronation of Reza Shah Pahlavi
1927	Britain recognized the independence of Ibn Sa'ud in the Treaty of Jeddah
1927	Iran's Bahrain claim submitted to the League of Nations
1928	Iran's reassertion of sovereignty over Hengam Island
1928	Negotiations begun toward the conclusion of an Anglo-Iranian treaty
1928	A thorough reexamination of Persian Gulf policy initiated by London
1929	The Great Depression and the introduction of cultured pearls hastened the decline of the Persian Gulf pearling industry
1929	Iran formally recognized Iraq and Ibn Sa'ud's Kingdom of the Hijaz and Najd
1930	An oil concession in Bahrain granted to the Bahrain Petroleum Company
1932	British air route transferred from the Iranian to the Arabian littoral
1932	Iranian naval ships arrive to the Persian Gulf
1933	A year of crisis in Anglo-Iranian relations: British flag hauled down at Basidu; Iranian customs *mudir* arrested by British officers
1934	An oil concession in Kuwait granted to the Kuwait Oil Company

1935	British naval facilities at Hengam and Basidu evacuated and moved to al-Jufayr, Bahrain
1937	Promulgation of the Nationality and Property Laws in Bahrain endeavored to turn wealthy traders from Iran into Bahraini citizens
1938	Reform movements in Kuwait, Dubai, and Bahrain
1941	Iran invaded by British and Soviet forces; Reza Shah forced to abdicate

Introduction

The geopolitical rivalry between the Gulf Arab states and Iran has its origins in the interwar period, the period between the Paris Peace Conference in 1919, which marked the end of the First World War, until 1941 when the Persian Gulf became a theater of the Second World War. The interwar period was a formative period because it marked a transition from a Gulf society characterized by symbiosis and interdependency to a subregion characterized by national divisions, sectarian suspicions, rivalries, and political tension. The introduction of Iranian nationalism to the Persian Gulf waterway, islands, and littoral and the unprecedented interventions of the British government in the Arab shaykhdoms including Kuwait, Qatar, Bahrain, Dubai, Abu Dhabi, Sharjah, and Ras al-Khaimah, constituted a watershed in the history of the Persian Gulf, disrupted centuries of unrestricted movement, refashioned frameworks of exchange between the two shores, and forged an acute Arab-Iranian dichotomy that would characterize the Persian Gulf into the twenty-first century.

Cultural animosity between Arabs and Iranians has been centuries in the making. A prominent example is the way that Arabs are depicted in the *Shahnameh*, the epic tale of Persian kings composed more than a thousand years ago. Its author, Ferdowsi, derided Arabs as an uncivilized people who drank camel's milk and ate lizard meat. In the nineteenth and twentieth centuries, some Iranian intellectuals have even gone so far as to trace Iran's weaknesses back to its conquest in the seventh century by "barbaric" Arab nomads.[1] Persians, too, have been scorned and mocked by Arabs. The difficulties faced by immigrants from Iran who have tried to gain acceptance in the tribally organized Arab societies of the Gulf are exemplified by the moniker ʿAjam, a pejorative term that denotes "foreigners" but is used almost exclusively

[1] David Menashri, *Post-Revolutionary Politics in Iran: Religion, Society, and Power* (London: Frank Cass, 2001), pp. 237–238.

of Persians. The hardening of Arabs' attitudes toward Iran was prominently reflected in the nomenclature – the Arabian Gulf – which was introduced into the political discourse during the interwar period, but would gain particular prominence during the heyday of Gamal Abdel Nasser.

Religious differences, which are also cultural differences, have their roots in antiquity. The Persian Gulf is the epicenter of the Sunni-Shi'i divide, the origins of which can be traced back to the early days of Islam and the struggle for succession in the Muslim world after the death of the Prophet Mohammad. Since the Battle of Karbala in 680, in which Hussein, a direct descendant of the Prophet was defeated by the Umayyad Caliph, the cry for revenge by his supporters has divided the Muslim community. At that time the defeated supporters of Hussein became like a dissident faction – the Shi'a. In the subsequent centuries, persecution and exclusion of the Shi'a at the hands of the Sunnis perpetuated the rivalry between the communities of the two major traditions of Islam. The conversion of Iran to Shi'i Islam further divided Arabs and Persians. But the split did not conform to national or geographic lines. Arab Shi'a have long been a minority in most Arab countries, and a majority in Iraq and Bahrain.

Indeed, the Persian Gulf basin sits astride the region's major geographical, cultural and religious fault lines. And yet, even while the Gulf's inhabitants dwell in the clefts and ridges of these sectarian fault lines, there has been at least as much impetus for cooperation and interdependence between them as there has been for division. For millennia, the upper and lower Gulf littorals comprised an integrated societal unit – united by linguistic, cultural, religious, tribal, maritime, and commercial factors – the inhabitants of the two shores having more in common with each other than with the nomadic or agricultural peasant societies dwelling on the Iranian and Arabian plateaus. The Gulf's physical location between the Zagros Mountains of Iran and the foreboding deserts of Arabia encouraged the inhabitants of the northern and southern littorals to supply their needs from within and through economic connections with each other.[2]

[2] Lawrence G. Potter, "Introduction" to *The Persian Gulf in History*, ed. Lawrence G. Potter (New York: Palgrave Macmillan, 2009), pp. 1–24. See also Lawrence G. Potter, "Society in the Persian Gulf: Before and after Oil," CIRS Occasional Paper No. 18 (Georgetown University in Qatar, 2017).

It was during the period between the First World War and the Second World War that this integrated and interdependent Persian Gulf civilization came to be characterized by rivalry and competition. The form that the Arab-Iranian conflict in the Gulf has taken today has less to do with ancient religious and ethnic divides and more to do with the introduction of modern political forces – namely, imperial intervention, state formation, and the rise of nationalism. The introduction of Iranian nationalism into the Persian Gulf during the interwar period, a period that roughly corresponds to the rule of Reza Shah Pahlavi (1921–1941),[3] and the challenge that Iran posed to the dominant imperial power in the region elicited an unprecedented degree of imperial intervention in the smaller tribal societies situated around its perimeter. To obstruct Iranian ambitions in the Gulf, British policy makers decided to reinforce the authority of the Gulf's ruling shaykhs. These actions expedited a process whereby tribal rulers were transformed into absolute monarchs. This process was underway before the advent of oil. Britain's policy of denying Iran a role to play also laid the foundations of the modern security architecture in the Gulf, which excludes Iran and relies upon an outside security guarantor.

This book tells a story of the formative period in the history of the Persian Gulf with particular attention to the roles of the main political actors, Iran, Britain, and the Arab shaykhdoms. With regard to the Arab shaykhdoms, Bahrain and the Trucial States are presented as case studies that can shed light on the role of the smaller, tribal societies centered around port towns on the Arabian littoral of the Persian Gulf, during the interwar period. The book examines the revival of Iranian national ambitions in the Persian Gulf under Reza Shah Pahlavi, the challenge that Reza Shah's assertive Persian Gulf policy posed to Britain's hegemonic position in the Persian Gulf, the challenge it posed to the Arab shaykhdoms under British protection, and the effect of these dynamics on the dense web of Arab-Iranian relations in the Gulf. It investigates the Arab shaykhs' relationships with Britain during the interwar period when Iran contested Britain's position in the Gulf and the independent status of the Arab shaykhs under Britain's protection. It surveys the different expressions of Iranian nationalism and

[3] Reza Khan's rise to power began in 1921 when he became the minister of war. In 1923 he became the prime minister and in 1925, after deposing Ahmad Shah Qajar, he was proclaimed the Shah of Iran and took the name Reza Shah Pahlavi.

patriotism among Iranian immigrant communities in the Gulf Arab shaykhdoms and the perceptions and responses of the shaykhs and inhabitants of the Arabian littoral to this phenomenon. It also explores how local actors, such as merchants, state officials, and military men influenced and responded to efforts by states to create or challenge boundaries, to control movement, and to sanction or limit contact between individuals in the contested frontier region.

Reza Shah's Persian Gulf policy was strongly influenced by a particularly virulent strain of anti-colonial, nationalist impulses that emerged in Iran in the aftermath of the First World War. The highly visible British presence in the Persian Gulf was a lightning rod for the vital expression of anti-British sentiment during the war and in its aftermath. Britain's support for the Al Khalifa shaykhs of Bahrain, and the Al Qasimi shaykhs who claimed Abu Musa and the Tunbs – like their support for Shaykh Khaz'al in Khuzestan and other semi-autonomous tribal chiefs in the south – was viewed as part of a colonial strategy that was designed to deny Iran its territorial sovereignty and independence. Under Reza Shah, Iran contested Britain's claim to be the protector of Arab shaykhs in the Persian Gulf and challenged its position as the main security provider in the Persian Gulf waterway. Nationalist sentiments were expressed in territorial terms: the entire Persian Gulf, including the islands, waterway, and the shaykhdoms on the Arabian littoral, were depicted as usurped Iranian frontiers. Iran's claim to be the only legitimate sovereign in the Persian Gulf – a claim that resonated in the minds of many Iranian people – gained the shah some leverage that he could use to reduce British influence in southern Iran and loosen British authority in and around Iran's territorial waters.

Reza Shah succeeded in extending the authority of the central government over Iran's ports, islands, and territorial waters. The British government was obliged to relinquish its assets and evacuate its posts on the Iranian side of the Gulf, and the modern Iranian navy and customs administration came into being. One area in which the shah failed was in his policy toward the Arab shaykhdoms of the Persian Gulf: Reza Shah's government sought to establish relations with the Arab shaykhs of the southern littoral and, at the same time, promoted its claims to be the rightful sovereign over their domains. The Arabs' fear of Iran strengthened their reliance on British protection allowing Britain to further entrench its position on the Arabian littoral and making it all the more difficult for Iran to successfully appeal to the shaykhs. While Reza Shah's efforts to assume responsibility for policing the Gulf met with limited success, the introduction of Iranian nationalism into the Gulf waterway engendered both feelings of pride on the part of Iranians as well as feelings of superiority that, at times, produced destructive consequences. Heavy-handed treatment of travelers from the lower Gulf by Iran's port authorities sowed the seeds of resentment and mistrust. This stifled the flow of goods and people to and from Iran. Furthermore, harsh enforcement of new policies that were intended to bring about national unity prompted waves of emigration from Iran's southern coastal areas to the Arab shaykhdoms of the lower Gulf.

Iran's repudiation of foreign interference and its articulation of an assertive, anti-colonial, and nationalist policy brought about a watershed in British imperial strategy in the Persian Gulf. Iranian assertions in and around the Gulf posed a direct challenge to Britain's position and engendered an abrupt shift from indirect to direct forms of imperial penetration in the Arab shaykhdoms and a gradual transfer of its locus of power from the Iranian to the Arabian littoral. This was especially manifested in Bahrain where the imperative to stymie Sunni-Shi'i tensions and deny Iran a pretext to continue intervening in the affairs of Bahrain brought about the forced retirement of Shaykh 'Isa bin 'Ali Al Khalifa, the hereditary ruler, and the establishment of a modern state administration under the aegis of the government of India. Similarly, British protection of Dubai's ruler, Shaykh Sa'id bin Maktum Al Maktum, curtailed his autonomy and brought him to the brink of a palace coup, but enabled him to survive it. The neighboring shaykhdoms, Abu Dhabi, Sharjah, and Ras al-Khaimah, also became an arena of growing foreign intervention owing to their strategic value as a civil and military air route. Finally, the transference of Britain's main Persian Gulf naval base in 1935 from the Iranian island of Hengam to al-Jufayr in Bahrain cemented the archipelago as the linchpin of British strategy in the Persian Gulf on the eve of the Second World War.

The political awakening that ignited Iran spread like wildfire to the Iranian immigrant communities dwelling in Arab port towns such as Manama, Kuwait, Dubai, and Abu Dhabi. Their flamboyant expressions of patriotism, which included wearing the Pahlavi cap and trousers, marching about in military formation, singing anthems, and waving flags, drew sharp protests from the Arab inhabitants who had no sympathy for Iran. Iranian immigrants who thrived under the

British protective apparatus were increasingly perceived as agents of colonial exploitation. In the 1930s, young people in Bahrain protested the employment of Iranians and other foreigners in the oil company, which they viewed as an enterprise that should exclusively benefit Bahrainis. Their protest was reflected in the formulation of a new discourse that focused on the dichotomy between the "Arab nation" and the Iranian "foreigner." Members of another immigrant group, the Hawala, were also resented in some quarters for different reasons. The Hawala were Sunni merchants from Iran that exhibited Persian appearance and characteristics to varying degrees, though many of them began to emphasize Arab origins to gain greater acceptance in tribal societies during the interwar period. Their transnational connections and involvement in the sea trade kept them relatively prosperous even while the pearl merchants lost out during the pearling crash and the economic depression of the 1930s. The Hawala maintained their access to political and economic patronage while other traditional elites whose fortunes were degraded began to lose clout and influence.

By the beginning of the Second World War, the crystallization of an historic process was increasingly becoming evident in the shaykhdoms whereby revenues from external sources paid directly to the rulers' purses began to weaken their dependence on revenues derived from merchant activity. External revenues dramatically restructured the political and economic foundations of the shaykhdoms.[4] Moreover, the special relationship between the rulers and the British – which had previously worked to the advantage of the merchants by providing protection for their economic activity – ceased to be an advantage for the merchants and was now an acute source of friction. New ideas were gaining currency in Kuwait, Bahrain, and Dubai, including ideas about national rights and popular representation in decision-making bodies. The 1938 reform movements in Bahrain and Dubai were fueled in part by Arab-Iranian antagonisms and resentment about British interventions that were administered in the name of protection. In Bahrain, Hawala merchants and disenfranchised Sunni Arabs composed a critique that cast British imperialism and tribalism as the root of Bahrain's social ills. These activists began to articulate alternative frameworks of identity, along national and ethnic lines. Intermittent

[4] See Jill Crystal, *Oil and Politics in the Gulf: Rulers and Merchants in Kuwait and Qatar* (1990; Repr., New York: Cambridge University Press, 1995).

calls for "Arabization" or "Bahrainization" – political goals that were by no means coterminous – divulged the new fault lines crisscrossing the social and political landscape of Bahrain. Moreover, the perceived significance of these new fault lines was beginning to transcend the significance formerly attached to religious divides.

The sharp rise of Iranian nationalism and British interventionism in the Persian Gulf during the interwar period bore out profound consequences among the tribally organized societies situated around its perimeter. An era of fluid identities and unfettered movement of people was eclipsed by the drawing of political boundaries and the regulation of national status. Inhabitants of the Gulf region who had long enjoyed access to multiple social and economic worlds were compelled to chart out their destinies in line with the emerging geopolitical fault lines. Modern notions of citizenship and national status vied for significance with traditional frameworks of identity, such as tribe and religious sect. The movement of goods and people previously determined by nature became subjected to the intrusion of the centralizing structures of Iran and the emerging Arab states. The entrance of nationalism forged an acute dichotomy between Persians and Arabs in the Gulf, and its application to the entire depth and breadth of the waterway forged an acute geopolitical rivalry that endures to this day.

1 *States and Tribes in the Premodern Gulf*

It is the opinion of ancient historians that the cradle of civilization, even of the human race, is the Persian Gulf; that the inhabitants of its islands were the first to launch a sail upon the water and to brave the dangers of long voyages between the East and the West.[1]

Ameen Rihani, 1930

The Persian Gulf has been variously shared and contested by tribes and states since time immemorial. Before the introduction of modern political forces, the most conspicuous constant was its constant changeability – the configuration and reconfiguration of frontier zones in line with the construction of imperial space or the expansion of tribal authority. The Persian Gulf in antiquity was an arena of waxing and waning empires variously based in Mesopotamia or on the Iranian plateau. After the rise of Islam, the Persian Gulf was dominated by Muslim dynasties that gained control over trade routes linking the commerce of the Indian Ocean to the thriving urban centers of the interior. Trade, it has been argued, gave rise to a unique relationship between the inhabitants of the northern and southern Gulf littoral, who shared more linkages with each other than with the agrarian and nomadic societies of the interior.[2] The allure of trading ventures in the East brought Portuguese, British, Dutch, and French traders into contact with Persian Gulf states and tribal principalities. During the Age of Imperialism the port towns of the Persian Gulf became increasingly integrated into the wider Indian Ocean maritime trading system.

In the eighteenth century, the British East India Company edged out its European rivals on the Indian subcontinent. In the nineteenth century, it undertook the herculean task of eliminating piracy in its vital transportation route thorough the Persian Gulf. The Persian Gulf

1 Ameen Fares Rihani, *Around the Coasts of Arabia* (London: Constable, 1930), p. 271.

2 See Hala Fattah, *The Politics of Regional Trade in Iraq, Arabia, and the Gulf: 1745–1900* (Albany: State University of New York Press, 1997).

under the *Pax Britannica*, as the era of British supremacy came to be called, was subdued by a series of maritime truces between the British government and the Arab shaykhs of the southern littoral. In the 1880s and 1890s, the British deepened their commitment by means of the "exclusive agreements" according to which the British government undertook the conduct of relations with foreign powers on behalf of the shaykhs. These agreements blocked the influence of Britain's imperial rivals and prevented regional powers from exerting any meaningful influence in the Persian Gulf. The expanding Saudi state was similarly incorporated into the system in 1915 with a treaty that bound Ibn Sa'ud to respect British influence in the Gulf Arab shaykhdoms. On the Iranian littoral, *ad hoc* arrangements with various tribal chiefs of southern Iran, and an agreement with the Shaykh of Mohammerah in particular, helped the British to consolidate their political and military control over the strategic waterway and nascent oil industry.

The Persian Gulf from the Dawn of Civilization to the Rise of the British

The world's oldest known civilization, Sumer, developed in Mesopotamia at the head of the Persian Gulf. It was conquered around 2,334 B.C.E. by Sargon the Great and turned into the first recorded empire in history. He boasted in his inscriptions that the merchant ships of Dilmun (Bahrain) and Magan (Oman) docked in his Mesopotamian ports.[3] The first known polity to control the northern littoral from Mesopotamia to the Gulf of Oman was the Median Empire, a state that grew out of the confederation of ancient Iranian tribes. In the sixth century B.C.E., Cyrus the Great united the Median and Persian tribes and led them in a conquest of territory that spanned three continents. Iranian domination of the Persian Gulf was ended during the conquests of Alexander the Great but restored in the seventh century when the Sassanid dynasty (224–651 B.C.E.) conquered the whole of the Persian Gulf – its northern and southern shores.

The Arabian Peninsula since times immemorial was home to nomadic tribes, although several regional states developed on its perimeter, including the Kingdoms of Saba, Hadramawt, and Awsan in

[3] Harriet E. W. Crawford, *Dilmun and Its Gulf Neighbors* (Cambridge: Cambridge University Press, 1998), pp. 1–2, 104.

the territory of present-day Yemen. But the coming of Islam in the seventh century created, for the first time, a single unified polity in the Peninsula, organized not around the tribal concept of kinship, but around the principle of a common faith. With Muhammad's successors at the helm, the Bedouin armies burst out of the Arabian Peninsula, took possession of the Byzantine province of Syria, and then went on to overwhelm the entire Persian Sassanid Empire. The Arab-Muslim conquest of Iran changed its linguistic, religious, and cultural makeup almost beyond recognition. The subsequent invasion by Turkic and Mongol tribes gave rise to strong dynasties such as the Seljuk Empire, which later gave way to a succession of weak dynastic empires whose waxing and waning authority overlapped with that of smaller regional states and tribal polities.

The Safavid dynasty (1501–1736) reunited Iranian territory under central rule, reestablished Persian as the official language of Iran, and established Twelver Shiism as the official religion of the realm. Though the Safavids were the strongest force in Iran, they exercised less than complete authority over Iran's nomadic tribes, particularly the Kurds, Turkomans, Baluch, and Arabs. Most of the Arabs, who dwelled along the Persian Gulf littoral and in Khuzestan, retained their Sunni faith.[4] The Safavids' greatest rival was their Ottoman neighbor to the west. Their rivalry was galvanized by the Sunni-Shiʿi schism. The Ottoman-Safavid frontier that ran through Mesopotamia and the Persian Gulf became a zone of conflict and competition. Here, the notion of the Persian Gulf as a frontier zone deserves special attention.

Hala Fattah, in her seminal work on the politics of regional trade, observes that imperial frontiers were never defined in an exact manner: "Both the Ottomans and the Persians continued to treat them as buffer zones, or strongholds, a no-man's-land defended by tribal armies in the pay of either empire, or sometimes of both."[5] Kaya Şahin in her study on Ottoman state-building highlights the interdependent nature of tribe and state on the Ottoman-Safavid frontier: both the Ottomans and the Safavids relied on their alliances with the semi-autonomous tribal power centers in the periphery to establish and maintain their military and political influence in the area. The frontiers were very

[4] See Richard Tapper, "Introduction," *Tribe and State in Iran and Afghanistan*, ed. Richard Tapper (New York: Croom Helm, 1983), pp. 1–75.

[5] Fattah, *The Politics of Regional Trade*, p. 32.

fluid, she notes. "Constant skirmishes occurred, intelligence peddlers traveled between the two sides, fortresses changed hands, allegiances were quickly shifted and restored, and commercial activity took place despite the tensions."[6]

Merchant activity was a unifying factor that brought the people of the northern and southern littorals of the Persian Gulf into closer relations with each other than with the peoples of the interior. Geographically, the Persian Gulf is an extension of the Indian Ocean and its economic orientation has always been outward toward the Indian subcontinent. After the spread of Islam in the seventh century, the spice trade was dominated by Muslim seafarers who transported spices from the trading emporiums in India to ports in the Persian Gulf and the Red Sea. During the Age of Exploration, the region's trade was transformed when European trading nations entered the commercial and political power map. Moreover, this was the Golden Age of Piracy. Trade vessels loaded with gold, spices, and silk from the rich markets in India were particularly vulnerable in the narrow Strait of Hormuz where marauders lay in wait inside the long, deep inlets nestled in the craggy cliff walls. Persian, Arab, and Indian pirates were joined by European privateers – individuals authorized by their governments to attack foreign vessels during wartime. One astute chronicler noted "there was only one rule of law at sea in those days, to destroy one's rivals and make as much money as possible in the shortest possible time."[7]

States, Tribes, and European Trading Companies

The Portuguese were the first of the European powers to play a major political, economic, and military role in the Persian Gulf waterway following the momentous voyage of Vasco de Gama to the Indian Ocean in 1498. In 1507, Portuguese explorer Alfonso de Albuquerque captured the Kingdom of Hormuz and its dependency, Muscat. Albuquerque turned the trade-based Arab city-state, formerly a tributary of the mainland rulers of Fars and Kerman, into a Portuguese vassal. In 1521, a joint Portuguese-Hormuzi naval expedition subdued Bahrain

[6] Kaya Şahin, *Empire and Power in the Reign of Süleyman: Narrating the Sixteenth-Century Ottoman World* (New York: Cambridge University Press, 2013), p. 92.

[7] William McFee, *The Law of the Sea* (Philadelphia: Lippencott, 1950), p. 139.

and gained Portugal control over Bahrain's rich pearl banks. By 1554 the Portuguese had eliminated Ottoman sea power and established a monopoly over the lucrative East-West trade.[8]

The tide was turned with the establishment of the Safavid dynasty (1502–1736) and particularly, the rise of its greatest monarch, Shah Abbas I (1587–1629). Shah Abbas built a new infantry and artillery and embarked on an ambitious campaign to recover Herat and Mashhad from the Uzbeks and parts of Mesopotamia and the Caucasus from the Ottomans. After those victories, he turned his attention to territories held by the Portuguese in the Persian Gulf. In 1602 his forces ousted the Portuguese from their fort in Bahrain. He made contacts with European trading nations, namely the British and the Dutch, offering them trading privileges in Iran, in exchange for their help in establishing control over Iran's Persian Gulf littoral. In 1622, with the reluctant help of the British East India Company he drove the Portuguese out of Qeshm Island and Hormuz.[9]

The British East India Company had arrived in the Persian Gulf hoping to profit from the spice trade with India. The company's agents reached an agreement with Shah Abbas leading to the establishment of trading posts, first at Jask in 1616 and then inland at Shiraz and Isfahan in 1617. After the defeat of Hormuz in 1622, the company was awarded a monopoly on the silk trade and commercial privileges at the nearby port of Bandar Abbas. The establishment of a British trading post in 1622 and then a Dutch trading post in 1623 marked the rise of Bandar Abbas as a regional emporium for trade in a wide variety of merchandise including horses, gold, silver, silk, dyes, spices, rice, and sugar. While initially there was cooperation between the British and Dutch companies, the better part of the next 150 years was characterized by Anglo-Dutch imperial rivalry in the Persian Gulf, a rivalry that was variously played out at Bandar Abbas, Basra, Bushehr, Bandar Rig, and Kharg Island. The French East India Company entered the Gulf in 1664 and by the time of Napoleon

[8] Rudi Matthee, "The Portuguese Presence in the Persian Gulf: An Overview," in *Imperial Crossroads: The Great Powers and the Persian Gulf*, eds. Jeffrey Macris and Saul Kelly (Annapolis, MD: Naval Institute Press, 2012), pp. 1–12.

[9] Sadeq Nash'at, *Tarikh-e Siyasi-ye Khalij-e Fars* (Tehran: Kanun-e Ketab, 1344/1965), pp. 132–139.

Bonaparte, they had taken the place of the Dutch as Britain's most formidable European rival.[10]

From the Battle of Hormuz in 1622 until the rise of British supremacy in 1820 no single regional or European power was able to assert hegemony over the Persian Gulf waterway. It was an era of ever-shifting alliances between regional states, foreign powers, and tribal principalities. Two or more powers often combined forces against a third to defeat it, as was the case when the Ya'rubi Imam of Oman combined forces with the British and Dutch East India Companies to drive the Portuguese out of Muscat (1650) and reassert control over the East African coastal area.[11] One of his successors enlisted the help of the Qasimi Arabs (pl. Qawasim) of Ras al-Khaimah to attack Bahrain in 1715. Initially they were repelled by Safavid forces but in 1717 they succeeded not only in defeating the Safavids at Bahrain but also in occupying Larak and Qeshm.[12] Fortunes were again reversed when Nader Shah came to the throne (1736–1747) and unified Iranian territory with armies composed mostly of tribal units. He also built a navy based at Bushehr with ships purchased from India's shipyards and crews staffed with Arabs from Iran's coastal region: it was used to recapture Bahrain and also intervene in the Sultanate of Muscat. His successors, however, did not manage to maintain a grip on the Persian Gulf coastal areas that he had subdued.

Iranian weakness during the rule of the Zand dynasty (1750–1797) left a power vacuum in the Persian Gulf that smaller tribally organized polities expanded to fill. Tribal rulers manipulated the regional power equation to their own ends, playing one foreign power off against another, against a state ruler, or against competing tribal rivals. The triangular relationship between the Dutch East India Company, the semi-independent Arab shaykhs of the Iranian littoral and the Zand state can serve as an apt example. In 1753 Karim Khan Zand authorized the Arab shaykh and hereditary Governor of Bushehr, Nasir Al Madhkur, to use military force to recapture Bahrain from the Omani garrison that held it. The Shaykh of Bushehr enlisted the help of Mir

[10] Sir Percy Sykes, *A History of Persia*, Vol. 2 (1915; Repr., New York: RoutledgeCurzon, 2004), pp. 188–197.

[11] A. J. R. Russell-Wood, *The Portuguese Empire, 1415–1808: A World on the Move* (Baltimore, MD: The Johns Hopkins University Press, 1998), p. 24.

[12] Lawrence Lockhart, *The Fall of the Safavi Dynasty and the Afghan Occupation of Persia* (Cambridge: Cambridge University Press, 1958), p. 115.

Nasr al-Sa'di, the Shaykh of Bandar Rig, and recaptured the archipelago, but soon a disagreement arose between the two shaykhs over the matter of farming the revenues from Bahrain. Mir Nasr countered Nasir Al Madhkur's tactics by inviting the Dutch East India Company to rent Kharg Island, a nominal dependency of Bandar Rig. The Dutch, having just lost their position at Basra, accepted his invitation and established a fort and trading post there. Once established on Kharg, the Dutch found themselves wedged between the shaykhly family of Bandar Rig and the Zand state, which aimed to regain its hold over the independent shaykhs of the Persian Gulf littoral. Ultimately, in 1765 the Dutch lent naval assistance to Karim Khan Zand for an attack on Bandar Rig but were expelled from Kharg Island during the fighting.[13]

Another constant in the history of the premodern Gulf is the constant movement of tribes in search of resources and greater autonomy. The Persian Gulf of the eighteenth century was defined by two migratory patterns – the migration of semi-sedentarized tribes from the Arabian coast to the Iranian coast and the migration of nomadic tribes from the Arabian interior to the coastal areas. The first trend is illustrated by the Qasimi migration northward: in the chaos that ensued after the death of Nader Shah in 1747, tribesmen of the Qasimi confederation established a presence at Lingah, Qeshm, Laft, and Shinas.[14] Initially, they were viewed by Karim Khan Zand as a protective barrier against the expansion of other local power centers and were encouraged to settle along the Iranian coast in greater numbers.[15]

The second trend, the migration of nomadic tribes to the coast, is illustrated by the establishment of the Bani 'Utub and the Banu Ka'b on the Arabian littoral. At the head of the Gulf, a group of clans from the Najd, collectively known as the Bani 'Utub, became established in Kuwait.[16] By 1756 the leadership of Sabah bin Jabir, the patriarch of

[13] John R. Perry, "Mir Muhanna and the Dutch: Patterns of Piracy in the Persian Gulf," *Studia Iranica* 2 (1973), pp. 79–95.

[14] "Historical Sketch of the Joasmee Tribe of Arabs; From the Year 1747 to the Year 1819, Prepared by Mr. Francis Warden, Member of the Council at Bombay," in *Records of the Emirates: 1820–1960*, ed. Penelope Tucson, Vol. 1 (Archive Editions, 1990), pp. 239–252.

[15] Shahnaz Razieh Nadjmabadi, "The Arab Presence on the Iranian Coast of the Persian Gulf," in *The Persian Gulf in History*, ed. Lawrence G. Potter (New York: Palgrave Macmillian, 2009), p. 133.

[16] B. J. Slot, *The Origins of Kuwait* (Leiden: Brill, 1991), pp. 70–72.

the Al Sabah ruling family, was acknowledged over Kuwait's expanding mercantile center.[17] In 1766 the Al Khalifa branch of the Bani 'Utub confederation left Kuwait for Zubara, a pearl fishery and thriving transit port on the Qatari Peninsula. In 1783 the Al Khalifa wrested Bahrain from the Al Madhkur Governor of Bushehr. Like the Bani 'Utub, the Banu Ka'b was a confederation of tribes that originated in central Arabia. By the 1750s they had established a presence on the Ottoman-Iranian frontier east of Basra, in the area called Arabistan (later Khuzestan). The Banu Ka'b fought both for and against the Ottoman and the Zand dynasties, choosing whichever side offered the best advantage to the tribe at a given time. The enhanced position they gained from association with the powerful states, enabled the Banu Ka'b to dominate other tribal groups in the area.[18] By the 1780s, the preeminent shaykh, Jabir al-Ka'bi, ruled over a semi-independent shaykhdom in Arabistan.

In the end of the eighteenth century, another group of tribes, the Bani Yas, were beginning to make their presence felt on the inside of the Hormuz Strait, along the Arabian littoral. The Bani Yas was a confederation of nomadic tribes whose economic livelihood was centered on camel herding in the hinterland and whose leadership was based at Liwa oasis. When fresh water was discovered on Abu Dhabi Island in the 1760s, wells were dug, palm frond houses were built, date gardens were planted, and in the 1790s the principal shaykh of the Bani Yas took up residence there. Abu Dhabi village continued to grow and attracted an increasing number of tribesmen from the hinterland, some of whom pooled their resources and bought boats for pearl diving.[19] Abu Dhabi suffered a blow in 1833, when the sizeable Al Bu Falasa (later Al Falasi) subsection of the Bani Yas headed by Shaykhs 'Ubayd bin Sa'id bin Rashid and Maktum bin Butti bin Suhayl, emigrated en masse to the neighboring town of Dubai, after the failure to resolve a dispute with the Ruler of Abu Dhabi.[20] Dubai,

[17] Alan Rush, *Al-Sabah: History and Genealogy of Kuwait's Ruling Family 1752–1987* (London: Ithaca Press, 1987), p. 197.

[18] Willem Floor, "The Rise and Fall of the Banu Ka'b: A Borderer State in Southern Khuzestan," *Iran* 44 (2006), pp. 277–315.

[19] Frauke Heard-Bey, "The Tribal Society of the UAE and Its Traditional Economy," in *Perspectives on the United Arab Emirates*, eds. E. Ghareeb and I. al-Abed (London: Trident Press, 1997), p. 106.

[20] For a genealogical chart of the Bani Yas tribe and its subsections and branches, see Hammad Khatiri, *Awthaq Ma'ayyir fi nasab Bani Yas wa-al-Manasir* (Abu

with its larger population, would soon outpace Abu Dhabi in terms of its economic significance.

By the closing years of the eighteenth century, two maritime powers competed for dominance at the narrow entrance to the Strait of Hormuz – the Omani state with its seat of rule at Muscat and the large Qasimi tribal confederation. The preeminent Al Qasimi shaykh, based at Ras al-Khaimah, ruled the southern Gulf from Sharjah to the Musandam Peninsula and also claimed as his dependents the smaller shaykhs who exercised authority at Lingah, Kong, and Charak as well as Sirri, Abu Musa, the two Tunbs, and Laft, a port on Qeshm Island.[21] Qasimi ports harbored the largest ocean-going vessels in the Gulf, employed 8,000 pearl divers, and put 400 boats out to sea. Their trade extended from India to the Red Sea.[22] Their main competitors were the Omani Arabs of Muscat, who had colonies of their own including the Makran coast and the eastern coast of Africa. Their ships docked at ports from Bombay to Yemen, carrying about 40,000–50,000 tons of cargo per year, mainly spices, coffee and dates. In 1800 the Imam of Muscat reached an agreement with Fath ʻAli Shah that allowed him to farm the customs revenues of Bandar Abbas, Hengam, and Qeshm.[23] By the 1830s, the predominance of the Arab population on the northern Gulf littoral from Mohammerah to the Sea of Oman impelled one visitor to remark in his travel log: "The Persian side of the Gulf is nearly abandoned to the Arabs .... The Arabs indeed may be said to possess all the shores of the Gulf."[24]

The Rise of British Supremacy

The British defeat of the French in 1757 at the Battle of Plassey in India marked the beginning of British formal rule in India. The British East India Company used two main routes of transportation between the

Dhabi: Wizarat Shu'un al-Ri'asa Markaz al-Watha'iq wa-al-Buhuth, 2007), pp. 107–116.

21 "Historical Sketch of the Joasmee Tribe of Arabs; From the Year 1747 to the Year 1819," in *Records of the Emirates*, Vol. 1, pp. 239–252.

22 Charles E. Davies, *The Blood Red Arab Flag: An Investigation into Qasimi Piracy 1797–1820* (Exeter: University of Exeter Press, 1997), pp. 226–234.

23 Willem Floor, *Bandar Abbas: The Natural Trade Gateway of Southeast Iran* (Washington, DC: Mage, 2011), p. 58.

24 John Kitto, *Uncle Oliver's Travels: Persia*, Vol. 2 (London: William Clowes, 1838), pp. 107–108.

Mediterranean Sea and the Indian Ocean: the first involved an overland journey through Egypt that linked the Mediterranean with the Red Sea, and the second involved an overland journey through parts of the Ottoman Empire that linked the Mediterranean with the Persian Gulf. The Persian Gulf route, which made use of ports at Basra, Kuwait, and Bushehr, was convenient and direct, but it was remarkably hazardous. Owing to frequent tribal wars and the pestilence of piracy, passage though the Persian Gulf waters was fraught with dangers. Merchant vessels were particularly vulnerable at the narrow Hormuz Strait where marauders could lie in wait inside the long deep inlets nestled in the craggy cliff walls of the Musandam Peninsula.[25] By the end of the seventeenth century the British position in the Persian Gulf had vastly improved as compared with its imperial rivals but piratical activities of the sea-faring tribes and coastal people was a big liability.

The security of the Persian Gulf route became an urgent imperative for Britain when Napoleon's expedition to Egypt in 1798 deprived them momentarily of the Red Sea route.[26] The British acted quickly to form an alliance with the powerful Sultan of Oman, but in doing so, they inadvertently made themselves enemies of Oman's rivals, the Qawasim. The Omani-British "Treaty of Friendship" signed in 1798 generated a great deal of business for Muscat to the detriment of its rival: it brought in tariffs for rent of the docks, opened new markets for Oman's coffee and pearl exports, grew Muscat's fleets, and increased the Omani presence in the Persian Gulf waterway.[27] Soon after, the Qawasim became tributaries of the first Saudi-Wahhabi state. Imbued with Wahhabi religious zeal, they escalated the maritime warfare on Oman and its patrons. As a result of British cooperation with Oman, the British were treated as enemies by the Qawasim and British shipping was subjected to a heretofore unprecedented level of attacks, raiding, and plundering.[28]

[25] James Onley, "Britain and the Gulf Shaikhdoms, 1820–1971: The Politics of Protection," CIRS Occasional Paper No. 4 (Georgetown University in Qatar, 2009), p. 31.

[26] John F. Standish, "British Maritime Policy in the Persian Gulf," *Middle Eastern Studies* 3, no. 4 (1967), pp. 335–340.

[27] H. Moyse-Bartlett, *The Pirates of Trucial Oman* (London: McDonald, 1966), pp. 20–26.

[28] Davies, *The Blood Red Arab Flag*, pp. 37–44, 242–251.

The escalating attacks prompted the British East India Company in 1809 to send an expeditionary force against the "Pirate Coast" centered around Ras al-Khaimah and against the Qasimi strongholds on the Iranian coast, Lingah, Laft, and Shinas.[29] The sea was reasonably quieted for about three years, after which the severity and frequency of attacks returned to its former level. By 1818, Muhammad 'Ali Pasha had crushed the Saudi state and Ras al-Khaimah had become a sanctuary for prominent Wahhabi refugees and the war on Oman was renewed with particular zeal. A year later, in 1819 the company decided to put an end to the piracy once and for all. They dispatched their second expeditionary force against Ras al-Khaimah, destroyed the fleet, occupied the fort, and set the structures ablaze. The Qawasim and the remnants of the Saudi-Wahhabi state fled from the burning town. After the fall of Ras al-Khaimah, the expeditionary force continued on, delivering punishing attacks to the Qasimi positions in the other parts of the Gulf.[30]

In 1820, the British Indian government was able to impose a treaty on Sultan bin Saqr, the Qasimi chieftain, called "The General Treaty for the Cessation of Plunder and Piracy by Land and Sea."[31] To forestall the evolution of new antagonisms, similar truces were signed with the other shaykhs of the coast of Oman including the chief of the Bani Yas tribal confederacy based in Abu Dhabi, and three smaller shaykhs, the rulers of Dubai, Ajman, and Umm al-Quwain. The contracting parties, the "Trucial shaykhs" as they came to be called, committed to a cessation of plunder and piracy on land and sea. Vessels belonging to the "friendly Arabs" were to fly a red-and-white flag and were obligated to be at peace with the British government and with each other.[32]

To supervise and enforce the General Treaty, the government of India stationed a Political Agent on Qeshm Island. In 1822 the post was moved to Bushehr, on the Iranian coast, and was combined with

[29] Charles Umpherson Aitchison, ed. *A Collection of Treaties, Engagements and Sanads Relating to India and Neighboring Countries: Relating to Aden and the Southwestern Coast of Arabia*, Vol. 11, 5th ed. (Calcutta: Government of India, 1933; Repr., Liechtenstein: Kraus-Thomson, 1973), pp. 197–199.

[30] Donald Hawley, *The Trucial States* (London: Twayne Publishers, 1971), pp. 98–114.

[31] Aitchison, *A Collection of Treaties, Engagements and Sanads*, Vol. 11, pp. 240–249.

[32] Ibid.

the older post of Bushehr Political Resident (established in 1763 by the British East India Company). In the same year the Residency was subordinated to the government of Bombay (1822–1873), an administrative subdivision of British India. Chief among the responsibilities of the Political Resident (hereafter, the Resident) was the task of supervising the independent Arab shaykhs of the Arabian littoral to ensure their compliance with the anti-piracy truces. The Persian Gulf Squadron was created to support him in this capacity.[33] Its naval supply depot was established at the port of Basidu, on the northwest extremity of Qeshm Island. Basidu was viewed as a strategic position from which the British could maintain their control over the lower Persian Gulf.[34] As the incidence of piratical episodes tapered off, the function of the Resident widened to include responsibilities such as the suppression of the slave trade; the suppression of gun-running; the operation and protection of the Indo-European telegraph lines and British-Indian post offices, the quarantine service, and the lighting and buoying service; and the provision of services to British subjects and British protected persons in the Gulf.

The Resident was aided in his responsibilities by a skilled cadre of "native agents" who served as his eyes and ears in the principal ports and islands situated around the Gulf's perimeter.[35] Drawing upon the network of local brokers that had been cultivated by the East India Company, the government of India established native agencies in key locations around the Gulf including Sharjah (1823), Lingah (1830), Bahrain (c. 1816), Gwadar on the Makran coast (1880), and Muscat (1809).[36] In keeping with the tradition established by the company, native agents were recruited from among the affluent Indian, Arab, and Persian merchants who conducted business in and around the Persian Gulf. The transnational connections and multilingual abilities of local merchants engaged in the sea trade were particularly suited for keeping

33 James Onley, *The Arabian Frontier of the British Raj: Merchants, Rulers, and the British in the Nineteenth Century Gulf* (New York: Oxford University Press, 2007), p. 45.

34 FO 317/12291: Foreign Secretary to the Government of India, January 6, 1927, with enclosure: "Précis of correspondence relating to British position at Basidu and Henjam, 1821–1926."

35 See James Onley, "Britain's Native Agents in Arabia and Persia in the Nineteenth Century," *Comparative Studies of South Asia, Africa and the Middle East* 24, no. 1 (2004), pp. 129–137.

36 Onley, *The Arabian Frontier of the British Raj*, p. 234.

the Resident apprised of local developments.[37] After the passage of time, the title "Residency Agent" took hold. Their vital role in providing the Bushehr-based Political Resident with authentic intelligence on a wide variety of matters affecting British interests is evident from the steady stream of reports that he complied, including the annual administration reports of the Persian Gulf Political Residency, annual trade reports, and special memoranda written on myriad issues as they arose. Between 1900 and 1910 British officers were appointed to the various political agencies that were subordinated to the Resident in Bushehr replacing most of the native agents who had previously worked in that capacity; however, local merchants continued to serve in political roles under the supervision of the British officers.[38] A prominent example is the agency at Sharjah, a post that was held by Arab merchants from the ʿAbd al-Latif "al-Serkal" family and passed from father to son.[39]

Figure 1 The British Persian Gulf Political Residency in Bushehr.
Source: *The Times History of the War*, Vol. 11 (London: Printing House Square, 1917), p. 339. Photo by Lovat Fraser.

[37] Ibid., pp. 64–103. [38] Onley, "Britain's Native Agents," p. 135.
[39] "Al-Serkal" refers to the honorary title awarded by the British.

The Resident's spacious, Indian-style headquarters in Bushehr with its cadre of well-trained servants stirring about the grounds, underscored the impression expressed by none too few visitors that southern Iran appeared to be more of a precinct of the British Indian Empire than part of the sovereign Qajar state.[40] Viceroy Lord Curzon painted a vivid picture of that impression in his eminent work *Persia and the Persian Question*:

> The Union Jack fluttering from the summit of the Residency flag-staff is no vain symbol of British ascendancy in Bushire. The steamers lying at the anchorage are with scarcely an exception British steamers; the goods that crowd the stalls in the bazaars are British or Indian goods; the rupee is as readily, nay more readily, accepted than the kran. There must be many a Persian who has contrasted the smart bodyguard of the British Resident with the slatternly escort of the native Governor. In appearance and structure the English quarter of the town is not unlike an Indian station.[41]

The establishment of formal relations with the Qajar Shahs, who exercised little influence in the provinces, was clearly a second priority in British strategy, and when the relationship did materialize, it was an outgrowth of the East India Company's imperative to protect the western approach to India. The first permanent mission to Tehran, whose minister was formally styled "Envoy Extraordinary and Minister Plenipotentiary," was established in 1807 by the government of Bombay, as a means of blocking Napoleon's drive toward India.[42] After 1857 the Foreign Office took over responsibility for the Tehran Legation, giving its minister a rank in the Foreign Service that was one step lower than that of ambassador. It was agreed that the Resident in Bushehr would report directly to the minister in Tehran though he would continue dealing with the local authorities in cases affecting the lives and properties of British subjects in the southern province of

[40] Denis Wright, *The English amongst the Persians: Imperial Lives in Nineteenth Century Iran* (London: I.B. Tauris, 2001), pp. 63–64; L. P. Elwell-Sutton, *Persian Oil: A Study in Power Politics* (London: Lawrence and Wishart, 1955), p. 55.

[41] George Curzon, *Persia and the Persian Question*, Vol. 2 (London: Longmans, Green and Co., 1892; Repr., London: Elibron Classics, 2012), p. 236.

[42] J. G. Lorimer, *Gazetteer of the Persian Gulf, Oman, and Central Arabia*, Vol. 1: Historical, ed. Richard Lockington Birdwood (Calcutta: Superintendent of Government Printing, 1915; Repr., Archive Editions, 1986), p. 2099.

Fars.[43] The responsibility that the Resident had always exercised in the south of Iran was formalized in 1878 under his new title as "Consul-General for Fars and the coasts and islands of the Persian Gulf, being within the dominions of Persia."[44]

The conversion of the Bushehr Residency from a Company agency to a political office in 1820 was not without its mishaps. The government of Bombay, the subdivision of British India that the Resident answered to after 1822, found itself in an embarrassing position when the officer it promoted to Political Resident, Captain William Bruce, concluded an agreement on his own initiative with the Governor of Shiraz. The unauthorized agreement dated August 6, 1822, acknowledged that Bahrain had "always been subordinate to the Persian Province of Fars and provided that British vessels could be loaned to the Governor of Fars should they be required for the re-conquest of Bahrain."[45] Once aware of these proceedings, the Bombay government quickly disavowed them and dismissed Captain Bruce from his post. Letters were dispatched to the Governor of Shiraz and the Al Khalifa Shaykh of Bahrain disowning the agreement and affirming the shaykh's independence. The agreement was also disavowed by the shah who resented that the Governor of Shiraz had concluded such an agreement without his knowledge.[46]

The Persian Gulf under the Pax Britannica

The Qajar government's ineffective control of Iran's frontier provinces and lack of an effective navy provided an opportunity for the steady growth of a network of British institutions that situated the Persian Gulf firmly but informally within the precincts of the greater British Indian Empire. The suppression of piracy paved the way for the introduction of steam navigation to the waterway that was previously deemed too treacherous. The Calcutta and Burmah Steam Navigation Company, formed in 1856, set up lighthouses in Persian Gulf islands, headlands, and anchorages, and buoyed the Gulf's shoals and channels. In 1862 it became the British India Steam Navigation Company,

43 Wright, *The English amongst the Persians*, pp. 63–64.
44 *The London Gazette*, January 3, 1879.
45 J. B. Kelly, "The Persian Claim to Bahrain," *International Affairs* 33, the Royal Institute of International Affairs, no. 1 (January 1957), pp. 57–59.
46 Ibid.

and it established a regular mail and transportation service from Bombay to Basra, stopping at Karachi, Gwadar, Muscat, Jask, Bandar Abbas, Lingah, Bahrain, Bushehr, al-Faw, and Mohammerah.[47]

In the 1860s the Qajar Shah granted concessions that allowed the construction of two telegraph lines along the Iranian Persian Gulf littoral, in transit from London to Bombay. Telegraph offices were opened in Bushehr, Hengam Island, Jask, and Gwadar. Agreements and arrangements were made with local shaykhs and khans for the protection of the cables and for the safeguarding of the offices and their British and Indian staff. The advent of steam navigation and telegraph communication along the Iranian littoral dramatically increased the importance of the Persian Gulf in British imperial thinking and protecting the vital transportation and communication lines was increasingly viewed as essential to the maintenance of the British position in India.

The Arab Shaykhs and British Protection

Since the show of force against the Qawasim and the imposition of the General Maritime Treaty, the Gulf Arab shaykhs increasingly viewed the British as a powerful regional actor and increasingly sought to draw them into further interventions on their behalf. They frequently tried to persuade the Resident to intervene in their disputes with other actors in the Persian Gulf. Initially the British denied these requests because the Bombay government did not want to get drawn into the internal politics of the Arabian Peninsula; however, changing political circumstances eventually drew the British into deeper commitments to the shaykhdoms.

The General Treaty of 1820 was not entirely effective. It had prohibited plunder and piracy of ships, but did not prohibit acknowledged wars between shaykhdoms at sea.[48] As a result, many hostile aggressions were committed under the title of acknowledged war, especially during the pearling season.[49] In 1835, the new Resident, James Morrison, saw fit to suggest a different kind of truce that he hoped would close that loophole. He convened a meeting to recover property that was seized by tribesmen from Abu Dhabi during a raid on ships

47 Lorimer, *Gazetteer of the Persian Gulf,* Vol. 1: Historical, pp. 2441–2442.
48 Aitchison, *A Collection of Treaties, Engagements and Sanads*, Vol. 11, p. 199.
49 Ibid.

from Sharjah. During that meeting he proposed a truce whereby the shaykhs would commit not to engage in hostilities at sea under any circumstances during the entire six-month pearling season, and he offered the services of the Persian Gulf Squadron to enforce the truce. The two shaykhs viewed the truce favorably, as did the shaykhs of Dubai, Ras al-Khaimah, Ajman, and Umm al-Quwain who were invited to join.[50]

In 1836 when the Resident offered to renew the truce, all the signatory shaykhs agreed. Thereafter the truce was renewed on an annual basis, until, in 1853, at the request of the shaykhs, the truce was made permanent. The "Treaty of Peace in Perpetuity" obligated all Gulf Arab shaykhs to prevent hostilities at sea between their subjects and dependents; punish their subjects and afford compensation in the case of infractions; and not retaliate if attacked, but rather report the incident to the Resident or naval officer.[51] This cast the British in the role of mediator, requiring them to mediate disputes between tribes, broker settlements, and obtain reparation for any injuries inflicted by one party on another.[52]

Some observations made by Paul Dresch, who carried out fieldwork among tribesmen in Yemen, can shed light on why the Gulf Arab rulers viewed these agreements as advantageous in light of the traditional tribal customs of the Arabian Peninsula. Dresch explains that from the point of view of the Yemeni tribesmen, a dependent is "on the honor" of his protector, meaning he is in the charge of his protector and must be defended by him.[53] If someone offends the dependent, it is considered a disgrace to the protector. To wipe out the disgrace, the protector must obtain compensation or avenge the victim because if the offender gets away without punishment, he has not only offended the protector's honor but has also humiliated him by revealing his inadequacy as a protector.[54] According to tribal norms, if someone has a claim against the dependent of another, he is to appeal to the

[50] James Onley, "The Politics of Protection in the Gulf: The Arab Rulers and the British Resident in the Nineteenth Century," *New Arabian Studies* 6 (November 2004), pp. 71–74.

[51] Onley, "The Politics of Protection in the Gulf," pp. 73–74; Aitchison, *A Collection of Treaties, Engagements and Sanads*, Vol. 11, pp. 199–200.

[52] Onley, "The Politics of Protection in the Gulf," pp. 73–74.

[53] Paul Dresch, *Tribes, Government and History in Yemen* (Oxford: Clarendon Press, 1989), p. 59.

[54] Onley, "The Politics of Protection in the Gulf," pp. 57–58.

protector, not the dependent.[55] The protector is expected to act as mediator and arbitrate a settlement between his dependent and the third party. Once a settlement is reached, the protector becomes the guarantor of the settlement.[56]

James Onley applies Dresch's insights to the Arabian context, and argues that from the perspective of the Gulf Arab shaykhs who signed the "exclusive agreements," the British government took "upon its honor" the responsibility to mediate on behalf of the shaykhdoms and represent their interests in any dispute involving a third party. The British had become, as one British official put it, the "arbiter and guardian of the Gulf."[57] For the shaykh, the protection of a regional power carried both advantages and disadvantages. External protection helped a shaykh reinforce his position within his shaykhdom. He was better able to channel much needed resources to his dependents and fend off the attempts of rivals to capture his leadership position. However, relations with an outside power created an additional role for the shaykh, that of mediating between the tribesmen and the outside power. If the interests of the tribesmen clashed with the interests of the protector, the shaykh was faced with a serious dilemma: if he sided with his people he faced the prospect of external intervention, but if he sided with an external power, his authority would be undermined in the eyes of his people.[58]

The Al Khalifa shaykhs of Bahrain were not a party to the myriad treaties concluded between 1820 and 1861 with the Trucial shaykhs, with the exception of several agreements relating to suppression of the slave trade.[59] This was because the British were extremely reluctant to assume a greater responsibility for the protection of Bahrain. James Onley has shown that the shaykhs of Bahrain, ever casting about for a protector to secure the greatest possible degree of autonomy, frequently tried to persuade the Resident to protect them from regional actors. The numerous appeals were refused because the government of Bombay did not want to get drawn into the internal politics of Bahrain and its dependencies.[60] Lacking British support, the rulers of Bahrain

[55] Dresch, *Tribes, Government and History in Yemen*, p. 61.
[56] Onley, "The Politics of Protection in the Gulf," pp. 57–58.
[57] Confidential Foreign Office Memorandum of 1908, quoted in James Onley, "The Politics of Protection in the Gulf," p. 30.
[58] Onley, "Britain and the Gulf Shaikhdoms," pp. 1–44.
[59] Aitchison, *A Collection of Treaties, Engagements and Sanads*, Vol. 11, p. 192.
[60] Onley, "Britain and the Gulf Shaikhdoms," pp. 1–15.

maneuvered in the local power map with an eye to securing the greatest possible degree of independence. From the advent of the Political Residency in 1820 until the year 1861, they intermittently submitted to the authority of the Amir of the Najd, the Sultan of Muscat, the Iranian Governor of Fars in Shiraz, and the Ottoman Governor of Baghdad.[61]

In 1861, the British finally saw fit to admit the Shaykh of Bahrain to the Perpetual Maritime Treaty, at his own request.[62] But the subsequent raids that he carried out against his dependents in Qatar were viewed by them as gross violations of his commitment to the treaty. The punishments inflicted on him by British gunboats formed the subject of several protests from the Qajar government, which viewed the shaykh as an Iranian subject owing to his periodic submission to Iranian authorities, most recently in March 1860. After a flurry of dispatches between the Resident and the India Office and between the India Office and the Foreign Office, Foreign Secretary Lord Clarendon addressed a response to the Iranian government, in which he related the circumstances of the shaykh's commitment to the anti-piracy agreement and Britain's commitment to maintaining the peace in the Persian Gulf waterway. In his correspondence, he intimated that should Iran become capable of maintaining the peace at sea, Britain would happily divest herself of this responsibility and he granted that, to whatever extent possible, the British government would notify Iran before undertaking future operations against the Shaykh of Bahrain.[63] Lord Clarendon's statement of April 29, 1869, was cited by successive Iranian governments as one the proofs of the validity of Iran's claim to sovereignty over Bahrain.

The Consolidation of British Hegemony

Greater assertiveness, first on the part of regional powers and then later on the part of European powers, drew the British into deeper commitments with the ruling shaykhs of the Arabian littoral. In 1880 the Shaykh of Bahrain came under pressure when the Ottoman government engaged in various attempts to extend its authority into his domain. Desirous of avoiding further interventions by the Turks,

[61] Onley, "The Politics of Protection in the Gulf," pp. 46–53.
[62] Ibid., pp. 52–53. [63] Kelly, "The Persian Claim to Bahrain," pp. 64–65.

the shaykh entered into an agreement with the British according to which he undertook to abstain from entering negotiations or making treaties with any foreign power without the consent of the British government.[64]

Similar incidents drew the British into further commitments with the Trucial shaykhs. After a series of secret meetings between Iranian authorities and the Shaykhs of Abu Dhabi and Dubai, it came to light in 1887 that Iran's new Governor of Gulf Ports (the *Darya Begi*) endeavored to place the Trucial Coast under Iranian suzerainty. Similar to what had been done in Bahrain, the British government undertook to conduct foreign relations on behalf of the Trucial shaykhs, in exchange for assurances that they would exclude the representatives of foreign governments from their domains.[65] When Britain's imperial rivals, namely France and Russia, revived an interest in the Persian Gulf, the British moved to formalize these assurances within the framework of the 1892 "exclusive agreements," binding on the signatory shaykhs, their heirs, and successors. Kuwait and Qatar signed similar agreements in 1899 and 1916, respectively. With the consent conferred by these agreements, the British took upon themselves the responsibility for protecting the shaykhs' independence from outside threats as well as managing foreign relations on their behalf.[66]

On May 5, 1903, fresh indications of Russian ambitions in the Gulf elicited the most decisive statement of Britain's policy in the Persian Gulf to date, when Foreign Secretary Lord Lansdowne declared to the House of Lords:

> First, we should protect and promote British trade in the Gulf. Secondly, we should not exclude the legitimate trade of others. Thirdly, we should regard the establishment of a naval base or a fortified port in the Gulf by any other power as a very grave menace to British interests, and we should certainly resist it by all the means at our disposal.[67]

Later that year, Lord Curzon, Viceroy of India, escorted by four ships in the service of the Royal Navy and Royal Indian Marine, embarked

[64] Lorimer, *Gazetteer of the Persian Gulf*, Vol. 1: Historical, pp. 736–739; and Muhammad Morsy Abdullah, *The United Arab Emirates: A Modern History* (London: Croom Helm, 1978), pp. 24–25.
[65] Ibid.
[66] Aitchison, *A Collection of Treaties, Engagements and Sanads*, Vol. 11, pp. 256–260, 262.
[67] "The Persian Gulf," *The Argus* (Melbourne), May 16, 1903.

on a tour of the Persian Gulf designed to demonstrate to the world that Britain was the unquestioned master of the area.[68] Lord Curzon was received with pomp and ceremony in the Arab shaykhdoms, as the representative of the paramount power that provided them with protection from outside aggressions. In 1906 the shaykhs were presented with Arabic copies of the principal agreements that were in force as well as a copy of Curzon's interpretive speech.[69] The language used in Lord Curzon's 1903 address to the Trucial shaykhs, illustrates why they viewed these agreements as an advantage (emphasis added):

> Chiefs, out of the relations that were thus created, and which by your own consent constituted the British Government the guardian of inter-tribal peace, there grew up political ties between the Government of India and yourselves, whereby *the British Government became your overlords and protectors*, and you have relations with no other Power. Every one of the States known as the Trucial States has bound itself, as you know, not to enter into any agreement or correspondence with any other Power, not to admit the agent of any other Government, and not to part with any portion of its territories. These engagements are binding on every one of you, and you have faithfully adhered to them. *They are also binding in their reciprocal effect upon the British Government, and as long as they are faithfully observed by the Chiefs there is no fear that anyone else will be allowed to tamper with your rights or liberties.*[70]

During his elaborate tour of the Gulf, an argument with Iranian authorities prevented Lord Curzon from disembarking at Bushehr. Curzon, who planned to visit the Residency mansion, angrily cancelled the visit when Iranian authorities insisted that he abide by certain diplomatic protocols – protocols that would have subordinated his rank as Viceroy of India beneath that of the Governor of Fars.[71] Britain's refusal to recognize Iranian authority in the southern provinces was not soon forgotten in Tehran.

The hire of Belgian customs administrators by the Qajar government at the turn of the century and their efforts to establish customs offices in the southern ports and islands where British influence held sway

[68] "Indian Viceroy's Tour," *New York Times*, November 16, 1903.
[69] IOR/L/P&S/7/195: Political Resident to the Government of India, March 18, 1906, with enclosures.
[70] Lorimer, *Gazetteer of the Persian Gulf*, Vol. 1: Historical, p. 2638.
[71] Shiva Balaghi, "Nationalism and Cultural Production in Iran, 1848–1906," PhD dissertation (University of Michigan, 2008), pp. 201–203.

provoked a number of fresh disputes between Iran and the British government. Among the places earmarked for the construction of Iranian customs houses were three small islands, Abu Musa, Greater Tunb, and Lesser Tunb.

The British government recognized the Al Qasimi shaykhs of Sharjah and Ras al-Khaimah as the owners of Abu Musa and the Tunbs, while Iran viewed these islands as an integral part of its sovereign territory. Anticipating that the dispute over these islands would be revived, the government of India asked Shaykh Saqr bin Khalid Al Qasimi, then Ruler of both Sharjah and Ras al-Khaimah, to fly his flags on Abu Musa and Greater Tunb, which he did in the beginning of 1903. In April 1904, the Belgian director of customs at Bandar Abbas departed on a tour to inspect the islands where Iran intended to establish customs houses. Having found the shaykh's red-and-white flags erected on Abu Musa and Greater Tunb, he removed them, installed Iran's flag in their stead and stationed sentries to keep watch. He also installed an Iranian flag on Sirri Island, where no Arab flag flew. These events provoked a dispute between the Foreign Office's minister in Tehran and the Qajar government. The British minister became convinced that the Iranian foreign minister, Moshir al-Dowleh, had ordered the shaykhs' flags to be taken down at the instigation of the Russian government, which was still seeking to gain a foothold in the Gulf. Faced with an ultimatum from the British government, Iran's foreign minister agreed to issue instructions for the removal of the flags and expressed a hope that neither party would hoist flags in the two islands pending a settlement to the dispute. Notwithstanding that, the Resident instructed the Shaykh of Sharjah to rehoist his flags, which he did. In the absence of naval power sufficient to enforce its will, Iran's only recourse was through protest.[72]

The establishment of an Iranian customs house on Hengam Island in 1904 provoked considerable friction between the Qajar authorities

[72] IOR/L/P&S/18/B397: J. G. Laithwaite, "Status of Islands of Tamb, Little Tamb, Abu Musa and Sirri," August 24, 1928; Lorimer, *Gazetteer of the Persian Gulf*, Vol. 1: Historical, p. 2138; see also Koroush Ahmadi, "Islands and International Politics in the Persian Gulf: Abu Musa and Tunbs in Strategic Perspective," *Iranian Review of Foreign Affairs* 3, no. 1 (Spring 2012), pp. 31–33; and Mohammad ʻAli Bahmani Qajar, *Tamamiyat-e Arzi-ye Iran: Sayri dar Tarikh-e Marzha-ye Iran* (Tehran: Mu'assasah-ye Motala'at va Pezhuheshha-ye Siyasi, 1390/2001), pp. 144–145.

and the Arab tribesmen that inhabited the island. Hengam was a semi-autonomous tribal enclave, inhabited by Arabs of the Bani Yas tribal confederacy, and ruled by a relative of the Shaykh of Dubai. They migrated to Hengam in 1826 after receiving permission from the Sultan of Muscat who leased the island from the Qajar government.[73] They had intermarried with the Bani Yas of the Trucial Coast and their economic activity – mainly pearl diving and cargo transport – was interconnected with the Arabian littoral.[74] The reassertion of Iranian authority on Hengam and the attempt to collect taxes was an unwelcome development for the tribal inhabitants of the island. The Shaykh of Hengam, Shaykh Ahmad, cast about for protection, soliciting both the British government and the Sultan of Muscat. The crisis finally abated when the merchants of Hengam developed various means of getting around the customs dues. The British naval squadron and a coaling station were quietly transferred to Hengam in 1911 without reference to the Qajar government.[75]

Immigration to the Shaykhdoms from Southern Iran

The security of the Arab ports that thrived under British protection as contrasted with the instability and economic distress in Qajar Iran fostered waves of emigration from the northern to the southern littoral. Many Iran-based entrepreneurs who were engaged in the sea trade were attracted to the prospering port towns of the southern littoral, particularly Manama and the Trucial ports. Often these merchants were the businessmen who imported foodstuffs from India, such as rice, sugar, and coffee, and sold them in local shops or redistributed them to other population centers in and around the Persian Gulf.[76] When conditions for business became intolerable in Iran, they opted to open trading outposts in the Arab ports where the tax burden was light

[73] Muhammad Hasan al-'Aydarus, *al-Juzur al-'Arabiyya wa-l-ihtilal al-Irani namudhaj lil-'alaqat al-'Arabiyya al-Iraniyya: Dirasa Watha'iqiyya Arshifiyya*, Vol. 2 (Dubai: Dar al-'Aydarus lil-Kitab al-Hadith, 2002), p. 46.

[74] FO 416/83: Lieutenant Colonel Sir L. Haworth to the Government of India, July 20, 1928.

[75] IOR/L/P&S/18/B399: J. G. Laithwaite, "Status of Certain Groups of Island in the Persian Gulf," August 24, 1928; Lorimer, *Gazetteer of the Persian Gulf*, Vol. 1: Historical, p. 2138.

[76] Willem Floor, *The Rise and Fall of Bandar-e Lingah: The Distribution Center for the Arabian Coast 1750–1930* (Washington, DC: Mage, 2010), p. 14.

and the *Pax Britannica* prevailed. Most of them did not view this as a permanent move because they maintained branches on both sides of the Gulf as well as in the greater Indian Ocean trading area. It was often the case that such merchants would reside in one of the Persian Gulf port towns on the southern littoral during the winter and return to their homes in Iran during the hot season. Initially, the opening of business branches on the Arabian coast did little to change the orientation of trade because the bulk of the imports from India still passed through the Iranian port of Lingah before being redistributed to other ports or prepared for the journey inland.[77]

Immigration played a vital role in the formulation of the economic and political power structure of the Arab shaykhdoms. Immigrants whose business activities contributed to enlarging the ruler's purse and prestige were highly sought after. Among the most valuable and influential newcomers were wealthy entrepreneurs from Iran and financiers from India. Indians, most of whom were Hindu, came to the shaykhdoms as British subjects and represented British business interests. Another important group of immigrants during this formative period was the Hawala – Sunni Muslims from southern Iran who claimed that their heritage was on the Arabian Peninsula. Their transfer from the northern to the southern littoral of the Persian Gulf was depicted as a "return" to the land of their forebears.[78] These newcomers were depicted by the local Arabs as foreigners because of their Persian dress, language, customs, and manners. But unlike their Indian counterparts, their Sunni faith and their claim to Arab ancestry enabled them to more easily gain acceptance by the dominant group.

The first wave of immigration to the southern littoral began around the middle of the nineteenth century, when the Qajar government began to extend its authority to Iran's southern ports. In 1850 the Al Madhkur family in Bushehr lost its position, after a 13-year struggle with the central government arising out of the shaykh's failure to produce the increased taxes demanded of him. The arrival of Iranian officials was an unwelcome development for Bushehr notables who had hitherto prospered under the circumstances of local autonomy.[79]

[77] Mohammad T. Razavian, "Iranian Communities of the Persian Gulf: A Geographical Analysis," PhD dissertation (University of London, 1975), p. 375.

[78] Lorimer, *Gazetteer of the Persian Gulf,* Vol. 1: Historical, pp. 754–755.

[79] Vanessa Martin, *The Qajar Pact: Bargaining, Protest and the State in Nineteenth-Century Persia* (London: I.B. Tauris, 2005), pp. 29–47.

From the 1870s the whole Dashti district, of which Bushehr was the capital, was plagued with troubles – drought, famine, disease, and rising crime – which encouraged further emigration. The flourishing pearl and entrepôt economy of Bahrain attracted many of these immigrants from the area of Bushehr, who may have viewed Bahrain as a part of Iran that was still outside of the reach of the central authorities.[80]

Members of the Shiʿi Safar family and the Shiʿi Bushiri family were among those who left Bushehr in the midst of its troubles, for better business opportunities in Bahrain. Their stories illustrate the manner in which the first generation of immigrants helped pave the way for the immigration of their family members and business associates. ʿAli Kazem Bushiri arrived in Manama around 1860 and worked as a laborer in the harbor and an errand boy for Hajji ʿAbd al-Nabi Khan Safar, also from Bushehr.[81] In 1872 he established a Persian shop in the market and accumulated a fortune by importing foodstuffs from Iran and India. He provided loans to fellow shopkeepers, especially Iranian immigrants who flocked to the town. One of the immigrants that he sponsored was his cousin and brother-in-law, Hajji ʿAbd al-Nabi Bushiri, who arrived in 1888 to work at his shop. This connection facilitated the transfer of his father-in-law, Ahmad Bushiri, to Bahrain in 1890. ʿAbd al-Nabi Bushiri established a partnership with ʿAli Kazem Bushiri and the two went into business as building contractors.[82]

A second wave of immigration to the shaykhdoms began in the 1880s and culminated in a massive influx of newcomers around the turn of the century. In the 1880s the Qajar government, heavily burdened with foreign debt, began to bring more of its southern ports under the authority of the central government. In 1899, after a 15-year struggle against the Qawasim, Lingah and Sirri Island were brought under central control. Confronted with high customs tariffs and deprived of the protection of an Arab shaykh, Arab merchants from this area began to shift their economic activities back to the land of their forebears. Some shifted their businesses to the Qasimi homeland

[80] Razavian, "Iranian Communities in the Persian Gulf," pp. 308–309.
[81] Onley, *The Arabian Frontier of the British Raj*, p. 107.
[82] ʿAli Akbar Bushehri, "ʿAmid al-ʿAʾila Shaykh al-ʿAjam ʿAli Kazem Bushehri," *Tarikh Mamlakat al-Bahrayn*, October 23, 2012, http://bahrain.svalu.com/1033.html (accessed February 18, 2013).

of Sharjah and Ras al-Khaimah but a greater number were attracted to the neighboring port of Dubai, where Shaykh Rashid bin Maktum offered them his personal protection and prime plots of land close to the creek.[83]

The Farook family is an exemplar of the Bastaki families that settled in Dubai at the invitation of Shaykh Rashid. Taking its name from the patriarch, Muhammad Farook al-Arshi, the family was based in Lingah, but also maintained houses in Bombay, Karachi, Bahrain, Dubai, and Paris. The family business was selling and distributing commodities such as textiles, building materials and particularly, pearls. Just before the turn of the century, Farook's second son, 'Abd al-Karim Farook, was one of the first five Bastaki merchants to build houses next to Dubai creek in the area that came to be known as the Bastakiyya quarter. Bastakiyya, characterized by its Persian wind tower architecture, was named for the town of Bastak in the Lingah district. During his lifetime, 'Abd al-Karim linked himself by marriage to four different Sunni families, among them the Al Qasimi ruling family of Sharjah and Ras al-Khaimah, and the 'Abd al-Latif and Fikri families also from Bastak.[84]

Some unofficial population estimates that were made during the first decade of the twentieth century can give an indication of the direction of population movement on the eve of the First World War. In that decade, the population of Kuwait was estimated to be about 35,000 souls of which an estimated 1,000 were considered Iranian nationals. That number consisted of about 20 wealthy entrepreneurs, 100 shopkeepers, 200 indigents, and the remainder craftsmen and laborers.[85] The total population of Dubai was estimated at around 2,075 souls, a number which included about 500 shopkeepers from Iran. Most of these were thought to be merchants from the Lingah district (including Bastak) who engaged in the trans-shipment and sale of foodstuffs and

83 Julia Wheeler and Paul Thuysbaert, *Telling Tales: An Oral History of Dubai* (Dubai: Explorer, 2005), pp. 68–69.

84 Mariam Behnam, *Zelzelah: A Woman before Her Time* (Dubai: Motivate, 1994), pp. 16–22. See also "al-Ayam al-Bahriniyya: al-Wajih al-Mohsin Mustafa bin 'Abd al-Latif al-'Abbasi, 1383–1307/1890–1964," *al-Ayam* (Manama), *Ramadan* 2, 1432 (August 2, 2011) www.alayam.com/alayam/Variety/97993/News.html (accessed May 6, 2019).

85 Lorimer, *Gazetteer of the Persian Gulf,* Vol. 1: Historical, p. 1051.

other commodities.[86] Manama's population was estimated at about 25,000, a number that included about 1,550 Iranians. Unlike in Dubai where the majority of the immigrants who arrived from Iran before 1904 were Sunnis, in Bahrain Shi'i immigrants from Iran outnumbered Sunni immigrants.[87] Also, in contrast to Kuwait and Dubai, where immigrants from Iran inhabited the same living quarters as the prominent tribal families, settlement in Bahrain was organized along the lines of multiple, distinct ethnic, and sectarian communities. Here it is worthwhile to consider the unique situation that was created in Bahrain where the greatest degree of sectarian differences was felt.

Bahrain, the British, and Qajar Iran

Like the other Gulf Arab shaykhdoms, Bahrain grew up as a pearling center and mercantile community based in a port town ruled by a Sunni Arab shaykhly family of Bedouin origin. The main religious distinction was between Sunni and Shi'i. The Shi'i segment could be further divided into two groups: the *Baharna*, native, nontribal Arab villagers who dwelled on the archipelago before the Al Khalifa gained power, and the Shi'i immigrants from Iran, called 'Ajam (foreigners) by the Arab population. The Baharna and the 'Ajam shared the same Shi'i faith, but spoke different languages, gathered around separate places of worship, inhabited different neighborhoods, and did not intermarry. Sunnis could be further divided into three main groups. The first group was composed of tribes, including the Al Khalifa, Al Jalahimah, Al Subah, Al Dawasir, Al Fadhil, Al Rumahi, Al Manan'a, Al Mosallam, Al Sada, Sudan, and Al Bin 'Ali. Some of these were, like the Al Khalifa, branches of the Bani 'Utub confederation, which arrived to Bahrain alongside the Al Khalifa, while others, such as the Dawasir arrived after the conquest.[88] The second Sunni group was comprised of "Najdis," merchants who took leave of their town or tribal abode in the Arabian interior to pursue business opportunities on the coast. Their Arab pedigree and Sunni faith enabled them to become close

[86] IOR/R/15/1/252: Residency Agent Sharjah ('Abd al-Latif) to Political Resident (Kemball), July 29, 1901; Frauke Heard-Bey, *From Trucial States to United Arab Emirates*, 2nd ed. (London: Longman, 1996), p. 242.
[87] Lorimer, *Gazetteer of the Persian Gulf*, Vol. 1: Historical, p. 1160.
[88] Muhammad Ghanim Al-Rumaihi, "Social and Political Change in Bahrain since the First World War," PhD thesis (Durham University, 1973), p. 50.

associates with the ruling family. The third Sunni group consisted of merchant families who depicted themselves as "Hawala." These were families that claimed Arab heritage and depicted their transfer to the Arab shaykhdoms as a "return" to the land of their forebears after a long sojourn in southern Iran. Hawala were also called 'Ajam, especially in the early days of their migration, because of their strong cultural and linguistic connection to Iran, but over time, many of them were able to appeal to their Sunni faith and claim to Arab heritage to facilitate their acceptance into the dominant group.[89]

Al Khalifa rule, like the tribal rule in the other shaykhdoms, was informal and decentralized. Some areas inhabited by tribal allies of the Al Khalifa, such as the abodes of the Dawasir in al-Budayyi' and al-Zallaq, enjoyed virtual autonomy from the ruling apparatus. The loyalty of the ruler's male family members and other tribal allies was maintained by the distribution of favors, such as subsidies, business concessions, and the rights to administer certain tracts of land. Most of Bahrain's cultivated land was appropriated over time by the ruler, Shaykh 'Isa bin 'Ali Al Khalifa, when the peasants who worked the land were unable to pay the taxes and fees that were demanded of them. Once acquired, plots of land, market properties, and entire villages were distributed among his male relatives, to be administered for their own gain, thereby ensuring their continued loyalty and acquiescence to his rule. These men, the subordinate Al Khalifa shaykhs, enjoyed virtual autonomy in their own estates, collecting taxes for their own purse, holding majlis, settling disputes, and providing law and order. The shaykhs enforced their will through the use of their armed retainers (*fidawiyya*) made up of Sunni Arabs, Baluchis, and freed African slaves. Through the coercive arm of the *fidawiyya*, shaykhs were known to be especially harsh in their extraction of forced labor (*sukhra*) and collection of taxes from the most vulnerable segments of society, namely the Baharna villagers.[90]

[89] Lorimer, *Gazetteer of the Persian Gulf*, Vol. 1: Historical, pp. 754–755; see also Clive Holes, "Dialect and National Identity," in *Monarchies and Nations: Globalization and Identity in the Arab States of the Gulf*, eds. Paul Dresch and James Piscatori (London: I.B. Tauris, 2005), p. 58.

[90] Fuad I. Khuri, *Tribe and State in Bahrain: The Transformation of Social and Political Authority in an Arab State* (Chicago: University of Chicago Press, 1980), pp. 49–52.

Toward the end of the nineteenth century, successful immigrant merchants were able to capitalize on the decentralized tribal administration to acquire tax-farming rights in certain commodities and the control of some market properties. This enabled them to employ immigrants from their own communities of origin and also afforded them a special status as the intermediary between the Al Khalifa and the immigrant community that they sponsored.[91] The story of Hajji ʻAbd al-Nabi Kal Awaz Kazeruni can serve as an example of how a Shiʻi merchant from Iran was able to leverage the tribally organized administration to acquire a considerable degree of wealth and status in Bahrain. Hailing from Kazerun, a town between Shiraz and Bushehr in the southern province of Fars, the Kazeruni family became firmly established in Manama by the end of the nineteenth century. By 1904, ʻAbd al-Nabi Kazeruni, the son of a shopkeeper, had acquired a contract to manage the cargo landing operations and warehouse on behalf of the Al Khalifa shaykh who held tax-farming rights in the harbor. He also received renumeration for serving as an interpreter for the shipping agent, Gray Paul & Co., and for provisioning the British men of war while they were stationed at Bushehr. He was recognized as the head of a small immigrant labor force composed of grocers and laborers who worked in the market.[92] By 1910 he had become the leader of al-Ma'tam al-ʻAjam al-Kabir, the Shiʻi house of mourning that provided a sense of community and spiritual fulfillment to Iranian immigrant laborers.[93] Between 1910 and 1913, together with the Bushiri, Dashti, and Shirazi families, ʻAbd al-Nabi Kazeruni helped to found Ettehad, the Iranian school for boys. The school was instrumental in the preservation of language, culture, and national identity among the children of Iranian immigrants to Bahrain.[94]

While the economic policies of the Al Khalifa family were favorable to the growth of immigrant communities in Bahrain, Fuad Khuri

[91] Nelida Fuccaro, *Histories of City and State in the Persian Gulf: Manama since 1800* (New York: Cambridge University Press, 2009), pp. 88–90.

[92] IOR/L/P&S/10/81: Major Cox, Officiating Political Resident in the Persian Gulf to the Secretary of the Government of India, No. 421, December 17, 1904, with enclosures.

[93] ʻAbdullah Sayf, *al-Ma'tam fi al-Bahrayn*, Vol. 1 (Manama: al-Matbaʻa al-Sharqiyya, 1995), pp. 109–111.

[94] Mai bint Mohammed Al Khalifa, *Mi'at ʻAm min al-Taʻlim al-Nizami fi al-Bahrayn: al-Sanawat al-Ula lil-Ta'sis* (Beruit: al-Mu'assasa al-ʻArabiyya lil-Dirasat wa-l-Nashr, 1999), pp. 105–107.

points out that the traditional tribal administration made it difficult for anyone outside of the Al Khalifa patronage system to obtain a satisfactory form of justice.[95] The massive influx of immigrants that accelerated after the 1860s created the problem of jurisdiction over foreigners in a country where "foreigner" was hard to define. Moreover, the particularly large presence of foreigners made it inevitable that a conflict involving foreign nationals would attract the attention of foreign governments and draw the British, as mediator, deeper into Bahrain's affairs.[96] The crises that unfolded in September 1904, which involved German and Iranian nationals, brought the matter to a head.

In September 1904, Shaykh 'Isa's nephew, Shaykh 'Ali bin Ahmad, and several of his *fidawiyya* assaulted an employee of the German firm, Wönckhaus and Co. Not satisfied with the actions taken by the British Political Agent, Robert Wönckhaus, owner of the firm, appealed to the German Consul in Bushehr.[97] Soon after that, a brawl broke out in the market between Shaykh 'Ali's men and a group of Iranian shopkeepers headed by 'Abd al-Nabi Kazeruni. The severity of the beatings inflicted on 'Abd al-Nabi's party by Shaykh 'Ali's *fidawiyya*, among other indications, pointed to Shaykh 'Ali's role in the deliberate escalation of the violence. The *casus belli* appeared to be an earlier episode in which Shaykh 'Ali's *fidawiyya* were punished after they were caught by 'Abd al-Nabi robbing the warehouse in the harbor. The injured Iranians refused to appear before the Shari'a court because it was composed of Sunni mullahs and Al Khalifa tribesmen whom they blamed for the assaults. 'Abd al-Nabi sent a telegram to Tehran on behalf of the Iranian community in Bahrain, describing their plight and appealing for the shah's protection.[98] The reply from Foreign Minister Moshir al-Dowleh bears witness to the absolute powerlessness of the Qajar government in relation to the affairs of Bahrain:

> I received your telegram regarding the assault on you by the Bahrain Arabs. Keep yourselves calm for I have had a long talk with the British Minister on the subject and I am sure he will take early steps to get the affair settled and get the culprits punished.[99]

[95] Khuri, *Tribe and State in Bahrain*, pp. 87–88. [96] Ibid.
[97] IOR/L/P&S/10/81: Major Cox to the Secretary of the Government of India, No. 420, December 17, 1904, with enclosures.
[98] Ibid. [99] Ibid., enclosure No. 4.

Desirous of proving its worth as a protecting power and precluding further intervention by Iran and Germany, the British forced Shaykh 'Isa, under threat of naval bombardment, to accept the rulings of a British tribunal, which called for the public flogging and banishment of Shaykh 'Ali and the ringleaders, and compensation for the injured parties.[100] For the Iranian nationals in Bahrain, this marked the beginning of their informal status as British protected persons, similar to the Indians and Europeans residing there. For Shaykh 'Isa, this intervention represented an encroachment on the traditional rights of the Al Khalifa family.[101] For the British government, these events contributed to a growing awareness that to effectively keep foreign governments out of Bahrain's affairs, it would need to effect an improvement in the administration of justice on the archipelago.

The Persian Gulf in a Changing Regional System

The first two decades of the twentieth century were witness to significant historical processes that paved the way for the emergence of a new political power map in the Persian Gulf region. The aging and decadent Ottoman Empire was in the last throes of a process of disintegration while British power and influence in the Persian Gulf reached its zenith. The discovery of oil in Iran in 1908 meant that British interests in the Gulf further expanded in the years prior to the First World War. The Anglo-Persian Oil Company (APOC) was formed in 1909 and it took over the D'Arcy concession of 1901.[102] Seeking to secure the investment, the British deepened their commitment to Shaykh Khaz'al Khan al-Ka'bi, the Ruler of Mohammerah (later Khorramshahr). In exchange for a guarantee of the security of the oil installations and company personnel, the British government committed to protect him from an unprovoked attack or encroachment by a foreign power and to support him to the extent of obtaining a satisfactory solution in the event of encroachment by the Iranian government on his jurisdiction,

[100] IOR/L/P&S/10/81: Major Cox to the Officiating Secretary of the Government of India, March 4, 1905, with enclosures.

[101] IOR/L/P&S/10/81: Petition from the Shaykh of Bahrain, *Sha'ban* 3, 1323 (October 2, 1905).

[102] In 1935 APOC was renamed the Anglo-Iranian Oil Company (AIOC) and in 1954 it became the British Petroleum Company (BP).

recognized rights, or property.[103] The largest refinery in the world was completed at Abadan in 1913, and on the eve of the First World War, the oil it produced assumed a new strategic importance when it began to replace coal as the main source of fuel for the Royal Navy.

The rise of nationalism in Iran in the late Qajar period transformed the nation's political landscape. Literature, historiography, cartography, and archaeology of the late Qajar period expressed a tangible sense of longing for the restoration of a strong and effective government, and the territorial sovereignty and cultural dominance of former days.[104] A greater sense of Iranian nationhood emerged particularly during the 1905–1911 Constitutional Revolution. All the urban classes participated in the revolt against arbitrary rule.[105] The nobility, 'ulama', and educated elites demanded greater liberty and emancipation from foreign domination. The revolution led to the establishment of a constitutional monarchy and the creation of the Majles. Nationalists had high hopes that constitutionalism would pave the way for the restoration of Iran's former glory. The importance of the Persian Gulf to Iranian national consciousness was expressed in the constitutional press where newspapers such as *Majles*, *Muzaffari,* and *Habl al-Matin* devoted special attention to elucidating the history of the Persian Gulf and the history of Bahrain with particular attention to the periods of Iranian preeminence.[106] But that enthusiasm was dampened when the revolution spiralled into chaos. In August 1907, an Anglo-Russian agreement divided Iran into a Russian zone in the north, a British zone in the south, and a neutral zone. The shah was no longer able to play the one off against the other. The central government disintegrated and autonomous power centers rose up throughout the provinces to fulfill the administrative functions that had once been Tehran's jurisdiction. These experiences would gradually give way to a new direction for Iranian nationalism,

[103] H. M. Government, Cabinet Office, "Historical Summary of Events in the Territories of the Ottoman Empire, Persia and Arabia Affecting the British Position in the Persian Gulf, 1907–1928," PG 13 (London: Committee of Imperial Defense, 1928; Repr., Archive Editions, 1987), p. 34.

[104] Firoozeh Kashani-Sabet, *Frontier Fictions: Shaping the Iranian Nation, 1804–1946* (Princeton, NJ: Princeton University Press, 1999), pp. 1–14.

[105] Homa Katouzian, *State and Society in Iran: The Eclipse of the Qajars and the Emergence of the Pahlavis* (London: I.B. Tauris, 2000), p. 50.

[106] Azita Logha'i, "Bahreyn dar Matbu'at-e Mashrutah (1322–1325)" *Faslnameh-ye Motala'at-e Tarikhi* 8, no. 33 (Summer 1390/2011).

exemplified by the growing perception among the elites of the need for a strong central government and a strong leader who could consolidate and centralize the country.[107]

In eastern and central Arabia, Ibn Sa'ud emerged as the dominant force, uniting the disparate tribes through conquests and alliances. By 1912 the Najd and eastern coast of Arabia, formerly under nominal Ottoman sovereignty, were in his hands. His rise to power as a regional player changed the calculations of the British-protected Arab shaykhs, who were continuously assessing the regional power equation with an eye to enlarging their own autonomy. Ibn Sa'ud was feared by the Gulf shaykhs, but he was also used by them, as a tool by which to play one rival power center off the other in an effort to maximize their freedom from outside interference. The appeal for protection from the Shaykh of Dubai to Ibn Sa'ud in the aftermath of the 1910 *Hyacinth* incident can serve as an apt example. In the midst of an arms blockade in the Persian Gulf, the British navy was much annoyed to find out that Dubai had become a center for arms trafficking. On December 24, 1910, acting on intelligence that an illegal arms shipment had landed in Dubai and was being stored in the houses of Ahmad bin Dalmuk and Thani bin Khalif, the HMS *Hyacinth* laid anchor off the coast of Dubai and a small armed party disembarked to search the houses. A firefight broke out during which the *Hyacinth* fired off shells. In the end, 37 Arabs were killed and a number of buildings were damaged. This harsh experience with "gunboat diplomacy" provoked resentment among the people of Dubai toward the British officials, the British navy, and the Indian traders that enjoyed British protection.[108] So dissatisfied was he with the treatment of the British that Shaykh Butti bin Suhayl, the Ruler of Dubai, attempted, albeit unsuccessfully, to obtain protection from Ibn Sa'ud.[109]

When Ibn Sa'ud captured al-Hasa' (also known as al-Ahsa'), a narrow strip of coastal land between Kuwait and Qatar, the British became convinced that he was in a position to pose a serious threat to their position in the shaykhdoms of the Arabian littoral. Consequently, they compelled him to sign a treaty in 1915, which recognized him as the independent Ruler of Najd, Hasa and Qatif and contained a clause

107 M. Reza Ghods, "Iranian Nationalism and Reza Shah," *Middle Eastern Studies* 27, no. 1 (January 1991), pp. 35–37.

108 Abdullah, *The United Arab Emirates*, pp. 32–37.

109 Ibid., p. 175.

according to which he pledged to abstain from interference in Kuwait, Bahrain, Qatar, and the Trucial States.[110] The treaty did not prevent the spread of Wahhabi ideology or sympathy for Ibn Sa'ud's cause among the inhabitants of the coast, but it did secure his recognition of the British position in the Arab shaykhdoms. At various times, Trucial shaykhs made appeals to him in contravention of their treaty commitments, but British officials reprimanded them and also put pressure on Ibn Sa'ud to abide by his treaty commitment. As it were, Ibn Sa'ud had an overriding interest in preserving the sympathy of the British government, and did not respond to their overtures.[111] Nonetheless, his presence remained powerful throughout the interwar years.

The imposition of heavy customs tariffs in southern ports, between 1901 and 1904 drove many affluent merchants away from Iran's port towns. Many of Manama's seasonal merchants decided to make Bahrain their permanent residence.[112] Shaykh Maktum bin Maktum intentionally attracted the better part of Lingah's merchants to settle permanently in Dubai by offering free parcels of land and a tax-free port. He also awarded a seat in his majlis to the most prosperous Hawala merchants. Once in Dubai, wealthy entrepreneurs ordered their big trading ships from India to stop in Dubai instead of Lingah, and by 1904 steamers from the British India Steam Navigation Company made Dubai their main port of call.[113] By the early 1920s, the homes of families from Fars province such as the Lari, Awadhi, Harmoodi, and Gerashi families were nestled beside the residences of the Al Maktum inner circle.[114] Natural disasters affecting agricultural production in southern Iran engendered another wave of immigration in the 1910s, this time consisting of destitute villagers and

110 H. M. Government, Cabinet Office, "Historical Summary of Events in the Territories of the Ottoman Empire, Persia and Arabia Affecting the British Position in the Persian Gulf, 1907–1928," PG 13 (London: Committee of Imperial Defense, 1928; Repr., Archive Editions, 1987), p. 10.

111 Rosemarie Said Zahlan, *The Origins of the United Arab Emirates: A Political and Social History of the Trucial States* (London: Macmillan Press, 1978), p. 87; Abdullah, *The United Arab Emirates*, p. 179.

112 H. J. Whigham, *The Persian Problem* (London: Isbister and Company, 1903), p. 51.

113 Lorimer, *Gazetteer of the Persian Gulf*, Vol. 1: Historical, pp. 2611–2612.

114 Report of the Acting *Kargozar* of Bandar Lingah, *Bahman* 28, 1301 (February 18, 1923), in *Gozideh-ye Asnad-e Khalij-e Fars: Ravabet-e Iran ba Keshvarha-ye Hawzeh-ye Khalij-e Fars va Tahavvolat-e Dakheli-ye anha*, Vol. 2 (Tehran: Daftar-e Motala'at-e Siyasi va bayn al-Milali, 1369/1990), p. 35.

agriculturalists, mostly Shi'i, who came seeking employment as craftsmen, builders, divers, pullers, guards, porters, and dock laborers.[115]

In the early years of the twentieth century, Bahrain could aptly be described as a microcosm of the ideological and political processes unfolding in the region. Bahraini society was witness to the increased sense of nationhood among Iranians in the late Qajar period and the revival of the Saudi-Wahhabi movement in the Arabian Peninsula. The transnational dimensions of these upheavals were manifest in the activities of immigrants whose businesses and familial origins linked the heads of wealthy merchant families with power centers outside the island. 'Abd al-'Aziz al-Qusaybi, a wealthy immigrant from the Najd, came into prominence as the representative of Ibn Sa'ud and leader of Bahrain's Najdi community. After Ibn Sa'ud established authority over al-Hasa' 'Abd al-'Aziz al-Qusaybi was said to have acquired a virtual monopoly over the trade between Bahrain and the emerging Saudi-Wahhabi state.[116] In a similar vein, 'Abd al-Nabi Kazeruni capitalized on the local tribal apparatus that was grounded in patronage politics by appointing himself Iran's representative in Bahrain.[117]

Iranian communities in Bahrain were not unaffected by the rise of nationalist impulses in Iran, especially during the 1905–1911 Constitutional Revolution. Tehran newspapers received letters from correspondents in Bahrain, affirming their patriotism and calling for the reassertion of Iranian sovereignty there and the sending of a *Kargozar* (agent of the foreign ministry) to the island.[118] The inspiration for such articles was said to be the man who styled himself Iran's representative in Bahrain, 'Abd al-Nabi Kazeruni.[119] With the collusion of Qajar authorities, he was issuing Iranian travel passes, known as *ilm-o-khabar*, for travelers proceeding from Bahrain to Iranian ports. These travel passes included a header that specified "for persons proceeding from one Iranian port to another," a blatant assertion that Bahrain was part

115 Razavian, "Iranian Communities in the Persian Gulf," pp. 181–182, 310–313, 370–371, 377.

116 IOR/R/15/1/319: Political Agent Bahrain (Daly) to Political Resident, March 23, 1922.

117 IOR/R/15/2/2: Political Resident Bushire to His Britannic Majesty's Chargé d'Affaires Tehran, July 2, 1910.

118 See for example, *Majles*, 21 *Rabi' al-Avval* 1325 (May 3, 1907); *Neday-e Vatan*, 2 *Jamadi al-Avval* 1325 (July 12, 1907), IOR/R/15/2/2.

119 IOR/R/15/2/2: Political Agency Bahrain to the Political Resident, July 13, 1907.

of Iran.[120] *Kargozars* in Iranian ports were issuing the same travel passes to Iranians departing for Bahrain. To ensure conformity in this system, they required the traveler to leave a deposit in cash or kind, to be refunded, provided that he returned with a pass endorsed by ʻAbd al-Nabi.[121] The discovery of ʻAbd al-Nabi's activities in 1910, and the Political Agent's desire to deport him, hastened efforts in London to frame an Order in Council, a type of legislation that would regulate Britain's extraterritorial jurisdiction over all foreigners in Bahrain.[122] The shaykh, however, opposed the idea of deporting him, and soon the events of the First World War gave the British government reason enough to postpone further intervention in Bahrain.

In anticipation of an Ottoman declaration of war, the decision was taken in October 1914 to send a British Indian expeditionary force to Bahrain. The show of force, it was thought, would reassure the Arab shaykhs and rulers of the Persian Gulf, including Khazʻal Khan and Ibn Saʻud, of Britain's commitment to protect them from Ottoman aggression. While the shaykhs appreciated Britain's commitment to their independence and autonomy, their support for the British against the Ottomans was a cause of dissention between the shaykhs and the local population. Due to the strength of Islamic sentiment, the local Muslim majority largely supported the Ottomans in the war. When transport ships carrying Indian troops anchored off the coast of Bahrain on October 23, 1914, they were not permitted to disembark owing to the tangible anxiety that was exhibited among the Muslim population of Manama. The 5,000 men and 1,200 animals onboard remained in their hot, cramped quarters until November 2 when they departed for the Shatt al-Arab. The Mesopotamia campaign commenced on November 6 when the expeditionary force bombarded the Ottoman fort on al-Faw Peninsula.

In November 1914, British and Indian troops invaded and occupied Basra and established garrisons to protect British oil installations in neighboring Abadan. Their campaign in Mesopotamia was aided by Shaykh Khazʻal who provided intelligence on Ottoman movements and the Shaykh of Kuwait who provided financial support and allowed the use

120 See for example, a copy of an Iranian travel pass issued on October 27, 1924 to Hajji Mohammad Sharif in ʻAli Farahmand, "Engelis va Parvazha-ye Iran-zedayi az Khalij-e Fars," *Tarikh-e Ravabet-e Khareji*, no. 22 (Spring 1384/2005), p. 176.

121 IOR/R/15/2/2: Political Resident to Chargé d'Affaires Tehran, July 2, 1910.

122 IOR/R/15/2/2: Lieutenant-Colonel Cox to Sir Walter B. Townley, January 22, 1913.

of his harbor for evacuating the wounded. For his part in the war, Mubarak Al Sabah, the Kuwaiti shaykh, was promised independence after the dismantling of the Ottoman Empire. Shaykh Khaz'al was rewarded with a promise of protection for his heirs and successors.[123] The shaykhs' support for the British was, however, in contradiction with the anti-British sentiment that prevailed in the Muslim-majority societies under their rule.

Iran, despite its declaration of neutrality became a theater of the Great War. In the north it was invaded by Russia, in the West by the Ottomans, and in the south by the British. The demands of the invading troops during a time of drought and food shortage contributed to a prolonged famine, whose victims may have numbered in the millions. After the Russian Revolution of February 1917 halted Russian operations in Iran, the British became the dominant foreign military power. They further entrenched their position in the southern provinces with the creation of the South Persia Rifles, a locally staffed military force tasked with protecting their supply lines from brigandage and fending off tribal rebellions instigated by the German agent Wilhelm Wassmuss.[124] Hengam Island was turned into a support base for British operations in Mesopotamia and a canteen and recreation area was built for the squadron that was stationed there.[125] By the end of the war it served as Britain's de facto naval headquarters in the Persian Gulf.

States and Tribes in the Persian Gulf at the Dawn of the Modern Era

On the eve of the modern era of national boundaries and geopolitical fault lines, relations between individual Iranians and Arabs of the Persian Gulf issued from the long history of trans-migratory connections between the two shores. Trans-regional commercial networks, extensive cultural contacts, and overseas connections had fostered a dense of web of economic and social connections between Arabs, Iranians, Indians, and Europeans. Identities in the Gulf were fluid and could be negotiated according to different contexts and circumstances.

[123] H. M. Government, Cabinet Office, "Historical Summary of Events in the Territories of the Ottoman Empire, Persia and Arabia Affecting the British Position in the Persian Gulf, 1907–1928," PG 13 (London: Committee of Imperial Defense, 1928; Repr., Archive Editions, 1987), p. 34.

[124] Ibid., pp. 21–22.

[125] FO 317/12291: Foreign Secretary to the Government of India, January 6, 1927; with enclosure: "Précis of correspondence relating to British position at Basidu and Henjam, 1821–1926."

Political relations between Iran and the Arab shaykhdoms were governed by the British, the unquestioned hegemonic power in the region. British mastery of the Arab shaykhdoms was confirmed by the "exclusive agreements" dating back to 1892 and reinforced by their strategic collaboration with the Arab shaykhs during the first World War. Britain's military and economic control in southern Iran sprung from a web of ad hoc agreements concluded with the Shaykh of Mohammerah and minor khans in the south and was reinforced with the establishment of the South Persia Rifles, which further entrenched its military supremacy in Iran's coastal provinces. Tribal patronage of a foreign protecting power worked to the disadvantage of the Qajar state, severely undermining its authority in the far-flung provinces of the country. But British policies during the war contributed significantly to driving a wedge between tribal rulers who collaborated with the British and their dependents, most of whom opposed the collaboration.

Anti-British sentiment that proliferated during the war was a subject of cohesion for the Persian Gulf inhabitants – a disposition that crossed national and tribal lines. But the sense of identification with a modern nation-state or lack thereof was an element of divergence. Iran was possessed of a long history and tradition that existed within roughly the same territory. In contrast, the Gulf Arab shaykhdoms were relatively new tribal polities centered around port towns on the coast with undetermined borders in the hinterland. They were small in terms of population, military, and economic resources. The traditional tribal administrations of the shaykhdoms were informal and decentralized; their economic architecture was open to the inclusion of outsiders, especially wealthy outsiders, but the ruling apparatus remained the exclusive domain of the tribesmen.

Iranian nationalism that emerged in the late Qajar period and gained momentum during the constitutional era (1905–1911) placed an emphasis on pre-Islamic Persian culture and traditions. Even as yet, the ideology of nationalism had little touched ethnic minorities and tribal groups outside of Tehran. The primary frameworks for collective identity for many of the ethnic and linguistic minorities in Iran's Persian Gulf provinces, as with the tribes inhabiting the Arabian littoral, were variously based on tribe, locale, and religious sect. But the unique experience of Iran, forged when it was invaded by Ottoman, Russian, and British forces during the first World War would give rise to a new direction for Iranian nationalism. This would have profound ramifications for the tribes and ethnic minorities in Iran, the Iranian diaspora around the Persian Gulf and the tribally organized societies of Eastern Arabia.

2 *British Policy in the Persian Gulf between the World Wars*

For more than 100 years Great Britain has been the arbiter of the Gulf and it is mainly our prestige which had brought to an end the constant strife between Persian and Arab, and between conflicting Arab tribes, and which had rendered possible the virtual suppression of gun-running and the slave trade. This prestige is mainly the result of Naval power; and its outward and visible sign, especially to oriental eyes, is the British Flag.[1]

First Lord of the Admiralty, 1933

By the end of the First World War, Britain had secured a military hold over many of the Arab lands formerly under Ottoman rule. The administration of Palestine, Transjordan, and Mesopotamia was added to Britain's traditional areas of influence, Egypt, Sudan, the Arabian Peninsula, and the Persian Gulf. Britain's relationship with Kuwait, Bahrain, Qatar, and the Trucial States was governed by the "exclusive agreements," originating in 1892, which committed the British to their protection from external threats while preserving the autonomy of the ruling shaykhs. This is implicit in their official designation as states "under British protection" as distinguished from protectorates like Aden and the Sultanate of Egypt;[2] however, the distinction between "protectorate" and "protected state" soon became blurred in Bahrain. Compared with the other Gulf shaykhdoms, it was in Bahrain that the greatest degree of imperial intervention was felt. This was primarily due to the challenge that was posed to the British position in the Persian Gulf by the rise of nationalist feeling in Iran and the focus it placed on Bahrain.

The surge of nationalist sentiment in the aftermath of the Great War and the coming to the fore of Reza Shah Pahlavi was accompanied by a

[1] CAB 24/243: Memorandum by the First Lord of the Admiralty, September 1, 1933.
[2] Ibid., pp. 150–164.

sharp rejection on the part of Iran of Britain's claim to be the primary security provider in the Persian Gulf waterway. Reza Shah's government rejected the legitimacy of British supremacy in the Persian Gulf and counteracted it in many spheres. Moreover, the zeal of local officials, intent upon reviving Iran's historic role in the Gulf, presented a series of crises that tested the mettle of British supremacy. The challenge of Iranian nationalism to the British position in the Persian Gulf prompted the British government to conduct a thorough review of its policy, the result of which was an historic shift of its naval bases and administrative institutions from the Iranian to the Arabian littoral. Reza Shah's rise to independence and his introduction of a more assertive Persian Gulf policy provoked a great deal of excitement in London's halls of power, but ultimately British supremacy in the Persian Gulf survived the challenge. British military dominance persevered in the Gulf until 1971, when the British flag was hauled down voluntarily and for reasons largely unconnected with the situation in the Gulf.

Britain's Persian Gulf Policy, 1919–1939

The British administered the Persian Gulf as an informal domain of its Indian Empire.[3] Its integration was supported by telegraphic, postal, and aerial lines of communication, a quarantine service, and a lighting and buoying system. Moreover, British trade had acquired almost a monopoly on the commerce of Persian Gulf Ports.[4] The interwar years witnessed a dramatic growth of the importance placed on the Persian Gulf in British imperial strategy owing to its oil resources and oil potential. Having taken the decision to convert the fleet of the Royal Navy from coal to oil, British policy toward the Middle East became increasingly focused on securing access to oil resources. This pivotal transition was both strategic and risky: oil-powered ships were faster, more efficient, and required less manpower, but unlike the United States and Russia, the United Kingdom did not possess any significant oil resources. Thus, securing Britain's access to Iranian oil, and acquiring other sources of oil within the precincts of its formal and informal empire, became a major strategic priority. The Persian Gulf, with

[3] See James Onley, "Britain's Informal Empire in the Gulf, 1820–1971," *Journal of Social Affairs* 22, no. 87 (2005), pp. 29–45.

[4] Standish, "British Maritime Policy in the Persian Gulf," p. 346.

known oil reserves in Iran and suspected oil reserves in Mesopotamia and Kuwait, became a main pillar of imperial strategy. As the opening shots of the war were fired in 1914, the British government acquired a controlling interest in the Anglo-Persian Oil Company (APOC) to ensure that the British armed forces would have access to an adequate supply. By the end of the war, Iranian oil fields were producing one million tons annually.

When the Ottoman Empire entered the war, British strategy focused on securing its Persian Gulf oil facilities. They did so by sending troops to protect the installations at Abadan and by landing troops at al-Faw, which housed the main Ottoman fort on the Persian Gulf coast. Al-Faw was captured in 1914. Following that, the British advanced into Mesopotamia capturing Basra (1914), Baghdad (1917), and Mosul (1918). At the end of the war, Britain was given mandatory authority over Mesopotamia (Iraq) and also acquired Turkey's share in the Turkish Petroleum Company, the forerunner of the Iraq Petroleum Company. Access to Iraq's presumed oil resources became a subject of Anglo-French negotiations, and a formula for dividing Iraqi oil between them was reached at the San Remo Conference of 1920. By this time, the United States had also joined the quest for oil. American policy in the aftermath of the war, which was intent upon securing an "open door" for American commercial interests in the Middle East, stimulated heated and prolonged diplomatic disputes between the American and British governments during the interwar period.

The regulation of movement between and within states was also an outcome of the First World War, which had far-reaching implications for the dominions, colonies, protectorates, mandates, and other territories ruled or administered by the United Kingdom. Passports were introduced in British India at the start of the war under the Defence of India Act in 1914 and were made permanent under the Indian Passport Act of 1920. In the aftermath of the war, the British colonial apparatus realized the full potential of the passport as an instrument of political control and surveillance. British Indian passport booklets were issued to British subjects and British-protected persons. New travel regulations coming into effect during the war affected everyone in the Gulf from the wealthy merchants to the impoverished migrants. Inhabitants of the shaykhdoms who were in the employ of the British, namely the native agents and their families, were considered British protected persons and were eligible to receive the new passport booklets.[5] For the vast majority of the inhabitants of the Arab shaykhdoms, travel required the attainment a British-issued certificate of identity bearing an endorsement for the particular port or country he or she intended to enter. These certificates, variously referred to as passports, *ilm-o-khabar*, or travel permits, were required for entry to any of the Gulf Ports or India.[6] These were sharp indications that inhabitants of the Gulf who had long enjoyed access to multiple social and economic worlds were increasingly becoming subjected to the intrusion of imperialist structures.

The strengthening of Britain's political control in the Persian Gulf affected and was affected by the growth of anti-British feeling in the Arab shaykhdoms and aggressive anti-colonial nationalism in Iran. Opposition to the Anglo-Iranian Agreement of 1919, seen as prejudicial to the sovereignty of Iran, and the fall of the Iranian foreign minister who concluded it, attested to the strength of anti-British feeling in Iran. Likewise, agitations for the renewal of Iranian sovereignty over Bahrain were a precursor to the dramatic imperial interventions of 1923 designed to put an end to sectarian fighting and blunt Iran's interference on the archipelago. Most significantly, the coming to the fore of a stridently nationalist military leader in Iran and his introduction of a more aggressive policy in the Persian Gulf was the forerunner of the storm that would culminate in a historic shift of Britain's strategic bases from the northern to the southern littoral of the Persian Gulf.

The acquisition of new territories by Britain necessitated an extensive reorganization of the bureaucracy to incorporate the newly acquired mandates into the system. In February 1921 the Middle East Department was created within the Colonial Office under the direction of Sir Winston Churchill. The Masterton-Smith Committee appointed by the Cabinet and named for its chairman, Sir James Masterton-Smith,

5 "File 13/1 III Registration of passports of British subjects etc." British Library: India Office Records and Private Papers, IOR/R/IOR/R/15/2/1393, in Qatar Digital Library, www.qdl.qa/en/archive/81055/vdc_100023643127.0x00000a (accessed April 10, 2017).

6 "File 29/7 II Passport and Visa Regulations," British Library: India Office Records and Private Papers, IOR/R/IOR/R/15/2/1749, in Qatar Digital Library, www.qdl.qa/en/archive/81055/vdc_100026405052.0x00003b (accessed April 10, 2017).

recommended that responsibility for the Arabian littoral of the Persian Gulf should remain with the Resident at Bushehr answerable to the India Office, but that he should be authorized to communicate directly with the Colonial Office on certain matters related to oil and Ibn Sa'ud.[7] These recommendations were adopted by the Cabinet, although for considerable time, Sir Percy Cox, the High Commissioner for Iraq, remained the channel of communication with Ibn Sa'ud, owing to the close relationship between them. Subsequently, in 1924 the Bushehr Resident was informed that he was directly responsible to the India Office for the internal administration of all the states on the Arabian littoral of the Persian Gulf, including Kuwait, Bahrain, the Trucial States, and Muscat; however, he was responsible to the Colonial Office on all matters that might react on Arab politics in general, including Iraq, oil, and Ibn Sa'ud. After Ibn Sa'ud was recognized as the independent Ruler of the Hejaz and Najd, by the May 20, 1927 Treaty of Jeddah, the lion's share of responsibility for the emerging Saudi state devolved upon the Foreign Office.[8]

By June 1926, the severe problems of jurisdiction and overlapping administrative authority in territories of the Middle East had formed the subject of a debate in the House of Lords.[9] Citing the strategic necessity of defending the oil fields and the Imperial Airways routes through the Persian Gulf, the Air Ministry urged the Cabinet to set up another inter-departmental subcommittee, along the lines of the Masterton-Smith Committee, to reassess the political machinery in the Persian Gulf.[10] Britain's relations with the new sovereign in Iran reached a new low point when in May 1927 Reza Shah Pahlavi announced the end of capitulations in one year's time and in December lodged a claim to Bahrain in the League of Nations. Whitehall's decision to undertake wide-ranging negotiations with the Iranian government in the autumn of 1928 toward the conclusion of a general comprehensive agreement and the need to equip the minister in Tehran with an outline of British policy objectives prompted a comprehensive

[7] CAB 24/126: Memorandum by the Secretary of State for the Colonies, July 11, 1921.
[8] CAB 24/242: Memorandum by the Secretary of State for the Colonies, June 9, 1933.
[9] House of Lords (Hansard), Debate, June 30, 1926, Vol. 64, Cols. 678–86.
[10] CAB 24/195: Memorandum by the Secretary of State for Air, May 8, 1928.

reevaluation of Britain's Persian Gulf policy on the eve of his departure for Tehran.[11]

The ad hoc Persian Gulf Sub-Committee of the Committee of Imperial Defense was set up on June 25, 1928, by the prime minister at the request of the Cabinet to examine British policy in the Gulf in light of the changes taking place in Iran. The major challenge that Britain faced was the challenge of Reza Shah's rise to political power and his bid to weaken British authority in the south of Iran and in the Persian Gulf. In affirmation of this, the Secretary of State for India, in his memo of October 11, 1928, cites the events that had transpired during that year – the reassertion of Iran's claim to Bahrain, the Tunbs, and Abu Musa; Iran's reassertion of central authority on Hengam Island; Iran's advancement of a claim to suzerainty, if not to dominion, over Muscat and the independent Arab states of the Arabian littoral of the Gulf; Iran's bid to assume responsibility for control of quarantine; lighting and buoying; and policing against the slave trade and arms traffic; the uncertainty of the air route along the Iranian coastline; and Iran's nonrecognition of Iraq. In his memo, he concluded that Reza Shah intended to leave no effort unstrained to secure the total elimination of the former influence of Great Britain, not merely from the Iranian shoreline, and from those islands the Iranian ownership of which was not in dispute, but from the Persian Gulf as a whole.[12]

The Persian Gulf Sub-Committee met a total of four times over the course of an inquiry that lasted just under a year. Owing to differences of opinion, no conclusion was reached on the primary question – that of coordinating political control in the Persian Gulf – but the committee's interim report forms what is, perhaps, the clearest statement of British policy toward the Persian Gulf during the interwar period. It concluded that the maintenance of British supremacy in the Persian Gulf was more essential to the security of India and to imperial interests at the present time than it had been in the past. It was believed that British interests were exposed to dangers not less in degree, though differing in kind, from those to which they had been liable in the past. Modern developments, such as air power and cross-country traction, and the probability of the construction of a railway between northern

[11] CAB 23/59: Conclusions of a Meeting of the Cabinet, November 5, 1928.
[12] CAB 24/197: Memorandum by the Secretary of State for India, October 11, 1928.

Iran and the Gulf, had increased the potential risks to which the interests of the British crown were exposed.[13]

The committee reaffirmed Lord Lansdowne's declaration of 1903 that to maintain British supremacy it was necessary to prevent any foreign power from establishing a naval base or fortified port in the Persian Gulf, or air undertakings within striking distance of the Gulf. It avowed that Britain must retain sufficient harbor facilities in the Gulf for its navy and determined that Britain should press on with the measures required to establish and secure its strategic and civil air routes along the shores of the Gulf. The report declared that Britain should endeavor to maintain the status quo in its entirety on the Arabian littoral and to maintain the status quo to "the utmost limit that political considerations will admit" on the Iranian littoral.[14]

The minister in Tehran was instructed not to try to obtain from the Iranian government an extension of the three-year lease granted earlier that year for the operation of the civil air route but to insist on Iran abiding by the spirit of the arrangements made with Imperial Airways. The establishment of a new air route on the Arabian side of the Gulf was viewed as a strategic imperative from a military point of view and the report averred that every possible effort should be made by political means to prepare the way for its development.[15]

Where questions in the Persian Gulf are concerned, the committee made a crucial admission that in many of the detailed matters in dispute between Iran and Britain, Britain's legal title was weak. Here it is worthwhile to cite the conclusions of the committee in full:

> In Persia there has been a strong revival of nationalism under the stimulus of the present Shah, who, after establishing the authority of the Central Government over the greater part of Persia, is now seeking to reduce our position in the Gulf. Though Persia is incapable of undertaking efficiently the functions we now fulfill, or of ejecting us by force, the weakness of our legal status, combined with Persia's membership in the League of Nations created for us a position of some difficulty.
>
> Our wisest course in the present circumstances is to avoid reference to the League of Nations if we can, and to endeavor to reach a general settlement with Persia …

[13] CAB 24/198: The Persian Gulf: Interim Report of a Sub-Committee of the Committee of Imperial Defense, October 29, 1928.
[14] Ibid., pp. 25–26. [15] Ibid.

On the Arabian shore of the Gulf our position is governed by a series of Treaties placing under our protection the territories of the rulers of Koweit, Bahrein, the Trucial Chiefs, and, for practical purposes, Muscat, the independence of which, however, His Majesty's Government and France jointly guarantee to respect. The rise of the Wahabi Chief, Ibn Saud, to hegemony over the greater part of the Arabian Peninsula is a disturbing factor in our political relations with the Chiefs concerned, as well as in the development of the southern air route.

The best way in which the menace of the Wahabis and the danger of their conquest or absorption of the Sheikhs can be averted is by securing the friendship of Ibn Saud. This will take time. In the meantime it is essential to support the Sheikhs by an active demonstration of our will and power to protect their legitimate rights in accordance with our Treaties. In the forthcoming negotiations with Persia our representative should have instructions that it is an essential part of our policy to defend the Sheikhs on the Arabian shore against the claims of the Persian Government.[16]

While the Foreign Office sought a general settlement with Iran that would be compatible with Iranian sovereignty and national aspirations, the India Office and the Bushehr Resident opposed any diminution of British influence in the Persian Gulf, fearing the effect that such would have on British prestige in the Arab shaykhdoms.[17] Bushehr Resident Sir Lionel Haworth (1927–1929) was particularly obstinate in his opposition to the idea of placating Iran's demands in the Persian Gulf – these coming at a time when Iran's new customs patrols were zealously capturing Arab dhows on the high seas and Iranian passport officers were forcefully distributing Iranian identity documents to residents of the Gulf Arab shaykhdoms. Haworth even went so far as to recommend that formal protectorates should be established over Bahrain, Kuwait, Muscat, and the Trucial Coast as a means of ensuring British supremacy against the threat of expansion by Iran and Ibn Sa'ud.[18] His recommendation, however, was rejected by the India Office on the basis that if the need arose, a more definite assertion of

[16] Ibid.
[17] R. M. Burrell, "Britain, Iran and the Persian Gulf: Some Aspects of the Situation in the 1920s and 1930s," in *The Arabian Peninsula*, ed. Derek Hopwood (London: George Allen and Unwin, 1972), pp. 63–64.
[18] FO 416/81: Sir R. Clive to Sir Austen Chamberlain, October 7, 1927, with enclosures.

responsibility "could be made and enforced on the basis of [the] existing political situation and sea power."[19]

While Haworth's recommendation to turn the shaykhdoms into formal protectorates was rejected, their increasing importance to Britain during the interwar period was evident from several other key developments. By 1923 Bahrain had been witness to the greatest degree of British intervention in any of the Gulf Arab shaykhdoms, the result of which was the establishment of a modern state administration under the aegis of the government of India and a series of reforms that laid the foundations of the emerging Arab state. Owing to these favorable conditions, Bahrain surpassed Kuwait in imperial planning as the future destination of choice for the headquarters of the Persian Gulf Political Resident. The entrance of American oil capital in 1928 and the discovery of large quantities of oil in 1932 made Bahrain a subject of Anglo-American relations, further drawing the Foreign Office into Bahrain's affairs. Finally, the transference of Britain's main Persian Gulf naval base in 1935 from Hengam to al-Jufayr in Bahrain cemented the archipelago as the linchpin of British strategy in the Persian Gulf on the eve of the Second World War. Anti-British feeling that seethed beneath the surface was addressed during the 1930s by a series of measures aimed at curtailing the privileges of foreigners and employing locals in the nascent oil industry.

The interwar years also witnessed the elevation of the Trucial States from relative obscurity to strategic importance. Formerly regarded as a tribal backwater, inimical to foreign visitors, the ambition to locate a strategic air route along the southern littoral as well as the prospect of oil had quickly made these little pearling hamlets essential to British imperial strategy. The conclusion of an air agreement with the Shaykh of Sharjah in 1932 and the subsequent decision to make Sharjah's Political Agent answerable to the Political Agent in Bahrain reflected Britain's growing dependence on the Trucial shaykhs for its paramount position in the Persian Gulf. The importance of the Trucial States to Great Britain was further underscored when the India Office decided to send a British political officer in 1939. He came and went, residing in

[19] H. M. Government, Cabinet Office, "Historical Summary of Events in the Territories of the Ottoman Empire, Persia and Arabia Affecting the British Position in the Persian Gulf, 1907–1928," PG 13 (London: 1928; Repr., Archive Editions, 1987), pp. 89–90.

Sharjah for a few months at a time owing to the persistence of the inherited wisdom that this was a dangerous posting.[20]

The establishment of the air route along the southern littoral was accomplished only with an unprecedented degree of coercion on the part of the British government. The Trucial shaykhs put up a great deal of resistance fearing the repercussions among their tribesmen on account of allowing the British to dig a firmer foothold in the shaykhdoms. The early steps toward establishing landing facilities were literally forced on the rulers. Such was the case with Ras al-Khaimah where tribesmen came out to fire on a British fuel barge that was landed against the wishes of the ruler – the British Resident arrived with two warships and sufficient threats to ensure compliance.[21] In June 1932, the British brought sufficient pressure to bear on the Ruler of Sharjah to persuade him to sign an air agreement in defiance of the opposition from within his own family. The air route along the southern littoral was inaugurated in the beginning of October 1932 when a plane from Imperial Airways landed in Bahrain and then Sharjah in route to India.[22] A stop in Kuwait was added to the route in January 1933.

After five years of negotiations toward a comprehensive Anglo-Iranian treaty, the fall of Teymurtash and the shah's cancellation of the D'Arcy concession in the end of 1932 put the talks in abeyance. Iran's demand that as part of any agreement, Britain should recognize at least one of its territorial claims in the Persian Gulf – Bahrain, Abu Musa or Greater Tunb – was a demand that the British government had never been willing to consider.[23] The end of the Mandate in Iraq and the unification of Saudi Arabia in 1932 precipitated the transfer of responsibility for Persian Gulf affairs from the Colonial Office back to

[20] H. M. Government, Cabinet Office, "Historical Summary of Events in the Persian Gulf Shaikhdoms and the Sultanate of Muscat and Oman, 1928–1953," PG 53, in *The Persian Gulf Historical Summaries 1907–1953*, Vol. 2 (Archive Editions, 1987), p. 138.

[21] "File No 13/3-I of 1951. Sharjah Air Agreement (Aerodrome facilities at Sharjah)." British Library India Office Records and Private Papers, IOR/R/IOR/R/15/2/938, in Qatar Digital Library, www.qdl.qa/en/archive/81055/vdc_100025642054.0x000031 (accessed September 21, 2015).

[22] Nicholas Stanley-Price, "Imperial Airways and the Airfield at Sharjah, 1932–1939," *Liwa: Journal of the National Center for Documentation and Research* 3, no. 6 (December 2011), p. 34.

[23] Administration Report of the Persian Gulf Residency for the Year 1932, pp. 3–4.

the India Office.[24] The oil crisis was ameliorated by a new agreement reached between APOC and the Iranian government on May 29, 1933. But new challenges arose when Iran began actively seeking British withdrawal from Hengam and Basidu.[25]

Reza Shah's introduction of a modern navy in the end of 1932 and the zealous conduct of its officers sent shock waves around the Persian Gulf. On the eve of the arrival of six warships ordered from Italy, several debates took place between the various governmental departments concerned as to the danger of aggression by Iranian warships to the Arab shaykhs of the southern littoral and the procedure that should be adopted in the event that one of the Iranian warships should desire to visit an Arab port.[26] After considerable discussion, the Bushehr Resident was authorized to obtain declarations from the Gulf Arab rulers stating that they wished to receive notification through British channels in advance of any visits by Iranian warships. In the event that the Iranian navy intended to try to lay claim to a territory claimed by an Arab ruler under British protection, it was to be resisted by force, and ships captains were authorized to counter by force any act of aggression against subjects of the Gulf rulers.[27]

Britain's principal cause of complaint against the fledgling Imperial Iranian Navy was its frequent interference with dhows owned and piloted by inhabitants of the Arab shaykhdoms, most of whom were viewed as the dependents of Arab shaykhs. What was particularly vexing for the British government was the seizure of Trucial dhows by Iranian warships in the territorial waters of the Arab shaykhdoms, in the territorial waters of islands claimed by Arab shaykhs, and in the territorial waters of Muscat.[28] On several occasions, Iranian authorities professed not to know that their visits to the coastal waters of the

[24] CAB 24/242: Memorandum by the Secretary of State for the Colonies, June 9, 1933; CAB 23/76: Conclusions of a Meeting of the Cabinet, July 26, 1933.
[25] See Chapter 4.
[26] FO 416/89: Minutes of an Interdepartmental Conference held at the India Office on Monday, July 20, 1931.
[27] Annual Report on Persia for the Year 1932, p. 37, in *Iran Political Diaries 1881–1965*, eds. R. M. Burrell and R. Jarman, Vol. 9 (Archive Editions, 1997). (Hereafter, references to the Annual Reports on Persia that can be found in this set of 12 volumes will be referred to by their year and page number.)
[28] Annual Report on Persia for the Year 1933, p. 43; Annual Report on Persia for the Year 1934, p. 14; Annual Report on Persia for the Year 1937, p. 12.

southern littoral were considered trespassing.[29] In the words of a British naval officer, local Iranian authorities were prone to "aggravate the Arabs by announcing everywhere that they own the whole Gulf, including the Arabs' own territory and do everything they could to create ill-feeling."[30]

The Bushehr Resident and the officers of the Royal Navy repeatedly decried the damage that was being done to British "prestige" by the failure to protect inhabitants of the Gulf shaykhdoms from molestation by the Iranian customs and naval authorities. Numerous cases were recorded in which Iranian naval and customs officers carried out their board and search operations on Trucial dhows with particular zeal, firing on them, taking crews to shore for investigation, even putting nakhodas and crews on trial.[31] Each of these cases formed the subject of a protest to the Iranian government, though it was nearly impossible for the British government to diplomatically obtain redress for damages done.[32] The Commander in Chief of the East Indies Station warned of the consequences of failure in his letter of September 10, 1928, saying that, owing to the continued delays in diplomatic channels, "the trust hitherto reposed by the Arab sheikhs on the British Government, and even their trust in the British navy, which they have regarded as their best friend is being seriously undermined." Further, the aggressive attitude of the Iranian authorities and private individuals in the Gulf is increasing, and the lengthy and ineffectual method of dealing with it is "damaging the prestige of Great Britain" in the eyes of both shaykhs and Iranians.[33] Captain Hector Boyes, senior naval officer in the Persian Gulf (1927–1930), put it quite bluntly when he said, "[W]hile not permitting the Arabs to be armed at sea, we permit the Persian motor dhows to attack them."[34]

[29] See for example, Annual Report on Persia for the Year 1934, p. 15.

[30] IOR/R/15/1/280: Senior Naval Officer Persian Gulf (SNOPG) to Commander in Chief, East Indies Station (CinCEI), August 17, 1928.

[31] See for example, Administration Report of the Persian Gulf Residency for the Year 1934, p. 18; and Administration Report of the Persian Gulf Residency for the Year 1936, pp. v, 30, in *The Persian Gulf Administration Reports 1873–1957*, Vol. 9 (Archive Editions, 1986). (Hereafter, references to the Persian Gulf Administration Reports which can be found in this set of 12 volumes will be referred to by their year and page number.)

[32] Annual Report on Persia for the Year 1934, p. 14.

[33] FO 416/83: CinCEI to Admiralty, September 10, 1928.

[34] IOR/R/15/1/280: SNOPG to CinCEI, August 17, 1928.

The imperative of preserving British "prestige" fueled the decision to send a Royal Navy destroyer flotilla to the Persian Gulf in the late summer of 1933. A series of crises that occurred at Hengam and Basidu during that summer brought Iran's newfound pattern of assertion in the Persian Gulf to a crescendo. The hauling down of the British flag at the port of Basidu on Qeshm Island by a group of Iranian naval officers in August 1933 caused much commotion in the Arab shaykhdoms where Iran's actions were viewed as an open insult and act of defiance against England.[35] Wild stories circulated of Britain's impending retreat from the Gulf. In an effort to restore the confidence of the Arabs, the British government took the decision to send a flotilla to show the flag in the ports and islands of the Persian Gulf. In September 1933, the First Destroyer Flotilla of the British Mediterranean Fleet, consisting of nine warships, arrived to Hengam where they were joined by the senior naval officer on the HMS *Shoreham*. It proceeded to make a tour of the Persian Gulf stopping over in Kuwait, Bahrain, Doha, Dubai, Abu Dhabi, and the smaller ports of the Trucial Coast. State banquets were attended by sailors in full military regalia and ceremonies were staged. The Trucial shaykhs had an opportunity to inspect the honor guards, tour the ships, and examine the quality of the machinery and weapons systems.[36] All this was designed to provide practical proof of Britain's naval superiority and its firm intention of protecting its Arab friends against Iranian aggressions.

The lack of legitimacy for the ongoing British presence at Basidu on Qeshm Island was thrust into the spotlight by the high degree of publicity afforded to the arrest of the customs mudir by British military men in the fall of 1933. When the Iranian government began to consider referring this complaint to an international tribunal, the British government was forced to acknowledge, internally, the weakness of its own case. After a report by the Law Officers of the Crown determined that Britain's case for Basidu would not stand up in the court of international law, the decision was taken, in principle, on October 25, 1934, to prepare for the evacuation of Hengam and Basidu; however, action was postponed pending the efforts to secure basing on the southern littoral and to give the Resident adequate time

[35] See Chapter 5.

[36] IOR/R/15/2/491: Translation of an article which appeared in *al-Thagr* newspaper of Basra, dated *Jamad al-Thani* 21, 1332 (October 9, 1933).

"to prepare public opinion" and counteract the loss of prestige that such a withdrawal could signify.[37] Land was purchased from the government of Bahrain without it being disclosed to the ruler or to the public that the land was intended for use by the Royal Navy. When the Shaykh of Bahrain was notified in April 1935 that the British naval base would be relocated to Bahrain, he penned a letter to the Political Agent saying that he welcomed the transfer with great pleasure.[38] Circulars were distributed on the coast to explain the reasons for the transfer. Then on April 5 and 11, respectively, the British flags at Hengam and Basidu were ceremoniously hauled down and the transfer of the moorings, buoys, anchors, provisions, coal, recreational gear, furniture, and flagstaffs were carried out without incident.[39] The policy of gradual withdrawal of British interests from the Iranian littoral was carried further in the autumn when the telegraph stations on Hengam and Chabahar were handed over to Iranian administration. By the end of the year, the British minister in Tehran was able to state that "the Gulf had lost its position as the main storm-centre in Anglo-Iranian relations."[40]

Iran's seizure of dhows originating from the Arab shaykhdoms and Muscat continued and the British minister in Tehran warned the Iranian foreign ministry that if these incidents did not cease, the ships of the Royal Navy would be authorized to use force to prevent such incidents from occurring. This threat won the British minister an oral assurance that Iranian warships were being instructed not to inspect dhows outside of Iran's territorial waters.[41] In 1937 Iran's nonrecognition of travel passes (single-page identity documents issued by the British) belonging to residents of the Arab shaykhdoms was extended to include all those in possession of a British or British Indian passport that contained a visa for any of the Arab states in the Persian Gulf. Already in 1935 the British had begun equipping British-protected

37 Annual Report on Persia for the Year 1933, p. 39; FO 416/93: Sir John Simon to Mr. Knatchbull-Hugessen, March 4, 1935.

38 H. M. Government, Cabinet Office, "Historical Summary of Events in the Persian Gulf Shaikhdoms and the Sultanate of Muscat and Oman, 1928–1953," PG 53, in *The Persian Gulf Historical Summaries 1907–1953*, Vol. 2 (Archive Editions, 1987), p. 47.

39 FO 416/93: Extract from the Senior Naval Officer's Persian Gulf Intelligence Report for March and April 1935.

40 Annual Report on Persia for the Year 1935, p. 8.

41 Annual Report on Persia for the Year 1937, p. 13.

residents of Kuwait and Bahrain with multiple passports enabling them to sidestep harsh treatment by Iran's port authorities.[42]

By September 1938, the likelihood of war in Europe had come to overshadow the various local questions in the Persian Gulf. Despite a declaration of neutrality, Reza Shah's friendly relations with Nazi Germany were a cause of concern for the British who feared that in the event of hostilities the Abadan oil refinery could fall into German hands. The Soviet government had a graver assessment of the situation. It raised alarm bells over the large number of German nationals on Iranian territory and the risk that they posed to the interests of the Allied powers. Some of them, it was assumed, were spies and agents of the Nazis. Following Germany's invasion of the Soviet Union in June 1941, the Allied powers viewed the newly opened Trans-Iranian railway as an attractive option for the transport of critical war supplies from the Persian Gulf to Soviet locations, but the shah's declared neutrality obstructed its use as such. Finally, on July 19, 1941, the Soviet and British governments came together on the first of what would become a series of joint memoranda, demanding that the shah enact measures to reduce the number of Germans residing in Iran. The shah's refusal to cooperate became the pretext for the joint British and Soviet invasion of Iran which began on August 25, 1941. Iran's fledgling army and navy were rapidly overwhelmed and the oil fields and the railroad were seized. When the Allies' demand for the surrender of German nationals was not granted, Soviet troops entered Tehran. Reza Shah was sent into exile, leaving his 21-year-old son, Mohammad Reza Pahlavi, to replace him on the throne.[43]

The Persian Gulf in Anglo-Iranian Negotiations

Between the years 1928–1932 wide-reaching negotiations took place between Reza Shah's court minister, 'Abdolhossein Khan Teymurtash, and Britain's minister in Tehran, Sir Robert Clive (1926–1931), the aim of which was the conclusion of a bilateral treaty to resolve all outstanding issues between the two governments. The two sides failed

[42] Ibid., p. 15; IOR/L/P&S/12/3792: Minute paper, P. E. Grombie, January 11, 1935.

[43] Miron Rezun, *The Soviet Union and Iran: Soviet Policy in Iran from the Beginnings of the Pahlavi Dynasty Until the Soviet Invasion in 1941* (Leiden: Institut Universitaire de Hautes Études Internationales, 1981), pp. 356–373.

to reach an agreement and a treaty never materialized, but here it is worthwhile to examine the conduct and content of these negotiations because doing so can provide valuable insights about British policy toward Iran, the Arab shaykhdoms, and the Gulf.

The negotiations failed because of a disagreement about territory. Iran maintained that Britain did not offer sufficient compensation to persuade it to renounce its claim to Bahrain. The British government refused to afford any legitimacy to Iran's claim to Bahrain, viewing it as an independent Arab shaykhdom under British protection. Teymurtash's proposal – that a renunciation of Iran's claim to Bahrain might be possible if Iran were to be compensated by the positive recognition of one of its other territorial claims in the Gulf, such as Abu Musa or Greater Tunb Island – was not something that the British government was prepared to contemplate.

British objectives during these negotiations were to secure a lease for Hengam Island where they already maintained a naval base; to obtain a renunciation of Iran's claims to Bahrain, Abu Musa, and the Tunbs; and to reach settlements on questions surrounding the Slavery Convention of 1882, the Zahedan railway, lighting and buoying in the Persian Gulf, the transfer of wireless and telegraph stations and to reach a settlement regarding debt incurred by Iran during the First World War.[44] To achieve these objectives the British government relied upon a strategy of being able to bluff or mislead Iran into accepting concessions that were not really concessions at all.[45]

The British government did not anticipate the degree to which Iran's territorial claims and ambitions in the Persian Gulf would dominate the discussions, though the writing was on the wall. The first indication was the referral of Iran's Bahrain claim to the League of Nations on November 22, 1927. Britain's position from the start was that a *sine qua non* of any treaty was Iran's abandonment of its claims to Bahrain. Iran's position was that Bahrain was an inalienable part of Iranian territory, and its citizens would not allow the government to renounce

44 Ibid.; FO 416/84: Sir Clive to Sir Austen Chamberlain, December 22, 1928.

45 FO 416/83: Lord Cushendun to Sir R. Clive, November 7, 1928; FO 416/84: Sir Austen Chamberlain to Sir R. Clive, February 9, 1929; FO 416/89: Memorandum on Basidu, August 24, 1931; FO 416/92: Sir John Simon to Sir R. Hoare, November 29, 1933.

its rights to Bahrain without an adequate *quid pro quo*.[46] Iran's position was hardened by Russian support. The Soviet government – ever trying to limit British influence in Iran – saw the strategic value of Bahrain, and urged Teymurtash not to relinquish Iran's claim, lest the British turn it into a naval base that could pose a menace to Iran in the future.[47] Encouraged by the Russians, the Iranian government believed that Bahrain was one of its most valuable – if not the most valuable – bargaining chips, and demanded considerable remuneration in exchange for a renunciation of its claim.

The second indication that Iran's territorial ambitions would dominate the talks was the announcement in August 1928 of Iran's nonrecognition of the independence of the Gulf Arab shaykhdoms and its nonrecognition of Britain's special relationship with them. This came about during a series of correspondences after an Iranian customs patrol seized an Arab dhow off the coast of Greater Tunb, which was claimed by Iran. The British government asserted that the island was owned by the Shaykh of Ras al-Khaimah and that he was under British protection as per the treaties in force between them.[48] The Iranian government rejected the notion that the shaykh was independent and rejected Britain's claim of protecting him "on the pretext of having treaties."[49] In September fresh instructions were sent from Tehran to the provincial authorities affirming that travelers from Kuwait, Muscat, the Trucial States, and Bahrain were to be regarded as Iranian citizens.[50]

In response, the British provided Iran with a copy of the 1892 "exclusive agreement" between the British government and the rulers of the Trucial Coast (according to which the Arab rulers committed themselves not to enter into correspondence with any foreign power other than the British).[51] The Iranian foreign ministry reiterated its

[46] FO 416/84: Sir Clive to Sir Austen Chamberlain, January 8, 1929; FO 416/87: Sir Clive to Sir Austen Chamberlain, July 29, 1930; FO 416/91: Mr. Hoare to Sir John Simon, September 8, 1932.
[47] Rezun, *The Soviet Union and Iran*, p. 132.
[48] FO 416/83: Mr. Parr to M. Pakravan, August 4, 1928.
[49] FO 416/83: Acting Minister of Foreign Affairs (Pakravan) to His Majesty's Chargé d'Affaires (Parr), *Amerdad* 30, 1307 (August 21, 1928).
[50] IOR/L/P&S/12/3792: Decypher, Sir R. Clive, "Text of a circular of September 1925 as to passports of natives of Arab littoral," December 20, 1928.
[51] FO 416/83: Mr. Parr to Lord Cushendun, August 24, 1928; Mr. Parr to M. Pakravan, September 7, 1928.

"indisputable right" to Tunb (Greater Tunb Island was often referred to simply as "Tunb" in official correspondences) and added that the Iranian government could not recognize the aforementioned treaties as valid.[52] Around that time, a semi-official paper, *Habl al-Matin*, called for the renewal of Iran's protectorate over Muscat and other small shaykhs of the coast of Oman.[53] Britain's senior naval officer reported on some local intrigues that appeared to support a rumor that Iranian officials were instructed to open direct negotiations with the Trucial Coast without reference to Great Britain.[54] These shadowy claims to territory on the Arabian littoral were cleverly used by Teymurtash as a pressure point. Privately, he told Britain's minister in Tehran, Sir Robert Clive, that he was not aware of any claims to the Arab shaykhdoms and that if a compromise could be found in regards to Bahrain, Iran would disinterest itself in the affairs of the Trucial Coast.[55] A second protest was submitted to the League of Nations on January 5, 1929, against a new Bahraini law that barred Iranian nationals from entering Bahrain without a passport.[56]

At the start of these negotiations the British found many indications that the Iranian government had adopted a deliberate, provocative policy of challenging British supremacy throughout the Persian Gulf.[57] A memorandum by the Secretary of State for India drew attention to a series of incidents that had marked the summer of 1928 – the reassertion of Iran's claim to Bahrain, Abu Musa, and Greater Tunb; challenges to British authority at Hengam and Basidu; indications that Iran wanted to supplant Britain's role in the conduct of humanitarian and international obligations, which included lighting and buoying, and

52 FO 416/83: M. Pakravan to Mr. Parr, *Shahrivar* 29, 1307 (September 20, 1928).

53 H. M. Government, Cabinet Office, "Historical Summary of Events in the Territories of the Ottoman Empire, Persia and Arabia Affecting the British Position in the Persian Gulf, 1907–1928," PG 13 (London: 1928; Repr., Archive Editions, 1987), p. 91.

54 IOR/R/15/1/282: SNOPG to the Political Resident, August 13, 1928, and December 17, 1928; IOR/R/15/1/282: Shaykh Sa'id bin Hashr Al Maktum to 'Isa bin 'Abd al-Latif, *Jamad al-Awwal* 22, 1347 (November 5, 1928).

55 FO 416/84: Sir Clive to Sir Austen Chamberlain, January 8, 1929, January 19, 1929, and March 6, 1929.

56 The League of Nations, *Official Journal*, March 1929, p. 351; Ministry of Foreign Affairs to Ministry of the Interior, *Dey* 15, 1307 (January 5, 1929), in *Gozideh-ye Asnad-e Khalij-e Fars Jazayer-e Khalij-e Fars*, Vol. 1 (Tehran: Daftar-e Motala'at-e Siyasi va bayn al-Milali, 1372/1993), p. 140.

57 FO 416/83: Lord Cushendon to Sir R. Clive, November 7, 1928.

the suppression of traffic in slaves and arms. The India Office also marveled at Iran's advancement of a claim "so fantastic as to be unbelievable, to suzerainty, if not dominion, over Muscat and the independent Arab states of the Arabian littoral."[58] It concluded that Iran "has definitely thrown down the glove and ... intends to leave no effort unrestrained to secure the total elimination of the former influence of Great Britain, not merely from the South Persian shore, and from those islands the ownership of which is not in dispute, but from the Gulf as a whole."[59]

As various crises arising out of the actions of local officials were brought to the attention of Teymurtash, he professed to have only a vague understanding of the particulars in the Persian Gulf. In view of that, Sir Robert Clive suggested that Sir Frederick Johnson, Britain's Resident in Bushehr, and Captain Boyes, Britain's senior naval officer in the Persian Gulf, should be brought to Tehran for consultations, and Teymurtash welcomed the opportunity. During the meetings, which took place in mid-February 1929, Teymurtash posed questions and heard British viewpoints on a wide range of subjects relating to the Persian Gulf. According to Clive's account, Teymurtash was particularly interested in hearing Captain Boyes elucidate on the methods used by smugglers to outsmart Iranian customs patrols and land contraband goods on Iranian soil. Captain Boyes explained that most of the smuggling from Bahrain was carried on by Tangestani boats (originating from the coastal area south of Bushehr) while the smuggling from Dubai was conducted by Arab dhows.[60]

On the contentious issue of Bahrain, Clive shared his personal opinion that if Iran were prepared to renounce its claims to Bahrain, the British government might be willing to recommend to the shaykh that he should permit an Iranian consul to reside in Bahrain. Teymurtash took note and inquired as to whether it would also be possible to have an Iranian consular agent in Dubai, where he understood there was a sizeable Iranian colony. Sir Frederick Johnson explained that there was no British agent there as it had never been considered safe to

[58] CAB 24/127: Memorandum by the Secretary of State for India, October 11, 1928.
[59] Ibid.
[60] FO 416/84: Sir Clive to Sir Austen Chamberlain, February 16, 1929.

send one and that therefore it was unlikely that an Iranian agent would be allowed.[61]

During that meeting, Teymurtash questioned why the British flag continued to be flown from a flagstaff on Iranian territory in Bushehr. Clive explained that it had flown there for a good number of years and that its removal was likely to cause a "bad impression" on the Arab coast.[62] But he offered that as part of the would-be agreement, the government of India might be willing to consider transferring the Persian Gulf Residency to some place outside of Iranian territory, and Teymurtash viewed the suggestion positively. Finally, Teymurtash expressed a keen interest in the subject of lighting and buoying in the Gulf and asked Captain Boyes to indicate on a map the points where lights and buoys existed. He expressed his opinion that Iran should take over these functions and stated that he was anxious for a conference to take place on the subject.[63]

An outline of the proposed general treaty was presented to Teymurtash on August 10, 1929. The first article provided for mutual recognition and nonaggression between the two contracting parties to include the British Mandate in Iraq and the Gulf Arab shaykhdoms under British protection. The British proposed the inclusion of a list of each of the Arab shaykhs by name to secure Iran's recognition of their sovereignty and independence and recognition of Britain's role as protector and sole intermediary in their foreign affairs. After seeing this, Teymurtash objected to the inclusion of Bahrain, but then accepted Clive's suggestion that the issue of Bahrain should not be discussed in isolation, but rather considered in relation to the treaty as a whole and in relation to the concessions that Britain was prepared to make to secure the treaty. At Clive's suggestion, the two negotiators began to view the would-be agreement in terms of a balance sheet, such that Iran's concessions could be compared at a glance with a list of Britain's concessions.[64] The trouble, of course, was reaching a mutual understanding of what constituted a concession while both sides continued to employ tactics of bluff and deception.

After the exchange of a draft outlining the terms for a lease of Hengam in February 1929 the British were optimistic about the prospect of maintaining their naval facilities on the island. Teymurtash's

[61] Ibid. [62] Ibid. [63] Ibid.
[64] FO 416/85: Sir R. Clive to Mr. A. Henderson, August 10, 1929.

counterdraft of the lease was viewed by London as an acceptable basis for discussion; however, they soon learned that Iran's condition for granting a lease was the positive recognition of at least one of Iran's territorial claims, not including Basidu. Britain's withdrawal from Basidu – while it was a welcome outcome – was not viewed by Iran as a concession. Teymurtash proposed to Clive that the granting of a lease for Hengam would be possible in exchange for recognition of Iran's claim to Greater Tunb.[65] According to another scheme, he proposed that a lease of Hengam would be possible in exchange for an assortment of concessions, including Britain's support for a border rectification in Baluchistan; increased revenue from the Anglo-Persian Oil Company; assistance in the purchase of airplanes and warships; and a promise of goodwill in the event that Iran should apply for a loan in the future.[66]

British draft treaties contained a clause according to which Iran would acknowledge that Abu Musa and the Tunbs were owned by the rulers of Sharjah and Ras al-Khaimah and another clause to the effect that Britain would acknowledge Iran's sovereignty over Sirri Island. Britain's position on Sirri, like its position on Basidu, was a bluff. In internal memos, the British admitted Iran's ownership of Sirri, but aimed to use the fact that Sirri was also claimed by the Qasimi Arab shaykhs, and the fact that Britain had never officially acknowledged Iranian sovereignty, to make Sirri look like a positive gain for Iran in the negotiations balance sheet. They hoped that this could ameliorate the political fallout that Teymurtash would face in giving up Iran's claim to Abu Musa and the Tunbs.[67] However, Teymurtash did not fall for it. In his counter draft of August 9, 1929, he stated that Iran's ownership of Sirri was not in question. He also reiterated that Abu Musa and the Tunbs were unquestionably Iranian islands and expressed hope that in the future, Iran would be able to impose her authority on "this part of her empire."[68]

Clive recalled that during a private discussion about the draft article relating to Abu Musa and the Tunbs, Teymurtash admitted that control of Greater Tunb was more important to Iran than control of Abu Musa because it was closer to Iran's shoreline and because the Iranian

65 FO 416/87: Sir R. Clive to Mr. A Henderson, October 5, 1930.
66 Annual Report on Persia for the Year 1932, p. 25.
67 FO 416/83: Lord Cushendun to Sir R. Clive, November 7, 1928.
68 FO 416/85: Teymurtash to Sir R. Clive, *août* 9, 1929.

government believed that it was being used by the Arabs as a regular depot for smuggling. Teymurtash proposed that the Iranian government should be allowed to negotiate directly with the shaykh who claimed the island. Clive reminded him of Britain's capacity as the protecting power of the Trucial shaykhs and also warned that if the Iranian government tried to seize the island, it would create a most serious incident.[69] Besides their commitment to the Trucial shaykhs, the British also placed high importance on Tunb because of the lighthouse that it hosted. The British remained intransigent in their demand that any treaty must contain a renunciation of Iran's claim to Abu Musa and the Tunbs.

In October 1930, Clive reported on a suggestion by Teymurtash that Iran would be content with a long lease of Tunb.[70] He proposed that if the shaykh would agree to lease the island to Iran for 50 years, Iran would pay him whatever rent it received from Britain's lease of Hengam. He added that the shaykh would be allowed to retain his guard and that he would be exempt from customs dues.[71] This proposal was viewed with interest by the British, who approached Shaykh Selim bin Sultan, Ruler of Ras al-Khaimah, with the proposal of a lease. Shaykh Selim agreed in principle and provided them with a document listing the terms according to which he would allow the Iranian government to lease the island; however, his terms were so restrictive that they were never communicated to the Iranian government because it was presumed that Iran would not accept them.[72]

Teymurtash suggested a variety of ways in which Britain could compensate Iran for the loss of Bahrain.[73] Teymurtash's first proposal was the outright sale of Bahrain. He proposed that the British government should admit Iran's claim to Bahrain, and that in return, Iran

[69] FO 416/85: Sir R. Clive to Mr. A. Henderson, August 31, 1929.

[70] FO 416/87: Sir R. Clive to Mr. A. Henderson, October 5, 1930.

[71] IOR/L/P&S/12/3709: Memorandum, "Suggestion That the Island of Tamb Might Be Leased to Persia," November 14, 1930.

[72] FO 416/88: Consul-General Biscoe to Government of India, May 11, 1931, with enclosure: Statement of the Conditions Required by the Ruler of Ras al-Khaimah; CAB 24/247: Memorandum by the Standing Ministerial Sub-Committee for Questions Concerning the Middle East on Proposed Negotiations with the Shah, January 23, 1934.

[73] For a good summary of these proposals in Persian, see Shohreh Jalalpur and Shiva Jalalpur, "Engelestan va Jodayi-ye Bahreyn va Iran," *Faslnameh-ye Motala'at-e Tarikhi* 8, no. 33 (Summer 1390/2011), pp. 200–201.

would sell her rights to the British government, after which the British government could keep it or turn it over to the shaykh. He explained to the British minister that the sale of Bahrain would serve more for "saving face" then for providing Iran with a large sum of money and he guaranteed that the press and the Majles would joyfully accept that solution.[74] On another occasion, Teymurtash suggested that in exchange for the renunciation of Iran's claim to Bahrain, the British should offer support for a rectification of the Iran-Iraq border in the area near Khanaqin, where oil drilling was taking place on the Iraqi side.[75] In August 1929 he proposed that Iran could recognize the independence of Bahrain if Britain could forgive Iran's "war debt," take responsibility for British claims against Iran, and provide Iran with 10 gunships for the policing of its waters against contraband traffic.[76] In August 1930 he again proposed to trade Bahrain for a military aid package, consisting of 10 warships, an unspecified number of airplanes and seaplanes, an agreement to educate Iranian air and naval cadets for 25 years, total debt forgiveness, the right to appoint an Iranian consul in Bahrain, and further unspecified concessions.[77] The open-ended nature of Teymurtash's proposals prompted further discussions during which Clive learned that his demands were not in fact quantitative, but qualitative – Iran wanted Britain's acquiescence to Iran's rise as a regional power and its assistance in making Iran such.[78]

In response to all of these proposals, Clive reminded Teymurtash that his government did not admit Iran's claim to Bahrain as valid and that, therefore, no compensation was justified, but he entertained the idea of helping Teymurtash find a face-saving solution. During one conversation, Clive tried to persuade Teymurtash and the acting foreign minister, Mohammad 'Ali Foroughi Zoka' al-Molk, of the advantages that Iran would gain under the proposed treaty: Britain offered a nonaggression clause, the surrender of Britain's "rights" at Basidu, payment of rent at Hengam, the gift of three wireless installations, renunciation of the perpetual most favored nation privileges under the treaty of 1857, and the remission of Iran's war debt. Mohammad 'Ali

[74] FO 416/84: Sir Clive to Sir Austen Chamberlain, January 8, 1929.
[75] FO 416/90: Mr. Hoare to Sir John Simon, February 17, 1932.
[76] FO 416/85: Teymurtash to Sir R. Clive, *août* 20, 1929.
[77] FO 416/87: M. Foroughi to Sir R. Clive, *août* 9, 1930.
[78] FO 416/85: Sir R. Clive to Mr. A. Henderson, August 21, 1929; and FO 416/87: Mr. A. Henderson to Sir R. Clive, September 18, 1930.

Foroughi, a career diplomat and college professor, wryly offered an explanation: as substantial as these advantages were, he said, they would not strike the Iranian mind as adequate compensation for the loss of Bahrain. No Iranian, he said, had ever contemplated the need to repay what Britain called the "war debt."[79]

By various means, the Iranian government both encouraged and exploited the growing irredentist feeling toward the Arab shaykhdoms as a means of exerting pressure on the British. This was particularly evident in the hardening of Iran's passport policy, which treated the inhabitants of the Arab shaykhdoms as Iranian citizens, subject to Iranian law. The presence of a large number of Iranian nationals in the shaykhdoms was further exploited toward these ends. This is implicit in a letter that Foroughi penned on September 23, 1930, in his capacity as foreign minister in which he explained:

> Regarding the travelers inhabiting the southern coasts of the Persian Gulf in general and a number of travelers from Muscat (who have gone) to the Khorasan regions in particular, I have the honor to state that as the Imperial Government have not recognized the form of government of the states of the southern coast of the Persian Gulf and as they (the Persian Government) have no relations with them, and as, on the other hand, no census has ever been made of a large number of Persians who are residing on the southern coasts of the Persian Gulf, and who have no identity papers or passports, and as it has often been observed that the holders of passports or identity papers issued by the sheikhs of the Gulf coasts are Persians, who for the lack of a guardian, were compelled to take out traveling papers from the latter sheikhs, and, therefore, for these reasons it was not possible to recognize such papers and issue visas on them, instructions have been issued by the Imperial Government to the frontier officials to issue exit and entry passes to travelers coming from the southern coasts of the Gulf on their entry into Persian territory against the payment by them of statutory fees.[80]

The negotiations were derailed in September 1932 when the British government was notified that the ships of the new Iranian navy arriving from Italy required the use of the naval facilities on Hengam. The British government was asked to take the necessary steps to ensure that

[79] FO 416/87: Sir Clive to Sir Austen Chamberlain, July 29, 1930.
[80] FO 416/87: Persian Minister of Foreign Affairs (Foroughi) to His Majesty's Minister (Clive), September 23, 1930.

ships of the Royal Navy would cease to be stationed there.[81] The British government reacted to the news with alarm, interpreting the note as a request for immediate evacuation. After receiving instructions from London, Sir Reginald Hoare, the new British minister in Tehran (1931—1935), approached Teymurtash and inquired whether it might be possible for the British and Iranian navies to share Hengam. Teymurtash admitted that this might be possible, and he said he would be grateful if details about the topography of Hengam could be sent to the war ministry so that this request could be considered. Then he intimated that perhaps a way could be found to share the facilities on Hengam if only the question of Bahrain could be settled.[82] But before the new proposals for Bahrain could be studied, the cancellation of the D'Arcy concession and the fall of Teymurtash in November 1932 brought negotiations to a dramatic halt.[83]

Serious negotiations toward a comprehensive bilateral agreement were not resumed after the fall of Teymurtash. Numerous crises, such as the storm that followed from the hauling down of a British flag on Basidu by Iran's new navy, produced an atmosphere that was not conducive to negotiations.[84] The British government revised their earlier draft treaty in January 1934 in hopes of restarting the talks, but new intrigues on the part of some Iranian officials at Greater Tunb prevented the British from returning to the negotiating table.[85] By 1935 hopes of achieving a general treaty with Iran had given way to a preference for dealing with issues on an individual basis.[86]

[81] Ministry of War to Ministry of Foreign Affairs, *Shahrivar* 23, 1311 (September 14, 1932), in *Gozideh-ye Asnad-e Khalij-e Fars*, Vol. 1, p. 556.

[82] FO 416/91: Acting Minister of Foreign Affairs (Ghaffari) to His Majesty's Minister (Hoare), September 19, 1932; Ministry of Foreign Affairs to Ministry of War, *Shahrivar* 31, 1311 (September 22, 1932), in *Gozideh-ye Asnad-e Khalij-e Fars*, p. 563; FO 416/91: Memorandum, "Record of an Interview with Teymurtash," September 20, 1932. See also Mohammad 'Ali Foroughi to the Ministry of Foreign Affairs, October 2, 1932, in *Gozideh-ye Asnad-e Khalij-e Fars*, p. 565.

[83] Administration Report of the Persian Gulf Residency for the Year 1932, pp. 29–30.

[84] See Chapters 4 and 5.

[85] CAB 24/247: Memorandum by the Standing Ministerial Sub-Committee for Questions Concerning the Middle East on Proposed Negotiations with the Shah, January 23, 1934; Annual Report on Persia for the Year 1934, pp. 3–4.

[86] Annual Report on Persia for the Year 1935, p. 5.

British Supremacy in the Eyes of Arabs and Iranians

Britain's overwhelming successes in the contest of strength speaks nothing of the contest for the hearts and minds of the Persian Gulf residents. The highly visible British presence in the Persian Gulf rose up as a sharp bone of contention between Arabs and Iranians during the interwar years. For Iranians, symbols of British ascendancy such as the Abadan refinery, the Hengam naval base, and the Bushehr Political Residency were persistent reminders of national humiliation and defeat. Paradoxically, the same institutions were a source of satisfaction for the Trucial Arabs who viewed them as affirmation of the coercive power of their protector. As the entrance of Iranian nationalist policies into the Persian Gulf waterway converted the once interdependent Gulf civilization into a contested border region – these symbols took on a meaning that far outweighed their material value.

The political significance of powerful symbols is manifest in the contrasting perceptions of the British Residency. The Persian Gulf Residency was a fortified mansion with an Indian guard that occupied the most exposed section of the Bushehr coast. What made it particularly awkward was that the bulk of the duties performed by the Resident from his headquarters on Iranian soil was the supervision of the treaties with the Arab shaykhs whose independence Iran did not recognize.

A letter dated July 24, 1924, illustrates how one local Iranian port official, known as Mo'ezzeh al-Soltan, apprehended the symbolic importance of the British Residency. In the letter to the foreign ministry, he reports on a rumor that the British were considering bringing the Shaykh of Bahrain to Bushehr. He warns that this could be a ploy designed to bedazzle the shaykh with manifestations of British power and dominance on Iranian soil. He writes:

> From the moment that he disembarks until he reaches the building of the General Consul … he will see all of the British institutions (the water distiller and ice house, the lighthouse, the massive telegraph device, the multiple telegraph buildings, the wireless station, the sepoy guard station … the clubhouse which is one of the British political masterpieces that the Arabs are intimidated by) and will see that this side of the Gulf, like Bahrain, is under the agencies and domination of the British, and if he has any

inclination toward Iran, through excitement and delight it will completely disappear.[87]

Another powerful and contested symbol was the Union Jack fluttering from the summit of the Residency flagstaff. With its flag by day and its beacon by night, the Residency flagstaff served as a guidepost for mariners and British men-of-war, contributing to the common perception that Bushehr was more of a British than an Iranian port-city. But the very symbol that was a source of resentment for Iranians was a source of gratification for the Arabs. One British Resident, Sir Lionel Haworth (1927–1928), noted,

> In regions such as the Persian Gulf the flag of a country has an importance such as it held in Europe in Medieval times, such as till recently were possessed by the colours of a regiment when carried into battle. For many years ... our flagstaff has been situated outside the British Residency at Bushire. The Persians have now demanded its removal within the Residency. In Europe this would be a small matter; to the Arab the British flag is the symbol of Britain's greatness. It may well be asked why this sudden request. It is a demand following upon other similar demands. The Persian Government knows better than most Englishmen the psychological result of such an act and the effect that such a removal will have upon Persian and Arab alike.[88]

The government in Iran was inundated with reports of flag offenses in and around the Persian Gulf. A letter addressed to the chairman of the Majles on behalf of the Iranian community in Bahrain, warned of the sneaky tactics of the British Political Agent who arranged for the transfer of a British flag from the roof of a building to a flagpole. He laments that the flagpole was erected in a place that was specially prepared for it in the soil of Bahrain. Implicit in the meaningful distinction between a flag draped on a building and a flag flown from a flagstaff emplaced in the ground, was the perception of the flagstaff as a symbol of territorial demarcation. A circular that went out from the Iranian foreign ministry in 1931 instructed foreign embassies and legations that the use of flagpoles placed in the ground was forbidden

[87] Head *Kargozar* of the Persian Gulf Ports (Bushehr) to the Ministry of Foreign Affairs, *Asad* 2, 1303 (July 24, 1924), in *Gozideh-ye Asnad-e Khalij-e Fars*, Vol. 1, pp. 73–74.

[88] Sir Lionel Haworth, "Persia and the Persian Gulf," *Central Asian Society Journal*, Vol. 16, pt. 4 (1929), pp. 495–509.

to foreigners at all times. It further specified that national flags could only be displayed on their respective national holidays.[89]

Surveillance of the political landscape gave local officials and military men an opportunity to advertise their vigilance and dedication to the nationalist cause. In early 1930, for example, a field commander heard a rumor that British flags had been erected on Abu Musa and the Tunbs. The document trail gives witness to a flurry of excitement as the army dispatched a customs launch to investigate the rumors and instructed the foreign ministry to take action diplomatically.[90] The customs officer went to Greater Tunb only to find that the rumors pertained to flags that were temporarily hoisted during the course of a hydrographic survey.[91] Not wasting an opportunity, he returned to Lingah and advertised that he had been sent to Greater Tunb to look for buildings to convert into an Iranian customs house.[92] Having gotten it wrong that time, the war ministry was exultant when it was finally able to report with certainty that the Shaykh of Sharjah had hoisted his red flag on the wood pole that the British had placed in the soil of Abu Musa expressly for that purpose.[93]

For Iran, the exclusion of foreign symbols from the landscape became a vital expression of control in a frontier region beleaguered with territorial loss and uncertainty. One particularly symbolic act was the hauling down of the British flag at Basidu by a group of Iranian naval officers on July 31, 1933.[94] In his statement to the war ministry, senior naval commander Gholam ʿAli Bayandor related his pleasant surprise at seeing the British (Indian) officers run away while his ship approached Basidu. Seeing that no British warship was anchored there, he and his crew disembarked. Then the four Iranian seamen marched to the flagstaff with drum and fife, he said, lowered the flag, raised the Iranian flag in its stead and gave it military honors. For Bayandor, the

89 Annual Report on Persia for the Year 1931, p. 3.

90 Ministry of War Chief of Staff to Ministry of Foreign Affairs, *Esfand* 5, 1308 (February 24, 1930) and Ministry of Foreign Affairs to British Legation, *Esfand* 5, 1308 (February 24, 1930), in *Gozideh-ye Asnad-e Khalij-e Fars*, Vol. 1, Tehran: Daftar-e Motalaʿat-e Siyasi va bayn al-Milali, 1372 (1993), p. 351; IOR/R/15/1/282: SNOPG *Triad* to Political Resident, March 14, 1930.

91 FO 416/86: Sir R. Clive to Mr. A. Henderson, April 18, 1930.

92 IOR/R/15/1/282: SNOPG *Triad* to Political Resident, March 12, 1930.

93 Ministry of War to Ministry of Foreign Affairs, *Aban* 9, 1311 (October 31, 1932), in *Gozideh-ye Asnad-e Khalij-e Fars*, Vol. 1, p. 371.

94 See also Chapter 4.

removal of the British flag and the hoisting of the Iranian flag in its stead was an assertion of Iranian authority on a contested piece of territory.[95]

The hauling down of the British flag by Iranian naval officers caused much commotion in the Arab shaykhdoms where Iran's actions were viewed as an open insult and act of defiance against England.[96] According to the stories that circulated in the Arab shaykhdoms, the Iranian commander threw the flag on the ground, stamped on it, and then tore it into shreds.[97] British imperial officers and military men emphasized the disastrous effect of this incident on Arab opinion. The British Resident wrote to his superiors saying it was a common boast of the Iranians that they would have the British out of the Gulf very soon.[98] The Political Agent at Kuwait, Colonel Dickson, related that the Shaykh of Kuwait was quite outspoken about the bad effect that the rumors were having in his town. People, he said, were wondering what action the British would take in the matter as a deliberate insult against them appeared to have been committed. Moreover, in Kuwait, he added, "Persians are looked upon as being such utterly irresponsible beings, as to be quite capable of appearing before Kuwait and bombarding the place."[99]

The issue of a circular by the British government, reporting on the rehoisting of the British flag and the "regret" of the Iranian government over the incident, went some distance to suppress rumors of Britain's retreat. The most optimistic report came from Britain's Residency Agent at Sharjah, who said, "The people of the Oman Coast now laugh at the Persians on account of their previous talks about Basidu."[100] Notwithstanding this, the informational circular did not wholly mollify fears among the inhabitants of the Arabian coast that

95 Mohammad 'Ali Bahmani Qajar, "Naqsh-e Niru-ye Daryayi va Bayandor dar Ekhraj-e Engelisha az Hengam va Basa'idu," *Faslnameh-ye Motala'at-e Tarikhi* 7, no. 27 (Winter 1388/2009), pp. 88–89.

96 FO 371/16957: Lieutenant Colonel H. R. P. Dickson, Political Agent Kuwait to Political Resident, August 29, 1933.

97 "Letter from Kuwait," *al-Thagr* (Basra), September 3, 1933.

98 IOR/R/15/1/282: Resident at Shiraz to Government of India Simla, August 15, 1928.

99 FO 371/16957: Lieutenant Colonel H. R. P. Dickson, Political Agent Kuwait to Political Resident, August 29, 1933.

100 IOR/R/15/2/491: Residency Agent Sharjah ('Abd al-Latif) to Political Agent Bahrain (Gastrell), *Rajab* 12, 1352 (October 31, 1933).

Britain was a declining power. Charles Belgrave, adviser to the Shaykh of Bahrain, mentioned in a letter how several of the Arabs in Bahrain, Sunnis and Shi'a, expressed their views that the British were being too lenient. It was their conviction that the British were letting Iran off too lightly and that this was bound to bear out consequences in the future.[101] Ultimately, it took the arrival of the First Destroyer Flotilla, consisting of nine modern battleships, to counter the rumors that Britain's power was waning.

Rumors and gossip were conspicuous features of the contentious relations between Arabs and Iranians in the Persian Gulf during the interwar period. A salient example is the stories that proliferated in the aftermath of Iran's reoccupation of Hengam Island. According to a report written by the British senior naval officer, the stories that circulated in Lingah boasted of the defeat of the Royal Marines by the gallant Iranian troops and Iran's recapture of the island.[102] He went on to describe how the officer commanding Iranian troops at Hengam was engaging in "propaganda" work, "taking care to see that the seed he sows has a chance of taking root along the Trucial Coast."[103] The main points were summarized as follows:

> When might was right England ruled the world and Persia and everyone else had to submit to her big guns and now might is no longer right and there is the League of Nations and the law and Persia knows the law just as well as England does. Everything has to be decided by the League of Nations now and before the League of Nations everyone is equal and Persia is as good as England in fact better because Persian politicians are more clever than the English ones and that is why you see England is becoming a weaker power and Persia is getting stronger.[104]

Bahrain formed another fitting subject for various machinations designed to shake the confidence of the Arabs in the British government. In September 1928 the Bushehr Resident reported on an exchange in which the chief of police (*nazmiyyeh*) informed him that Britain had agreed to hand Bahrain over to Iran in exchange for the granting of overflight privileges to Imperial Airways.[105] In the same month, the director of finance at Bandar Abbas arrived in the Bahrain

[101] IOR/R/15/2/491: Belgrave to Gastrell, September 16, 1933.
[102] IOR/R/15/1/280: SNOPG to CinCEI, August 17, 1928.
[103] IOR/R/15/1/282: SNOPG to Political Resident, August 28, 1928. [104] Ibid.
[105] IOR/R/15/1/282: Political Resident to Minister at Tehran, September 17, 1928.

harbor as a passenger onboard a German ship. He used the opportunity to communicate to the Iranians resident in Bahrain that he had been appointed to Bahrain as an official and that he would return after receiving his instructions from the Iranian government. After his departure, a rumor circulated to the effect that the Iranian vessel *Pehlevi* would arrive to Manama shortly to bring the Iranian officials who would take charge of its law court and customs house.[106] To a large extent, the receptivity of such rumors was directly related to a person's status and relative proximity to British authorities. The urban neighborhoods of Manama, for example, were said to be full of talk about the Iranian possession of Bahrain, while the Al Khalifa did not take these rumors seriously. Charles Belgrave, adviser to the Shaykh of Bahrain, mused in his diary that Shaykh Hamad "didn't show much interest in [Iran's claim to Bahrain] and merely said that they never lost a chance of claiming it but thanks to the British government they would not get it."[107]

Indeed, a major point of contention between Arabs and Iranians during the interwar years was British supremacy in the Persian Gulf and Britain's protection of the Arab shaykhs of the southern littoral. In the eyes of Iranians, Britain's support for Shaykh 'Isa in Bahrain, the Qasimi shaykhs who claimed Abu Musa and the Tunbs, and other shaykhs of the southern littoral was analogous to their support for Shaykh Khaz'al and other semi-autonomous tribal chiefs in Iran's southern provinces. Their cultivation of protégés among the Gulf Arab shaykhs was viewed in Iran as a colonial "divide and rule" tactic that was devised to prevent Iran from asserting authority over all of its sovereign territory. Thus, the highly visible British presence in the Persian Gulf and involvement in the shaykhdoms was a lightning rod for the vital expression of anti-British, Iranian nationalist sentiment.

The Arab shaykhs of the Persian Gulf along with their dependents and the foreigners who dwelled inside their tribal domains were long accustomed to viewing British supremacy in the Gulf as the necessary obstacle to aggressions from regional or foreign powers. Symbols of British supremacy, such as the flags flying at Bushehr and Hengam and the modern British warships laying offshore, were tangible reminders

106 IOR/R/15/1/282: Political Agent Bahrain (Barrett) to the Undersecretary to the Political Resident, September 11, 1928.

107 Charles D. Belgrave, Personal Diaries (1926–1957), January 4 and November 7, 1928.

of the power of the protector. At the advent of a more aggressive Persian Gulf policy on the part of Iran during the interwar years, the resilience of these symbols was watched like a kind of barometer that attested to Britain's level of commitment to the maintenance of security in the Persian Gulf. Britain's abstention from the use of force against Iran, dictated by its will to protect its interests in Iran, was at times perceived as weakness by the shaykhs and merchants of the Arabian littoral. During the period of heightened tension that accompanied Reza Shah's rise, a perpetual cause of excitement among the Arabs inhabiting the southern littoral was the persistence of rumors that Iran would soon effect the complete withdrawal of the British from the area of the Persian Gulf waterway.[108]

[108] IOR/R/15/1/282: Resident at Shiraz to Government of India Simla, August 15, 1928.

3 *The Rise of Reza Khan and Iran's Persian Gulf Policy, 1919–1925*

[T]he visit to Bushire of the War Minister [Reza Khan] . . . sent a violent jar through the whole framework of administration in the South.. . . One thing is certain; the present is a stage of transition. So far as the British position on the Persian side of the Gulf is concerned a great and rapid change is taking place which will of course react on the Arabian side.[1]

Political Resident in the Persian Gulf, April 1922

The Persian Gulf comprised a central theme in the anti-colonial, nationalist discourse in Iran after the First World War. The highly visible British presence in the Persian Gulf was a lightning rod for anti-British protest and a constant reminder of the nation's weakness and exploitation at the hands of foreigners. From Iran's perspective, Britain's special relationship with the shaykhs of the Arabian littoral was no different from its support for Shaykh Khaz'al in Arabistan and other semi-autonomous tribal chiefs and khans in southern Iran – it was a deliberate policy that was designed to subvert the exercise of Iranian authority over its sovereign territory. But the rise of a powerful military leader in Iran on the wings of the nationalist forces already at work combined with a spirited national discourse surrounding Iran's historical and rightful frontiers heralded a new era in the history of the Persian Gulf. Reza Khan's extension of central authority over the periphery appeared to be the beginning of a campaign that would culminate in the restoration of Iran's lost frontiers and the revival of its former greatness. The assertion of central authority over Arabistan (whose name reverted to Khuzestan) was viewed in Iran as a decisive step in the country's more ambitious goal of reducing British influence in the Persian Gulf waterway, islands, and littoral.

[1] Administration Report of the Persian Gulf Residency for the Year 1922, p. 8.

Iranian Nationalism in the Aftermath of Invasion

Iran's unique experience during the course of the Great War gave rise to a new direction for Iranian nationalism. Hoping to avoid entanglement in the war, Iran declared neutrality. Despite that, Iran was invaded by Ottoman, Russian, and British troops causing its collapse as an independent political entity. In 1919 a British military force (the North Persia Force or "Norperforce") remained in Iran on the pretext of preventing the incursion of Bolshevism.[2] In 1920 Russian forces returned on the pretext that British forces remained in Iran.[3] In the aftermath of the war, the chief foreign policy goal for Iranian statesmen was Iran's political, economic, and territorial emancipation from foreign powers.

The Versailles episode can attest to the strength of national feeling and the primacy of territory in Iranian nationalist ambitions. In 1919, Iranian statesmen sought to have a seat at the Congress of Versailles to request wartime reparations and territorial rectification.[4] Iranian Foreign Minister Prince Firuz Mirza Nosrat al-Dowleh, in his letter to British Foreign Secretary Lord Curzon, argued that justice would be served if the powers would act to rectify Iran's century-old territorial disputes in its northern and western frontiers. He provided Curzon with a map of Iran's claims to territories in Turkey, Iraq, and the Caucuses.[5] Curzon balked at what he viewed as "extravagant demands" and suggested that Iran could gain the support of the British government if it were prepared to put forward a more modest request.[6] But Nosrat al-Dowleh refused to modify the proposed "rectification" of Iran's frontiers.[7] In his view, this territory was Iran's natural right and destiny.[8] Despite having been warned of the lack of British support

[2] CAB 24/116: Telegram from Viceroy, Foreign and Political Department, December 6, 1920.

[3] Rouhollah K. Ramazani, *The Foreign Policy of Iran: A Developing Nation in World Affairs, 1500–1941* (Charlottesville: University Press of Virginia, 1966), p. 189.

[4] FO 608/100/11: FM Mamalek to the President and Delegates of the Conference and the Preliminaries of Peace at Paris, February 1919.

[5] FO 608/100/11: Memorandum Handed to Lord Curzon by Prince Nosrat ed-Dowlah, November 13, 1919; and Earl Curzon to Sir P. Cox, November 28, 1919; see also *Nosrat al-Dowleh: Majmu'ah-e Moqatibat, Asnad, Khatirat, va-'Asr-e Firuz Mirza Firuz*, Vol. 2, ed. Mansoureh Ettehadieh (Tehran: Ketab-e Siyamak, 1990).

[6] Ibid. [7] Ibid. [8] Kashani-Sabet, *Frontier Fictions*, pp. 150–152.

for their demands, a five-man Iranian delegation headed by 'Ali Qoli Khan Ansari Moshaver al-Mamalek arrived at Versailles, but Lord Curzon made sure that they were neither admitted nor heard.[9]

Likewise, the failure of the 1919 Anglo-Iranian Agreement attested to the nationalists' will to terminate foreign domination of Iran. Secretly negotiated between Lord Curzon and Hasan Vusuq al-Dowleh, the Anglo-Iranian treaty was characterized by its opponents as an agreement that would have granted the British a monopoly over the economic and military affairs of Iran.[10] The treaty was signed without approval from the Majles, but it soon became clear that fierce opposition from within and without would prevent it from ever being executed.[11] The subsequent fall of Vusuq al-Dowleh's government in 1920 attested to the strength of the nationalist and anti-British feeling in Iran. As its first act of business, on June 22, 1921, the Fourth Majles unanimously nullified the 1919 Anglo-Iranian Agreement. In fact, the Fourth Majles exhibited the most assertive nationalist resolve to date: its members manifested strong anti-British sentiments and for the first time began to challenge Britain's economic and political supremacy in Iran.[12]

With the advent of the Fourth Majles, the anti-foreign tone of the Persian language press reached a shrill pitch. Russia was preoccupied with its own revolution and the British were viewed as the dominant threat to Iran's independence. Newspapers churned out articles decrying British imperialism in Iran and asserting Iran's right to "fight for independence and for the integrity of the country against the encroachments of powerful and imperialist governments."[13] The activities of Lord Curzon, the architect of British imperial strategy in Iran, were a focus of scrupulous reporting. One Shiraz newspaper, *Bahr-e Fars*, reported that he gave a speech in which he mentioned the possibility

[9] Ibid.

[10] CAB 24/145: War Cabinet Memorandum, Eastern Report No. CXXXIV, August 21, 1919.

[11] Homa Katouzian, "The Campaign against the Anglo-Iranian Agreement of 1919," *British Journal of Middle Eastern Studies* 25, no. 1 (May 1998), pp. 5–46.

[12] Cyrus Ghani, *Iran and the Rise of Reza Shah: From Qajar Collapse to Pahlavi Power* (New York: I.B. Tauris, 2000), p. 232.

[13] *Tufan*, December 19, 1921, in *Iran Political Diaries 1881–1965*, eds. R. M. Burrell and R. Jarman, Vol. 6 (Archive Editions, 1997), p. 130.

of the British government seizing Iran's Gulf Ports in view of the unsettled condition of the country.[14]

Papers cast Britain as the colonial oppressor that continuously undermined the central government by arming the tribes in Arabistan, and the separatist movements in Khorasan and Kurdistan. It was alleged that as part of their strategy to dominate Iran, they exploited existing antagonisms between tribal chiefs, "induced tribes to revolt and set them quarrelling with one another" and purposefully stirred up disturbances.[15]

The Rise of Reza Khan and the Persian Gulf

The experience of a humiliating foreign occupation during the Great War had greatly contributed to the militarization of Iranian nationalism and this paved the way for the nationalists' embrace of a military solution to Iran's predicament. Moreover, inept and corrupt leadership on the part of the Qajar government had given rise to a desire for radical change on the part of the nationalists, who began to search for a strong leader to restore the country's pride, and consolidate and centralize the country.[16] Their goals found fulfillment in the February 21, 1921, military coup of Reza Khan, a bold, nationalist officer in the Cossack Brigade.[17] Accompanied by Sayyed Zia' al-Din Tabataba'i, a journalist and one of the leaders of the Constitutional Revolution, Colonel Reza Khan entered Tehran with his troops meeting little resistance.

In a speech addressed to his countrymen shortly after the coup, Reza Khan presented his vision for the nation:

> We came to Tehran to apply the stewardship of the country and the centralization of the government in its true sense ... a government that would not just be a spectator to the misery and plight of the nation, a government which would respect the army as the supreme means of the country's welfare ... a government which does not unscrupulously give Muslim public funds to lazy parasites and self-indulgent people, a government which does not make the capital city of Muslims the focus of subjugation and cruelty, a government

[14] IOR/L/P&S/10/1017: British Legation, Tehran (R. Bridgeman) to Qavam al-Saltaneh, October 19, 1921.

[15] See for example, *Ettehad*, September 4, 1921, and *Tufan*, November 4, 1921, in *Iran Political Diaries*, Vol. 6, p. 84.

[16] M. Reza Ghods, "Iranian Nationalism and Reza Shah," pp. 35–45.

[17] Ibid.

Figure 2 Reza Khan as minister of war.
Source: Wikimedia Commons. Photo by Antoin Sevruguin.

which does not abandon the thousands of hungry and poverty-stricken within its territory ... a government which will not be a puppet of foreign powers, a government that does not shed its honor every day or tolerate the humiliation of the country for several hundred thousand *tomans* of debt.[18]

Despite the military coup, Reza Khan did not become head of state overnight. Within a few weeks, Ahmad Shah appointed Sayyed Zia' prime minister, and Reza Khan, Sardar-e Sepah, chief of the army. While Zia''s days in office proved to be few, Reza Khan engaged himself in unifying and reorganizing the army, and gradually converting the government into a military administration with himself at the helm.

During the years of Reza Khan's service as chief of the army and later minister of war (1921–1923), Iran's foreign policy was more a product of the numerous prime ministers than Reza Khan. The Russo-Persian Treaty of 1921, for example, which cancelled Iran's debt to Russia and annulled the capitulations that had been granted to the former Tsarist government, was negotiated by Iran's former Prime Minister Hasan Pirnia before the coup and signed by Seyyed Zia'

[18] Hossein Makki, *Tarikh-e Bist Saleh-ye Iran*, Vol. 1 (Tehran: Sepehr, 1357/1978), p. 255.

within a week of his appointment to the premiership.[19] As Reza Khan worked to eliminate enclaves of autonomous tribal rule and extend martial control across the country, further strides were taken by the prime ministers in the diplomatic arena. In his military campaigns of 1921 Reza Khan crushed the rebellion of Kuchak Khan in Gilan. By the end of August 1922, he had suppressed the Kurdish revolt in Azerbaijan as well. These victories enabled Seyyed Zia''s successor, Ahmad Qavam (Qavam al-Saltaneh), to compel the British and then the Russian forces to withdraw from the north of Iran.

The suppression of provincial revolts and tribal rule was applauded by most politically aware Iranians inside and outside the capital.[20] With the threat of Russia removed, at least for the meantime, and the suppression of separatist movements underway, the remaining resentment was channeled fiercely against the British, who exhibited no signs of withdrawal. The press provided a constant commentary on the British "colony-seeking policy" in the East in general, and in Mesopotamia (Iraq) and the Persian Gulf in particular.[21] An excerpt from an article that appeared in *Ettehad* titled "Aggressions of the British" can illustrate:

> News received during the last few days from Bushire and Bahrain is bad indeed. What does our southern neighbor desire from us? This tyrannical government has adopted an intolerable attitude toward Persia during the last few years which has caused economic losses to the country as well as heavy casualties. All Islamic countries have been afflicted with the same sort of tyrannies and cruelties. We still hear the bitter cries of Indians and Mesopotamians who clamor for their legal and due rights and entreat the world for help and assistance. We would like to understand how the Durbar of London justifies itself in exercising proprietary rights in our country. They beat and kill Persians, land troops at Bushire, and foment discord amongst the Persians and Arabs in Bahrain. Our incapable government merely watches the situation, and we wonder to whom we shall complain.[22]

[19] M. Reza Ghods, *Iran in the 20th Century: A Political History* (Boulder, CO: Lynne Rienner, 1989), p. 71.

[20] Ghods, "Iranian Nationalism and Reza Shah," pp. 35–45; see also FO 416/71: Translation of an article in *Iran*, March 29, 1922, "signed by 265 persons, most of whom were workers in the Bazaar."

[21] See for example, excerpts from *Ettehad*, September 4, 1921, and *Shafaq-e Sorkh*, December 10, 1922, in *Iran Political Diaries*, Vol. 6, pp. 84, 336–337.

[22] *Ettehad*, "Aggressions of the British," May 25, 1923, in *Iran Political Diaries*, Vol. 6, p. 511.

The press churned out articles describing the tactics that the British used to subjugate Iran – negotiating treaties with tribal chiefs and khans in Iran without respect to the central government; treating Iran's oil wells, telegraphs, and postal services as British domains. Moreover newspapers called for an end to the capitulations, foreign monopolies, and special privileges for foreigners that had been inaugurated by the corrupt Qajar leadership.[23] The British repeatedly petitioned the Iranian government to check the anti-British tone in the press, and even exercise censorship.[24] The Iranian government jailed some editors, as a result of constant British pressure, but, wherever it could, continued to encourage the nationalistic, anti-colonial spirit as a means of putting pressure on the British.[25]

Iran's military agenda and foreign policy were coordinated to secure the withdrawal of foreign forces. Prime Minister Ahmad Qavam terminated the contracts of British financial advisers and Reza Khan refused to sign the employment contracts of British and Swedish military advisers.[26] Just as the Majles began questioning the prime minister about the presence of British troops in the Persian Gulf, Reza Khan was preparing to send a garrison to Bushehr.[27] After the arrival of the garrison in the end of October 1922, the prime minister sent a note to the British government, announcing the organization of adequate Iranian forces at Bushehr and requesting that the British withdraw from the southern ports of Iran.[28] When they did not withdraw, Reza Khan paid a visit to Bushehr.

23 See excerpts in *British Documents on Foreign Affairs – Reports and Papers from the Foreign Office Confidential Print. Part II, From the First to the Second World War, Series B, Turkey, Iran, and the Middle East, 1918–1939*, eds., Robin Leonard Bidwell, Kenneth Bourne, and Donald Cameron Watt, Vol. 6 (Frederick, MD: University Publications of America, 1985), pp. 280–281.

24 IOR/L/P&S/10/1017: Political Resident (Trevor) to the Foreign Secretary of the Government of India (Sir Denys Bray), February 1, 1922; and H. B. M. Vice Consulate Resht to H. B. M. Minister Tehran (Loraine), September 13, 1922.

25 IOR/L/P&S/10/1017: British Legation Tehran (R. Bridgeman) to Lord Curzon, October 10, 1921; and "Intelligence Summary No. 24, for week ending October 15, 1921," in *Iran Political Diaries*, Vol. 6, p. 219.

26 Ghani, *Iran and the Rise of Reza Shah*, p. 237.

27 FO 416/71: Sir P. Loraine to the Marquess Curzon of Kedleston, November 14, 1922.

28 "Intelligence Summary No. 40, for week ending October 7, 1922," in *Iran Political Diaries*, Vol. 6, p. 284; FO 416/71: Sir P. Loraine to the Marquess Curzon of Kedleston, November 14, 1922.

Reza Khan's visit to Bushehr, in the end of November 1922 was the year's most significant event as far as the Iranian ports were concerned. This visit was, ostensibly to receive the shah on his return from Europe, but Reza Khan also had some other objectives in mind.[29] First he inspected the barracks of the newly arrived Bushehr garrison. Then he held meetings with the British Resident and the director of the Anglo-Persian Oil Company who was on a visit in Bushehr. In his meeting with the Resident he immediately inquired about the British (Indian) troops at Bushehr, reiterating that Iranian troops had arrived and requesting that the British troops be removed. The Resident replied, saying that the Iranian garrison posted to Bushehr was small and promised that if it was strengthened and proved capable of maintaining order, that the British government would view the request to remove its troops more favorably.[30] Following that meeting, Reza Khan went out and issued a proclamation:

> With reference to the numerous letters received by me from the inhabitants regarding the stay of foreign troops in the Gulf ports, I take this opportunity to point out that the said troops were sent there at the end of the international war owing to the weakness of the central government in Tehran and as guards of the frontiers. But now that, by the grace of God, the extended sphere of the army and military organizations have removed all imaginable difficulties from every point of view, the remainder of the above mentioned troops will return and there will be no cause for anxiety on the part of the inhabitants.[31]

After his meeting with the Resident, Reza Khan conversed with the director of the Anglo-Persian Oil Company and shared his view of the military progress. The director recalled the conversation in a letter saying that Reza Khan "was more or less at ease in his mind regarding the situation in the north and felt that the time had now come to turn his attention to the south."[32] His ambition was "to see [Iranian] troops at every port who would maintain the reputation of the central government and put down smuggling."[33] He made it quite clear that he "actively resented the claims to autonomy of the various chiefs of the Persian Gulf littoral," and said that he intended to obtain a Cabinet decision to place tribal shaykhs directly under his

[29] FO 416/72: Sir P. Loraine to the Marquess Curzon of Kedleston, February 4, 1923, with enclosures.
[30] Ibid. [31] Ibid. [32] Ibid. [33] Ibid.

authority so that they could be adequately controlled and prevented from going astray.[34]

The troops arriving to Bushehr were received as heroes by the local population.[35] And while unconvinced at first, even the British came to appreciate the security that they provided.[36] Previously, the Bushehr hinterland had been under the control of shaykhs, khans, and tribes who were accustomed to levying what they viewed as "road protection fees" on caravans and travelers.[37] Ambushes, robbery, gun-running, and blackmail were commonplace. Even the town of Bushehr had witnessed a handful of murders between 1913 and 1921. The small colony of foreigners at Bushehr lived in dangerous conditions, despite the British Indian battalion stationed there, and providing for their security was a constant concern.[38] The British eventually conceded that if Reza Khan could provide adequate security for their interests in the Persian Gulf Ports, British troop strength in the ports could be significantly reduced.[39] The Resident was aware that British troops on Iranian soil were increasingly viewed as a symbol of national shame: Persian newspapers' calls for the British to evacuate their troops from the Persian Gulf pleased public opinion in Iran's port cities, he said.[40]

Indeed, the rapid progress toward unification, modernization, and security captured the Iranian imagination. Reza Khan's extension of the central authority over Khorasan, Azerbaijan, and Gilan appeared to be the beginning of a campaign that would culminate in the restoration of Iran's lost frontiers and the revival of its former greatness. For Iranians, there was no reason to think that these efforts should not extend into the Persian Gulf until the British were ousted altogether

[34] Ibid.

[35] Administration Report of the Persian Gulf Residency for the Year 1923, p. 7.

[36] Annual Report on Persia for the Year 1922, p. 32.

[37] For a detailed description of life in Bushehr and travel in the hinterland, see the memoir of Cecil John Edmonds, *East and West of Zagros: Travel, War and Politics in Persia and Iraq 1913–1921*, ed. Yann Richard (Leiden: Brill, 2010), pp. 33–49.

[38] Ibid.

[39] FO 416/72: Viceroy to Secretary of State for India, April 30, 1922; FO 371/9036: "British Troops in South Persia," Minutes, December 10, 1923.

[40] Administration Report of the Persian Gulf Residency for the Year 1923, pp. 23–24.

and Iran's former possessions and influence were restored there as well.[41] Following the stationing of the garrison at Bushehr, garrisons arrived to Lingah and Bandar Abbas.[42] In a speech given at a patriotic reception for the garrison posted to Lingah, one local man expressed a hope that the Iranian army would go on to recover Bahrain and (Trucial) Oman.[43] An article published in *Ettehad* declared that "the arrival of Iranian troops in Arabistan is a forerunner of good news that Persia will soon be able to recover the ports and islands wrested from her in the Gulf."[44]

The central government pursued various means of loosening the grip of the British Empire in the Persian Gulf and extending the authority of the central government to the southern precincts. Already in December 1921, the Ministry of Foreign Affairs had raised the question of the right of the British administration to administer quarantine in the Gulf. It determined that the administration of quarantine, when necessary, was the duty of the sanitary officers of the Iranian government and issued instructions to the local customs administration not to pay the British for quarantine expenses (as they had done for the past 20 years).[45]

Another initiative begun in 1922 was the attempt to expand consular services in the Gulf. One official tasked with realizing this ambition, departed for Kuwait with the intent of opening a consulate there. He was stopped by the officials of the British administration and informed that, before pursuing that course of action, he would first need to get permission from the Shaykh of Kuwait, through the proper channel: the British Persian Gulf Administration.[46] It was attempted again in 1924. This time the Iranians tried to appease the British with a diplomatic letter: the Iranian vice-consul at Basra wrote to the British agent at Kuwait, saying that Kuwait was within his consular district, and

41 *Ravabet-e Dowlat-e Shahanshahi ba Keshvarha-ye Howzeh-ye Mas'uliyat-e Edareh-ye Nohom-e Siyasi dar Panjah Saleh-ye Shahanshahi-ye Pahlavi: Emarat-e 'Arabi-ye Mottahedeh, Bahreyn, 'Oman, Qatar* (Tehran: Edareh-ye Entesharat va Madarek, 1976), pp. 32, 51.

42 "Intelligence Summary No. 6, for week ending February 10, 1923," in *Iran Political Diaries*, Vol. 6, p. 449.

43 Administration Report of the Persian Gulf Residency for the Year 1923, p. 29.

44 *Ettehad*, October 10, 1923, excerpted in *Iran Political Diaries*, Vol. 6, p. 616.

45 Annual Report on Persia for the Year 1922, pp. 64–65.

46 High Commissioner Baghdad to Political Agent Kuwait, February 25, 1922, in *Records of Kuwait*, Vol. 6, p. 674.

that at the request of Iranian nationals resident in Kuwait, he would be sending a consular representative to issue Iranian identity certificates, and asked that the necessary assistance be rendered him.[47] When he did not get a favorable reply, he asked Tehran to intervene. Tehran made the same request of the British minister at Tehran – to allow an Iranian consular agent to enter Kuwait. The British referred Tehran's request to the Shaykh of Kuwait, Ahmad al-Jabir Al Sabah, but the shaykh denied the request, saying that he regarded it as an encroachment on his jurisdiction over foreign subjects. His answer was conveyed to Tehran through the British channels.[48]

The Agency of Local Actors

Iran's local actors, including police, port officials, military men, and newspaper correspondents, imbued with patriotic zeal were eager to participate in the struggle to liberate Iran from foreign domination. They expressed their nationalist sentiment in territorial terms, viewing the islands, waterway, and even the Arab shaykhdoms on the southern littoral as usurped Iranian frontiers. Many of them viewed their role as that of assisting the government and the army in reconquering the islands in the Persian Gulf, regaining the allegiance of the shaykhs on the southern littoral and driving the British out of the Gulf. Often the actions of local officials, who believed they knew better than Tehran, outstripped official policy. Despite numerous complaints from the British government, Tehran was loath to censure them, if their actions appeared to go in line with the national goals of territorial integrity and political independence. Tehran also appreciated that minor clashes in the Persian Gulf were an effective means of putting pressure on the British.

Local authorities in Iran's port towns were also hypersensitive to anything that could be interpreted as an affront to national pride. For example, the chief of police (*nazmiyyeh*) in Khuzestan came across a map and forwarded it to his superiors because he noticed that the sea next to Khuzestan was labeled the "Gulf of Basra." He says that this is

47 IOR/R/15/5/98: Political Agent Kuwait to Political Resident, August 12, 1924.

48 FO 416/74: Consul-General to Mr. MacDonald, August 19, 1924; IOR/R/15/5/98: Political Agent Kuwait (More) to Persian Consul Basra, September 9, 1924; and Administration Report of the Persian Gulf Residency for the Year 1924, p. 28.

a cause for concern, because he was accustomed to seeing this part of the map labeled as either the "Iranian Gulf" or the "Persian Gulf."[49]

Surveillance of the political landscape gave local officials and military men an opportunity to advertise their vigilance and dedication to the nationalist cause. The Governor of Gulf Ports wrote to Tehran to report that some quarantine papers carried by a British ship, contained the offending phrase "British Basidu."[50] In another instance, the Iranian consul in Karachi wrote to Tehran to inform of Britain's interference in Muscat:

> The office of the British India Steam Navigation Co. Limited has written a letter to this consulate saying that passengers that want to go to Muscat need to be inoculated against a plague. The Imperial government views Muscat as an integral part of the Imperial territory, therefore it forwards a copy and translation of the aforementioned company's letter.[51]

Preoccupation with finalizing the nation's borders also engendered a sense of entitlement to lands that were historically under Iranian suzerainty. This is implicit in a letter written by Iran's consul in Baghdad, on September 19, 1926, in which he advises "the Iranian government, for the sake of building its future, needs to carefully watch events in Kuwait."[52] In support of his assertion, he says, "Iranian nationals make up the majority of the population of Kuwait."[53] He goes on to explain that Iranian citizens have historical rights to Kuwait because "to this day they have been contributing to the water and the soil and commerce and wealth of Kuwait."[54] His immediate concern – and reason for writing – was a rumor going around that the territory of Kuwait could be joined to the territory of the Najd, and that if this

[49] Chief of Police Khuzestan to Police Administrative Headquarters, *Esfand* 17, 1311 (March 8, 1933), in ʻAli Farahmand, "Engelis va Parvazha-ye Iran-zedayi az Khalij-e Fars," *Tarikh-e Ravabet-e Khareji*, no. 22 (Spring 1384/2005), pp. 229–230.

[50] Ministry of Foreign Affairs to Ministry of the Interior, *Azar* 16, 1312 (December 17, 1933), in Mohsen Ganjbakhsh Zamani, "Piruzi-ye Iran bar Engelis dar Nabard-e Basaʻidu," *Tarikh-e Ravabet-e Khareji*, no. 22 (Spring 1384/2005), pp. 245–246.

[51] Consulate of Iran Karachi to Ministry of Foreign Affairs, *Ordibehesht* 3, 1316 (April 13, 1937), in *Gozideh-ye Asnad-e Khalij-e Fars*, Vol. 2, pp. 495–496.

[52] Consulate of Iran Baghdad to Ministry of Foreign Affairs, *Shahrivar* 27, 1305 (September 19, 1926), in *Gozideh-ye Asnad-e Khalij-e Fars*, Vol. 2, pp. 530–535.

[53] Ibid. [54] Ibid.

were to occur, Iran would have a big powerful Arab state on its border. He says that this would be dangerous for two reasons: it would pose a danger from the national perspective (it would be an Arab state), and it would pose a danger from the religious perspective (it would be a Sunni, Wahhabi state). To prevent this from happening, he urges the Iranian government to intervene and to consider the idea of annexing Kuwait to Iran.[55]

One class of civil servants whose role was instrumental in shaping Iran's policy in the Persian Gulf was the network of foreign ministry agents (*Kargozars*) operating in Iran's Persian Gulf port towns. The *Kargozari* system had been set up in the first half of the nineteenth century in response to the commercial expansion arising from the capitulations extended to Russia and Britain.[56] *Kargozaris* (agencies) were established in important cities, especially cities that drew much foreign commercial activity, including Bushehr, Bandar Abbas, Lingah, and Mohammerah (later Khorramshahr). Traditionally, the *Kargozar*s handled issues involving foreigners on behalf of the Ministry of Foreign Affairs such as settling disputes over trade and property and cases of theft.[57] The *Kargozars* were also passport officers, responsible for issuing travel documents and regulating the entrance and exit of foreigners. In the post First World War drive to consolidate Iran's frontiers and challenge British authority in the Persian Gulf, the *Kargozar*s became pivotal figures in the conduct of Arab-Iranian relations in the Persian Gulf. While continuing to serve as the central government's representatives vis-à-vis foreigners entering and exiting Iranian ports, they also increasingly took on the role of intelligence gathering. The head *Kargozar* in the Persian Gulf was based at Bushehr and he was aided by subordinate *Kargozars* at Lingah and Bandar Abbas: together they became the government's eyes and ears in the Persian Gulf, providing a steady flow of reports on the conditions prevailing in Iran's coast and islands, news from the Arab shaykhdoms, the activities of the British officials in the Persian Gulf, the movements of the

[55] Ibid.
[56] Vanessa Martin and Morteza Nouraei, "The Role of the Karguzar in the Foreign Relations of State and Society of Iran from the Mid-Nineteenth Century to 1921: Part 1: Diplomatic Relations," *Journal of the Royal Asiatic Society of Great Britain and Ireland* (Third Series) 15 (2005), pp. 261–277.
[57] Ibid.

British navy, and the attitude and activities of the merchants who traversed the Gulf.

A good example of the role of the *Kargozars* in the evolution of Iran's Persian Gulf policy are their detailed reports and recommendations concerning Hengam Island which precipitated Tehran's reassertion of authority over the island in the dramatic events of 1927–1928. In February 1923, the head *Kargozar*, whose title was Mobayyen al-Mamalek, notified the foreign ministry that smuggling on Hengam was costing the government a good deal of money. He advocated sending an Iranian official who would be loyal to the country and would not accept bribes. He also suggested the possibility of sending a troop detachment to arrest the Arab shaykh whose collusion with the British had been preventing the effective administration of Iranian authority on the island.[58] His successor, known as Mo'ezzeh al-Soltan, continued the efforts in regard to Hengam. In his report, he underscored the strategic importance of the island and again urged the government to send an official who would represent the Imperial government.[59] These dispatches led to the appointment of a tough customs clerk in 1926 and culminated in the reestablishment of military authority on Hengam in 1928, effectively closing the curtain on decades of semi-autonomous rule by an Arab shaykh.[60]

Given their close contact with traffic in people and goods from the southern littoral, the foreign ministry commissioned numerous reports from the *Kargozars* on the history and politics of the port towns of the lower Gulf, with particular attention to Iranian and Shi'i communities. Reza Khan's visit to Bushehr in 1922, and the stationing of a garrison there, followed by the stationing of garrisons in Lingah and Bandar Abbas in 1923, generated a tangible sense of excitement among the *Kargozars* of the Persian Gulf Ports that Iran might also be strong enough to regain an influence on the Trucial Coast (which they called "the coast of Oman" the "ports of Oman" or simply "Oman").

58 Head *Kargozar* of the Persian Gulf Ports (Bushehr) to the Ministry of Foreign Affairs, *Dalv* 22, 1301 (February 12, 1923), in *Gozideh-ye Asnad-e Khalij-e Fars*, Vol. 1, pp. 532–533.

59 Head *Kargozar* of the Persian Gulf Ports (Bushehr) to the Ministry of Foreign Affairs, *Azar* 17, 1302 (December 9, 1923); and Ministry of Foreign Affairs to Head *Kargozar* of the Persian Gulf Ports (Bushehr), in *Gozideh-ye Asnad-e Khalij-e Fars*, Vol. 1, pp. 537–540.

60 See Chapters 4 and 5.

The Trucial States were viewed by the *Kargozars* as former Iranian possessions and places where Iran might be able to regain an influence owing to the large presence of Iranian nationals and the prominent role that they played in politics and society.[61]

Iran and the Trucial States

Abu Dhabi was rocked by a bloody palace coup in August 1922. Mohammad 'Ali Sadid al-Saltaneh, the seasoned *Kargozar* of Bandar Abbas, forwarded a letter that he received from an informant in Dubai describing the murder of Shaykh Hamdan bin Zayid bin Khalifa, Ruler of Abu Dhabi, by his brother, Sultan.[62] The informant, an Iranian national residing in Dubai, begins by saying that Hamdan "had allowed the oppression and extortion of 'Ajam (Iranian) shopkeepers."[63] He and his brothers, Khalifa, Saqr, Sultan, and Muhammad, "had been violating their rights and giving them difficulties. Even the Arab community is given difficulties," he wrote.[64]

In connection with the coup, the *Kargozar* of Lingah, known as Hisham al-Vozara, provided a précis on the historical connection between Abu Dhabi and Iran. He begins the story in 1898, when the Qajar government sent an official to Lingah to unseat Shaykh Muhammad Al Qasimi and recover Iranian sovereignty over that port.[65] After that incident, "the shaykhs of [Trucial] Oman sought to be under the protection of the Iranian government," he says.[66] One of the shaykhs who petitioned the Iranian government was Shaykh Zayid bin Khalifa Al Nuhayyan (the father of Hamdan), he adds.[67] In conclusion,

[61] See for example, *Gozideh-ye Asnad-e Khalij-e Fars*, Vol. 2, pp. 15–49.

[62] "Report arriving from Dubai to the *Kargozar* of Bandar Abbas dated *Zihajjeh* 15, 1340 (September 9, 1922)," in *Gozideh-ye Asnad-e Khalij-e Fars*, Vol. 2, p. 19.

[63] Ibid. [64] Ibid.

[65] Qasimi rule of Lingah ended in 1887 when the Qajar government imprisoned the governor, Shaykh Qadhib Al Qasimi, but after 12 years, Shaykh Muhammad Al Qasimi, a descendant of the former governors of Lingah, attacked the town and held it until 1899.

[66] "Report #69 of the *Kargozar* of Bandar Lingah to the Head *Kargozar* of the Persian Gulf Ports (Bushehr) dated *Sonboleh* 24, 1301 (September 19, 1922)" in *Gozideh-ye Asnad-e Khalij-e Fars*, Vol. 2, p. 25.

[67] Ibid.; Following the ouster of Shaykh Muhammad bin Khalifa Al Qasimi from Lingah, Shaykh Zayid began correspondence with the new Iranian Governor of Lingah (the *Darya Begi*). Lorimer says, "When the negotiations were detected

"Shaykh Zayid was in the mercy of the Iranian government authorities, and Shaykh Hamdan, his successor, was killed. Use when appropriate," he says.[68] In February 1923, when a war broke out between the shaykhs of Abu Dhabi and Dubai, the Lingah *Kargozar* reminds the ministry in his report that "Abu Dhabi, like the other ports of Oman, was formerly in Iran's possession."[69]

The head *Kargozar* of the Persian Gulf Ports reported to Tehran on the "criminal conduct and abuse of the Arab shaykhs toward Iranian subjects."[70] He provided information gleaned from an informant in Dubai, that in February 1923, Shaykh Hashr bin Maktum, the brother of the ruling Shaykh of Dubai, went into a gathering of "Bahrainis" whom he also refers to as "Iranian subjects," arrested them on the charges of illegal activity, imprisoned them, and confiscated their property. One of them he struck and injured with a knife. In addition to these types of abuses, the informant said that the Iranians resident in the ports of Oman (Trucial Oman) were being forced to acquire foreign nationality papers.[71] The head *Kargozar* appealed to the foreign ministry to issue instructions for how to deal with these cases, so that he could "provide comfort to the Iranian citizens who suffer oppression" under the Arab rulers.[72]

The *Kargozars* were also keen to report on British activity along the Trucial Coast, albeit their information on the British was largely based on rumor. Mohammad 'Ali, *Kargozar* of Bandar Abbas, scrupulously

the Shaykh had already sent two horses as a present to Lingah, had differentiated himself from his neighbors by flying a green flag in place of the one prescribed by the treaty of 1820, and had received a sword of honor from the Shah of Iran and a commendatory epistle, bearing the royal seal, which was publicly read in an assembly in Abu Dhabi." He was reminded of his treaty obligations and the correspondence stopped. See J. G. Lorimer, *Gazetteer of the Persian Gulf, Oman, and Central Arabia*, Vol. 1, pp. 744–747.

68 Ibid.

69 "Report #280 of the Acting *Kargozar* of Bandar Lingah to the Head *Kargozar* of the Persian Gulf Ports (Bushehr) dated *Dalv* 28, 1301 (February 17, 1923)," in *Gozideh-ye Asnad-e Khalij-e Fars*, Vol. 2, p. 30.

70 Head *Kargozar* of the Persian Gulf Ports (Bushehr) to the Ministry of Foreign Affairs, *Hamal* 18, 1302 (April 8, 1923), in *Gozideh-ye Asnad-e Khalij-e Fars*, Vol. 2, p. 45.

71 "Report #321 of the Acting *Kargozar* of Bandar Lingah dated *Hut* 26, 1301 (March 18, 1923)," in *Gozideh-ye Asnad-e Khalij-e Fars*, Vol. 2, p. 46.

72 Head *Kargozar* of the Persian Gulf Ports (Bushehr) to the Ministry of Foreign Affairs, *Hamal* 18, 1302 (April 8, 1923), in *Gozideh-ye Asnad-e Khalij-e Fars*, Vol. 2, p. 45.

maintained a file containing copies of the treaties between the British and the Trucial shaykhs and sent translations of the treaties to the foreign ministry.[73] Other *Kargozars* evinced no knowledge of these treaties. For example, in September 1922, Shaykh Rashid, the Ruler of Umm al-Quwain, passed away and the Lingah *Kargozar* warned that a subsequent leadership struggle "would also give the British officials an opportunity to interfere there."[74] Apparently, he did not realize that Umm al-Quwain was a signatory to the British-sponsored "Exclusive Agreement" of 1892 and an oil exploration concession of 1922. In another instance, the *Kargozar* of Lingah believed a wildly exaggerated rumor that the British signed an agreement with the Shaykh of Sharjah, promising to arm him and make him sovereign over all the other "shaykhs of Oman" (Trucial shaykhs), if he would give them a quarter of his revenues and allow them to build institutions and fly the British flag over Sharjah.[75] He evinced no knowledge that the Shaykh of Sharjah, like the Shaykh of Umm al-Quwain, already had long-standing treaty relations with the British and hosted a British agency in his domain.

The reports of the *Kargozars* on the history and contemporary events of the Trucial Coast reveal that these Iranian port officials viewed the entire southern littoral – from Kuwait to Muscat – as usurped Iranian frontiers, where the Iranian residents suffered under the yoke of Sunni Arab rulers. Qatar (also called Zubara, the name of the fortified town), which was incorporated into the Trucial system in 1916, was viewed by Mohammad 'Ali as one of Iran's lost territories.[76] While relating the history of Bahrain in a letter to the foreign ministry, he explains that Zubara was formerly a dependency of Bahrain and writes, "here the

[73] "Head of the *Tazkera* Office of the Persian Gulf Ports (Mohammad 'Ali) to the Ministry of Foreign Affairs, *Esfand* 6, 1306 (February 26, 1928)," enclosing report #314, *Jadi* 6, 1301 (December 28, 1922), in *Gozideh-ye Asnad-e Khalij-e Fars*, Vol. 1, pp. 102–106.

[74] "Report #66 of the *Kargozar* of Bandar Lingah to the Head *Kargozar* (Bushehr) dated *Sonboleh* 24, 1301 (September 19, 1922)," in *Gozideh-ye Asnad-e Khalij-e Fars*, Vol. 2, p. 36.

[75] "Report #16 of the *Kargozar* of Bandar Lingah to the Head *Kargozar* (Bushehr) dated *Hamal* 10, 1302 (March 31, 1923)," in *Gozideh-ye Asnad-e Khalij-e Fars*, Vol. 2, p. 93.

[76] The idea that Zubara (Qatar) was part of Bahrain and therefore part of Iran captured Iranians' imagination. See also Pirouz Mojtahed-Zadeh, *Security and Territoriality in the Persian Gulf: A Maritime Political Geography* (London: RoutledgeCurzon, 2003), pp. 139–140.

government of Iran can take possession of Qatar as well."[77] Throughout 1922, Mirza Khalil, the acting *Kargozar* of Lingah, and his replacement, Hisham al-Vozara, refused to allow subjects of the Trucial States and Muscat (in addition to subjects of Bahrain) to enter Iranian ports with British-issued travel passes, claiming that travelers from the Trucial Coast and Muscat are Iranian subjects.[78]

Bahrain: Between the British and Iran

The British role in Persian Gulf islands, such as Bahrain, Hengam, Abu Musa, and the Tunbs, was a focal point for the vital expression of anti-British sentiment in the aftermath of the Great War. From the perspective of many Iranians resident in the Gulf, British sponsorship of Shaykh ʻIsa, the Ruler of Bahrain, was akin to its sponsorship of Shaykh Khazʻal in Iran – equally insidious, equally illegitimate, and equally mutable. From their point of view, the British exploited the sectarian divide between Sunni and Shiʻi in Bahrain to cement their "divide and rule" policy, which kept Iranian Bahrain separated from Iran. Moreover, the sectarian fighting in Bahrain, especially the uprising of the Shiʻi Arabs in February 1922, mirrored the outbreak of sectarian and secessionist uprisings that raged in the provinces. Newspapers declared that the British intentionally pitted Bahrain's Sunni and Shiʻi communities against each other as part of their colonial strategy to rule the island, and vigilant state authorities advertised their dedication to the Bahrain cause, seeking by various means to put Iran's claims to sovereignty into force.[79]

A small group of Iranian nationals residing in Bahrain provided the vital link between Bahrain and Iran in the early years of Reza Khan's rise. This was a group of about 40 men, petty shopkeepers and labor migrants, who coalesced around the person of ʻAbd al-Nabi Kazeruni,

[77] Head of the *Tazkera* Office of the Persian Gulf Ports (Mohammad ʻAli) to the Ministry of Foreign Affairs, dated *Esfand* 6, 1306 (February 26, 1928)," with enclosure (a copy of Mohammad ʻAli's report #314, December 28, 1922), in *Gozideh-ye Asnad-e Khalij-e Fars*, Vol. 1, p. 43.

[78] Administration Report of the Persian Gulf Residency for the Year 1922, p. 23.

[79] See for example, *Shafaq-e Sorkh*, *Safar* 1, 1341 (September 23, 1922); and an open letter to the Ministry of Foreign Affairs from Shaykh al-Islam Isfahani dated December 23, 1923, in *Ruzshumar-e Tarikh-e Muʻasir-e Iran*, ed. Hedayatollah Behbudi, Vol. 2 (Tehran: Mu'assaseh-ye Motalaʻat va Pezhuheshha-ye Siyasi, 1385–1388/2006–2010), p. 569.

one of the more prominent Shi'i merchants from Iran. Calling themselves the "patriots of Bahrain," members of this group, most of whom had roots in the Bushehr district, submitted numerous petitions to the head *Kargozar* and to the foreign ministry complaining of the indeterminate state of affairs in Bahrain, and appealing for the protection of the Iranian government. A letter from one individual, Kazem Reza-Zadeh Bushehri, can serve as an example. It reads:

> I have a heart full of sorrow, that we are a handful of Iranian citizens caught under foreign pressure. Each day of our lives provides different examples of the battles we face ... for example the warrant for false accusation of theft, and a one year prison sentence ... they beat us with a rod and sometimes take away all of our rights."[80]

The *Kargozars* advertised their willingness to go to Bahrain as representatives of Iran, and also urged the central government to bring its policies in line with its claim to sovereignty over Bahrain – particularly its policies in regard to travel documents, customs fees, and postal services.[81] The zeal of petty officials for the Bahrain cause can be seen in a letter of May 27, 1922, from the *Kargozar* of Bandar Abbas, in which he alerts the foreign ministry to a bureaucratic oversight that was contrary to Iran's claim to Bahrain: in the annual fiscal report drawn up by the Belgian customs administration, Bahrain was described as part of the British Empire and customs dues were levied on Bahrain as if it were a foreign country. He notes that the same report did not mention the Trucial States and Muscat as British territories, and wonders: Why was Bahrain identified this way?[82] After receiving his letter, the foreign ministry turned to Lambert Molitor, the Belgian director of customs, and asked him to account for this contradictory policy. Molitor responded saying that as long as there was no Iranian rule, no Iranian military force, and no Iranian customs

80 Head *Kargozar* of the Persian Gulf Ports (Bushehr) to Ministry of Foreign Affairs, *Jowza'* 14, 1301 (June 5, 1922), in *Gozideh-ye Asnad-e Khalij-e Fars*, Vol. 1, p. 36.

81 IOR/L/P&S/11/173: "Proposed visit to Bahrein of Kargozar, Bushire," March 25, 1922–May 4, 1922; Head *Kargozar* of Arabistan (Mohammerah) to Ministry of Foreign Affairs, *Dhu al-Hijja* 9, 1341 (July 23, 1923), in *Gozideh-ye Asnad-e Khalij-e Fars*, Vol. 1, p. 54.

82 "Report #9 of the *Kargozar* of Bandar Abbas (Mohammad 'Ali) dated *Jowza'* 5, 1301 (May 27, 1922)," in *Gozideh-ye Asnad-e Khalij-e Fars*, Vol. 1, pp. 43–45.

administration in Bahrain, it would be "extremely strange" to exempt Bahrain from customs duties.[83]

While negotiations were underway regarding the transfer of post offices from British to Iranian administration, a multitude of voices called for the inclusion of Bahrain in the Iranian postal administration.[84] These included local authorities, merchants, and Majles members.[85] Beginning in June 1922, the Shiraz newspapers *Estakhr* and *'Asr-e Azadi*, aided by 'Abd al-Nabi Kazeruni's "Nationalist Party," put out a spate of articles calling for the establishment of an Iranian post office in Bahrain.[86] In the latter half of the year, the articles began to demand specific actions from the Iranian government: one article called upon the government to appointment deputies in the Majles to represent Bahrain's interests and another one called upon the government to send a *Kargozar* to Bahrain.[87] The press campaign widened when articles appeared in Tehran newspapers, such as *Shafaq-e Sorkh* and *Setareh-ye Iran*, demanding to know which concrete steps the government was going to take to make good on Iran's claim to sovereignty over Bahrain.[88]

The Ahmad Qavam government chose the occasion of the postal conference to try to assuage public opinion concerning Bahrain. A postal conference was convened in December 1922 by the British government to conclude the details of the transfer of six southern post offices to Iranian administration. On the instructions of his government, the Iranian delegate to the postal conference reminded the British authorities that Bahrain was also an integral part of Iranian territory and managed to persuade the British (Indian) delegate to include Iran's contention in the conference proceedings.[89] But this gesture was not enough to alleviate the clamoring. The Shiraz paper, *'Asr-e Azadi*, berated the Iranian government for its failure to provide comfort to

[83] General Customs Office of Iran (Molitor) to the Ministry of Foreign Affairs, July 4, 1922, in *Gozideh-ye Asnad-e Khalij-e Fars*, Vol. 1, p. 30.
[84] CAB 24/155: Foreign Countries Report, No. 69, May 17, 1922, p. 5.
[85] Behbudi, *Ruzshumar-e Tarikh-e Mu'asir-e Iran*, Vol. 1, p. 283, and Vol. 2, pp. 289 and 569.
[86] IOR/R/15/1/319: *Estakhr*, July 25, 1922, and *'Asr-e Azadi*, July 30, 1922.
[87] See Mahdi Abdalla al-Tajir, *Bahrain: 1920–1945, Bahrain, the Shaikh and the Administration* (New York: Croom Helm, 1987), p. 31 and footnotes.
[88] IOR/R/15/1/319: *Shafaq-e Sorkh*, *Safar* 1, 1341 (September 23, 1922); Behbudi, *Ruzshumar-e Tarikh-e Mu'asir-e Iran*, Vol. 2, p. 569.
[89] Annual Report on Persia for the Year 1922, pp. 43–44.

Iranians settled in Bahrain in the simple matter of establishing a post office on an island that was claimed by Iran. The paper alleged that 30,000 Iranians in Bahrain were afflicted by a British consul and his agents and the deputies of the Majles did not pay the least attention.[90]

In May 1923 the outbreak of sectarian violence in Bahrain – this time involving Iranian nationals – was swept up in the march of Iranian nationalism. Violence erupted on May 10 as the result of a quarrel in the Manama market between Najdis and Iranians – namely the nationalist faction led by 'Abd al-Nabi Kazeruni. The Iranians promptly sent telegrams to Tehran, addressing their appeals to Reza Khan, the speaker of the Majles and the minister of foreign affairs. Their calls for help fueled articles in the Persian language press, then in its second year of a campaign to revive Iran's claim to Bahrain, and also resulted in the introduction of a motion to allow Bahrain to appoint a deputy to the Majles.[91]

In May 1924 the General Staff of the Iranian army demonstrated a keen interest in the possibility of supporting Bahraini opposition figures with the aim of reintroducing Iranian influence on the "island".[92] The army had received some petitions from Mohammed Amin Khonji, a wealthy Sunni merchant from Lingah residing in Bahrain, who sought to involve Iran in Bahraini affairs to the detriment of the British whose policies were harming his business. In his letters, Khonji described how the people of Bahrain – reputable merchants, tribesmen, pearl divers, and nakhodas – suffered immensely under the yoke of British imperial rule. He related how those who opposed British policies faced various forms of oppression including imprisonment without trial, confiscation of their property, and banishment from the island. He went on to describe how several prominent members of the Al Khalifa family, Shaykh Ibrahim bin Khalid and his younger brothers, nephews of Shaykh 'Isa, were banished from Bahrain by the British. He expressed a hope that the fugitives would accept his advice to travel to Lingah and urged the Iranian government to offer them

[90] IOR/R/15/1/319: *'Asr-e Azadi*, January 25, 1923.

[91] See for example, *Shafaq-e Sorkh*, *Khordad* 2, 1302 (May 24, 1923); FO 416/73: Sir P. Loraine to the Marquess Curzon of Kedleston, April 17, 1923.

[92] Bahrain is referred to as an island in the Iranian archival documents. Army General Staff to Prime Minister, *Sowr* 22, 1303 (May 19, 1924) with attachments in *Faslnameh-ye Motala'at-e Tarikhi* 8, no. 33 (Summer 1390/ 2011), pp. 238–249.

protection if and when they arrive. In addition, he suggested that Iran should offer tax and customs exemptions to Bahrain merchants to help win over the hearts of the Bahrain people and bring them back under Iranian authority.[93]

The Renewal of Claims to Bahrain and Abu Musa

During the period 1923–1924, numerous governments rose and fell in Tehran and Iran was in no position to seriously pursue its territorial claims in the Persian Gulf. Nevertheless, government ministers continued to give verbal and written notice of Iran's claims to satisfy domestic pressures. The 1923 Abu Musa episode can attest to this. A prominent merchant and constitutionalist, Hajji Mohammad Mo'in al-Tojjar Bushehri, who held the concession to mine red oxide on Hormuz Island, hoped to sell the mineral to the British firm, Messrs. Strick and Co.; however, rather than pay his price, the firm reached an agreement with the Shaykh of Sharjah to purchase red oxide from the island of Abu Musa, an island also claimed by Iran. Mo'in al-Tojjar agitated for the renewal of Iran's claim to Abu Musa but his appeals were unsuccessful. Then in April 1923 after the outbreak of violence in Bahrain, rumors abounded that Iran might refer its grievances about Bahrain to the League of Nations. Naturally, al-Tojjar became an advocate of this course of action and urged the government to couple its claim to Bahrain with its claim to Abu Musa and refer both to the League of Nations.[94] Minister of Foreign Affairs Mohammad 'Ali Foroughi handled the situation by issuing an official protest to the British Legation asserting Iranian sovereignty over the islands, and mentioning Iran's earlier protest of 1904. He warned that because the islands were Iran's possessions, the British did not have the right to hire the red oxide on Abu Musa to the Shaykh of Sharjah.[95]

At times, the Iranian government stirred up nationalist sentiment in the population by giving credence to populist ambitions in the Persian

[93] Ibid.

[94] FO 416/72: Sir P. Loraine to the Marquess Curzon of Kedleston, April 27, 1923; Annual Report on Persia for the Year 1923, pp. 31–32.

[95] FO 416/72: Persian Minister of Foreign Affairs (Foroughi) to Sir P. Loraine, May 23, 1923; FO 416/72: Sir P. Loraine to the Marquess Curzon of Kedleston, May 29, 1923; For a later account of these exchanges from Iran's perspective, see Report of the First Political Office to the Minister of Foreign Affairs, *Dey* 14, 1305 (January 5, 1927), in *Gozideh-ye Asnad-e Khalij-e Fars*, Vol. 1, pp. 289–291.

Gulf, but by doing so, it diminished its own room for maneuver, and found itself forced to react to the very passions it had created. The formal adoption of new passport regulations is a case in point. In October 1921, the head *Kargozar* notified his superiors that British officials were issuing travel documents to Iranians resident in Bahrain. This, he said, constituted interference in Bahrain, contrary to the sovereignty of Iran, and he requested that the ministry provide some instruction in the manner of dealing with this issue.[96] The foreign ministry reacted by dispatching one of its employees to instruct port officials on the procedure for handling travel documents in a way that was consistent with Iran's claim to Bahrain.[97] By June 1922, Iranian port officials began impounding British-issued travel documents that Bahrainis presented and issuing Iranian travel documents in their stead.[98] The central government then found itself pressed from two sides. On the one side, the British Legation brought pressure to bear on the foreign ministry, demanding that it reverse this policy, while on the other side, myriad voices from within and without pleaded with Tehran to bring its Persian Gulf policies in line with national sovereignty and independence.[99] Ultimately, the foreign ministry sided with the surge of nationalist feeling and sent official written instructions to treat Bahrainis as Iranian citizens.[100]

Tehran's formal adoption of this policy would have a profound effect on trade and travel between the two shores of the Persian Gulf throughout the interwar years and beyond, and no subsequent

[96] Head *Kargozar* of the Persian Gulf Ports (Bushehr) to Ministry of Foreign Affairs, *Mehr* 28, 1300 (October 20, 1921), pp. 32–35.

[97] Behbudi, "23 June 1922" in *Ruzshumar-e Tarikh-e Mu'asir-e Iran*, Vol. 2, pp. 247–248.

[98] Administration Report of the Persian Gulf Residency for the Year 1922, p. 23.

[99] Head *Kargozar* of the Persian Gulf Ports (Bushehr) to Ministry of Foreign Affairs, *Mehr* 28, 1300 (October 20, 1921); Head *Kargozar* (Bushehr) to Ministry of Foreign Affairs, *Dalv* 11, 1300 (January 31, 1922); and *Kargozar* of Bandar Abbas to Head *Kargozar* (Bushehr), *Jowza'* 5, 1301 (May 27, 1922), in *Gozideh-ye Asnad-e Khalij-e Fars*, Vol. 1, pp. 32–36, 38, and 43; see also a letter reproduced in Samaneh Bayrami, "Chalesh-e Iran va Engelestan bar sar-e Hakemiyyat bar Bahreyn,"*Faslnameh-ye Motala'at-e Tarikhi* 8, no. 33 (Summer 1390/2011), pp. 127–166; and Behbudi, *Ruzshumar-e Tarikh-e Mu'asir-e Iran*, Vol. 1, p. 283, and Vol. 2, pp. 289, 583, 739.

[100] FO 416/73: Political Resident to Foreign and Political Department Simla, April 25, 1923; Sir P. Loraine to the Marquess Curzon of Kedleston, July 14, 1923; Jalalpur and Jalalpur, "Engelestan va Jodayi-ye Bahreyn va Iran," p. 199.

government would reverse it. When the government that issued the passport instructions fell, Percy Loraine, the British minister in Tehran, appealed again to the foreign ministry to cancel the instructions affecting Bahrain travelers.[101] But the new minister of foreign affairs, Mohammad Mosaddeq (best known for his role in the nationalization of the oil industry in 1951), told Loraine that the instructions had been issued by the previous government and that although the new government (of Hasan Pirnia Moshir al-Dowleh) did not intend to raise the issue of Bahrain, it was not willing to cancel the previous government's instructions to treat Bahrainis as Iranian citizens.[102] Canceling the instructions, he explained, would be viewed by the public as a total abandonment of Iran's claim to Bahrain. He went on to say that Iran refused to abandon the claim for moral and sentimental reasons: the island had formerly been an Iranian possession, Iran had never renounced her claim, and public opinion would not consent to a renunciation of the claim unless good cause could be shown for doing so. Loraine asked him, off the record, whether the Iranian government would ever consider submitting the issue to third-party arbitration (a suggestion that later earned a rebuke from Lord Curzon). Mosaddeq replied, off the record, that yes, the Iranian government would probably be amenable to arbitration.[103]

While some ministers tried to keep the issue contained, the Persian newspapers and Iranians resident in Bahrain kept the issue alive, cultivating the narrative of Iranian Bahrain groaning under the foreign yoke. The Bahrain "Nationalist Party" sent letters to Persian newspapers and lobbied government officials for protection. The Iranian Consul at Najaf issued a statement inviting them to come to his consulate and register as Iranian citizens.[104] Zeyn al-'Abedin Rahnema, a Majles member, supporter of Reza Khan, and editor of the newspaper *Iran,* published a letter addressed to the foreign ministry, saying:

[101] IOR/R/15/1/320: Sir P. Loraine to the Marquess Curzon of Kedleston, October 31, 1923.

[102] Ibid. [103] Ibid.

[104] FO 416/73: Sir P. Loraine to the Marquess Curzon of Kedleston, July 14, 1923; L. B. H. Haworth to the Foreign Secretary of the Government of India (Sir Denys Bray), September 1, 1927, in *Arabian Boundaries 1853–1960*, eds. G. Blake and R. Schofield, Vol. 12 (Archive Editions, 1988), pp. 112, 120.

First of all, Bahrain is in the Iranian Gulf and is an inalienable domain of Iran, yet, there is no Iranian government official there, so must the people there be trapped by the pressures of the foreign officials? Second, if Bahrain's postal fees are in line with the rates of the interior provinces, then why is there a foreign stamp attached to the shipments that arrive from Bahrain? Third ... the government does not have a post office in Bahrain, and the Bahrain post office was not among those transferred [to Iranian authority] at the Bushehr postal conference, yet the importance of Bahrain, if it is not greater than the Gulf provinces is also not less, and if all of the Bahraini people really desire to have an administrator and officials from the government of Iran, then it is not clear: why has the sending of government officials and the opening of government agencies [there] not yet been ventured? Now, please ... take the necessary measures to open government offices and send *bona fide*, competent officials to Bahrain and the other islands of the Gulf to comfort the people.[105]

One colorful individual, ʻAli Asghar Khan Jahanbani, the commander of the Bushehr garrison, tried to position himself as the liaison between Bahrain and the Iranian central government. When the Ministry of War learned in April 1924 that the officer had visited Bahrain and received a very warm reception, it commissioned a full report from him, and asked him to include his "analysis of the Iranians of Bahrain and the views and feelings of the local people."[106]

ʻAli Asghar wrote to the foreign ministry saying that he had met Shaykh Hamad Al Khalifa, the Ruler of Bahrain, in January when the shaykh came to Lingah to hunt. "Upon seeing me," he said, the shaykh "expressed joy at the arrival of the troops to the ports and especially the building of the new barracks."[107] He said that the British, "upon hearing of the meeting between us ... urgently recalled the Shaykh to Bahrain."[108] Later, the officer was traveling on board a mail steamer of the British Indian service, and he disembarked at

105 Office of the Newspaper *Iran* to the Ministry of Foreign Affairs, *Ghows* 28, 1302 (December 20, 1923), in *Gozideh-ye Asnad-e Khalij-e Fars*, Vol. 1, p. 58.
106 Head *Kargozar* of the Persian Gulf Ports (Bushehr) to Ministry of Foreign Affairs, *Hamal* 19, 1303 (April 8, 1924); Ministry of Foreign Affairs to the Ministry of War, *Sowr* 10, 1303 (April 30, 1924), in *Gozideh-ye Asnad-e Khalij-e Fars*, Vol. 1, pp. 61 and 63.
107 Ministry of War to the Ministry of Foreign Affairs, *Sowr* 18, 1303 (May 8, 1924), in *Gozideh-ye Asnad-e Khalij-e Fars*, Vol. 1, p. 63.
108 Ibid.

Manama. In his report about this encounter he rhapsodized about the patriotism of the Iranians resident there:

> The tender Iranians, who numbered more than 12,000, and who have long dreamed of seeing and welcoming one of the Iranian army officers, gathered *en masse* in the city and shouted, "Long live the chief of the mighty Iranian army! Long live the commander of the troops of Iran and the ports!" Even the policemen all shouted loudly and cheered .... I went also to Ettehad, the Iranian school of Bahrain, and the school children there sang an anthem.[109]

'Ali Asghar went on to say that if the government would just issue the authorization it could have 12,000 soldiers in Bahrain who would expel the British. He added that although he was unable to meet with Shaykh Hamad Al Khalifa during this visit, he knew that the shaykh was troubled by the British and was "an extraordinary advocate of compliance with Iran."[110] The major reported that he was in regular contact with the shaykh, that he was well informed of the events in Bahrain, and ready to be of service to the Iranian government.[111] In the Iranian port towns, the colonel continued to advertise his intimate knowledge of Bahrain affairs and his meetings with prominent Bahraini figures.[112]

Soon it became clear that the instructions issued to the *Kargozars* to treat Bahrainis as Iranian citizens in regard to travel documents were more of a cheap way to please public opinion than a real challenge to British authority. This is illustrated by a report that one of the local officials sent to his superiors in Tehran. Hajji Mirza Mehdi Khan, the *Kargozar* of Arabistan based in Mohammerah, explains in his letter, "Since I arrived to Mohammerah, there has been an effort in regard to the people of Bahrain." His task, he says, is to execute new procedures designed to prevent British officials from intervening in Iran's sovereign affairs and to "encourage by various means the Iranian-ness" of the residents of Bahrain. Thus, he says, whenever anyone wants to travel to Bahrain, they come to my office and I issue them an Iranian *tazkera* (travel pass). But the problem with this, he writes, is that in Bahrain, it is the British authorities that issue travel passes, not the Iranian authorities. Moreover, people are being permitted to leave Bahrain with these

[109] Ibid. [110] Ibid. [111] Ibid.

[112] "Report #907 of the *Kargozar* of Bandar Abbas (Mohammad 'Ali) dated *Hut* 22, 1301 (March 13, 1925)," in *Gozideh-ye Asnad-e Khalij-e Fars*, Vol. 2, p. 89.

British-issued passes. There is also a problem in regard to Iran's policy about visits to the Shi'i shrines in Najaf and Karbala, he writes. In accordance with his instructions, he routinely refuses to issue travel documents to pilgrims. However, once denied, he laments, these pilgrims simply go to the British authorities who readily issue their own permits for the journey.[113] His letter, in no small way, underscored the futility of trying to put into force Iranian territorial claims by the issuance or nonissuance of travel documents. And the subtext was a not so subtle hint to the authorities in Tehran that they needed to back up Iran's claims with force.

Iranians wanted more than words, they wanted Reza Khan and his army to mount a real challenge to British interference in and around the Gulf. A Shiraz paper proclaimed:

> We complain of the illegal intervention of the British in the domestic affairs of Persia, and state that, although Persia has managed to organize an adequate and capable army, the British still maintain soldiers in the Gulf ports, and there are still 800 Indian soldiers at Bushire singing British hymns and songs in Persian territory. They still maintain strongly their influence and prestige in Bahrain and Qatar where British postage is still used in place of Persian postage. They keenly incite the Persians to show hostility and opposition to the Arabs, and the Shi'a against the Sunni. They bathed the poor Persians in blood, on the pretext of which they landed troops at that island. They urge the Arabs to attack the Persians, in order to compel the latter to denounce Persian citizenship and to apply for British citizenship and passports.[114]

The situation in Bahrain had fast become the epitome of British imperial policy, which aimed to deprive Iran of its legitimate rights in the Persian Gulf. Bahrain was more than the sum of its parts – it was a symbol of all the past Iranian frontiers in the Persian Gulf that had been usurped by foreigners and whose restoration to Iranian sovereignty must be achieved.

113 *Kargozar* of the Foreign Affairs of Arabistan (Mohammerah) to Ministry of Foreign Affairs, *Saratan* 18, 1303 (July 9, 1924), in *Gozideh-ye Asnad-e Khalij-e Fars*, Vol. 1, p. 71.

114 "The Cry of Persia," *Baharistan*, November 24, 1923, in *Iran Political Diaries*, Vol. 6, p. 638.

Arabistan and the Persian Gulf

By the time that Reza Khan assumed the office of prime minister in October 1923, he had come to be perceived as the leader of a national liberation movement. He had also gained favor in the eyes of the British officials in Iran, who viewed him as an indispensable keeper of order and stability.[115] His accession to political power was the catalyst for a significant reduction of British troops in the Persian Gulf Ports.[116] The nationalist press admitted that the withdrawal of British troops was an improvement, but called upon him to do more to roll back Britain's imperialist policy in Iran.[117] He was called upon to repudiate Britain's claim that Iran held war debt, to deal with the issue of their illegal possession of land on Iran's southern shores and in the Persian Gulf, to deal with the issue of Bahrain, to deal with British complicity in the Gulf smuggling business, and to deal with their interference in Arabistan.[118]

Reza Khan's accession to the premiership allowed him to amass larger amounts of money for his military modernization, recruitment, acquisitions, and training.[119] He eyed Arabistan not only because it was the only remaining province that had not yet been penetrated by the authority of the central government but also because he had come to appreciate the potential of Arabistan's oil industry to provide much-needed revenues for the military. In the summer of 1922 he had tried to recruit soldiers locally and gain a foothold there, but then in a catastrophic turn of events, a whole column of soldiers in route to Ahvaz were ambushed and routed by tribesmen.[120] The British still supported Shaykh Khaz'al as a partner in securing the oil fields and the Anglo-Persian Oil Company, based at Mohammerah and Abadan. Reza Khan

[115] Touraj Atabaki and Erik J. Zürcher, *Men of Order: Authoritarian Modernization under Atatürk and Reza Shah* (London: I.B. Tauris, 2004), pp. 19–20.
[116] FO 371/9036: "British Troops in South Persia," Minutes, December 10, 1923; and Sir P. Loraine to Foreign Office, December 20, 1923.
[117] *Karun*, July 1, 1924, in "Intelligence Summary No. 27 for Week Ending July 5, 1924," in *Iran Political Diaries*, Vol. 7, p. 85.
[118] Ibid.
[119] FO 416/72: Sir P. Loraine to the Marquess Curzon of Kedleston, May 23, 1923.
[120] Steven R. Ward, *Immortal: A Military History of Iran and Its Armed Forces* (Washington, DC: Georgetown University Press, 2009), p. 138.

tried to persuade them that an extension of Iran's authority to Arabistan was more advantageous to them than their continued support of Shaykh Khaz'al, and that the oil installations would be better protected by Iranian forces than local notables and tribesmen.[121] Furthermore, British ongoing support for Khaz'al over the interests of Iranian national unity and independence fueled popular hostility.[122] In October 1923, Tehran demanded that Khaz'al surrender his possessions to the government. He refused and Reza Khan began to prepare for a military operation in Arabistan.

In November 1923, the *Kargozar* of Arabistan, based at Mohammerah, who viewed British activity in Arabistan closely, sent reports to the foreign ministry to inform that British war ships were harbored in Mohammerah and Abadan.[123] Foreign Minister Forughi sent angry messages to London and the British Legation in Tehran, protesting the unannounced visit of warships to Iranian ports and demanded their immediate departure from Iran's waters. After further correspondences, in which the British pointed out that Abadan and Mohammerah are both sea ports open to international use, Forughi limited his complaint to the use of the Karun River to reach Mohammerah.[124] (Mohammerah had an approach from the sea as well as from the Karun.) Forughi avowed that the Karun is an inland Iranian waterway and that visits of warships to ports and internal waters of a foreign state was a "breach of the rights" of Iranian sovereignty and contrary to international law.[125]

This time, Iran's contention was acknowledged by the British. The British Resident was aware that for many years the *Kargozars* had been protesting the intrusion of British ships into the Karun River, and, given the strengthened central authority in Iran, he believed that Britain would need to concede on this issue. In the end, the British promised to provide monthly reports on the movements of British ships in

121 FO 416/72: Sir P. Loraine to His Majesty's Consular Officers at Bushire, Shiraz and Ahwaz, January 10, 1923; Sir P. Loraine to the Marquess Curzon of Kedleston, May 23 and June 4, 1923.
122 Kashani-Sabet, *Frontier Fictions*, pp. 164–167.
123 FO 416/74: Lieutenant-Colonel Prideaux to Chargé d'Affaires, Tehran, May 16, 1924.
124 FO 371/9036: "British Warships at Karun," November 16, 1923–November 27, 1923; FO 416/74: Lieutenant-Colonel Prideaux to Chargé d'Affaires Tehran, May 16, 1924.
125 Annual Report on Persia for the Year 1923, p. 23.

the Gulf, with advance notice of visits to Iranian ports, and in turn Reza Khan promised to notify the *Kargozars* that the specific visits outlined in the reports are approved.[126] While the British perceived their interests undamaged, aside from the hassle of added paperwork, Reza Khan had established an early framework that would later assist him in preventing British warships from entering and exiting Iran's territorial waters and ports at whim.[127]

At this time Reza Khan also began to work toward developing Iran's own naval forces. His long-term goal was to substitute Iranian influence for British influence throughout the Persian Gulf. His short-term goal was to develop the ability to take over the policing functions in the Gulf that were being carried out – insufficiently, in his view – by the British navy. Initially he sought to acquire some smaller patrol vessels that could be employed against gun-running, which undermined his efforts to disarm the civilian and tribal population. Negotiations with Germany that began in 1923 resulted in the purchase of a vessel in 1924 named the *Pehlevi*.[128] It was widely advertised in the press as a battleship made by the best manufacturers in Germany.[129] However, it turned out to be a disappointment for residents of Bushehr who gathered in the harbor to witness its arrival. An American official gives an amusing account of this episode:

I have the honor to report certain observations regarding the Persian Navy in view of Persia's demands that the policing of the Gulf to stop illicit arms traffic should be assigned to Persia instead of Great Britain. The largest vessels in the Persian navy are the Persepolis and Muzafferi, neither of which can be moved. One of these attempted a trip to Bombay some years ago, but as it was constantly on the point of sinking, the Captain refused to take it out again. In fact, both are expected to drop to the bottom soon. The crews strike for their pay at intervals, but are rounded up by the military and taken on board or to jail. The pride of the navy is the motor launch "Pehlevi" [Pahlavi], delivered this year by a German firm, – or almost delivered, as she ran out of provisions and fuel a few miles down the Gulf and the crew

126 FO 371/9036: Sir P. Loraine to Foreign Office, November 27, 1923.

127 *Ravabet-e Dowlat-e Shahanshahi ba Keshvarha-ye Howzeh-ye Mas'uliyat-e Edareh-ye Nohom-e Siyasi dar Panjah Saleh-ye Shahanshahi-ye Pahlavi*, p. 55.

128 Mohammad Gholi Majd, *Great Britain and Reza Shah: The Plunder of Iran, 1921–1941* (Gainesville: University Press of Florida, 2001), pp. 293–294.

129 Administration Report of the Persian Gulf Residency for the Year 1924, pp. 20–21; George Gregg Fuller quoted in Majd, *Great Britain and Reza Shah*, p. 293.

rowed to Bushire. A Persian crew was placed on board, under a German deck hand, promoted to Captain. The crew, unpaid, began to sell the ship's fittings in the bazaar, so a guard was detailed from the army to save the navy from itself. Then some army guns were placed on deck, and the "Pehlevi" was ordered to Mohammerah. The whole town turned out to witness the departure, – the event being only marred by the inability of the crew to find out how to get started. The ship was carried up the harbor by the tide, but her anchor was dropped in time to save her. She eventually reached Mohammerah, and will be left there for some time because of the expense of fuel. There are two armed launches now under the Customs Administration; one has been out of repair for over a year, and the other is at Mohammerah. A fine sailing craft was purchased in place of one launch, but the motor installed is too small to move the launch against strong currents. This and another sailing craft are the only vessels acting against smugglers. They [the ship's crew] frequently capture prizes and if their pay is not received, they can live by levying on the smugglers.[130]

Another addition to the navy was made in 1925 when an Iranian resident of Basra purchased a vessel from the British and made a gift of it to the government. The vessel was renamed *Khuzestan* because it was to be employed against the supporters of Shaykh Khaz'al.[131]

In January 1925, Reza Khan mounted the decisive campaign against Khaz'al Khan when 3,000 soldiers marched on Arabistan, thwarting his drive to carve out an independent Arab state on part of the Iranian homeland. His successful campaign to subdue the rebellion of Shaykh Khaz'al was symbolic for Iranian nationalists and was cheered in every major city.[132] New provincial divisions were drawn, and the name Arabistan was replaced with Khuzestan, a geographical term from time immemorial. Similarly, Mohammerah became Khorramshahr and the Shatt al-Arab became Arvand Rud.[133] The changes that took place in this fertile, oil-rich province at the head of the Persian Gulf reflected the calculated policies of nationalization and Persianization that were being pursued throughout the multiethnic, multilingual country. Having cemented Arabistan securely inside the Iranian territorial framework, Reza Khan began to turn his attention to the oil industry

[130] Ibid., p. 292. [131] Annual Report on Persia for the Year 1925, p. 82.

[132] Richard W. Cottam, *Nationalism in Iran* (Pittsburgh: University of Pittsburgh Press, 1979), pp. 113–114.

[133] Svat Soucek, "Arabistan or Khuzistan," *Iranian Studies* 17, no. 2/3 (Spring–Summer 1984), pp. 195–213.

there, to boundary disputes with Iraq, and to the imperative of weakening British influence in and around the Persian Gulf waterway.

The victory over Shaykh Khaz'al appeared to many in Iran as a decisive moment. The Khuzestan campaign symbolized a major victory over British imperial policy in Iran and provided Reza Khan and the army with enormous political credit in Iran's nationalist circles.[134] It also generated new political and military imperatives – that of establishing sovereignty over Iran's frontiers in and around the Persian Gulf and forcing foreign powers, namely Britain, to recognize its sovereignty. These imperatives would become the central tenets of Iran's policy toward the Persian Gulf during the reign of Reza Shah Pahlavi.

134 Stephanie Cronin, *The Army and the Creation of the Pahlavi State* (London: I.B. Tauris, 1997), pp. 206–207.

4 *Reza Shah's Persian Gulf Policy, 1925–1941*

The awakening of the Iranian nation and its restoration of power and political independence, with the decline of the Qajar dynasty and the rise of the Pahlavi dynasty, ushered in a stage which would have been previously unimaginable and it endeavored to shorten the reach of the foreign colonizers as far as possible in the area of the Persian Gulf, which is Iran's undisputable political and natural frontier.[1]

An Official Pahlavi History, Tehran, 1976

Reza Shah's Persian Gulf policy was a blend of grandiose vision and pragmatic realism. He embraced the nationalists' ambition of ousting the British and regaining Iran's historic role as the dominant power in the Persian Gulf waterway, and adopted the short-term goal of reasserting Iranian authority in Iran's ports, islands, and territorial waters. Toward these ends he established a small modern navy and an armed customs preventative service for the policing of Iran's territorial waters, and passed legislation to define Iran's territorial waters and regulate the visits of foreign warships. Despite this, Britain remained dominant in the Persian Gulf and Iran lacked the power of coercion to assert authority in ports and islands where British influence held sway. Given that weakness, the shah employed tactics of bluff and intrigue to try to put into force Iran's territorial claims while employing the tactics of bargaining to gain from the British as many concessions as possible. These tactics rendered the Persian Gulf a volatile environment in which Iran's attempts to challenge British authority fostered tension and ignited passions.

A prominent way in which Iran challenged British authority was in its policy toward the Arab shaykhdoms of the southern littoral. Reza

[1] *Ravabet-e Dowlat-e Shahanshahi ba Keshvarha-ye Howzeh-ye Mas'uliyat-e Edareh-ye Nohom-e Siyasi dar Panjah Saleh-ye Shahanshahi-ye Pahlavi*, pp. 32–33.

Shah's government did not recognize the sovereignty of the Arab shaykhdoms nor did it recognize the shaykhs' treaty relations with the British. Bahrain, claimed by Iran, was treated as the flagship issue; the press reiterated Iran's claim to sovereignty over Bahrain and cultivated the narrative of Iranian Bahrain groaning under the foreign yoke. Abu Musa and the Tunbs, also claimed by Iran, were focal points of nationalist angst. Iranian policy and rhetoric also left the door open for claims to Kuwait, Qatar, Abu Dhabi, Dubai, Sharjah, Ras al-Khaimah, as well as Muscat and Oman. The nationalist aspiration to assert sovereignty over the entire Persian Gulf waterway and littoral was a tool that the shah employed to gain some leverage against the British in his efforts to loosen British authority in and around Iran's territorial waters.

As a means of fortifying his posture vis-à-vis the British, the shah embarked on a policy of securing friendly relations with Iran's Muslim neighbors. This was manifested in the conclusion of a Treaty of Friendship with Turkey in April 1926 and a Treaty of Friendship and Security with Afghanistan in November 1927. It was further underscored by the conspicuous efforts made to obtain an understanding with Iraq in spite of the numerous thorny issues, including disputes over the treatment of Iranian nationals residing in Iraq, the activities of certain frontier tribes that undermined Iranian sovereignty, and toughest of all – the boundary in the Shatt al-Arab (Arvand Rud). Iran formally recognized Iraq on April 25, 1929, and appointed a diplomatic representative to Baghdad. After further reference to the League of Nations the boundary question was resolved in the framework of the July 4, 1937, treaty and protocol.[2] The Reza Shah government also forged a relationship with Ibn Sa'ud, concluding a Treaty of Friendship with the "King of the Hijaz and Najd" in August 1929 that led to the establishment of an Iranian embassy in Jeddah.[3] The will to free Iran of economic encumbrances and disputes on the northern frontier was prominently exhibited in the Saadabad Pact of July 1937, a treaty of nonaggression between Iran, Turkey, Afghanistan, and Iraq that was named for the shah's palace in which it was concluded. Iran's "good neighbor policy" was vitally necessary as a means of saving energy for

[2] Ramazani, *The Foreign Policy of Iran*, pp. 258–276.
[3] Banafsheh Keynoush, *Saudi Arabia and Iran: Friends or Foes?* (New York: Palgrave Macmillan, 2016), pp. 53–56.

its showdown with the British over the issue of sovereignty in the Persian Gulf waterway, islands, and littoral.

The Pahlavi State

After a failed attempt to convert Iran into a republic, Reza Khan established a new dynasty with himself on the throne. In the end of October 1925 the Majles introduced a resolution to overthrow the Qajar Shah. The resolution was pushed through despite opposition from some of its prominent deputies, including Sayyed Hasan Modarres and Mohammad Mosaddeq. It was supported by a broad cross-section of the Iranian populace, the 'ulama', the bazaar merchants, and the majority of the journalists. Most of the Qajar elites supported the change of dynasty, and many who did not explicitly support it, passively acquiesced. Many Iranian statesmen and former leaders of the Constitutional Revolution, who had been wary of a military dictatorship, supported Reza Khan, having ascertained that the country's momentum was with him.[4] On December 12, 1925, Reza Khan was declared Reza Shah Pahlavi by a constituent assembly. 'Abdolhossein Khan Teymurtash, whose support had been instrumental in bringing Reza Khan to the throne, orchestrated the formal events of his coronation.[5] With his ascension to the throne, the role of the Cabinet and the Majles was reduced to a minimum.

Consequently, the British evacuated the remainder of their Indian troops from Persian Gulf Ports, relinquishing security to Iran's own forces.[6] This was regarded as a victory for Iranian nationalism to the credit of the new shah and his army.[7] The army received considerable recognition in the capital for its stabilizing role; however, outside of the capital, its repressive and arbitrary practices began to foster resentment. An American official described the mood in Bushehr on the eve of Reza Shah's coronation:

> I have the honor to report several recent incidents which show that the Persian army is not yet the unmixed blessing a person in Teheran is led to believe. It has made transportation safer and enabled the collection of greater

4 Katouzian, *State and Society in Iran*, pp. 306–308.
5 Ghani, *Iran and the Rise of Reza Shah*, pp. 380–386.
6 FO 416/78: Mohammed 'Ali Foroughi to Sir P. Loraine, *Farvardin* 20, 1305 (April 10, 1926).
7 FO 416/78: Intelligence Summary No. 4 for the Period ending February 20, 1926.

revenues, but the arbitrary action of men and officers is creating great dissatisfaction in the remoter provinces. Bushire offers a good opportunity to understand military conduct in the provinces. The main difficulty is that the troops' pay is six months in arrears, although some units have been paid up to four months. They are always penniless or in debt, so their undisputed power is their chief source of income. The vacant house of a wealthy merchant was commandeered for the temporary use of officers, and no compensation was offered – or expected. Goods are taken from the bazaars as fancy indicates, and the transfer of the units will relieve them of the necessity of payment. The taxi drivers were forced to carry so many free army passengers that, whereas taxis could formerly be obtained anywhere, they have completely disappeared and no one would think of restarting such a business.... Thus the first time the Persian Government has stationed troops in Bushire has not increased its popularity.[8]

By 1926, the regime's military character was evident. The army became the principal institution of the Pahlavi state and the focus of Iranian nationalism.[9] The military administration expanded at the expense of the civil administration. Authority, which had been in the hands of the traditional elites, passed to individuals who had neither pedigree nor education. Given the magnification of the army's size, importance, and budget, the financial and administrative malpractices of the former era became amplified. The shah tolerated, and even encouraged unscrupulous practices as a means of ensuring the ongoing support of his generals.[10] Repressive measures were introduced to give the military greater control over the civil life of the country. The press, for example, was subjected to strict censorship.[11] Journalists who overstepped the limits of criticism were intimidated, beaten, imprisoned and killed, and the number of Persian periodicals dropped dramatically, from the hundreds that circulated during the constitutional era, to a mere 18 during the reign of Reza Shah Pahlavi.[12]

[8] George Gregg Fuller quoted in Majd, *Great Britain and Reza Shah*, pp. 110–112.
[9] Cronin, *The Army and the Creation of the Pahlavi State*, p. 182.
[10] Ibid., pp. 199–221.
[11] For an expanded discussion on that topic, see Karim Soleimani, "Press Censorship in the Reza Shah Era, 1925–1941," in *Culture and Cultural Politics Under Reza Shah: The Pahlavi State, New Bourgeoisie and the Creation of a Modern Society in Iran,* eds. Bianca Devos and Christoph Werner (New York: Routledge, 2014), pp. 181–198.
[12] Cyrus Rumi, *Shenasnameh-ye Matbu'at-e Fars: Az Aghaz ta Emruz* (Shiraz: Entesharat-e Navid, 1323/2009), pp. 16–17.

The persistent challenge of semi-independent tribes and competing nationalist movements in places like Khorasan, Azerbaijan, and Baluchistan kept the shah preoccupied with military affairs while the day-to-day conduct of domestic and foreign affairs devolved upon his energetic and capable court minister, 'Abdolhossein Khan Teymurtash (1925–1932). While Reza Shah was a semi-literate man from humble beginnings, Teymurtash was reputed to have been the most cultivated and educated Iranian statesman of his time. Born into nobility and educated in St. Petersburg, he had traveled extensively in Europe, become fluent in Russian and French, and was elected deputy to the Majles at 26 years of age. His name and his aristocratic background, bolstered by his role as the shah's most trusted adviser, enabled him to assume the leadership of much of the nationalist-oriented intelligentsia. He counted the prominent journalists as his close confidantes and was known to be a principal source and inspiration for much of their journalistic activity. His role as the intermediary between the shah and the Cabinet conferred on him far-reaching authority in the domestic and foreign policy spheres. Teymurtash represented the country's interests abroad, conducting wide-ranging negotiations and concluding agreements with foreign powers. As the powerful minister of court, Teymurtash exercised a degree of authority in Iran that was superseded only by that of Reza Shah.[13]

The Persian Gulf in Reza Shah's Domestic Policy

After having consolidated his power in the army and bureaucracy, Reza Shah embarked on an ambitious modernization program. Inspired by Kemal Atatürk, the reformist President of Turkey, Reza Shah implemented reforms designed to transform a religious and traditional society into a modern twentieth-century nation-state along the lines of a secular, European model. Numerous modernizing, secularizing, and westernizing reforms were decreed under the cover of a parliamentary façade. The shah established a standing modern army based on universal male conscription and extensive reserve units, a modern bureaucracy, a secular public education system, a secular

[13] Miron Rezun, "Reza Shah's Court Minister: Teymourtash," *International Journal of Middle East Studies* 12, no. 2 (September 1980), pp. 119–137.

judicial system, and a national bank and monetary system.[14] The country's transportation and communication systems were expanded and modernized. Hundreds of Iranians, including the shah's own son, were sent to Europe for education and technical training. Foreign diplomats were asked to use the designation "Iran" in official contexts, in place of "Persia." The Arabic lunar calendar was replaced with the Iranian solar calendar. Women were forced to remove the veil and men were forced to adhere to Western-inspired dress codes.

While secularizing and westernizing reforms did not penetrate deep beneath the traditional social and religious fabric of society, they did create a veneer of modernization in Iran. The shah's economic reforms aimed to change the traditional economy into a modern, independent, and self-sufficing economic system. The establishment of a strong centralized government allowed him to introduce centralized economic planning based on a strategy of import substitution and industrialization.[15] Trade controls and government incentives encouraged the growth of light industries for the production of textiles, sugar, tea, glass, tobacco, matches, leather, cement, soap, canning, chemicals, and munitions.[16] The growth of industry in the 1930s gave rise to the emergence of an urban, industrial working class and a professional middle class.

At the outset of his reign, the most urgent problem facing the new shah was the need to secure adequate sources of revenue to finance the modernization of the country. Despite that the largest oil refinery in the world operated on Iranian soil, Iran's share in the oil revenues contributed a relatively small amount to the overall state budget.[17] To finance the extensive development projects and at the same time avoid foreign debt, Reza Shah made recourse to indirect taxation. A prime example of this is the way in which he financed his most expensive project, the construction of the Trans-Iranian railway, which linked Tehran to the

14 Touraj Atabaki, "From Multilingual Empire to Contested Modern State," *Iran in the 21st Century: Politics, Economics and Conflict*, eds. Homa Katouzian and Hossein Shahidi (New York: Routledge, 2008), p. 49.

15 Willem Floor, "Industrialization in Iran 1900–1941," IMEIS Occasional Paper No. 25 (University of Durham, 1984).

16 Gholam Reza Moghadam, "Iran's Foreign Trade Policy and Economic Development in the Interwar Period," PhD dissertation (Stanford University, 1986), pp. 61–150; Massoud Karshenas, *Oil, State, and Industrialization in Iran* (Cambridge: Cambridge University Press, 1990), p. 77.

17 Between 13 and 16 percent for the period 1923–1937. Ibid., p. 82, table 3.4.

Persian Gulf and the Caspian Sea: a law passed in May 1925 imposed heavy taxes on the importation of tea and sugar, and the revenues generated from the tea and sugar monopoly were earmarked exclusively for the construction of the railroad. The importation of these consumer goods was to be replaced with domestic production through the development of Iran's own tea and sugar production plants. As no contracts were to be awarded to Britain or Russia, American and German firms provided the technical expertise needed to begin construction of the railroad and Danish and Swedish companies brought it to completion in 1939.[18] The construction of the Trans-Iranian railroad was intended to serve as visible proof of the renaissance of Iran under the Pahlavi dynasty.

While many embraced the rapid social and cultural changes, large segments of society were alienated due to the pace and manner in which reforms were imposed. The 'ulama' faced severe attacks on their power and privileges, losing their seats in the Majles and their control over educational and judicial institutions. They were also alienated by a secular-nationalist discourse that elevated Iran's pre-Islamic past over Shi'i Islam. Small shop owners and traditional craftsmen were put out of business by mechanized industry and state-financed enterprises. Tribes and ethnic groups, whose alternate loyalties were viewed as threats to modernization and progress, were ruthlessly suppressed. The Azeris, Kurds, Baluch, Bakhtiyari, and Qashqa'i were subjected to harsh economic and political pressure.[19] The new middle class also resented the state's growing penetration into their daily lives in matters such as forced conscription, forced unveiling, and European dress codes.[20] In parts of the country, especially in the southern rural towns, various strategies of resistance to these harsh intrusions of the state were met with painful consequences. Women who defied the ban on wearing the chador or veil, for example, risked being publicly

[18] Mir M. Hosseini, "Trans-Iranian Railway Completed," *Time Magazine*, August 18, 1938.

[19] Lois Beck, "Tribes and State in Nineteenth and Twentieth Century Iran," in *Tribes and State Formation in the Middle East*, eds. Philip S. Khoury and Joseph Kostiner (Los Angeles: University of California Press, 1990), p. 206.

[20] Ervand Abrahamian, *Iran between Two Revolutions* (Princeton, NJ: Princeton University Press, 1982), pp. 149–168.

humiliated by police who forcibly removed the banned clothing in the streets.[21]

The nationalist press was steady in its condemnation of British imperialist policies in Iraq, in Iran's oil industry, and in the Persian Gulf. The Soviet ambassador in Tehran endeavored to cultivate the anti-British tone in the Iranian press with encouragement and financial incentives.[22] The shah, helped by Teymurtash, enlisted the nationalist press to fan the flames of anti-British sentiment as a means of assuaging public opinion and deflecting criticism of the regime, often by expressing demands for the very policies that were about to be implemented. In the wake of his coronation, for example, the Shiraz press called upon the new shah to keep his eyes and ears open in the Persian Gulf and to show more authority in connection with the ports and islands where British influence still held sway.[23] Bahrain, Abu Musa, and Hengam were highlighted in the press as focal points of nationalist angst.[24] The government was not adverse to the possibility that press coverage of Britain's ongoing occupation of islands could serve to deflect criticism from its unpopular domestic reforms. When Jalal al-Din Hosseini, the editor of *Habl al-Matin*, a Persian language paper published in Calcutta, mounted a journalistic campaign in refutation of the British position regarding Bahrain – the shah described him as a fine patriot and rewarded him with government subsidies.[25] 'Ali Dashti, the editor of *Shafaq-e Sorkh*, encouraged by the shah, Teymurtash, and the Soviet government, devoted a good deal of journalistic energy to the Persian Gulf, making it a vehicle for the articulation of nationalist and anti-colonial feeling. A steady stream of articles inveighed against British policy in Bahrain saying that the British

[21] H. E. Chehabi, "The Banning of the Veil and Its Consequences," *The Making of Modern Iran: State and Society under Riza Shah: The Making of Modern Iran* (London: Routledge, 2003), pp. 193–210.

[22] FO 416/81: Sir R. Clive to Sir Austen Chamberlain, May 4, 1928; FO 416/82: Sir R. Clive to Sir Austen Chamberlain, January 15, 1929.

[23] Annual Report on Persia for the Year 1925, p. 44.

[24] See for example, *Shafaq-e Sorkh*, *Bahman* 8, 1306 (January 29, 1928); *Dey* 6, 1308 (December 27, 1929); *Dey* 7, 1308 (December 28, 1929); and *Mordad* 6, 1309 (July 28, 1930).

[25] FO 416/82: Sir R. Clive to the Government of India, April 21, 1928.

refused to recognize Iran's rights there and sought to crush the nationalist spirit in its earliest stages.[26]

Reclamation of Coastal Islands

In addition to Bahrain, two groups of islands factored into the disagreements between Iran and the British during the interwar period. The first group consisted of Abu Musa, Greater Tunb, and Lesser Tunb along with Sirri Island. Though Iran had maintained a garrison on Sirri since 1887 the British withheld formal recognition of Iran's sovereignty over Sirri, and offered formal recognition only in exchange for the relinquishment of Iran's claims to Abu Musa and the Tunbs. The second group, Qeshm and Hengam, were a bone of contention because they were being used by the British for military purposes owing to their strategic position at the narrow entrance to the Persian Gulf.

Hengam and Qeshm, the two strategic islands near Iran's shoreline, became a focus for the shah after the successful campaign in Arabistan. Tehran was aware that Britain's use of Hengam as a naval base was without legality and already in June 1923 requested the removal of British troops but to no avail.[27] In January 1926, Britain's basing rights at Basidu, a port on Qeshm Island, were called into question and the Iranian government began to search its archives to ascertain whether a concession had been granted.[28] Finding no record of a concession, an undersecretary recommended that the Ministry of Foreign Affairs should ask the British to provide documentation that would "clarify the extent of their concession," and if no documentation was forthcoming, to formally request that they evacuate.[29] In June 1926, the British chargé d'affaires received an oral request that the Iranian government might be informed on what documents the British

[26] *Shafaq-e Sorkh*, *Dey* 7, 1307 (December 27, 1928) and *Dey* 8, 1307 (December 28, 1928).

[27] Bahmani Qajar, *Tamamiyat-e Arzi-ye Iran*, p. 372.

[28] Head *Kargozar* of the Persian Gulf Ports (Bushehr) to the Ministry of Foreign Affairs, *Bahman* 4, 1304 (January 27, 1926), in *Gozideh-ye Asnad-e Khalij-e Fars*, Vol. 1, p. 398.

[29] "Report of the First Political Office of the Ministry of Foreign Affairs," *Ordibehesht* 16, 1307 (May 6, 1928), in *Gozideh-ye Asnad-e Khalij-e Fars*, Vol. 1, pp. 399–400.

government based their rights at Hengam and Basidu.[30] But no reply was forthcoming.[31]

On May 10, 1928, Iran sent a detachment of soldiers to restrain the recalcitrant Arab shaykh and reassert Iranian authority on Hengam. The troops departed for Hengam from Bandar Abbas in three ships. As they landed, the clerk in the telegraph enclosure cabled the Bushehr Resident to ask what action should be taken if the Iranian troops desired to enter the British enclosure. The reply was such that, because the telegraph enclosure was on Iranian soil, no objection should be made to Iran's use of it for military purposes, only that the officer commanding Iranian troops should be asked to do nothing that would endanger British lives or property.[32] However, a British ship's captain, who happened to be present for coaling when the Iranian soldiers landed, reacted according to his own understanding of the situation, and presented the Iranian commander with a note saying, "I cannot in any way allow [you] to enter the ground of the British concession."[33] Though the British captain was corrected and the Iranian troops proceeded to form an encampment inside the telegraph enclosure, the language of this note formed the subject of a protest from the Iranian government. The protest, dated July 22, 1928, pointed out that no concession had ever been granted for a British naval base at Hengam and requested that the British government should reprimand the "ignorant" captain.[34]

Following Iran's reoccupation of Hengam, rumors circulated that Iran also intended to dispatch troops to Basidu, the British enclave on Qeshm Island. In early September, the customs director of Bandar Abbas advertised that he had orders from Tehran to arrest the British caretaker at Basidu. He said that he did not recognize the British flag flying there and expressed his opinion that they would easily give way to Iran's resolute attitude at Basidu as they had done at Hengam in May.[35] On September 10, 1928, he boarded the gunboat *Pehlevi* at

[30] FO 371/11503: Harold Nicholson to Lieutenant Colonel Prideaux, July 5, 1926.
[31] Annual Report on Persia for the Year 1926, p. 28.
[32] FO 371/13065: Haworth to Parr, May 10, 1928.
[33] Ministry of War Army General Staff to the Ministry of Foreign Affairs, *Tir* 4, 1307 (June 25, 1928), in *Gozideh-ye Asnad-e Khalij-e Fars*, Vol. 1, p. 544.
[34] FO 371/13065: Haworth to Parr, May 13, 1928; Acting Persian Minister of Foreign Affairs to His Majesty's Chargé d'Affaires, *Tir* 31, 1307 (July 22, 1928).
[35] FO 416/83: SNOPG to CinCEI, September 10, 11, and 13, 1928.

night with a detachment of soldiers numbering about 30, intending to depart for Basidu. However, the British senior naval officer reported that after sighting the HMS *Triad* he cancelled his plans and returned to Bandar Abbas; rumors of an impending Iranian invasion continued to circulate.[36] In support of these rumors, one British memo reported that an Iranian intelligence officer from Bushehr went to Basidu on October 8, 1928, and delivered a speech, assuring the inhabitants that the British would soon evacuate and Iran would take control of Basidu.[37]

Introduction of an Armed Customs Preventative Service

Among the shah's immediate goals for the Persian Gulf was to develop the ability to take over policing functions that the British carried out, albeit insufficiently from his perspective. As the war minister, he had often complained that the British did not do enough to prevent gun smuggling, which impaired his ability to disarm the civilian and tribal population.[38] He later complained that the British did not do anything to prevent the smuggling of prohibited foodstuffs, especially tea and sugar, which cost the government a great deal of revenue.[39] The Belgian customs administrators believed that most of the smuggled goods were coming from Kuwait, Dubai, and Bahrain and tried to persuade the British government to use its position on the southern littoral to assist in preventing smuggling. They suggested that British agents should supervise cargo as it was being loaded in those ports and inspect ships' manifests, but their appeal was in vain.[40] The shah, in an effort to gain control over the contraband traffic, built coastal roads for military motor patrols and established the armed customs preventative service made up of five motor boats armed with machine guns.

[36] FO 371/13066: SNOPG to Admiralty, September 13, 1928.
[37] FO 371/13066: SNOPG to Mr. Parr, November 9, 1928.
[38] IOR/R/15/5/393/13: J. G. Laithwaite, "Persian Complaints of Smuggling in the Persian Gulf," October 1, 1928.
[39] In the beginning of 1929 customs authorities reported an annual loss to the Iranian treasury of 400–600 tomans due to smuggling. See Sir R. Clive to Sir Austen Chamberlain, February 2, 1929, FO 416/84. See also *Shafaq-e Sorkh*, *Aban* 28, 1307 (November 19, 1928) and *Ettala'at*, *Azar* 19, 1309 (December 10, 1930).
[40] FO 416/82: Intelligence Summary No. 26, for week ending December 24, 1927; and Sir R. Clive to Sir Austen Chamberlain, January 27, 1928.

Iranian customs agents were authorized to patrol the sea and intercept vessels that they believed were bound for the Iranian coastline.[41]

Among the first fruits of the customs preventative service were its pinpricks to British authority in and around disputed islands of the Persian Gulf. A provocation initiated by some local officials is a prime example. In the fall of 1925 customs officials at Lingah sent the motor launch *Azerbaijan* to Abu Musa to inspect the red oxide.[42] This action, instigated while the authorities in Tehran were on holiday, represented an effort by the local officials to use their newfound authority to try to put into force Iran's claims to the disputed islands. A British protest against these actions was met with a fresh declaration of Iranian sovereignty over Abu Musa.[43] In subsequent years, similar efforts by local officials to assert Iranian authority in and around the Gulf would thrust a wide range of Persian Gulf particulars into the purview of policy in Tehran.

Introduction of a Modern Iranian Navy

The establishment of a modern navy has been touted as one of Reza Shah's greatest achievements.[44] He faced many obstacles in this endeavor, not the least of which was the antagonism of the British whose navy enjoyed the dominant position in the Persian Gulf. Iran's lack of naval facilities and lack of trained seamen constituted substantial challenges. In 1926, the shah sent a group of five naval cadets to Italy for training. In the summer of 1928, Teymurtash visited Rome to negotiate the purchase of ships and a contract for technical assistance. The Italian government granted a tender to Italian firms for the construction of two gun boats and four motor patrol boats. In January

41 Bushire Residency Diary No. 4 for 1926 (Persian) for the month of April 1926, in R. Jarman, ed., *Political Diaries of the Arab World: The Persian Gulf 1904–1965*, Vol. 7 (Archive Editions, 1990), p. 351; FO 416/79: Persian Foreign Office to His Britannic Majesty's Legation at Tehran, *Tir* 15, 1305 (July 7, 1926).

42 FO 416/77: Consul-General Lieutenant Colonel Prideaux to Sir P. Loraine, October 9, 1925; *Golestan* (Shiraz), September 10, 1925.

43 FO 416/77: Lieutenant Colonel C. G. Crosswaite to M. Stas, Bushire, October 1, 1925; FO 416/78: Colonel Prideaux to Sir P. Loraine, May 28, 1926.

44 *Ravabet-e Dowlat-e Shahanshahi ba Keshvarha-ye Howzeh-ye Mas'uliyat-e Edareh-ye Nohom-e Siyasi dar Panjah Saleh-ye Shahanshahi-ye Pahlavi*, pp. 32–40, 51–54.

1929, an Italian officer, Commander Pierluigi Del Prato, was hired to help direct the development of the Iranian navy. He inspected Iran's vessels – five motor boats and two tugboats – and recommended that the best one (Khaz'al Khan's former yacht) should be refitted as a training vessel and the rest should be scrapped.[45]

Numerous editorials appeared, having received their inspiration from the highest quarters, urging the shah to expand Iran's naval forces. For example, the *Setareh-ye Jehan* on August 14, 1929, published an article on the necessity of Iran possessing a naval force in the Persian Gulf. The purchase of one 1,000-ton and four 300-ton ships were suggested for the protection of the coast and prevention of smuggling. A hope was expressed that in 50 years' time, Iran would rank among the leading naval powers of the world.[46]

As Iran's treasury lacked the funds necessary to make a payment on the Italian ships, Teymurtash explored the possibility of obtaining ships and technical expertise from Britain. On August 20, 1929, he offered to strike a bargain according to which Iran would renounce its claim to Bahrain in exchange for Britain's provision of 10 gun boats and the renunciation of Iran's war debt.[47] The British minister in Tehran, Sir Robert Clive, discussed the proposal with Teymurtash the following day. Clive made no attempt to hide his skepticism. He told Teymurtash that the provision of ships alone would not make a navy come into being. He estimated that naval officers would need at least 15 years' training and naval service before they could be put in command of a gunboat. He said he "felt very doubtful whether any Persian could ever be trained as a naval officer," and added, "practically the only Persians who had ever seen the sea or knew anything about it were the Persianized Arabs who lived on the Persian shore of the Gulf."[48] But Teymurtash refused to take such a pessimistic view. He said that Iran sought Britain's assistance in creating a small Iranian navy because Britain had the finest navy in the world and outstanding knowledge of the Persian Gulf. He said that Iran was prepared to

45 Massimiliano Fiore, *Anglo-Italian Relations in the Middle East, 1922–1940* (Farnham: Ashgate, 2012), pp. 126–127.

46 "Intelligence Summary No. 17, for Week Ending August 24, 1929," in *Iran Political Diaries*, Vol. 8, p. 388; see also *Shafaq-e Sorkh*, *Mordad* 31, 1308 (August 21, 1929) and *Iran-e Bastan*, *Aban* 4, 1312 (October 26, 1929).

47 FO 416/85: Teymurtash to Sir R. Clive, *août* 20, 1929.

48 FO 416/85: Sir R. Clive to Mr. A. Henderson, August 21, 1929.

recognize that Great Britain must always be the finest power in the Persian Gulf and that Iran was content with second place, but that she wished for Britain's assistance in establishing her right to second place and to have her territorial waters respected.[49]

Clive relayed Teymurtash's proposal to London where it was studied with interest. Of all the departments concerned, the Admiralty came out with the strongest support for the proposal because it was alarmed at Fascist Italy's attempt to gain influence in the region. Though the Foreign Office suspected that the British government was merely being used as a pawn in the negotiations between Italy and Iran, Clive was authorized to offer remission of one million pounds of Iran's war debt and a deal whereby Iran's payment of the remaining portion (£510,000) would cover the cost of the 10 vessels. However, when Teymurtash learned that Britain was not willing to give the warships free of cost he preceded with the purchase of ships from Italy without notifying the British that he had changed his mind.[50]

In October 1932 the ships ordered from Italy were delivered and the new Iranian southern navy was established with its base at Khorramshahr. Gholam 'Ali Bayandor, an infantry lieutenant in the Cossack Brigade, was appointed the highest ranking Iranian naval officer in the Persian Gulf.[51] In the first year after the ships arrived, the most senior naval officers onboard each ship were Italians who had been contracted by Iran for that purpose.[52] The ships acquired from Italy consisted of two 950 ton sloops equipped with four-inch guns, the *Palang* and the *Babr*, and four 331 ton gunboats equipped with three-inch guns, the *Karkas*, *Simorgh*, *Shahrokh*, and *Shahbaz*.[53] Sold to Iran as new, these ships were refurbished but Iran did not have the technical expertise to realize it.[54] By 1938 the shah had added a reconditioned gunboat, a tug boat, and a floating dock.[55] A Caspian

[49] Ibid. [50] Fiore, *Anglo-Italian Relations in the Middle East*, pp. 128–129.
[51] Ward, *Immortal: A Military History of Iran*, p. 144.
[52] Annual Report on Persia for the Year 1933, p. 75.
[53] *Ravabet-e Dowlat-e Shahanshahi ba Keshvarha-ye Howzeh-ye Mas'uliyat-e Edareh-ye Nohom-e Siyasi dar Panjah Saleh-ye Shahanshahi-ye Pahlavi*, p. 54; see also Richard Worth, *Fleets of World War II* (Cambridge, MA: Decapo, 2001), p. 138.
[54] Majd, *Great Britain and Reza Shah*, p. 295.
[55] Administration Report of the Persian Gulf Residency for the Year 1936, p. 59; Annual Report on Persia for the Year 1938, p. 43.

Figure 3 Rear Admiral Gholam 'Ali Bayandor.
Source: Ahmad Kasravi, *Afsaran-e Ma* (Tehran, 1323/1944–1945), p. 46.

Figure 4 Reza Shah inspecting the new southern navy in Bushehr with his son, the crown prince.
Source: Institute for Iranian Contemporary Historical Studies, https://bit.ly/2UYoXjn (accessed February 17, 2020).

flotilla was also established, which consisted of a four small patrol boats and a minesweeper.[56]

Nationalization of the Periphery

In pursuit of the goal of imposing national homogeneity on a country where more than half of the population was composed of ethnic minorities, the shah carried out an aggressive campaign of homogenization aimed at creating a unified, modern, secular, Persian-speaking country.[57] Arabistan, whose name reverted to Khuzestan after the defeat of Shaykh Khaz'al, is a prime example. This province, in the northwest corner of the Persian Gulf bordering Iraq, was populated by Lur, Bakhtiari, and Arab tribes, parts of them nomadic and parts of them settled. The most powerful of the Arab tribes was the Banu Ka'b who looked to Shaykh Khaz'al for leadership. They inhabited western Khuzestan and shared strong commercial, cultural, familial, and linguistic ties with Arabs in Iraq, and particularly in Basra. In western Khuzestan, where a majority spoke Arabic, education in Farsi was introduced. Arabic place names were Persianized – Mohammerah became Khorramshahr and the Shatt al-Arab became Arvand Rud.[58] Young men were conscripted into the national army. Land owned by Arabs was confiscated and non-Arabic-speaking people were offered economic incentives to settle in those lands. Industrial and agricultural projects and the growth of the oil industry further changed the ethnic mix of the province and diluted the once dominant Arab majority.[59] Reza Shah also undertook a vigorous campaign of attracting Iranians resident in Iraq back to Iran, and by 1929 a British dispatch concluded that many had returned and settled in Khuzestan.[60]

[56] Ward, *Immortal: A Military History of Iran*, p. 144.

[57] For estimations of Iranian demographics in the late Qajar period, see Charles Issawi, *The Economic History of Iran: 1800–1914* (Chicago: University of Chicago Press, 1971), p. 20, and Gad G. Gilbar, "Demographic Developments in Late Qajar Persia, 1810–1906," *Asian and African Studies* 11, no. 2 (1976), pp. 125–156.

[58] Soucek, "Arabistan or Khuzistan," pp. 195–213.

[59] Nikki R. Keddie, *Iran and the Muslim World: Resistance and Revolution* (New York: New York University Press, 1995), pp. 140–141.

[60] FO 416/84: Sir R. Clive to Sir Austen Chamberlain, December 22, 1928; Intelligence Summary No. 3 for the week ending February 3, 1929.

The economic stagnation and harsh centralization policies fueled chronic emigration from southern Iran in the 1930s. Thousands of young men fled by boat from Iran's coastal provinces to avoid mandatory conscription. Large numbers of labor migrants sought work in the Arab shaykhdoms, especially in Bahrain owing to active recruitment of semi-skilled laborers from Iran by the Bahrain Petroleum Company (BAPCO).[61] Countless others traversed the Persian Gulf in search of seasonal labor in the docks and warehouses of the Arab shaykhdoms. British reports noted that almost daily, immigrants from Iran could be seen arriving to the Arab Coast to escape the worsening conditions in Iran. One dispatch discussed the trial of some 2,000 "starving Persian refugees," who arrived to Kuwait in August 1932 only to be conveyed in dhows back to Iranian territory "free of charge" by order of the Kuwaiti ruler.[62] By 1938, the Bahrain government had rounded up and expelled 44 Iranian "indigents," defined as people who could not provide proof of a regular source of livelihood. The number of those who were arrested on suspicion of entering without a valid passport was in the hundreds.[63] By August 1938, the Iranian statistics and census bureau made a general observation that a number of the poor migrants who had gone to Bahrain in recent years were returning to Iran owing to the hardening of Bahrain's passport policy.[64]

While the British Persian Gulf Administration worked to help the Arab shaykhs prevent the dramatic influx of foreigners to their domains, the Iranian authorities worked to prevent Iranian citizens from fleeing. Myriad disparate narratives of emigrants and would-be emigrants can shed light on the migratory impulses that were prevalent in the Iranian ports and islands. The inhabitants of Basidu town, for example, planned to emigrate after the British evacuation in 1935, but were forced to stay put when Iranian authorities threatened to confiscate their property.[65] Another report tells of a party of 39 people that

[61] I. J. Seccombe and R. I. Lawless, "Foreign Worker Dependence in the Gulf, and the International Oil Companies: 1910–50," *International Migration Review* 20, no. 3 (Autumn 1986), pp. 559–560.

[62] Administration Report of the Persian Gulf Residency for the Year 1932, p. 54.

[63] IOR/R/15/2/494: Political Agent Bahrain to Political Resident (Fowle), June 14, 1938.

[64] Ministry of Interior to Prime Minister, *Mordad* 22, 1317 (August 13, 1938), in Bayrami, "Chalesh-e Iran va Engelestan bar sar-e Hakemiyyat bar Bahreyn," p. 162.

[65] FO 416/93: Mr. Knatchbull-Hugessen to Sir John Simon, April 2, 1935.

was apprehended by the Iranian navy while attempting to flee the Iranian coast with all their sheep and cattle in two dhows. When interrogated by the law court at Bushehr, the men declared that high-handed treatment by the road police and the military authorities in Dashti had persuaded them to migrate to the Arab side of the Gulf.[66]

Forced unveiling and mandatory dress codes prompted further waves of immigration in 1935 and 1936. On Hendurabi Island, which was home to a population of devout Sunni Arabs numbering about 300, road police (*amniyyeh*) tried to force the women to discard their veils. The community rose up against the police as well as the local customs mudir, bound them hand and foot, and then immigrated to Oman leaving the government officials in confinement.[67] The Bani Hamad tribe on Chiru, an outcropping of coastal land facing Hendurabi, moved to Kalba on the Oman Coast. They cited unveiling as their main grievance.[68] In the villages along the Shibkuh coast, *amniyyeh* officers reportedly forcibly shaved the beards on about 30 mullahs and qadis. This led to a wave of emigration from the small towns there to Bahrain, Oman, and the Trucial Coast.[69] For a community of about 8,000 Baharna who had resided in the Mohammerah district for several generations, unveiling was the "final straw." This community, which had been complaining of harsh treatment at the hands of Iranian officials for several years, finally emigrated en masse to Basra.[70]

At Bushehr, famine and economic conditions went from bad to worse in the 1930s, depleting its population and accelerating its decline as an independent trading center.[71] By 1944 its population

[66] Diary of the British Residency and Consulate General Bushire for the Month of May 1938, in *Political Diaries of the Persian Gulf*, Vol. 13, p. 82.

[67] Diary of the British Residency and Consulate General Bushire for the Month of October 1936 in *Political Diaries of the Persian Gulf*, Vol. 12, pp. 245–247.

[68] Abdullah, *The United Arab Emirates*, p. 248.

[69] Diary of the British Residency and Consulate General Bushire for the Month of October 1936 in *Political Diaries of the Persian Gulf*, pp. 245–247.

[70] IOR/R/15/2/486: Petition signed by 58 Bahrainis living at Basra to the Advisor, Bahrain Government, *Safar* 14, 1358 (April 4, 1939).

[71] Administration Report of the Persian Gulf Residency for the Year 1937, p. 4. See also, Intelligence Summary No. 11, for the period ending June 1, 1932; Intelligence Summary No. 16, for the period ending August 12, 1932; and Intelligence Summary No. 9, for the period ending May 5, 1934, in *Iran Political Diaries*, Vol. 9, p. 551.

stood at about 10,000, down from 15,000 in 1908.[72] Bandar Abbas entered a period of stagnation: despite the establishment of a spinning mill and a canning factory and the construction of a road linking it to Kerman, emigration and economic hardship kept the cold weather population steady at around 10,000.[73] Indeed, the port town most affected was Lingah whose population had dwindled from about 20,000 in 1919 to around 8,000 by the end of Reza Shah's reign.[74] By 1939, Lingah's role as a distribution center for goods from India had been completely eclipsed by the busier ports on the Trucial Coast.[75]

The Persian Gulf in Reza Shah's Foreign Policy

Political and economic emancipation from the Soviet Union and Great Britain was the focus of Iran's foreign policy throughout the rule of Reza Shah Pahlavi. The shah leveraged Iran's weakness to its advantage playing both ends against the middle, as a means of procuring a maximum degree of independence. The first foreign policy priority on the new shah's agenda was to forge an economic and commercial relationship with the Soviet Union that would end Iran's dependence on Russia. Toward that end, he sent his energetic and capable court minister to Moscow for talks that would result in the nonaggression and neutrality treaty of 1927 (whose terms also formed the basis of the subsequent agreements of 1931 and 1935).[76] The Iranian-Soviet agreement provided a momentary relief from the Soviet threat to the north, but it also enabled the Soviet Union to probe deeper into Iran's internal affairs. The Soviets feared that Iran would reach an

72 Lorimer estimated Bushehr's population to be around 15,000 at the beginning of the century and the British Admiralty estimated it at around 10,000 in 1944. See Lorimer, *Gazetteer of the Persian Gulf, Oman, and Central Arabia*, Vol. 2: Geographical, ed. Richard Lockington Birdwood (Calcutta: Superintendent of Government Printing, 1908; Repr., Archive Editions, 1986), p. 345; Admiralty, Naval Intelligence Division, *Iraq and the Persian Gulf* (Oxford, 1944; Repr., Archive Editions, 1987), pp. 156–157.

73 Ibid. p. 10; Admiralty, *Iraq and the Persian Gulf*, p. 163. See also "Bandar-e 'Abbas," *Encyclopædia Iranica*, Vol. 3, Fasc. 7, pp. 685–687; www.iranicaonline.org/articles/bandar-e-abbasi (accessed December 11, 2012).

74 Administration Report of the Persian Gulf Residency for the Year 1919, p. 10; Willem Floor, *The Rise and Fall of Bandar-e Lingah*, p. 154.

75 Admiralty, *Iraq and the Persian Gulf*, pp. 161–162.

76 Ramazani, *The Foreign Policy of Iran*, pp. 216–241.

accommodation with the British that would allow the British to threaten the Soviet Union from Iranian soil. Thus, the Soviet Union supported Iranian nationalism as a brake against British expansion. Soviet representatives warned Teymurtash of the strategic dangers inherent in allowing Imperial Airways to develop aviation rights along Iran's Persian Gulf littoral and they warned him not to surrender Iran's claim to Bahrain because of its strategic position in the Persian Gulf.[77]

By the end of 1927, British ascendancy in Iran was the main obstacle on Iran's path to full independence. They benefited from low taxes and customs rates, special courts for foreigners and other commercial advantages. British firms held commercial concessions for telegraphs, railroads, and, most prominently, oil.[78] The D'Arcy concession afforded the Anglo-Persian Oil Company (APOC) the exclusive rights to prospect for, exploit and export Iran's oil. Khuzestan, the site of APOC's oil installations, exhibited the attributes of a colonial mini-state, an overcrowded, undeveloped township that had grown up around an industrial center where "natives" labored under the supervision of British company managers.[79] Iran also had numerous grievances with Iraq, then under British mandatory rule, not the least of which was the unfair boundary delimitation in the Shatt al-Arab. According to the boundary in force the entirety of the Shatt al-Arab lay in Iraqi territory.[80] Finally, it was no secret that the Persian Gulf was viewed around the world as a "British Lake."[81] British warships anchored freely at Bushehr where the large Union Jack fluttered over the grandiose mansions housing the British Resident and his staff. The many vestiges of imperialist control on Iranian soil infuriated nationalist opinion and became the focal points of Reza Shah's dealings with the British.

77 Miron Rezun, *The Soviet Union and Iran*, pp. 130–134.
78 Ibid., pp. 242–309.
79 Kaveh Bayat, "With or without Workers in Reza Shah's Iran: Abadan, May 1929," in *The State and the Subaltern: Modernization, Society and the State in Turkey and Iran*, ed. Touraj Atabaki (London: I.B. Tauris, 2007), pp. 111–122.
80 Aliasghar Zargar, "A Historical Review of British Role [sic] in Iran-Iraqi Dispute [sic] on the Shatt al-Arab Waterway," *International Journal of Political Science* (Tehran) 1, no. 2 (Summer and Fall 2011), pp. 22–25.
81 Minister of Iran London to Ministry of Foreign Affairs, *Mehr* 11, 1307 (October 3, 1928), in *Gozideh-ye Asnad-e Khalij-e Fars*, Vol. 1, p. 134.

An important aspect of Iran's foreign policy under Reza Shah was the effort invested in defending Iran's sovereignty and interests as well as cultivating Iran's image abroad as a proud, independent, and friendly nation. Officials exhibited extreme sensitivity when Iran was criticized in foreign publications. The foreign press was monitored attentively, especially by Iran's diplomats abroad, and articles that contained references to Iran were translated and sent back to Tehran. Reports that portrayed Iran or Iranians in a negative light or assertions that disavowed what Iran believed to be its sovereign rights were deemed "worthy of a measure." In practical terms it meant that an official was given the task of articulating and disseminating a refutation or correction of the offending content.[82] Iranian diplomats were expected to be vigilant in monitoring press comments about Bahrain, for example, and countering any statement in the foreign press that disavowed Iran's claims to Bahrain.[83] Government ministers admitted that newspapers in Iran did not publish anything that was not in conformity with the wishes of the government; all the more so, it was assumed that a strong nation like Britain imposed its views on the press.[84] Consequently, the British government was blamed when negative comments appeared about Iran. On one occasion, the shah threatened to suspend diplomatic relations with Britain if it did not reprimand the editor of an offensive article or arrange for a "correction" to appear in a future issue.[85]

One of the channels through which Iran sought to promote a modern and independent image internationally was the League of Nations. The League of Nations, of which Iran was a founding member, was viewed in Iran with a mixture of interest and dissatisfaction. It was viewed with dissatisfaction because it appeared to be a body designed to serve the interests of the great powers of Europe to the disadvantage of the small nations. But it was also viewed with interest because of its potential as a means by which to play one

[82] See for example, "Letter received from the editor of *al-Islah* by the Iranian Embassy Kabul," *al-Islah*, August 19, 1939, IOR/R/15/1/359; see also Cameron Michael Amin, "The Press and Public Diplomacy in Iran, 1820–1940," *Iranian Studies* 48, no. 2 (2015).

[83] See for example, Minister of Iran London (Mirza Da'ud Khan Meftah) to Ministry of Foreign Affairs, *Jadi* 20, 1303 (January 10, 1925), in *Gozideh-ye Asnad-e Khalij-e Fars*, Vol. 1, pp. 77–80.

[84] Annual Report on Persia for the Year 1933, p. 28.

[85] Ibid., p. 8.

European power off against another. Among the more interesting functions of the League was its function as a tribunal for territorial disputes. In the beginning of 1927, the undersecretary for foreign affairs prepared an internal memo recommending that all the historical records and evidence for Iran's territorial claims in the Persian Gulf should be gathered so that Iran's legal experts could study the means of pursuing Iran's claims through the League.[86] The minister at Brussels sent policy recommendations relating to the Shatt al-Arab and the Persian Gulf.[87] A seasoned local official, Mohammad 'Ali Sadid al-Saltaneh, was sent to gather records from the *Kargozars*' Persian Gulf offices, which had been converted into passport offices when the capitulations were abolished.[88] Detailed reports were commissioned on the history and evidence for Iran's claims to Qeshm, Hengam, Bahrain, Sirri, Abu Musa, and the Tunbs. The project produced considerable excitement among the officials who compiled historic support for Iran's various claims and the foreign ministry instructed them to "keep quiet" about the findings, so that the government would have the advantage of choosing an opportune time to proceed.[89]

Reza Shah's first big move vis-à-vis Great Britain was the abolition of the capitulatory regime, which he had inherited from the Qajar dynasty. On May 10, 1927, the shah announced the abolition of capitulatory privileges in one year's time.[90] This gave the British government one year to conclude a new commercial agreement with respect to trade and the treatment of British nationals. In addition to securing their economic interests in the post-capitulations era, the British also hoped to renegotiate overflight privileges and landing facilities for Imperial Airways, a settlement of Iran's war-time debt; the recognition of Iraq; and new agreements with regard to the telegraphs, quarantine service, railroad

[86] First Political Office to the Ministry of Foreign Affairs, postscript, *Bahman* 13, 1305 (February 13, 1927), pp. 289–296.

[87] Minister of Iran Brussels to Ministry of Foreign Affairs, *Dey* 30, 1305 (January 21, 1927), in *Gozideh-ye Asnad-e Khalij-e Fars*, Vol. 1, pp. 297–303.

[88] Head of the *Tazkera* Office of the Persian Gulf Ports (Mohammad 'Ali) to the Ministry of Foreign Affairs, *Esfand* 6, 1306 (February 26, 1928), enclosing report #314, *Jadi* 6, 1301 (December 28, 1922), in *Gozideh-ye Asnad-e Khalij-e Fars*, Vol. 1, pp. 102–106.

[89] First Political Office to the Ministry of Foreign Affairs, Postscript, *Bahman* 22, 1305 (February 12, 1927), in *Gozideh-ye Asnad-e Khalij-e Fars*, Vol. 1, p. 291.

[90] Annual Report on Persia for the Year 1927, p. 3.

and pipeline.[91] The shah agreed upon the need for a settlement of all the outstanding issues between Iran and Britain and urged Britain's minister in Tehran, Sir Robert Clive, to lose no time in starting discussions with Teymurtash toward that end.[92]

Teymurtash signaled what he believed was his most valuable bargaining chip at the outset when he referred Iran's claim to sovereignty over Bahrain to the League of Nations.[93] In the letter, dated November 22, 1927, the Iranian government objected to the wording of the Jeddah Treaty signed between the British government and Ibn Sa'ud on May 20, 1927, which characterized Bahrain as a territory having "special treaty relations with the British government."[94] The letter cited Iran's earlier protest of 1869 and Lord Clarendon's reply as proof of its ownership of Bahrain and asserted that a private treaty between the Shaykh of Bahrain and the British government was contrary to the territorial integrity of Iran.[95] Through Iran's envoy in Cairo, an objection was also sent to Ibn Sa'ud, King of the Hijaz, who maintained close ties with the Pahlavi court.[96] Further protests were issued to the British on January 5, 1929, against a new Bahraini law that barred Iranian nationals from entering Bahrain without a passport and again on July 23, 1930, against the shaykh's granting of an oil concession.[97]

Though Teymurtash had requested arbitration from the League, privately he told Clive that he preferred to handle the Bahrain issue together with other outstanding issues in the context of bilateral negotiations with the British government.[98] The British government was

[91] FO 416/82: Sir Austen Chamberlain to Sir R. Clive, January 5, 1928.
[92] Annual Report on Persia for the Year 1927, p. 5.
[93] Bulletin of International News, Vol. 4 (Royal Institute of International Affairs, Information Department, 1927), pp. 332–333.
[94] FO 416/81: Acting Minister of Foreign Affairs (Pakravan) to Sir R. Clive, *Aban* 30, 1306 (November 22, 1927).
[95] Ibid. [96] Keynoush, *Saudi Arabia and Iran*, p. 50.
[97] The League of Nations, *Official Journal*, March 1929, p. 351; Ministry of Foreign Affairs to Ministry of the Interior, *Dey* 15, 1307 (January 5, 1929), in *Gozideh-ye Asnad-e Khalij-e Fars*, Vol. 1, p. 140; FO 416/87: M. Foroughi to Sir R. Clive, *Murdad* 1, 1309 (July 23, 1930); Ministry of Foreign Affairs, translation from the newspaper *The Near East*, June 5, 1930, in *Gozideh-ye Asnad-e Khalij-e Fars*, Vol. 1, pp. 172–173.
[98] FO 416/82: Sir Austen Chamberlain to Hovhannes Khan Mossa'ed (London), January 18, 1928; FO 416/81: Sir R. Clive to Sir Austen Chamberlain, December 28 and 29, 1927.

also keen to prevent international arbitration for a variety of reasons: arbitration, they feared, would undermine the confidence of the shaykhs who were in treaty relations with the British government and depended on it for protection against stronger regional powers; it would encourage the belief that the British government was weak in the Middle East; and it would set a dangerous precedent for other powers in the region, such as Ibn Sa'ud who might have wished to challenge Britain's position in Kuwait.[99] Satisfied that Teymurtash preferred to handle this outside of the League, the British government submitted a detailed refutation of Iran's claim to Bahrain to the League but informed the League's secretary general that the two countries would resolve the dispute within the context of bilateral negotiations.[100] During the course of subsequent negotiations, Teymurtash would several times reraise the specter of international arbitration, a threat that he knew posed some risk to the British and a threat that he apparently hoped to leverage to Iran's favor.[101]

The deadline for the end of capitulations drew closer and the two sides had failed to reach an agreement on all the issues under discussion (especially owing to the insertion of the Bahrain issue), so the end of capitulations was addressed separately in the framework of the Anglo-Iranian commercial agreement concluded on May 10, 1928, the day the abolition of capitulations took effect.[102] The agreement protected the rights of British citizens in Iran, but afforded Iran full autonomy in its customs policy.[103] Upon the conclusion of the commercial agreement, Teymurtash wrote to the British minister in Tehran, saying that the first round of negotiations was finished and signaled his expectation that the Persian Gulf would be a focus in the second round:

> The Iran of today hopes to see her relations with the British Empire established on a new basis: the equality of rights, community of interests and recognition of her legitimate aspirations. There is no need to mention the out-of-dateness of the existing treaties and conventions and Iran's abnormal

[99] IOR/R/15/1/320: Foreign Office (Curzon) to Sir P. Loraine, October 31, 1923.
[100] FO 416/81: Sir Austen Chamberlain to Sir R. Clive, December 6, 1928; FO 416/82: Sir Austen Chamberlain to Sir R. Clive, January 12, 1928; Sir R. Clive to Sir Austen Chamberlain, January 18, 1928.
[101] FO 416/83: Sir Clive to Sir Austen Chamberlain, January 8, 1929.
[102] Annual Report on Persia for the Year 1928, pp. 10–12.
[103] Ramazani, *The Foreign Policy of Iran*, pp. 243–247.

situation in the Persian Gulf and a host of other issues that were raised during our discussions. His Majesty's government consented in principle to revise and rectify this and the Persian Government highly appreciates its attitude.[104]

In that letter, Teymurtash wrote that he would do his best not to "brusquer the situation" in the Persian Gulf because he anticipated a happy ending to the negotiations.[105] This suggestion formed the basis of an unofficial arrangement agreed upon by both sides to maintain the status quo in the Gulf until a formal agreement could be reached; albeit the very definition of the term *status quo* would form the basis for a number of disagreements.

Having succeeded in abolishing capitulations to foreign powers, the Iranian government prepared for the final showdown with APOC. In July 1928, Teymurtash flew to Europe to impress upon John Cadman, the chairman of the company, the need to revise the terms of the original D'Arcy concession. This initiated a four-year period of negotiations during which Teymurtash endeavored to revise the original concession on terms that were more favorable to Iran.[106]

The Persian Gulf in Negotiations with Teymurtash, 1928–1932

Five years of negotiations that took place between ʻAbdolhossein Khan Teymurtash and Britain's ministers in Tehran, namely Sir Robert Clive, with the aim of resolving all outstanding issues between the two governments failed to result in an agreement. Over the course of numerous discussions, drafts, and counterdrafts, there emerged little sign of a considered strategy on the part of Iran to secure an agreement save an ambition to obtain whatever concessions it could through discussions or other means. From the start, Iran's objectives were defined in vague terms: to normalize Iran's status vis-à-vis Great Britain, and to secure Britain's recognition of Iran's "legitimate aspirations," particularly in the Persian Gulf.[107] Moreover, the Iranian government appeared to view the negotiations as a process through which to reach a more thorough understanding of Iran's interests

[104] FO 416/82: Teymurtash to Sir R. Clive, *mai* 10, 1928. [105] Ibid.
[106] Ferrier, *The History of the British Petroleum Company*, Vol. 1, pp. 599–602.
[107] FO 416/82: Teymurtash to Sir R. Clive, *mai* 10, 1928.

rather than as a series of steps taken to achieve a result. Ultimately, the scant progress Reza Shah made in asserting Iranian authority in the Persian Gulf was obtained by other means.

It is worthwhile to make three general observations about Iran's negotiating style as it was prominently expressed by Reza Shah's negotiator, Teymurtash. The first observation relates to the way in which Teymurtash afforded much weight to public opinion – whether real or manufactured. At various times, Teymurtash said that the public and the army would not forgive the government for renouncing any part of Iranian territory without an acknowledgment of Iran's rights and adequate compensation. But his use of the semiofficial nationalist press to encourage and manufacture public demand proved to be a double-edged sword because the more the press generated expectations, the more it limited the government's room for maneuver. The second observation is that the frequent crises that arose in the Persian Gulf during the discussions were accepted as part and parcel of the negotiation process. Local authorities were allotted wide latitude to challenge British authority throughout the Persian Gulf while the government tried to leverage the frequent crises to its favor. But, as an examination of the events will illustrate, the crises that frequently cropped up during the talks did not always work to Iran's advantage. The final observation relates to Iran's talent for exercising patience. The Iranian government appeared to be in no hurry to conclude an all-encompassing agreement, perhaps hoping that the longer the negotiating process lasted the greater the chance that Britain would unwittingly modify its stance or that circumstances would otherwise change in Iran's favor.

The insurmountable obstacle to concluding an agreement proved to be Iran's territorial claims in the Persian Gulf, and its claim to Bahrain in particular. Teymurtash stated that "the Persian government would never agree to a treaty which, on the face of it appeared to involve considerable territorial sacrifices by Persia."[108] Domestic constraints were a real obstacle, he said. He explained that there was a growing spirit of nationalism in general among Iranian army officers and an interest in the Persian Gulf in particular. During one conversation with Clive, for example, Teymurtash described how passions were stirred up when the war ministry received a report that a British flag had been hoisted on Greater Tunb.[109] It issued instructions to the customs officer at Lingah

108 FO 416/86: Sir R. Clive to Mr. A. Henderson, April 18, 1930.

109 Ibid.

to go and inspect the islands and report on the flags, and then requested that the foreign ministry would do its part diplomatically.[110] The Iranian Ministry of Foreign Affairs addressed a protest of the usual variety to the British Legation.[111] The customs mudir, on instructions from the army, visited the island and made inquiries concerning the visit of a British ship.[112] As it turned out, the ship's crew had temporarily hoisted a flag during the course of a hydrographic survey that was being carried out.[113] But the incident had given some army officers an opportunity to advertise their vigilance and devotion to the nationalist cause, and it had given the customs mudir an opportunity to advertise that he had been sent to Tunb to look for buildings to convert into an Iranian customs house.[114] Teymurtash described the incident as symptomatic: he said the army had been worked up to a fever pitch over issues in the Persian Gulf and asserted that if Iran were to give up any territory there as part of a treaty, this action "would create a feeling in the army that Iranian interests had been sacrificed."[115]

The particulars that arose during the ongoing negotiations were shaped to a large extent by the actions of Iran's civil and military authorities. Military men and local officials were eager to participate in the ongoing struggle to liberate Iran from foreign domination and defend its borders. Many of them viewed their role as that of assisting the government and the army in reconquering the islands in the Persian Gulf, reestablishing Iran's influence on the southern littoral, and driving the British completely out of the Gulf. Tehran allowed them considerable leeway when their actions appeared to go in line with the national goals of territorial integrity and political independence and appreciated that challenges to British authority in the Gulf were an effective means of applying pressure during negotiations.

Teymurtash seemed pleased to view the frequent tussles between the British and local officials as part and parcel of the negotiating process. For example, in mid-January 1929, the British government was

110 Ministry of War, Chief of Staff to Ministry of Foreign Affairs, *Esfand* 5, 1308 (February 24, 1930), in *Gozideh-ye Asnad-e Khalij-e Fars*, Vol. 1, p. 351.
111 Ministry of Foreign Affairs to British Legation, *Esfand* 5, 1308 (February 24, 1930), in *Gozideh-ye Asnad-e Khalij-e Fars*, Vol. 1, p. 354.
112 IOR/R/15/1/282: SNOPG *Triad* to Political Resident, March 14, 1930.
113 FO 416/86: Sir R. Clive to Mr. A. Henderson, April 18, 1930.
114 IOR/R/15/1/282: SNOPG *Triad* to Political Resident, March 12, 1930.
115 FO 416/86: Sir R. Clive to Mr. A. Henderson, April 18, 1930.

embarrassed when port officials prevented the crews of British warships from disembarking at Abadan and Bandar Abbas on the grounds that permission was not granted by authorities in Tehran.[116] The British navy was accustomed to calling at any Iranian port, greeting the local authorities upon arrival, and remaining as long as they pleased.[117] In the eyes of the British government, the obstruction to visits of British warships on the part of local officials was a breach of the "gentleman's agreement" to maintain the status quo until a final settlement could be reached. For Teymurtash, these unplanned incidents presented an opportune moment to introduce some of Iran's desiderata regarding the Gulf into the negotiations. While discussing these incidents, Clive recounted in his correspondence, Teymurtash showed him a draft bill that he had prepared for the Majles delineating the breadth of Iran's territorial waters and regulating the entry and exit of foreign warships. His proposed regulations called for the officers of British ships to obtain permission eight days in advance of entering Iranian ports. No more than two ships would be permitted to be in Iran's waters at any given time and visits would be restricted to 72 hours.[118] Clive countered this proposal by pointing out that three miles of territorial waters was a universally recognized limit and, apparently supposing that Teymurtash needed to be schooled in the affairs of state, explained that the visits of foreign warships should be established by executive regulations and not by the passing of a law. Teymurtash, he said, listened politely and agreed to settle the matter as part of the ongoing overall negotiations; but, he warned, if an agreement were not reached, he would proceed with passing the law on account of public opinion. The public, he said, was very ignorant and should understand what Iran's sovereign rights were.[119]

Another contentious issue that surfaced during discussion of the draft treaty was the British demand for the continuation of the 1882 Anglo-Iranian slavery convention, which stipulated that the British government was permitted to stop Iranian vessels suspected of

[116] Annual Report on Persia for the Year 1928, p. 29.

[117] *Ravabet-e Dowlat-e Shahanshahi ba Keshvarha-ye Howzeh-ye Mas'uliyat-e Edareh-ye Nohom-e Siyasi dar Panjah Saleh-ye Shahanshahi-ye Pahlavi*, pp. 57–61.

[118] FO 416/84: Teymurtash to Sir R. Clive, *janvier* 16 1929; Sir R. Clive to Sir Austen Chamberlain, January 18, 1929, and January 19, 1929.

[119] FO 416/84: Sir Clive to Sir Austen Chamberlain, January 31, 1929.

transporting slaves. The convention, signed by the Qajar government, was viewed by Iran as out of date and contrary to Iranian dignity. Reluctantly, the British included a draft of a new convention in their proposed treaty stipulating that British ships would stop and search suspect ships flying the Iranian flag only after requesting permission from the shah. However, the Iranian government rejected the proposal because it was not based on the principle of complete reciprocity. Teymurtash said that Iran would only allow the inspection of Iranian ships by Britain if Britain would allow the inspection of its own ships by Iran.[120] Devoid of reciprocal rights, Teymurtash refused to approve the draft convention, maintaining that the policing of Iran's territorial waters and the supervision of Iranian ships was an Iranian responsibility and not the responsibility of a foreign navy.[121] Similarly, Iran opposed a proposal put forward in the League of Nations to include the Persian Gulf and the Sea of Oman in a "special maritime zone" within which "native vessels" could be stopped and searched to ensure their compliance with the 1925 Arms Traffic Convention. Iran opposed this measure on the grounds that its provisions infringed on Iran's sovereignty over its own territorial waters.[122]

During discussions with Clive, Teymurtash indicated that it was Iran's firm intention to take responsibility for lights and buoys in the Persian Gulf. He said that Iran ought to do her share in Iran's territorial waters but wished to be guided by the British experts who were engaged in these functions.[123] The British inserted a clause in the first draft treaty to the effect that Britain and Iran should cooperate to provide lighting and buoying in the Persian Gulf waterway, but Teymurtash requested its removal. He said that this was not an issue for negotiations because Iran had a sovereign right to administer the lights and buoys in its own territorial waters. Instead, he proposed a small conference to enlist the assistance of the British government in transferring these responsibilities to Iranians.[124] Throughout these discussions, the British officials harbored doubts about Iran's genuine interest

[120] FO 416/84: Teymurtash to Sir R. Clive, *janvier* 13, 1929.
[121] CAB 24/241: Memorandum, May 23, 1933.
[122] The League of Nations, *Official Journal*, August 1931, pp. 1583–1586.
[123] FO 416/84: Sir R. Clive to Sir Austen Chamberlain, January 8, 1929, and February 16, 1929.
[124] FO 416/85: Teymurtash to Sir R. Clive, *août* 20, 1929.

in lights and buoys apart from the satisfaction of *amour-propre*, so they cast about for a gambit to satisfy Iran by giving it the outward appearance of responsibility while maintaining British control over the lights and buoys.[125]

After five years of negotiations, Teymurtash indicated that he had not managed to gain enough by way of concessions that would tempt Reza Shah to sign an agreement. Iran remained firm in its claim to sovereignty over Bahrain, Abu Musa, and the Tunbs and refused to recognize Britain's special position in the shaykhdoms. By the end of 1932, Tehran's refusal to grant overflight and landing privileges to Imperial Airways resulted in the transfer of the air route to the Arabian littoral, more firmly entrenching Britain's position in Kuwait, Bahrain, and the Trucial States. Negotiations with APOC had also reached a deadlock and falling oil prices were severely depressing Iran's treasury. On November 27, 1932, Reza Shah abruptly inserted himself into the picture, announcing the cancellation of the D'Arcy concession. The shah's actions can best be described as a brash response to an accumulation of grievances, not the least of which was the growing perception of Teymurtash as his rival.[126]

The Persian Gulf in Iranian Policy after Teymurtash, 1933–1939

Teymurtash returned from Europe only to be put on trial for trumped up corruption charges and was later murdered in his prison cell. After his downfall, there was no real effort on the side of Iran to negotiate an all-inclusive agreement with the British government. By many accounts, the agreement reached with APOC in April 1933 offered no real advantage over the terms of the original concession. In the Persian Gulf, Reza Shah resorted to the traditional tactics of bluff, intrigue, and bribery to try to gain whatever concessions he could. A greater role was delegated to Iran's diplomatic missions abroad, who received fresh instructions to bring before the world Iran's claim to a paramount position in the Persian Gulf: examples of this occurred at Tokyo where protests were made against the sale of Bahraini oil in

[125] Annual Report on Persia for the Year 1931, p. 39.
[126] Rezun, "Reza Shah's Court Minister," pp. 128–134.

Japan in Afghanistan where Iran's claim to Bahrain was ventilated in the local press; and in Baghdad where Iran's minister informed his Iraqi counterpart that Iran's activities in the Shatt al-Arab were just part of the shah's plan to oust the British altogether from the Persian Gulf.[127] While the American Congress was preparing to ratify the Arms Traffic Convention of 1925, the Iranian minister to Washington found a friend among the congressmen who managed to insert a reservation to the effect that the United States' consent to the convention "shall not be construed as denying any right of sovereignty which the Kingdom of Persia may have in and to the Persian Gulf, or to the waters thereof."[128]

Though the new Iranian fleet was no match for the British navy, the advent of Iranian warships in the end of 1932 bolstered Iran's capacity to assert its authority in and around the Persian Gulf waterway. Chief among its priorities was the assertion of Iranian authority at Basidu, Hengam, and the two Tunbs islands. The pandemonium that was caused in August 1933 when the Iranian navy hauled down the British flag at Basidu led to the eventual removal of the British naval bases from Iranian islands. This was regarded as a victory for the new Iranian navy and for a clever Iranian policy that leaned on tactics of bluff and intrigue to bring about a change in the circumstances. Britain's withdrawal from Iranian islands also served to harden Iran's position regarding Bahrain, Abu Musa, and the Tunbs.

Though serious negotiations were not resumed after the fall of Teymurtash, Reza Shah's government continued to echo the bargaining position that he had established, based on the principle of adequate compensation. Foreign Minister Sayyed Bagher Khan Kazemi told his British counterpart that Bahrain was really of no interest to Iran, being too far away from its shore, but, he said, public opinion felt very strongly and it could not be given away without something to show in return. He said that a settlement could be reached if the British government would help Iran assert her sovereignty over half of the Shatt al-Arab and over Abu Musa and the Tunbs, in exchange for Iran's recognition of Bahrain's independence and British treaty relations with the Arab shaykhs. The offer was again rejected by the

[127] Ibid.

[128] U.S. Department of State, *Foreign Relations of the United States: Diplomatic Papers*, 1934 (Washington, DC: Government Printing Office, 1951), p. 477.

British, on the grounds that Britain had neither the legal authority to revise the boundary in the Shatt al-Arab nor to give away islands that did not belong to Britain.[129] Protests were lodged over the issuance of Indian postage stamps surcharged "Bahrain" (1933) and over a Bahrain-Saudi transit dues agreement (1936).[130] Iran's claim, however, appeared markedly feebler after 1935 when the British established a naval base in Bahrain, at the invitation of the Al Khalifa ruler.

The Year of Crisis, 1933

The ink was barely dry on the new agreement between APOC and the Iranian government when Iranian authorities began a series of intrigues aimed at putting into force Iran's claim to Greater Tunb Island. In April 1933, the Governor of Bandar Abbas, the chief of police and a customs collector visited Greater Tunb to make inquiries about the lighthouse.[131] Preparations were underway for the visit of a French lighting expert who had been contracted to train Iran's naval officers to take over the responsibilities for lighting and buoying. The expert, Jacques Bénard, accompanied Rear Admiral Bayandor onboard the *Palang* for a tour of lights and buoys in the Persian Gulf. On July 23, 1933, the *Palang* visited Greater Tunb. A landing party, which included Bayandor and Bénard, drew a sketch plan and gave the lighthouse keeper a signed certificate saying that all was in order. The British protested this action in the name of the shaykh under British protection who claimed Tunb as his own, saying that the shaykh required prior notification for the visit of a warship to his island.[132] Later the shaykh, Selim bin Sultan, claimed that he received a letter from Tehran with an offer to lease Tunb Island. When he did not show the letter, British officials assumed that his statement was a bluff, when in fact, it was the substance of some indirect efforts on the part of Iranian officials to bring the island under Iranian authority.[133]

[129] FO 416/93: Mr. Knatchbull-Hugessen to Sir John Simon, April 2, 1935.

[130] IOR/R/15/2/139: HM's Minister Tehran to His Majesty's Secretary of State for Foreign Affairs London, October 12, 1932; IOR/R/15/2/172: Political Resident to Political Agent Bahrain, June 6, 1936.

[131] Guive Mirfendereski, "The Ownership of the Tonb Islands: A Legal Analysis," in *Small Islands, Big Politics: The Tombs and Abu Musa in the Persian Gulf*, ed. Hooshang Amirahmadi (London: Macmillan, 1996), p. 138.

[132] FO 416/92: Mr. Mallet to Persian Minister of Foreign Affairs, August 22, 1933.

[133] Annual Report on Persia for the Year 1933, p. 44.

Basidu, the British enclave on Qeshm Island, became a focus of Anglo-Iranian friction in the turbulent year of 1933. The exercise of British authority at Basidu was a persistent irritant to Iranian national pride and territorial sovereignty. In March some Iranian officials entered the British area and collected taxes from owners of date gardens, an action that became the subject of a British complaint to the government in Tehran. In April a customs official began using the British area as an observation point and carried out searches of dhows in nearby waters. He proudly told the British senior naval officer that he had instructions from his superiors at Lingah to enter the British area whenever he needed in the course of his duties. In July the governor of the south ports paid a visit to the caretaker, an Iranian in the employ of the British, and admonished him saying that the whole area of Basidu was Iranian territory.[134] These pinpricks to British authority, which took place when the British warships were out to sea, were just forerunners of the storm that was to break when four Iranian naval officers visited Basidu in an Iranian naval ship on July 31, 1933, and hauled down the British flag.[135]

When news of the incident reached the British government, Sir Victor Mallet, an early career diplomat serving in a temporary capacity as chargé d'affaires in Tehran, was instructed to lodge a protest with the Iranian government against the actions of the Iranian navy. Privately, he told Iran's Foreign Minister Mohammad 'Ali Foroughi that on account of the damage that was done to British "prestige," his government contemplated requiring visual reparation from Iran, along the lines of a flag rehoisting ceremony. He proposed that to make amends for what they had done, the crewmembers of the *Palang* would be required to attend a ceremony during which they would either salute the Union Jack or be dismissed from their duties. Faced with the threat of national humiliation, Foroughi told Mallet that the Iranian government disapproved of the actions taken by the crew's commander, Rear Admiral Bayandor, had reprimanded him, and had instructed him to refrain from interfering with British naval arrangements in the future. These statements, however, he refused to put in writing.[136] He also gave an account of how the

[134] Ibid., p. 33.
[135] FO 416/92: Sir R. Hoare to Sir John Simon, August 17, 1934.
[136] Annual Report on Persia for the Year 1933, p. 34.

shah had personally reprimanded Bayandor for his "ignorant" and "childish" actions.[137]

Despite the reinstatement of the British flag at Basidu a few days later, news of the incident spread fast among the inhabitants of the Persian Gulf coast towns giving rise to wild rumors of British withdrawal from the Persian Gulf. To restore confidence in the British, the Resident sent copies of a circular to all the Arab shaykhdoms announcing that the British flag had been rehoisted, and that the Iranian government regretted the incident and promised to investigate this and other complaints against the Iranian navy. At the same time, a destroyer flotilla, consisting of nine warships of the Royal Navy, was dispatched to the Persian Gulf to advertise that the British government intended to support her Arab friends against Iranian aggressions. The Iranian government responded by arranging for an article to appear in the Iranian press announcing that the British government had requested permission from Iran to send nine destroyers into the Persian Gulf and that the Iranian government had graciously granted permission.[138]

At this time Forughi was promoted to the office of prime minister, and the responsibility for foreign affairs devolved temporarily on the undersecretary, Mirza Anushirvan Khan Sepahbodi, pending the arrival from Baghdad of the new foreign minister, Sayyed Bagher Khan Kazemi (1933–1935). Sepahbodi, a relative of the deposed Qajar Shah, was a career statesman and patriot who had spent much of his time representing Iran overseas. As Iran's ambassador to Italy he played a leading role in the purchase of Iran's modern navy. He also represented Iran at the League of Nations, alongside Forughi. In September 1933, Sepahbodi was given a foretaste of the extreme sensitivity that would later send him packing his bags and returning home from an ambassador's post in Paris, when in 1938 Reza Shah abruptly broke relations with France in protest over a disparaging story that appeared in a French newspaper. The 1933 episode connected with Basidu also dealt Forughi a tough reminder about the precariousness of his own position, in a regime where civil servants were arbitrarily turned into scapegoats and supreme authority was based on fear.

137 Ibid.; Bahmani Qajar, "Naqsh-e Niru-ye Daryayi va Bayandor dar Ekhraj-e Engelisha az Hengam va Basa'idu," p. 94.
138 See for example, *Iran*, *Shahrivar* 23, 1312 (September 14, 1933).

The tempest that would be stirred by further insensitive conduct on the part of the British began when the shah learned how the actions of the Iranian navy had been characterized in English-language newspapers and, in tandem, learned of Forughi's role in generating the offending narrative.[139] Forughi was attributed with a statement to the effect that the British flag was hauled down at Basidu because of the "ignorance" of the Iranian navy. To make matters worse, Basidu was described as a "British possession" and the Iranian government was said to have "apologized" to the British government for the incident.[140] The shah was also aggravated by a report that the British were constructing something at Basidu and that a British naval guard was still posted there.[141] In his rage, the shah castigated Forughi, cursing him as a silly old fool who had been tricked by the British, and then had him "dragged" out of the room. Then the shah demanded that measures would be taken to make sure that the Persian press repudiated the British version of events.

Forughi and Sepahbodi came to Mallet and pleaded with him to make some concession that would help Forughi avoid the fate that had felled Teymurtash. Sepahbodi suggested that the shah's wrath could be quenched by the removal of the British naval guard from Basidu. Mallet said that if he suggested this to his government, the reply would probably be the opposite of what was hoped. Forughi begged Mallet to put a further communiqué in the press that would disavow the notion that Basidu was a "British possession" and that Iran had "apologized" for the removal of the flag.[142] He related that the shah, in spite of his rage, still wanted good relations, and reiterated his inability to understand why the British navy should pursue this vendetta against the Iranian navy because of a foolish act born of ignorance and inexperience.[143]

The next day, Sepahbodi addressed a further note to the British government, to the effect that a number of British marines had recently landed with machine guns at Basidu contrary to the rights of Iranian sovereignty. The Iranian government registered a protest against this

[139] See for example, *The Daily Mail*, "Union Jack Incident in Persia," September 16, 1933.
[140] Annual Report on Persia for the Year 1933, p. 36. See for example, *The Straits Times*, September 21, 1933.
[141] Ibid. [142] Ibid. [143] Ibid.

action and requested the immediate removal of the British troops from Basidu.[144] Mallet went to see Sepahbodi, returned the note, and warned that the British government could not accept this note if negotiations were to continue. Sepahbodi told Mallet that if he took the note back, he would surely be sent to prison. He said that he could not allow the shah to be humiliated in front of the Soviet deputy foreign minister who was due for a visit that very week. In his correspondence back to London, Mallet described a dramatic scene in which Sepahbodi tearfully begged him to remove the troops from Basidu and rescue Foroughi from impending ruin by correcting the false idea about Iran's "apology."[145] Mallet suggested to Sepahbodi that the naval guard could be removed in a month's time with the next visit of the destroyer flotilla, though he maintained that the British government had the right to send it again if desired. He also suggested that an official communiqué could be prepared to clarify Iran's position on the incident without the use of the word "apology."[146]

In the next meeting between Sepahbodi, Forughi, and the shah, the shah was reportedly in better spirits, and he was persuaded to accept the compromise arrived at between Mallet and the two ministers. He asked that Mallet arrange for a new official communiqué that would be devoid of the offensive language and would conclude with a pronouncement that the incident was closed. He agreed to take back the note demanding the withdrawal of British troops from Basidu, if Britain would remove the troops from there as soon as possible.[147] The new communiqué was prepared and Mallet stipulated orally that the question of the naval guard would be considered only after the shah's response to the new communiqué was known. Iran's response, in the form of a letter drafted by the new foreign minister, Bagher Kazemi (best known for his Cabinet appointments and proximity to Mohammad Mosaddeq during the fateful period of 1951–1953), was still being studied when the news broke that a British naval officer at Basidu had arrested the Iranian customs mudir and the Basidu crises entered its second phase.

On October 9, the Basidu customs mudir and his assistant went on board a dhow that was lying at anchor off the shore of the British

[144] FO 416/92: Mr. Mallet to Sir John Simon, September 21, 1933. [145] Ibid.
[146] FO 416/92: Mr. Mallet to Sir John Simon, September 22, 1933.
[147] FO 416/92: Mr. Mallet to Sir John Simon, September 23, 1933.

enclave and asked to see the nakhoda's papers. On his return to the shore, the British naval commander stopped him and asked him whether he did not know that Basidu was a British port. The mudir replied saying he considered Basidu and its waters to be Iranian territory and that he had acted in accordance with his instructions to carry out his duties in any part of Basidu. Viewing him as a troublemaker, the British naval officer took him into custody together with his assistant, brought them onboard the HMS *Lupin*, and the following day transported them to Bandar Abbas where they were handed over to the governor.[148]

News of the incident reached the British government before it reached the Iranian government. The British government tried to forestall a protest from the Iranian government by lodging a protest of its own against the conduct of the customs mudir before the Iranian government could enter a protest against his arrest. On October 14, a note was sent to the Iranian foreign ministry informing of the arrest and protesting the mudir's intrusion into the "British area" of Basidu. The British government asserted that the official's actions had been an infringement on the status quo according to which they exercised exclusive rights at Basidu.[149]

After the Iranian government gathered information on the arrest of the customs mudir, information was released to the press and the Majles was convened.[150] A debate was staged in which Kazemi responded to questions posed by the ministers and delivered a speech affirming that the Iranian government did not and would not recognize either a British area or British territorial waters or any right of possession at Basidu and that the government would defend the rights of Iran in this case as they had done in all other matters under the guidance of the shah.[151] During the speech he read the letter that he drafted in reply to the British:

[148] "Report from the Basidu customs mudir," *Mehr* 23, 1312 (October 15, 1933), in *Gozideh-ye Asnad-e Khalij-e Fars*, Vol. 1, p. 431; Annual Report on Persia for the Year 1933, p. 37.

[149] FO 371/16972: Mr. Mallet to Persian Minister of Foreign Affairs, October 14, 1933.

[150] Memorandum by the Finance Ministry, *Mehr* 24, 1312 (October 16, 1933), in Zamani, "Piruzi-ye Iran bar Engelis dar Nabard-e Basa'idu," p. 248.

[151] FO 371/16972: *Ettela'at*, October 22, 1933.

I have received with utmost surprise your note ... regarding the inexplicable treatment given to the mudir of customs at Basidu while the latter was performing his duties, and his removal to Bandar Abbas. It's a source of great surprise that the claim which was maintained by His Britannic Majesty's Government to a coal station at Basidu has gradually assumed another aspect, and that His Britannic Majesty's Government have now taken action as if they were the owners thereof and are preventing the exercise of the sovereign rights of [Iran] in that place, and have even called it a special British area and consider its territorial waters as being outside Iranian jurisdiction. The authorities of the Imperial Government do not know why the *status quo* has been invoked in this connection and with what justification the British naval authorities have taken this action, since the Imperial Government have not recognized, and will not recognize any British area or any sort of proprietary rights of the British Government at Basidu.[152]

This was followed by a rigorous press campaign in Iran. Impassioned articles avowed that the British had no standing whatsoever at Basidu and that the arrest of an Iranian official on Iranian soil was an insulting act on the part of a power that did lip service to the League of Nations.[153] The Iranian government issued instructions to its quarantine officials in the Persian Gulf to prevent the entry of any ship whose papers bore the designation "British Basidu."[154] Permission was also denied for visits of a British warship to Abadan, Hengam, and Bushehr saying that these visits were inopportune at such a juncture, though they later relented and allowed "unofficial" visits.[155]

In the course of subsequent conversations, Kazemi suggested what he thought would be adequate recompense for the arrest of the mudir: the British government should disavow the naval officers concerned, just as the Iranian government had disavowed the naval officers that earlier hauled down the British flag. Mallet told Kazemi that this was out of the question. Kazemi responded by saying that this incident had touched the nation to the quick and that, unless a satisfactory

[152] Ibid.; FO 371/16972: Persian Minister of Foreign Affairs (Kazemi) to Mr. Mallet, October 16, 1933; for the Persian text see, Zamani, "Piruzi-ye Iran bar Engelis dar Nabard-e Basa'idu," pp. 254–255.

[153] See for example, *Setareh'yé Djéhane*, October 27, 1933; and *Shafaq-e Sorkh*, October 25 and 31, 1933.

[154] Ministry of Foreign Affairs to Ministry of the Interior, *Azar* 16, 1312 (December 7, 1933), in Zamani, "Piruzi-ye Iran bar Engelis dar Nabard-e Basa'idu," p. 245.

[155] Annual Report on Persia for the Year 1933, p. 7.

settlement could be found, his government would be forced to refer the question of Basidu to international arbitration.[156] The Iranian minister in London made a similar statement about the necessity of referring the incident to a third party, and ultimately, it was the threat of international arbitration that turned the tide.[157]

When the Iranian government began to consider referring the incident to the international tribunal, the British government began to question the strength of its case. After a thorough review, its legal advisers concluded that Britain's case would not stand up in the court of international law. Thereafter, the Foreign Office called for a more accommodating posture at Basidu and began to contemplate a complete withdrawal of its facilities. In a subsequent conversation with Kazemi, Mallet softened his government's stance about the incident, saying that after receiving fuller reports, his government had formed a less grave view of the mudir's actions. He also let Kazemi know that the naval guard had been ordered to withdraw, but that British ships would continue to visit Basidu from time to time to preserve the "rights" claimed by the British government.[158]

In December 1933, British withdrawal from Basidu was confirmed by the Iranian customs mudir and the Baghdad press.[159] Kazemi went to the Majles on January 15, 1934, to announce that the matter of the mudir's arrest was closed. The whole incident was explained as being due to a mistake that was without malice or the intent to insult Iran. Kazemi said that the British cowed in the face of the indisputable arguments that Foroughi had prepared for the International Court of Justice. They were "forced to submit" to international law, he said, and evacuated Basidu "though they suffered from feelings of humiliation due to the removal of their flag and the loss of their bases."[160]

[156] Ibid., p. 38.
[157] FO 416/92: Foreign Office to Admiralty, November 25, 1933.
[158] Annual Report on Persia for the Year 1933, p. 39; see also "Report of a Meeting with the British Minister by Mir Kazemi," *Azar* 8, 1312 (November 29, 1933), in *Gozideh-ye Asnad-e Khalij-e Fars*, Vol. 1, p. 460.
[159] Ministry of the Interior to Ministry of Foreign Affairs, *Dey* 10, 1312 (December 31, 1933), in Zamani, "Piruzi-ye Iran bar Engelis dar Nabard-e Basa'idu," p. 282; Ministry of Foreign Affairs to Special Imperial Office, *Dey* 6, 1312 (December 27, 1933), in *Gozideh-ye Asnad-e Khalij-e Fars*, Vol. 1, p. 477.
[160] *Mozakerat-e Majles-e Shura-ye Milli*, *Dey* 25, 1312 (January 15, 1934), in Zamani, "Piruzi-ye Iran bar Engelis dar Nabard-e Basa'idu," p. 279.

In conclusion, he said, "Iran was able to force the British colonial giant to take yet another step back from the Persian Gulf."[161]

Change and Continuity, 1934–1939

By the end of 1933 it had become clear that the personal initiatives of military men, local officials, and even private citizens played a greater role in shaping events in the Persian Gulf than protracted negotiations in London and Tehran. Iran increasingly leaned on the tactics of bluffs and ploys instigated by local officials to slowly edge the British out of the Persian Gulf. In the period 1934–1939, Iranian officials vigorously hunted smugglers originating from the northern and southern littorals. The British lodged numerous protests on behalf of the Arab shaykhs against Iranian interference with Arab dhows on the high seas and in the territorial waters of Muscat, Kuwait, and Bahrain. Officials of the Iranian government attempted to bribe the headman of Greater Tunb to fly the Iranian flag.[162] When that failed they attempted in vain to negotiate a lease directly with the shaykh who claimed the island.[163]

The Iranian government made every effort to foster an impression that it was steadily assuming greater control over the Persian Gulf even as Britain's position veritably grew stronger. Laws defining Iran's territorial waters and regulating the visits of foreign ships were passed.[164] New regulations required foreign merchant ships to fly the Iranian flag when entering Iran's territorial waters.[165] Changes were demanded to the uniforms worn by British employees in Iranian port towns because they were deemed to have a colonial or military appearance.[166] Meanwhile, the Arab shaykhs of the southern littoral allowed the steady entrenchment of the British in their domains. This was prominently expressed in the transference of the British air route and naval base to the southern littoral in the 1930s.

Iran continued to keep the door open for a possible claim to the Arab shaykhdoms of the southern littoral and the Ministry of Foreign Affairs refused to send written replies to matters concerning them.

161 Ibid.
162 FO 371/17827: Residency Agent Sharjah ('Abd al-Latif) to Political Agent Bahrain, April 19, 1934.
163 Annual Report on Persia for the Year 1934, p. 16.
164 Ibid., p. 5.
165 FO 416/92: Intelligence Summary No. 11 for the Period Ending June 3, 1933.
166 Annual Report on Persia for the Year 1937, pp. 11–12.

In an internal memo, Kazemi recalled a conversation that took place in October 1933, during which he explained to Mallet:

If we are forced to give a very clear and explicit answer, we will have to discuss things that maybe you should not be so eager to hear, and if we remain silent, it is against our interest and in answer to the question such as on the topic of the dhows of Kuwait and Muscat and Dubai and Ras al-Khaimah and the British embassy, and repeated correspondence makes it clear to us that if we want to give an answer it is necessary to say that until now we do not recognize these shaykhs and certainly we cannot recognize their flags. You know what's in your correspondence that you specify. . . . We do not recognize your intervention with the shaykhs or the states located on the western shores of the Persian Gulf and references to them were of a purely private matter and if we want to be clear in this regard also if you want in writing we are forced to refer to this fact. So it is better that you not write about this type of problem in letters, because we do not plan to read it and give answers, but the problem can be addressed within the framework of the general treaty.[167]

The Iranian foreign ministry took the additional step of ordering its diplomatic officials not to communicate with British officials on matters regarding the shaykhdoms.[168]

Iran's passport policy, which treated the residents of the Arab shaykhdoms as Iranian citizens, further exacerbated the situation. In the spring of 1934, further instructions were issued to Iran's consulate in Iraq that if a traveler requested a visa to visit Iran but had a visa for Bahrain or Kuwait in his (British-issued) passport, the offending visa had to be removed from the passport before a visa for Iran could be granted.[169]

In his analysis of the situation, Sir Victor Mallet recalled that on several occasions he was approached quietly by staff of the foreign ministry requesting information about Britain's relationship with the shaykhdoms. Viewing this as an opportunity to school Iranian officials

[167] "Discussion with the British Chargé d'Affaires," Memorandum by the Ministry of Foreign Affairs, *Mehr* 23, 1312 (October 15, 1933), in Zamani, "Piruzi-ye Iran bar Engelis dar Nabard-e Basa'idu," pp. 256–258. See also Persian Minister of Foreign Affairs (Kazemi) to His Majesty's Chargé d'Affaires (Mallet), October 21, 1933, IOR/R/15/5/172.

[168] Consulate of Iran Karachi to Ministry of Foreign Affairs, Postscript, *Ordibehesht* 2, 1316 (April 23, 1937).

[169] FO 416/92: Sir R. Hoare to Sir John Simon, August 23, 1934; Annual Report on Persia for the Year 1934, p. 6.

on the political status of the Arab shaykhdoms, the British government decided to send the Iranian government copies of the agreements between the British government and the shaykhs of Kuwait, Bahrain, Qatar, and Muscat. This would complete the communication of September 7, 1928, when copies of the 1892 agreements with the Trucial shaykhs were sent to the foreign ministry. In a letter dated March 17, 1934, the minister in Tehran, Sir Reginald Hoare, provided copies of the "exclusive agreements" in force between the British government and the shaykhs, and he explained "all these rulers have placed the conduct of their foreign relations in the hands of His Majesty's Government."[170] To this communication Kazemi replied, saying:

> Not only does the Persian Government consider those of the agreements, treaties and concessions in question which relate to lands and places such as Bahrain etcetera, which are inseparable parts of Persian territory, to be neither official or valid but it considers the conclusion of such instruments by a third Power to be contrary to the principles of friendship, and protests strongly and vigorously against such a step which violates the rights of sovereignty and suzerainty of Persia in her own territory and waters.[171]

Kazemi's characterization of Iran's claims as "Bahrain etcetera" raised alarm in London because it appeared that Kazemi was intentionally leaving the door open for possible claims to additional territories in the Gulf. In writing he refused to disavow the shadowy claims; however, privately, he told Hoare that Iran had no concern with the Arab rulers and that matters could be easily settled if Iran could be withdrawn from the position that it had taken up.[172]

By means of intrigue and bribery, Iran's officials made a number of attempts to expropriate Greater Tunb. In April 1934, a report arrived to Sharjah that the Governor of Bandar Abbas and other officials had gone to Greater Tunb in a customs launch. According to this report, the party proceeded to the house of Mahmud, the representative of the Shaykh of Ras al-Khaimah, and questioned him. They asked him how

170 FO 416/92: Sir R. Hoare to Persian Minister of Foreign Affairs, March 17, 1934.

171 FO 416/92: Persian Minister of Foreign Affairs (Kazemi) to His Majesty's Minister (Hoare), *Ordibehesht* 10, 1313 (April 30, 1934).

172 FO 416/92: Mirza Seyyid Bagher Khan Kazemi to His Majesty's Minister (Hoare), *Ordibehesht* 23, 1313 (May 13, 1934); Mr. Knatchbull-Hugessen to Sir John Simon, December 15, 1934; FO 416/93: Mr. Knatchbull-Hugessen to Sir John Simon, January 9, 1935.

much rent the British warships gave to the shaykh. Mahmud replied saying he did not know. The Iranians asked him how much money he earned and whose flag he was flying on Tunb. They offered to reward him generously if he would lower the shaykh's flag and replace it with the Iranian flag. Mahmud said that he refused the offer and the Iranians left.[173] On April 26 the governor returned with the chief of police, the director of customs at Bandar Abbas, and an interpreter. Mahmud was again asked how much money he earned either from the shaykh or from the British government. They told Mahmud that if the island were to become Iranian property that he would receive double his salary.[174]

Further visits were paid to Tunb by vessels of the Iranian navy. In the end of August 1934, the *Palang* was sighted there. When questioned, the ship's captain, Gholam 'Ali Bayandor, said that he merely wished to anchor for the night, that it was the first time he heard that the island was claimed by the Shaykh of Ras al-Khaimah and said he did not know that the shaykh wished for notification of visits.[175] Later it was learned that the *Palang* had spotted a Dubaian dhow at Lesser Tunb and took it to Greater Tunb to search it. The search was carried out on the side of the island opposite to which the British warships were. Shortly after, the *Charokh* paid a visit. The captain said he considered Tunb to be Iranian territory and said he was looking for a deserter.[176] It later came to light that a party had landed and asked the headman where the customs house was and tried to coerce him to board the *Charokh*.[177] British Foreign Secretary Sir John Simon warned Kazemi that a total cession of such tactics was a precondition for the continuation of negations and also let him know that the British navy had been authorized to use force if an Iranian naval vessel were to be discovered at Tunb in the future.[178]

In the end of the year, Selim bin Sultan, the Shaykh of Ras al-Khaimah, who was in a dire financial situation owing to the decline of the pearl trade, apparently decided to try to lease his island to the

[173] FO 371/17827: Residency Agent Sharjah ('Abd al-Latif) to Political Agent Bahrain, April 19, 1934.
[174] Ibid. [175] FO 371/17827: SNOPG to India Office, September 1, 1934.
[176] FO 371/17827: Sir R. Hoare to Foreign Office, September 14, 1934.
[177] FO 371/17827: Political Resident to the Secretary of State for India, September 17, 1934.
[178] FO 371/17827: Sir John Simon to Sir R. Hoare, September 28, 1934.

highest bidder. On September 3, 1934, he wrote to the British Resident, Trenchard Craven William Fowle (1932–1939), saying that he would like to lease Greater Tunb to the British government, but indicated that if the government did not wish to lease it, he hoped that it would grant him permission to exercise his rights in this matter.[179] By the end of December the shaykh's flag had been removed from the island and it was rumored that Iranian officials were in communication with him concerning a lease. The Resident made inquiries and learned that the shaykh felt he ought to receive rent for the lighthouse on Tunb. Meanwhile, a resident of Tunb was approached, first by the Hengam customs mudir and then by the Shaykh of Qeshm, and asked to deliver an official letter to Tunb from Tehran. He also reported that the mudir of customs at Bandar Abbas planned to go to Tunb in February to collect customs dues and hoist the Iranian flag. Rumors spread around the Gulf that Iran's flag was soon to be raised over Greater Tunb Island. On March 19, the British Resident sent an ultimatum to the shaykh demanding that he replace his flag within 10 days or ownership of his island would be transferred to his cousin, the Shaykh of Sharjah. Shaykh Selim bin Sultan apologized to the British government, saying that he merely sought rent for his lighthouse on Tunb, and he agreed to rehoist his flag.[180]

The final series of events took place in the middle of April. A dhow came to Tunb from Lingah and landed an Iranian official believed to be from the customs service. He expressed surprise upon finding that the shaykh's flag flew again from the flagstaff. Two days later, another dhow arrived bringing the Governor of Bandar Abbas. He was intercepted by a British naval officer while attempting to deliver an official letter to the headman of Tunb. The letter when opened was found to contain copies of a decree in regard to elections to the Majles, signed by an official from Bandar Abbas. The governor was interviewed and then released. The British government determined that local officials, rather than Tehran, were responsible for these intrigues and elected not to pursue the issue.[181]

While Reza Shah's government failed to assert sovereignty over Abu Musa and the Tunbs, it succeeded in establishing a measure of control over the visits of British warships to its own ports and territorial

[179] Abdullah, *The United Arab Emirates*, p. 269.
[180] Annual Report on Persia for the Year 1934, p. 16. [181] Ibid.

waters. These regulations, issued on July 15, 1934, have been touted in official Pahlavi history as the most significant achievement of Reza Shah's Persian Gulf policy.[182] The new law declared a six-mile limit on Iran's territorial waters and an additional six-mile "zone of maritime supervision."[183] Though the regulation was on the law books, the British government continued to recognize a limit of only three nautical miles. Accordingly the British Admiralty was authorized to intervene in any attempt by Iranians to interfere with Arab dhows outside the three-mile limit and to protect them with force, if necessary.[184] The regulation established that foreign warships could only pass through Iran's territorial waters or call at Iran's ports if notification was made eight days in advance. Additional rules established procedures for the exchange of salutes, and formal calls between visiting captains and Iranian officials.[185]

After reference to the Foreign Office, Britain's new minister in Tehran, Sir Hughe Montgomery Knatchbull-Hugessen (1935–1939), tried to persuade the Iranian government to accept a modified arrangement. He said that the British government would notify Tehran in advance of visits but that for the sake of convenience, local officials would also be informed directly. He proposed that the Iranian government should issue instructions to the local officials to raise no objections to such visits in the absence of communication from Tehran. This was to permit the landing of naval vessels in the case of a sudden urgent need such as a medical illness or accident. He also proposed a special arrangement whereby British ships would be allowed to call at Abadan for the sole purpose of fueling with notification only to the local official and with exemption from the formalities of salutes and calls. The Iranian government rejected his proposals and informed him that local authorities were instructed to ignore British notifications and

182 Ministry of War to Ministry of Foreign Affairs, *Ordibehesht* 10, 1315 (April 30, 1936), in *Ravabet-e Dowlat-e Shahanshahi ba Keshvarha-ye Howzeh-ye Mas'uliyat-e Edareh-ye Nohom-e Siyasi dar Panjah Saleh-ye Shahanshahi-ye Pahlavi*, p. 165.

183 For a copy of the Persian text, see *Ravabet-e Dowlat-e Shahanshahi ba Keshvarha-ye Howzeh-ye Mas'uliyat-e Edareh-ye Nohom-e Siyasi dar Panjah Saleh-ye Shahanshahi-ye Pahlavi*, pp. 97–99.

184 Annual Report on Persia for the Year 1938, p. 6.

185 *Ravabet-e Dowlat-e Shahanshahi ba Keshvarha-ye Howzeh-ye Mas'uliyat-e Edareh-ye Nohom-e Siyasi dar Panjah Saleh-ye Shahanshahi-ye Pahlavi*, pp. 55–61.

await official authorization from Tehran for the visits of any foreign warships. However, Iran's realization of its reliance on British goodwill would soon render it more flexible in these matters.[186]

The year of 1936 heralded a turning point when the Iranian government began to view naval cooperation with the British as more advantageous than confrontation. In January, the Iranian government requested the granting of docking facilities at Bombay for the *Babr* and *Palang* as they needed to undergo repairs. The British government agreed to grant facilities unconditionally but addressed a letter to the Iranian foreign ministry contrasting Britain's cooperative attitude with Iran's stubborn stance. Consequently, Iran's Ministry of War was obliged to offer a more flexible arrangement for emergency fueling visits to Abadan along the lines of those proposed by Knatchbull-Hugessen. However, Iran was not willing to compromise on its requirement that advance notification must be given to Tehran before any foreign warship could enter Iran's ports or waters. The British government decided not to continue pursuing the matter and concluded in an internal memo that if necessity arose, ships of the Royal Navy would pass though Iran's territorial waters regardless of the published regulations. But by 1937 it became apparent that the Iranian government would be more flexible about emergency landings at Iranian ports than was previously thought. Gholam 'Ali Bayandor and other local officials admitted that they were instructed to be flexible in the event that a British warship needed to make an emergency landing, especially if seamen were in need of urgent medical attention. Though several minor incidents occurred with regard to the visits of foreign warships to Iranian ports during the period under discussion, the incidents were ironed out through correspondence between the British minister and the Iranian ministry of foreign affairs.[187]

By 1935 the Iranian government notified the British government that its experts had completed their examination of lights and buoys, and that arrangements were being made to take over the maintenance of the current installations and to install some new ones. French and Italian engineers had been hired to construct lights and beacons on various places of the Iranian coast and Kish Island.[188] After the failure

[186] Annual Report on Persia for the Year 1935, pp. 11–13.
[187] Annual Report on Persia for the Year 1936, pp. 4–7.
[188] Administration Report of the Persian Gulf Residency for the Year 1936, p. 6; Diary of the British Residency and Consulate General Bushire for the Month of

to negotiate the purchase of the existing lights and buoys, Iran notified the British of its decision to buy its own devices. Britain was asked to remove its devices as the new ones were phased in. Neville Chamberlain, the new prime minister in Britain, was of the opinion that the British government had no choice but to comply with this request and instructed the India Office to remove its equipment, which was admittedly out of date anyway.[189] By the close of the period under discussion, the British government had acquiesced to Iran's takeover of lights and buoys in its own territorial waters – a task that Iran was deemed incapable of doing 10 years prior when the initiative was first raised by Teymurtash.

The Outcomes of Reza Shah's Persian Gulf Policy

The Persian Gulf, which stood as a symbol of Iran's weakness, became a focus for the articulation of nationalist and anti-colonial feeling during the reign of Reza Shah Pahlavi. The shah's endeavor to extend the central authority over Iran's ports, islands, and territorial waters met with limited success: he compelled the British to withdraw their troops from Persian Gulf Ports and islands; introduced a small, modern navy into the Persian Gulf waterway; established regulations for the visits of foreign warships to Iran's ports and waters; and began policing its shoreline. He tried but did not succeed in getting the British to recognize Iran's claims to Bahrain, Abu Musa, and the Tunbs. Another area in which his government failed was in its policy toward the Arab shaykhdoms of the Persian Gulf: Iran sought to establish relations with the Arab rulers on the southern littoral and at the same time entertained shadowy claims to sovereignty over their domains. The Arabs' fear of Iran strengthened their reliance on British protection allowing the British to entrench their position along the southern littoral and making it all the more difficult for Iran to gain influence in the shaykhdoms.

While Reza Shah is remembered for the establishment of order and stability and for having created the institutions of a strong, centralized

October 1936, in *Political Diaries of the Arab World: Persian Gulf 1904–1965*, Vol. 12 (Archive Editions, 1990), pp. 245–247.

[189] FO 416/94: British Legation Tehran to Persian Ministry of Foreign Affairs, March 21, 1935; FO 416/96: Foreign Office to India Office, September 13, 1937.

state, he is not remembered for a strong Persian Gulf policy, in part because Iran's military weakness in the Persian Gulf was laid bare during the events of the Second World War. On the pretext of its collusion with Nazi Germany, British and Soviet troops reentered Iran despite the shah's declaration of neutrality. The Allied invasion began on August 25, 1941, when the HMS *Shoreham* open fired on the Iranian sloop *Palang*, harbored at Abadan, causing the ship to erupt in a massive ball of fire. Iran's senior naval commander, Gholam 'Ali Bayandor, narrowly escaped only to witness the further destruction of the Iranian navy from a small pier. He was later gunned down in the assault on Khorramshahr.[190] The oil field and the railroad were captured and the Iranian army was rapidly overwhelmed by British and Soviet troops. Reza Shah was forced to abdicate in favor of his son, Mohammad Reza Pahlavi, who replaced his father as shah on December 16, 1941.

While Reza Shah's efforts to assert authority in the Persian Gulf met with limited success, the introduction of Iranian nationalism into the Persian Gulf waterway bore colossal ramifications. The entrance of nationalism forged an acute dichotomy between Persians and Arabs. Harsh polices aimed at unifying the country prompted mass waves of migration from Iran's coastal areas to the Arab states of the southern littoral. Heavy-handed treatment of the inhabitants of the southern littoral disrupted centuries of movement and exchange between the two shores. The hostility of local authorities charged with implementing the more aggressive Persian Gulf policy left a legacy of popular hatred for the Pahlavi dynasty. Moreover, the introduction of Iranian nationalism marked a transition from a Gulf society once characterized by symbiosis and interdependency to a sub-region characterized by national divisions, sectarian suspicions, rivalries, and political tension. The conflict that emerged between the Iranian state and the Arab shaykhdoms of the Persian Gulf during the interwar period would continue to characterize Persian Gulf politics into the twenty-first century.

[190] Ward, *Immortal: A Military History of Iran*, pp. 156–157.

5 The Trucial States, Iran, and the British

[T]he increasing activities of the Persian Customs Service operating outside territorial waters and the generally aggressive attitude of the Persians, both officials and private individuals, are causing much ill-feeling on the Trucial Coast, where the Arabs, who have the greatest contempt for all Persians, both individually and as a nation, are with difficulty being restrained from taking direct action to protect themselves and obtain revenge. It is without any doubt true that it is only their fear of the guns of His Majesty's ships which has, so far, kept them under control.[1]

British senior naval officer, Persian Gulf, 1928

The introduction of Iranian nationalism into the Persian Gulf had a profound effect on the rulers and societies of the Trucial Coast,[2] particularly the port towns of Dubai, Abu Dhabi, Sharjah, and Ras al-Khaimah. While rulers and merchants were formerly pleased to view the British as their protector against the aggressions of regional powers, the events of the interwar years gave rise to a growing perception that this protection came at a very heavy cost. A growing assertiveness on the part of Iran forced the British to reconsider their support for Arab shaykhs and tribes in Iran's coastal areas and islands, and the Trucial shaykhs, whose traditional tribal domains included islands claimed by Iran, were caught in the cusp. What's more, the shaykhdoms became an arena of growing imperial intervention owing to their strategic value as a civil and military air route and to the development of the oil industry. During the course of the interwar years,

[1] IOR/R/15/1/280: SNOPG to CinCEI, August 17, 1928.

[2] Also known as "Trucial Oman," the "Trucial States," and the "Trucial Shaykhdoms," until 1971 and thereafter, the United Arab Emirates. They were small polities in terms of population, military, and economic resources, analogous to what Ernest Gellner calls "tribal proto-states." See Ernest Gellner, *Anthropology and Politics: Revolutions in the Sacred Grove* (Cambridge, MA: Blackwell, 1995), p. 184; and James Onley and Sulayman Khalaf, "Shaikhly Authority in the Pre-Oil Gulf: An Historical Anthropological Study," *History and Anthropology* 17, no. 3 (September 2006), pp. 189–208.

and largely due to the rise of Iran within the regional power equation, Britain's image in the shaykhdoms as a propitious protecting power was overshadowed by its image as a heavy-handed colonial overlord.

Reza Shah's efforts to bring the authority of the central government to bear over the contested frontier region caused an explosive situation between Arabs and Iranians in the Persian Gulf. Iran's introduction of board and search operations designed to catch smugglers turned zealous local officials into the vanguard for the extension of Iranian authority into the Persian Gulf waterway, which had hitherto been dominated by Arab seafarers. This turn of events hearkened back to the precarious situation in the Gulf before the *Pax Britannica*, when ships were subject to raiding and retaliation for the failure to pay taxes or tolls to the tribe or polity that controlled a particular area. The murder of a customs official on Hengam Island in 1927 by an Arab shaykh, Iran's reoccupation of that island, and its capture of an Arab dhow in 1928 brought the Arabs of the Trucial Coast to the brink of retribution. Britain's refusal to mediate on behalf of the Shaykh of Hengam, who was claimed as a dependent by the Shaykh of Dubai, and its inaction in the face of Iranian aggressions against Trucial Arabs were perceived as a sign that Iran was on the rise and British protection was useless. After having acquiesced to the British prohibition against consulting Iran, the Shaykh of Dubai elected to forestall an outbreak and ensure his own survival by adopting a strategy of rapprochement toward the Iranian authorities, and the sizeable and influential Iranian diaspora in Dubai was instrumental in bridging the gap.

The Trucial States: Between the British and Iran, 1919–1929

In the immediate aftermath of the first World War, both Iran and the emerging Saudi-Wahhabi state were taking their places as important components of the political power structure in the area. The striking difference between them was Ibn Saʿud's acquiescence to Britain's special relationship with the Trucial States versus Iran's rejection of this special relationship. In contrast to Ibn Saʿud, Reza Shah flagrantly challenged the treaty relationship in force between the British and the Trucial States.[3] Iran's policy toward the Trucial States was born partly

[3] FO 416/79: Persian Foreign Office to His Britannic Majesty's Legation at Tehran, *Tir* 15, 1305 (July 7, 1926).

out of pragmatic concerns, such as putting down the smuggling that robbed the treasury of much-needed customs income. But it was also buoyed by popular irredentist claims to areas that were historically under Iranian rule and areas that were populated by conationals, such as Kuwait, Bahrain, and the Trucial States.

The impression in Iran that most of the residents of the Trucial States were Iranian was not completely unfounded. A large portion of Dubai's population (and to a lesser extent the populations of Sharjah, Ras al-Khaimah, and Abu Dhabi) during the interwar years was made up of immigrants or children of immigrants from Iran. Residents of the Trucial States arrived to Iranian ports and presented travel documents with Persian names or family names that bore witness to their places of origin in localities such as Lar, Gerash, Evaz, Bastak, Janah, Galeh Dar, Heydarabad, Khor, and Kamir.[4]

In the absence of reliable statistics, sporadic estimates can give an indication of the strength of Dubai's ex-pat Iranian community. At the turn of the century, the total population of Dubai was estimated to be around 2,075 souls.[5] That number was said to include about 500 "Persian" shopkeepers.[6] By 1939, the total population of Dubai had grown to around 20,000.[7] In 1929 the number of immigrants from Iran was estimated to be between 4,000 and 5,000, and the majority was thought to be Arabs from the Lingah district (Hawala).[8] However, of those, about 2,000 were not claimed as subjects by Shaykh Sa'id, which suggests that most of this group numbering 2,000 probably identified as either Persian or Shi'i, and probably in most cases – both.[9] However, during the interwar years, an estimated 2,000–3,000 Hawala residing in Dubai were claimed as subjects of the shaykh, and the heads of several large and wealthy Hawala families were welcomed to attend his majlis. Though there were religious differences between the Hawala and Dubai's ruling family (the former being Shafi'i and the latter being Maliki) the Hawala were better equipped

[4] Report of the Acting *Kargozar* of Bandar Lingah, *Bahman* 28, 1301 (February 18, 1923), in *Gozideh-ye Asnad-e Khalij-e Fars*, Vol. 2, p. 35.
[5] Frauke Heard-Bey, *From Trucial States to United Arab Emirates*, p. 242.
[6] IOR/R/15/1/252: Residency Agent Sharjah ('Abd al-Latif) to Political Resident (Kemball), July 29, 1901.
[7] Zahlan, *The Origins of the United Arab Emirates*, p. 11.
[8] FO 416/84: Sir R. Clive to Sir Austen Chamberlain, February 16, 1929.
[9] FO 416/83: Major Dickson to Lieutenant Colonel Sir L. Haworth, July 5, 1928.

by their Sunni faith and claim to Arab ancestry to gain acceptance into the dominant group.

The immigration narrative of the al-Gurg family is illustrative of this historical process. In his memoirs, Easa Saleh al-Gurg, a prominent Emirati diplomat and businessman, relates how his family's migration from the Lingah district began in the later decades of the nineteenth century and was completed during the Reza Shah years:

[I]n my grandfather's time my family crossed the waters of the Gulf from the coastal plains of Iran, from the region known as Fars, and returned to our ancestral Arabia.... For some of us, particularly those families for whom the traditional ways of Islam and the way of life of the Arabs were of special importance and pride, there was another event which made the return to Arabia imperative. In the years after the end of the First European War ... a revolution in Iran brought to power Reza Shah Pahlavi.... Ironically, it was [his] attempts to reform many aspects of Islamic custom which encouraged many of the Sunni Arab families, living like my own on the coast, to return to Arabia. Not the least amongst the innovations to which the Arab families objected was the decision that women should go unveiled.... For the Arabs, on both sides of the Gulf, especially those from the old families of which mine was one, such proposals were wholly unacceptable.[10]

While the al-Gurg family is an exemplar of the wealthy Hawala immigrant families that integrated into the tribal society of the Trucial States during the height of the pearling era, the twenties and thirties also brought scores of immigrants having a different profile: these were the penniless villagers and agriculturalists, mostly Shi'a, who flooded to the shaykhdoms seeking employment as day laborers in the docks and the pearl banks.[11] While no definite numbers were recorded, varied eyewitness accounts attest to the immense growth of Iranian immigration to the shaykhdoms during these years. The British Political Agent in Bahrain noted in a memo of December 16, 1932:

When passing through the Sharjah bazaar ... I happened to notice that there were more Persians than I should have expected in such a place.... [W]hen

10 Easa Saleh al-Gurg, *The Wells of Memory: An Autobiography* (London: John Murray, 1998), p. 2.

11 Razavian, "Iranian Communities in the Persian Gulf," pp. 321–322; Nelida Fuccaro, "Mapping the Transnational Community: Persians and the Space of the City in Bahrain, c. 1869–1937," in *Transnational Connections and the Arab Gulf*, ed. Madawi al-Rasheed (New York: Routledge, 2005), p. 51; Fuccaro, *Histories of City and State in the Persian Gulf*, p. 93.

talking to Sheikh Sultan bin [Saqr] I brought the conversation [a]round to Persians and he confirmed the fact that considerable numbers were coming in to settle at Sharjah from various ports of the Persian littoral.[12]

The perception of Dubai, Abu Dhabi, Sharjah, and Ras al-Khaimah as Iranian colonies was particularly evident among the Iranian officials at Lingah and Bandar Abbas. They were aware of the historic connections between the Trucial Coast and the Lingah district and they knew that Iranian nationals were leaving southern Iran in droves seeking work on the other side of the Gulf. For them, the Trucial Coast was part of Iran's former empire, and territory that should be reincorporated into Iran when Iranian military strength would permit.[13] The introduction of passport policies that treated immigrants to the Arab shaykhdoms as Iranian citizens was aimed at assuaging these nationalist and irredentist sentiments.

Iran's imposition of heavy customs tariffs on tea and sugar at its principal ports in 1925 primarily affected the Hawala merchants who transported these goods from India to entrepôt ports, such as Dubai, and redistributed them to different markets around the Gulf. Many of them were merchants from villages in the Lingah hinterland including Lar, Bastak, Janah, Koohej, Evaz, and Gerash.[14] The new restrictions did not have an immediate effect, because clever-minded traders evaded the customs officers whenever possible and bribed them whenever necessary.[15] But beginning in the summer of 1926, Iranian customs agents were equipped with five launches armed with machine guns and authorized to begin intercepting vessels at sea, which they believed were bound for the Iranian coastline.[16] In particular, they

12 IOR/R/15/2/488: Political Agent Bahrain to Political Resident, December 16, 1932.

13 See Chapters 3 and 4.

14 Floor, *The Rise and Fall of Bandar-e Lingah*, p. 170.

15 Mohammad ʻAli Nikbin Tehrani, Customs Inspector Bandar Abbas, to *Sartip* Habibollah Khan Sheybani, Chief of the Army General Staff, *Tir* 12, 1306 (July 3, 1928), in *Faslnameh-ye Motalaʻat-e Tarikhi* 7, no. 25 (Spring 1388/2009), pp. 203–206; Bushire Residency Diary No. 18 for 1925 (Persian) for the Month of November 1925, in *Political Diaries of the Arab World: Persian Gulf*, Vol. 7, p. 311.

16 Bushire Residency Diary No. 4 for 1926 (Persian) for the Month of April 1926, in *Political Diaries of the Arab World: Persian Gulf*, Vol. 7, p. 351.

were instructed to search vessels originating from Dubai and Kuwait because the customs administration believed that these ports were the origin of most of the smuggling.[17]

In August 1926 the Residency Agent at Sharjah, reported that the Trucial shaykhs were growing angry about the molestation of Arab dhows at the hands of Iranian customs patrols, and were considering retaliating by seizing Iranian boats.[18] In accordance with the British-sponsored treaties, when a ruler's dependent was attacked he was obligated to refrain from retaliation, and instead notify the British Resident at Bushehr through his Residency Agent at Sharjah or notify the British naval officers who patrolled the Gulf waters. The British were expected to arbitrate the dispute, punish the offender, and exact compensation – something they had done numerous of times on behalf of the shaykhs.[19] Thus, the threat of retaliation that surfaced in August 1926 was for the shaykhs, a means of exerting strong pressure on the British to fulfill their obligation to arbitrate disputes and protect Arab shipping. The British Resident warned the Trucial shaykhs to restrain their men and not retaliate; but despite that, one of the dependents of Shaykh Sa'id bin Maktum, the Ruler of Dubai, took matters into his own hands.

The Struggle for Hengam

Hengam (Henjam in Modern Standard Arabic, or Henyam in Gulf Arabic), located just two kilometers southwest of Qeshm Island, is an Iranian island that had been inhabited by Arabs from the Al Bu Falasa section of the Bani Yas tribal confederation since 1857. They had migrated to Hengam at a time when Muscat leased the island from the Qajar government, and had remained there after the lease ended.[20] They had intermarried with the Bani Yas of the Trucial Coast and their commercial ventures were interconnected with that

[17] FO 416/79: Persian Foreign Office to His Britannic Majesty's Legation at Tehran, *Tir* 15, 1305 (July 7, 1926).
[18] IOR/R/15/1/277: Residency Agent Sharjah ('Abd al-Latif) to the Political Resident, August 25, 1926.
[19] See Chapter 1. [20] See p. 30.

tribe. Despite the Iranian Naturalization Act that was passed in 1894, they had never acknowledged Iranian sovereignty over themselves or over Hengam Island.[21] The Shaykh of Hengam, Shaykh Ahmad bin ‘Ubayd bin Sa‘id, was the father-in-law and maternal uncle of Shaykh Sa‘id bin Maktum Al Maktum, the Ruler of Dubai. In 1926, Iran reestablished a customs house inside the British telegraph enclosure and posted Mirza ‘Abd al-Khaleq there as the customs mudir. An Iranian customs inspector at Bandar Abbas described him as an honest man, and said that his unwillingness to accept bribes annoyed both the British and Shaykh Ahmad.[22] Shaykh Ahmad resented the mudir's collection of customs fees, viewing it as an infringement on his authority, letting it be known that he rejected Iranian overlordship and that he viewed himself as a dependent of the Shaykh of Dubai.[23]

Tensions between Ahmad and the Iranian authorities escalated to open confrontation on April 13, 1927, when an Iranian customs officer stopped a dhow belonging to Ahmad and seized some of its cargo.[24] Shaykh Ahmad and his men tried to strike back against the customs patrol, but it got away from them. They stormed over to the customs house, killed the customs mudir, pulled down the Iranian flag, and began to tear down the structure. The commander of HMS *Lupin* sent a naval party ashore and upon seeing them disembark, the attackers returned to their village.[25] When he heard that Iran was planning its response, the shaykh advertised that he would resist any force

[21] FO 416/83: Lieutenant Colonel Sir L. Haworth to the Government of India, July 20, 1928.

[22] Mohammad ‘Ali Nikbin Tehrani, Customs Inspector of Bandar Abbas, to *Sartip* Habibollah Khan Sheybani, Chief of the Army General Staff, July 3, 1928, in *Faslnameh-ye Motala‘at-e Tarikhi* 7, no. 25 (Spring 1388/2009), pp. 203–206; For an admission by the British to the statement of Mohammad ‘Ali Nikbin, see IOR/R/15/1/282: SNOPG to Political Resident, August 28, 1928.

[23] Al-‘Aydarus, *al-Juzur al-‘Arabiyya wa-l-ihtilal al-Irani namudhaj lil-‘alaqat al-‘Arabiyya al-Iraniyya*, Vol. 2, p. 47.

[24] FO 416/80: Intelligence Summary No. 8, for the Period ending April 16, 1927; Mohammad ‘Ali Nikbin Tehrani, Customs Inspector of Bandar Abbas, to *Sartip* Habibollah Khan Sheybani, Chief of the Army General Staff, July 3, 1928, in *Faslnameh-ye Motala‘at-e Tarikhi* 7, no. 25 (Spring 1388/2009), pp. 203–206.

[25] FO 371/11503: Secretary to the Resident to the Minister Tehran, April 14, 1927.

dispatched against him and, in the last event, would migrate with his followers to the Trucial Coast.[26]

It took an entire year for Iran to mount its response, but when it came it was a crushing blow to the shaykh's autonomy on Hengam Island. On May 10, 1928, Iran sent a detachment of soldiers to Hengam.[27] As they landed, the clerk inside the telegraph enclosure assured the commanding officer that the British government recognized Hengam as an Iranian island and that the shaykh would not be granted asylum in the enclosure or any assistance from the British whatsoever.[28] Initially, after hearing that he would have no British support, the shaykh sent a message to the commander of Iranian troops to the effect that he was ready to submit to Iranian authority, when in fact, preparations were underway to sneak away with his men and a number of women to Khassab, on the Musandam Peninsula.[29] In the hasty retreat, about 200 women and children were left behind. The Iranian garrison, now stationed at Hengam, did not permit the women to follow their husbands and they effectively became hostages in the hands of the Iranian army.[30]

When news of Iran's occupation of Hengam reached the coast, the Bani Yas went into an uproar. To further exacerbate matters, the officer commanding Iranian troops at Hengam advertised that Iran's next move would be the occupation of Ras al-Khaimah, (Greater) Tunb, and Abu Musa, a threat that particularly infuriated the Qasimi tribesmen of Ras al-Khaimah and Sharjah. Shaykh Ahmad, from his exile in Khassab, sent urgent letters to Shaykh Hashr Al Maktum who served as the Acting Ruler of Dubai, while his brother, Shaykh Sa'id, was away on the pilgrimage. In his letters, Ahmad proposed that all the Bani Yas of the mainland should help recover his island and women.[31] But Hashr, preferring a diplomatic course of action, turned to the Residency Agent at Sharjah, requesting permission to send an emissary to Bandar Abbas to negotiate with the governor there.[32] The Residency

[26] FO 416/83: Lieutenant Colonel Sir L. Haworth to the Government of India, July 20, 1928.
[27] Bahmani Qajar, "Naqsh-e Niru-ye Daryayi va Bayandor," p. 86.
[28] FO 416/82: Sir R. Clive to Sir Austen Chamberlain, May 11, 1928.
[29] Bahmani Qajar, *Tamamiyat-e Arzi-ye Iran*, p. 373.
[30] FO 416/83: Major Dickson to Lieutenant Colonel Sir L. Haworth, July 5, 1928.
[31] Ibid.
[32] FO 371/13065: Shaykh Hashr bin Maktum Dubai to the Residency Agent Sharjah, *Dhu al-Hijjah* 5, 1346 (May 25, 1928); Paraphrased Telegram from the

Agent, 'Isa bin 'Abd al-Latif, reminded Hashr that this would be a violation of the treaties and advised him to wait for instructions from the British Resident in Bushehr.[33] Hashr agreed to wait.[34]

Khan Bahadur 'Isa bin 'Abd al-Latif al-Serkal was a local businessman who served in the capacity of Residency Agent and functioned as the representative of the Political Resident to the Trucial shaykhs (1919–1935). His actual authority on the Trucial Coast was, perhaps, even greater than that of the individual rulers. He was the third member of his family to have served in this position, his father and his grandfather having held the position before him. He was responsible for interpreting Arabic for British officials, conveying messages from the Resident to the rulers, mediating disputes between rulers, and collecting debts owed to Indian merchants. He sent regular reports on Trucial affairs to the Resident and received instructions on how to handle each particular problem. He resided in Sharjah most of the year, but also had business investments in Ras al-Khaimah and Dubai. 'Isa's use and misuse of his position as Residency Agent enabled him to multiply his personal fortune and personal influence. Rumors suggested that he received annual protection subsidies from the rulers and also profited from debt collection. But because he did his job as an agent efficiently and as there was no obvious choice to replace him, the Resident retained him in spite of the misconduct that was revealed from time to time.[35]

In the immediate aftermath of Iran's reoccupation of Hengam, the British senior naval officer visited the Trucial Coast and Khassab and reported that the whole coast was in an uproar. The tribal inhabitants, he said, were particularly angry that the British had denied Shaykh Ahmad protection in the telegraph enclosure. He also reported that the men of Dubai wanted revenge: "they state that if it were not for British gunboats, they would come in the thousands, seize Qeshm Island and Hengam, and kill every Persian on the islands," he warned.[36] They also

Resident in the Persian Gulf to the Secretary of State for the Colonies, June 13, 1928 (received 3.36 am).

33 FO 371/13065: Residency Agent Sharjah to the Political Resident, May 28, 1928.

34 FO 371/13065: Shaykh Hashr bin Maktum Dubai to the Residency Agent Sharjah, *Dhu al-Hijjah* 7, 1346 (May 27, 1928).

35 Zahlan, *The Origins of the United Arab Emirates*, pp. 28–30.

36 FO 371/13065: Resident in the Persian Gulf to the Secretary of State for the Colonies, June 13, 1928 (received 3.36 am).

threatened that unless they obtained satisfaction, they would send parties to murder every Iranian official on the Iranian coast and would kill every Iranian on the Arab coast as well.[37]

Shaykh Hashr explained to ‘Isa that, as Acting Ruler of Dubai, it was his duty to arrange a peace and return Shaykh Ahmad to Hengam. He proposed to mediate with Iran on behalf of Shaykh Ahmad. He said, “If the Persians refuse my advances, then I can take more forcible measures.”[38] His brother, Shaykh Jum‘a Al Maktum, threatened that if the British did nothing to help, the shaykhs were prepared to tear up the treaties, be done with the air route, and massacre all the Iranians that could be found on the Arab coast.[39] Hashr and Jum‘a’s reactions were clear indications that they viewed the situation through the lens of long-established custom according to which the ruler’s honor, repute, and adequacy as protector hung on his ability to either arbitrate a resolution to Ahmad’s dispute with Iran or exact compensation for the wrongs that were done to him.

‘Isa continued to restrain Hashr and Jum‘a, reminding them that a dialogue with Iranian officials would be a violation of the treaty commitments and ordered them to wait for instructions from the Resident. At the same time, ‘Isa urged the Resident to act in accordance with Britain’s commitments to the shaykhdoms lest Britain should lose its standing on the coast. The Resident, in agreement with ‘Isa, attempted to persuade his superiors that Britain was obligated by her treaties to act as intermediary with the Iranian government on behalf of the shaykhs.[40] But this was to no avail. He was informed that the British government viewed Hengam as an Iranian island, that the treaties with the Trucial shaykhs did not pertain to Hengam and that Shaykh Ahmad should be encouraged to settle the matter himself with the Iranian authorities.[41]

The Iranian officer commanding troops at Hengam engaged in various efforts to compel Shaykh Ahmad to submit to Iranian

[37] Ibid.
[38] FO 416/83: Major Dickson to Lieutenant Colonel Sir L. Haworth, July 5, 1928.
[39] Ibid.
[40] FO 371/13065: Political Resident in the Persian Gulf to the Secretary of State for the Colonies, June 13, 1928; Sir Lionel Haworth to Sir Deny Bray, June 21, 1928.
[41] FO 371/13065: Viceroy, Foreign and Political Department to the Secretary of State for India, June 18, 1928; Secretary of State for the Colonies to the Political Resident in the Persian Gulf, June 19, 1928.

authority, sending letters both to him and to the subordinate shaykhs of Hengam offering them safety (*aman*) if they would return to Hengam. By this time, Shaykh Sa'id, the Ruler of Dubai, was on his way back from Mecca. The steamship that he traveled on stopped at Lingah where he was visited in his cabin by a prominent merchant and a close friend who urged him not to let Ahmad accept the Iranian overtures from the officer. According to the friend, the Iranians intended to arrest him just as they had done with Khaz'al Khan, the Shaykh of Mohammerah.[42]

On June 30, Shaykh Sa'id reached Dubai and took charge of the situation. In a long meeting together with his brothers, Hashr and

Figure 5 Shaykhs Jum'a bin Maktum and Sa'id bin Maktum Al Maktum.
Source: Wikipedia Commons.

[42] FO 416/83: Major Dickson to Lieutenant Colonel Sir L. Haworth, July 5, 1928.

Figure 6 The senior naval officer, the Shaykh of Dubai, the Shaykh of Hengam, and their entourages.
Source: National Maritime Museum, Greenwich, London.

Jum'a, Sa'id endeavored to explain the dilemma to the Assistant Resident, Major Dickson. He said that if his treaty forbade him to deal with any foreign power except through the British that the British were then obligated to arbitrate for him on behalf of Shaykh Ahmad. If they would not do that, he explained, as Ahmad's protector, he was obligated to act as intermediary and negotiate with Iran. Sa'id also explained that he and the merchants of Dubai had invested a good deal of money in Shaykh Ahmad and the pearl divers of Hengam and that their boats, about 40 in number, were high and dry at Hengam during the pearling season.[43] He pressed the British to use their good offices with Iran to at least secure the release of the women and property:

Surely you English must look after the interest of an Arab of the Trucial Coast if he gets in trouble on the Persian side, for we are under your protection. Similarly if a Persian is ill-treated on the Arab side, you English will, of course, settle the matter and will not allow Persia

[43] Ibid.

to interfere. [Therefore] you must at least offer your good offices to Sheikh Ahmad and his Dubai nationals now [that] he is in trouble with Persia.[44]

It was during this meeting that the shaykhs reiterated their threat to reciprocate Iran's treatment of the Trucial Arabs by targeting the Iranian nationals residing in Dubai: if Ahmad was not permitted to hold property on Hengam Island, they said, "we will make a law and confiscate the houses and property of all Persians in Dubai – we have 2,000 of them."[45] If Ahmad were to accept the Iranians' offer to return, the reciprocal principal would apply, Jum'a explained. He said that if Ahmad were to return to Hengam and be harmed by the Iranians, the Bani Yas of the mainland could not be restrained from taking revenge. "We know our mandate (*na'raf taklifna*)" he said. The Bani Yas would attack both Hengam and also the Iranian immigrant community of Dubai.[46]

The Seizure of an Arab Dhow off the Coast of Greater Tunb

In the beginning of July 1928, an Iranian customs patrol, which, unbeknownst to the British or to the Trucial Arabs had been operating near Greater Tunb, seized an Arab dhow near the southern coast of the island. It was taken, together with its cargo and passengers, to Lingah.[47] The dhow was from Dubai and flew the Trucial flag.[48] The British immediately began addressing sharp letters to Tehran, focusing on the status of Tunb: the seizure of an Arab dhow, carried out under the orders of Iranian authorities in the territorial waters of an island claimed

[44] Ibid. [45] Ibid. [46] Ibid.

[47] The sources differ as to the date of the capture. Shaykh Sa'id bin Maktum reported that it occurred on July 6 (*Muharram* 18, 1347). The officials of the Iranian customs office involved reported that the capture occurred on July 7 (*Tir* 16, 1307). The SNOPG believed that it occurred around July 20. For the Iranian report see, Finance Ministry to the Ministry of Foreign Affairs, *Shahrivar* 30, 1307 (September 19, 1928), in *Gozideh-ye Asnad-e Khalij-e Fars*, Vol. 1, p. 328; for Shaykh Sa'id's report, see Shaykh Sa'id bin Maktum to the Residency Agent Sharjah, *Rabi' al-Awwal* 21, 1347 (September 7, 1928), IOR/R/15/1/282; see also SNOPG to Admiralty, July 30, 1928, FO 371/13009.

[48] IOR/R/15/1/288: Shaykh Sa'id bin Maktum to Residency Agent Sharjah ('Abd al-Latif), *Rabi' al-Awwal* 21, 1347 (August 6, 1928).

by an Arab shaykh was a challenge to the Trucial shaykh's claim to ownership of the island.[49] The Iranian government held that the seizure of the boat was justified because it was carrying smuggled sugar and because it viewed Tunb and Abu Musa as inseparable parts of Iranian territory.[50]

When news of the captured dhow reached the Trucial Coast, it caused great agitation, increasing the hostility against the Iranian nationals that had already been ignited by Iran's occupation of Hengam. Initial reports circulated on the Trucial Coast that there were 15 or 16 women on board the dhow and that they were taken to Lingah and robbed of their jewels, their money, and even their clothes.[51] The Arabs, especially the husbands of the women believed to be in Iran's hands, demanded the dispatch of three armed dhows to rescue the seized vessel and attack the Iranian customs vessel operating against their shipping.[52] Shaykh Sa'id restrained them, but demanded British assistance and protection, in accordance with the terms of the "Exclusive Agreement" of 1892 and Lord Curzon's address to his father in 1903, of which he held a copy.[53] He pointed out that the British were accustomed to punishing the Arabs quickly when they committed an act of aggression at sea and demanded an equally quick response to this aggression committed by the Iranians.[54] Day after day passed with no news about the women presumed to be in captivity and the possibility of an outbreak loomed large. 'Isa moved from his home at Sharjah to a temporary residence in Dubai to keep tabs on the situation and urge Sa'id to keep his people restrained.[55] Britain's senior naval officer in the Persian Gulf delivered the message to Sa'id that the British minister in Tehran was

[49] FO 371/13009: Viceroy, Foreign and Political Department to the Secretary of State for India, August 4, 1928.

[50] In Iranian diplomatic correspondences, "Tunb" refers to Greater Tunb Island. FO 371/13010: Acting Minister of Foreign Affairs (Pakravan) to His Majesty's Chargé d'Affaires (Parr), *Amerdad* 30, 1307 (August 21, 1928).

[51] IOR/R/15/1/282: SNOPG to CinCEI, July 30, 1928.

[52] IOR/R/15/1/282: SNOPG to Political Resident, July 31, 1928.

[53] IOR/R/15/1/282: SNOPG to CinCEI, July 30, 1928.

[54] FO 371/13009: Political Resident to Secretary of State for India, August 2, 1928.

[55] IOR/R/15/1/280: SNOPG to CinCEI, August 17, 1928.

demanding the immediate release of the women and their property.[56] Nevertheless, time passed without result and it was believed that the only thing that kept the Arabs restrained was their fear of the guns of British ships.[57] When the British learned that the husbands of the women aboard the captured dhow were preparing to raid the property of Iranians, a British gunboat arrived just in time to deter the raid. The Resident arranged for a gunboat to remain at Dubai to keep tabs on the situation and relay messages about what was being done in Tehran.[58]

Meanwhile, a similar incident proved instructive to the shaykhs who were reassessing the efficacy of British Persian Gulf policy. The seizure of an Arab dhow by Iranian officials near Sirri Island was resolved forthwith in the spring of 1928 when the Shaykh of Qatar sidestepped British authorities and warned the Iranian officials in Lingah that he would retaliate against Iranian owned dhows in his harbor if the incident were not settled satisfactorily. The dispute was promptly resolved and news traveled fast. The British Resident in Bushehr observed that the Arabs must have noticed the difference in speed with which results were obtained through threat of force as opposed to British mediation.[59]

The ongoing acquiesce to the British on the part of the ruling Shaykh of Dubai severely undermined his authority in the eyes of his people. The wealthy and influential merchants of his shaykhdom, who were increasingly viewing the British as a rival to their own influence on the ruler, urged Sa'id to cancel the treaties and eject the British from Dubai's affairs. One merchant in particular, Muhammad bin Ahmad bin Dalmuk Al Falasi, led the effort to pressure Sa'id to cancel the British treaties and pushed for a military campaign against Iran.[60] He was a member of the Al Bu Falasa clan, and rumored to be the

[56] IOR/R/15/1/282: SNOPG to Political Resident, August 5 and 7, 1928.
[57] IOR/R/15/1/282: SNOPG *Triad* to Political Resident and CinCEI, August 5, 1928.
[58] IOR/R/15/1/282: Secretary of State for India to Political Resident, August 3, 1928; and Political Resident to the Government of India, August 6, 1928.
[59] IOR/R/15/1/282: Political Resident to the Foreign Secretary to the Government of India Simla, June 17, 1929.
[60] IOR/R/15/1/280: SNOPG to CinCEI, August 17, 1928.

wealthiest pearl merchant in Dubai. He was known for his hostility toward the British since the *Hyacinth* incident of 1910 (which had targeted his father).[61] He also shared family ties with one of the propertied Arabs of Hengam, Muhammad bin Hamad bin Dalmuk, who in the midst of the troubles with Iran, quit the island and resettled his family in Ras al-Khaimah.[62]

Muhammad bin Ahmad allied himself with the Rashid branch of the Al Bu Falasa clan. Sa'id's uncle, Shaykh Rashid bin Maktum, was a former Ruler of Dubai (1886–1894) and his sons, Shaykh Mani' bin Rashid and Shaykh Hashr bin Rashid, constituted the main challenge to Shaykh Sa'id's leadership position. The Rashid branch of the ruler's family were joined in their opposition by the Butti branch, comprised of the sons of the former ruler, Butti bin Suhayl (1906–1912) as well as other merchants who belonged to the Al Bu Falasa section of the Bani Yas tribe, such as Muhammad bin Ahmad and Muhammad bin Bayat.[63] The Al Bu Falasa oppositionists, headed by Shaykh Sa'id's cousins, expressed their advice and grievances through the ruler's majlis.

The ruler's majlis functioned like a barometer giving an indication of how much consent the ruler enjoyed as the manager of the tribe's affairs. Customarily, it also functioned like an advisory body because to maintain his position of authority, the ruler needed to be guided by the advice of the elites on which his authority depended. A loss of support from the men in the ruler's informal majlis was an indication that the ruler's position was insecure. Traditionally, if the ruler were to lose the confidence of his majlis, or a large enough faction of it, he would be vulnerable to a palace coup and his leadership position would be captured by one of his male relatives. Informed by history and custom, Shaykh Sa'id, the Ruler of Dubai, believed that to remain in his leadership position, he needed to placate the objections of the anti-British faction that was coalescing in his majlis around his cousin, Shaykh Mani' bin Rashid. Satisfying their objections depended on his ability to compel the British to fulfil their obligation as protector and,

[61] See Chapter 1.
[62] Administration Report of the Persian Gulf Residency for the Year 1929, p. 47.
[63] Mohammad Morsy Abdullah, "Changes in the Economy and Political Attitudes, and the Development of Culture on the Coast of Oman between 1900 and 1940," *Arabian Studies* 2 (1975), pp. 126, 167–178.

in doing so, demonstrate to his dependents the advantage of remaining under British protection.

In the end of the summer, Shaykh Sa'id still held out hope that he could induce the British to fulfill their treaty obligations. This is reflected is the statements that he and his brothers made to Captain Boyes, the British senior naval officer, on August 9, 1928. Boyes represented their statements as follows:

> The Persians are claiming everything in the Gulf now; if we were not bound by the treaties we should send armed parties and deal with them properly, as our fathers did; but we have the treaties and we may not deal with another nation except through the Great Government; you have punished us quickly enough in the past when we have not kept to the treaties, now let us see you keep to them and help us as quickly as you used to punish us; we applied to you for help in the case of our blood relative, the Sheikh of Henjam, three months ago, nearly, and so far as we can see you have done nothing about it. These matters are the first in which we have asked for British help. The British Government until now has had its rights and privileges from the treaties, now let us see how it regards its responsibilities, and if it does not act in the way we say it ought to, then we will finish with the British Government and finish with the treaties. If you give way before the Persians it means that you are becoming a weak Power, and for a weak Power, we have no use. When asked what they would do if they finished with the treaties they at once got very excited, and shouted: "Never you mind! That is our business. We have our plan all ready made up, and it will be all right, but it is our business and not yours, and we shall not tell you anything about that." They pointed out that the whole Trucial Coast was watching events to see what the British Government would and could do. They said: "So far we have had only promises from you – promises – promises – promises. When are we going to see some actions." The difficulty of working through diplomatic channels was again explained to them, and they promised to be patient a little longer, but pointed out that a sheikh rules by personality and not a powerful police force, and if they cannot show results to their people very soon their power will go, and in spite of all their efforts their men will break out and probably leave the port in dhows at night.[64]

The following day, Captain Boyes sent word to Shaykh Sa'id that the dhow and passengers had been released. This gave cause for hope that the situation on the Trucial Coast would settle down; however, rumors

[64] IOR/R/15/1/280: SNOPG to CinCEI, August 17, 1928.

soon reached Dubai that the Iranian customs officials had confiscated all they had and dispersed them in Lingah in a state of beggary.[65] The British notified Sa'id that they were seeking pecuniary compensation from Tehran for the seizure of the dhow and for the goods that were confiscated.[66] But two unresolved issues remained – the fate of the women detained at Hengam and the compensation for the dhow that was seized near the coast of Tunb.

Iranian officials tried to make a direct connection with the Ruler of Dubai through Hawala merchants who maintained connections on both sides of the Gulf. On August 13, a letter was received in Dubai from a merchant at Lingah saying that the Iranian director of customs proposed to come in a steam launch to interview Sa'id about the incident; when Sa'id received the communication through the Hawala merchant residing in Dubai he refused the proposition, informed the British, and Captain Boyes ordered his patrols at Dubai to prevent any Iranian officials from coming ashore.[67]

Captain Boyes learned that Shaykh Sa'id wished to visit his uncle, Ahmad, who had now moved to Bukha. He offered to bring Sa'id to Bukha in the HMS *Triad* and the shaykh accepted his offer. However, on August 19, the night before the *Triad* arrived, the shaykh's informal majlis convened and the shaykh was persuaded not to board the British warship.[68] The opinion of the majlis was summarized as follows:

We have had British warships anchored off Dubai now for three weeks; the people are expecting an answer about the inhabitants of Hanjam and about [compensation for] the captured dhow. They see the warships continually changing but there is always one here; they come and go but never do we get any answer from them; the Shaikh goes off to the ships but never brings any answer back; the people are getting tired of it all and are beginning to doubt; either the Shaikh is telling lies or else the British Government is unable to do anything for us; if the people see the Shaikh go away in the British man-of-war, the people will at once say he has been sent for to make a formal

[65] Ibid.

[66] IOR/R/15/1/282: HMS *Lupin* to Political Resident at Shiraz, August 7, 1928; IOR/R/15/1/280: SNOPG to CinCEI, August 17, 1928.

[67] IOR/R/15/1/282: SNOPG to the Political Resident, August 13, 1928; IOR/R/15/1/280: SNOPG to CinCEI, August 17, 1928.

[68] IOR/R/15/1/282: SNOPG to the Political Resident, August 22, 1928.

settlement of both matters, and then when he comes back with no answer the patience of the people will give out and there will be riots and all sorts of trouble.[69]

The shaykh left for Bukha in his own boat after requesting that the British warships be withdrawn so as not to arouse the expectations of the people until there was good news to communicate.[70]

In early September, Iranian officials managed to insert some misinformation about the dhow incident into a Basra newspaper, *The Times of Mesopotamia*, which further inflamed the Arabs of the coast.[71] The article purported to quote an official statement by the British minister in Tehran on the result of investigations into the incident. It said that, according to the investigations, the owner of the dhow was an Iranian subject; furthermore, the cargo was contraband and therefore justifiably confiscated. The article inferred that the investigation was final and that the case was closed.[72] While it was true that the Iranian government claimed the owner of the dhow as an Iranian national, it was not true that the British government had accepted this claim or closed the case. The senior naval officer paid an urgent visit to ʻIsa to tell him that the article was false, hoping he could do some damage control among the Arabs on the coast. He was further asked to collect evidence as to the names, tribes, and places of residence of the owner of the dhow, and its captain, crew, and passengers, to contest Iran's claim that the dhow was owned by an Iranian national.[73]

Around this time, a government circular was issued stating that Iran recognized no Arab rulers on the southern littoral and that all persons belonging to and arriving from Muscat, Qatar, the Trucial Coast, Kuwait, and Bahrain were to be considered as Iranian subjects and issued Iranian passports.[74] It was according to that logic, that ʻOtayba bin Rashid, the dhow's nakhoda, and Badr bin Muhammad, the

[69] SNOPG to Political Resident, August 23, 1928, quoted in Abdullah, *The United Arab Emirates*, pp. 259–260.
[70] Ibid.
[71] IOR/R/15/1/282: SNOPG to the Political Resident, Persian Gulf, September 10, 1928.
[72] IOR/R/15/1/282: SNOPG to the Political Resident, October 29, 1928, with enclosure, "Persians and Arabs in the Persian Gulf."
[73] IOR/R/15/1/282: SNOPG to the Political Resident, September 10, 1928.
[74] IOR/R/15/1/282: Political Resident at Shiraz to Government of India Simla, September 17, 1928.

dhow's owner, despite being Arabs of the Bani Yas tribe, were being treated by Iranian port officials as Iranian citizens.

Shaykh Sa'id provided a statement in which he affirmed that the owner, nakhoda, and female passengers were all Arabs of the Bani Yas tribe and residents of Dubai "since the time of their fathers and grandfathers."[75] Iran's claim – that the other male passengers were Iranian citizens – was not contested. Sa'id stressed the insulting nature of the incident and reminded the British of their duty to obtain compensation:

The Arabs do not agree to their women being captured by the Persians at sea and kept in Lingah creek as a show. We are very thankful and grateful [for their release]. But the detention of a boat at Lingah for such a period is surprising. And as the British government had on several occasions, taken fines from the Arabs when they transgressed at sea, the government should now take it for us from the Persians.[76]

Meanwhile, efforts to obtain compensation for the dhow seized off the coast of Tunb were impeded due to Iran's claim to sovereignty over the island. Shaykh Selim bin Sultan, the Ruler of Ras al-Khaimah was asked to produce documents verifying his ownership of the island, but conclusive documents could not be found. His blunt statement on the matter, summarized by the British senior naval officer, is particularly illustrative of the shifting perceptions along the Trucial Coast:

What is all this business of having to find documents to prove that Tanb belongs to me? When you wanted to put a lighthouse on Tanb you had no doubt in your mind about who owned it because you asked the Sheikh of the Qawasim tribe for permission; you would not have asked him if anybody else owned it. What is happening to England these days? You seem to be frightened of Persia. If you are not frightened of Persia, why don't you tell them honestly to mind their own business or else you [will] punish them the same as you would punish me. If you are frightened of Persia, it means that you are no longer any good as a nation and the Trucial treaties are no longer worth anything. Why do you argue with the Persians? From what I hear, Persia thinks she has become a big nation and as is good as England. If that is so, then England must be a really small nation. Why do you not go to war

[75] IOR/R/15/1/282: Shaykh Sa'id bin Maktum Dubai to the Residency Agent Sharjah, *Rabi' al-Awwal* 21, 1347 (September 7, 1928).
[76] Ibid.

with these Persians and finish with them? Is England just a bully that can hit a small people like a coast[al] tribe, but is afraid of Persia?[77]

The senior naval officer replied, saying that Britain had fought and won the Great War and was now determined to exercise patience to prevent bloodshed. The shaykh responded, acknowledging the wisdom of avoiding bloodshed, but reiterating his firm belief that this policy was motivated by fear, and uttering what he felt was the most pressing question: "How much more of the Gulf will you give up to the Persians?"[78]

For the shaykhs who were constantly evaluating and reevaluating the regional power equation and their own place in it, the fate of the Shaykh of Hengam was particularly worrying. By mid-September 1929, the British gave Shaykh Sa'id a final answer on the matter of Shaykh Ahmad, saying that the British government would not arbitrate his case, nor would it allow Sa'id to arbitrate. Ahmad, they said, would need to face the Iranian officials on his own.[79] Thus, Shaykh Ahmad was faced with two dim prospects – that of abandoning the women and property at Hengam or negotiating with Iran. The Iranian officer commanding troops at Hengam had been sending messages to Shaykh Ahmad, inviting him to return and promising the abolition of the customs house. Finally, the shaykh replied saying that he would accept the offer if he had a repetition of the promise from Tehran.[80] After that, two Iranian envoys from Hengam went to Bukha and invited the shaykh and all his people, except the actual murderers, to return to Hengam.[81] On September 20, Ahmad sent two representatives to Hengam to negotiate the terms.[82] An agreement was reached and Ahmad and his men returned. According to the agreement, the government would reestablish a customs post at Hengam. If after three months its revenues did not justify its existence, Ahmad would be allowed to run his own customs

77 IOR/R/15/1/282: SNOPG to the Political Resident, September 10, 1928.
78 Ibid.
79 FO 371/13066: Political Resident in the Persian Gulf to the Foreign Secretary to the Government of India, September 14, 1928.
80 IOR/R/15/1/282: SNOPG to Political Resident, August 28, 1928.
81 FO 371/13066: SNOPG to the Political Resident, September 15, 1928.
82 FO 371/13066: Political Resident to the Government of India, September 20, 1928.

on payment of a fixed amount to the government.[83] It was no matter that British lawyers were still trying to figure out the question of Ahmad's nationality: in the eyes of the Arabs, this arrangement amounted to Ahmad's submission to Iranian overlordship.[84]

Six months later, an attempt to overthrow Shaykh Sa'id was orchestrated by the opposition within his family. Given the strength of anti-British sentiment in Dubai, the coup attempt was an event that Sa'id anticipated; however, what he did not foresee was the way in which British support and the changing economic circumstances in Dubai would allow him to survive the predicament despite a lack of support from influential members of his family. Throughout the crises of 1928–1929, Shaykh Sa'id had repeatedly warned the British that their refusal to arbitrate on his behalf had completely undermined his authority and that his adherence to the treaties, which his people now considered worthless, had cost him the support of powerful families of Dubai.[85] His ongoing support for the British in matters that hurt their pocketbooks – particularly his support for the collection of debts owed by leading merchants to the Indian financiers – coalesced into the uprising of April 1929. The uprising, orchestrated by Muhammad bin Ahmad bin Dalmuk, had the aim of making his son-in-law, Shaykh Mani', ruler while Shaykh Sa'id was away on a trip to the hinterland. Citing a letter to the majlis, in which Sa'id offered to resign for the good of the tribe, Muhammad bin Ahmad persuaded the tribal elders to accept Shaykh Mani' as his replacement.[86] Ultimately, the coup was reversed by the intervention of 'Isa, the Residency Agent employed by the British, and the arrival to the town of Bedouin tribesmen who came to show their support for Shaykh Sa'id.[87] By summertime, the full

[83] Bushire Residency Diary (Persian) No. 8 for the Month of October 1928, in *Political Diaries of the Arab World: Persian Gulf*, Vol. 8, pp. 178–179.

[84] IOR/R/15/1/282: Political Resident to Senior Naval Officer, August 29, 1928; SNOPG to Political Resident, September 10, 1928.

[85] FO 371/13066: SNOPG to the Political Resident, September 15, 1928; Obaid A. Butti, "Imperialism, Tribal Structure, and the Development of Ruling Elites: A Socio-Economic History of the Trucial States between 1892 and 1939," PhD dissertation (Georgetown University, 1992), p. 166.

[86] Said, "The 1938 Reform Movement in Dubai," p. 250.

[87] Fatma al-Sayegh, "Merchants' Role in a Changing Society: The Case of Dubai, 1900–1990," *Middle Eastern Studies* 34, no. 1 (January 1998), pp. 87–102; Zahlan, *The Origins of the United Arab Emirates*, p. 54; Abdullah, *The United Arab Emirates*, pp. 126–127.

nature of the opposition's grievances was laid bare: 60 of Dubai's pearling boats were unable to proceed to the pearling banks because the debt-ridden merchants were not able to obtain advance payments necessary to buy supplies. The leaders of the opposition that had tried to unseat Shaykh Sa'id were on the verge of bankruptcy, including Muhammad bin Ahmad bin Dalmuk, Muhammad bin Bayat, and Shaykh Mani'.

The closing years of the 1920s were marked by a tangible sense on the Trucial Coast that Iran was gaining influence and British power was waning. Rumors circulated that Iran was preparing to evict the British from Bahrain and Basidu.[88] There were reports that ships' captains were being ordered to pull down their Arab flags and hoist Iran's flag when entering the port at Lingah. Residents of the Arab shaykhdoms who tried to enter Iranian ports with British travel documents were imprisoned and their travel documents were torn up.[89] Iranian officials continued to seize boats suspected of smuggling, often leading to harsh treatment and humiliation of the passengers.[90] By the end of 1929, the Resident reported that owing to these difficulties, maritime traffic between Iranian and Arab ports had been reduced to a minimum.[91] The apparent weakness of the British was among the reasons given for the harsh resistance of the Trucial shaykhs to providing facilities for a British air route along the southern littoral.[92] The introduction of the Iranian navy in 1932 and the nationalist zeal of its captains and crews would further intensify the fears in the shaykhdoms that Iranian military men were capable of violent aggression and they had little confidence that the British government would "see them through" in the event of an incident.[93]

[88] IOR/R/15/1/282: British Consular Agency Lingah to the Political Resident, August 17, 1928; Political Resident to Minster at Tehran, September 17, 1928.
[89] Mr. Knatchbull-Hugessen to Sir John Simon, December 15, 1934, in *British Documents on Foreign Affairs*, Vol. 27, p. 223.
[90] Summary of News from the Arab States for the Months of April, May, and June 1928, in *Political Diaries of the Arab World: Persian Gulf,* Vol. 7, p. 90.
[91] Administration Report of the Persian Gulf Residency for the Year 1929, p. 5.
[92] IOR/R/15/1/282: Political Resident to Government of India Simla, August 23, 1929.
[93] Administration Report of the Persian Gulf Residency for the Year 1932, p. 58. See also Report of a tour on the Trucial Coast by the Officiating Political Agent, Bahrain from September 22 to 27, 1934, IOR/R/15/1/280.

Dubai-Iran Relations in the 1930s

Compensation to the victims of the 1928 dhow incident was not forthcoming until March 1930, and ultimately it was the government of India – not Iran – that footed the bill.[94] These events taught Shaykh Sa'id an important lesson about the efficiency of British mediation. From that point forward the shaykh began to display a strong preference for finding local solutions to local problems. In future incidents concerning Iran, he increasingly availed himself of Iranian offers for direct cooperation.

Iran renewed its offers of friendship to the ruling Shaykh of Dubai. This was fostered by an impression in Iran that the various shaykhs of the southern littoral could be "attracted to the side of Iran."[95] Moreover, there was considerable substantiation of some rumors that Iranian officials had been instructed to cultivate direct communications with the shaykhs of the Trucial Coast without reference to Great Britain.[96] In May 1930, the British became aware that the Iranian Governor of Gulf Ports was sending letters to Shaykh Sa'id through an intermediary, asking for his help in settling some local matters, namely crimes involving persons of Iranian ancestry, whose families had long been settled in Dubai.[97]

Shaykh Sa'id was also asked to serve as the intermediary between Iran and the other shaykhs of the Trucial Coast. There was an organic connection between Iran and Dubai, owing to the large number of Iranian immigrants in Dubai and owing in particular to the wealth and proximity of some of them to the ruling family. This was reflected in a dispute that rose up in 1930 concerning two dhows that were owned at Ajman and detained at Lingah. The inspector of customs at Lingah sent a letter to Shaykh Sa'id through one of the influential merchants in Dubai. In the letter he described a proposal for resolving the situation

[94] IOR/R/15/1/282: Residency Agent Sharjah ('Abd al-Latif) to Secretary to the Political Resident (Fowle), March 20, 1930.

[95] See for example, Hajji Ra'is Hasan to Ministry of Foreign Affairs (Tehran), *Esfand* 9, 1311 (February 28, 1933), in *Gozideh-ye Asnad-e Khalij-e Fars*, Vol. 2, pp. 57–58; and Samaneh Bayrami, "Chalesh-e Iran va Engelestan bar sar-e Hakemiyyat bar Bahreyn," pp. 127–166.

[96] IOR/R/15/1/282: Shaykh Sa'id bin Hashr Al Maktum to 'Isa bin 'Abd al-Latif, *Jamada al-Ula* 22, 1347 (November 5, 1928); SNOPG to the Political Resident, August 13, 1928 and December 17, 1928.

[97] FO 416/86: Sir R. Clive to M. Foroughi, May 17, 1930.

and asked Sa'id to convey the message to the Shaykh of Ajman. To help persuade Shaykh Sa'id to play the role of the go-between, the Iranian customs inspectors allowed several motor dhows belonging to Sa'id to land cargo at Lingah without paying customs dues.[98]

Subsequently, when Dubai merchants became embroiled in fresh disputes with Iranian customs authorities, Sa'id negotiated directly with Iranian authorities, quietly and without reference to British authorities. In February 1934, for example, he engaged in correspondences with the Iranian authorities through an Iranian merchant whose business, Hajji Rais Hassan and Company, had branches in Dubai and Lingah. The complaint that Sa'id sent to the Lingah customs mudir, was on behalf of a Dubai merchant whose boats were molested by the customs officers at Lingah. Sa'id's direct appeal to Iran got the attention of the shah's Special Imperial Office, which directed the foreign ministry to provide the shaykh with a prompt response.[99] For the Iranian government, whose earlier request to have an Iranian consular agent in Dubai was refused by the British, this was viewed as a strategic opportunity to bypass the British and forge separate ties with the shaykhs of the southern littoral.[100]

Sa'id's dealings with Iran came to the attention of the British Resident in April 1936 when several of his letters to Iran were intercepted. The first was a letter addressed directly to the Iranian foreign minister in which Shaykh Sa'id appealed for help in bringing an absconded debtor to justice. He related how an Iranian national, a resident of Lar, had absconded from Dubai without paying his debts to merchants in Dubai and Abu Dhabi. He asked the foreign minister to instruct the police authorities to either assist in recovering the money or to send the man back to Dubai.[101] He had sent a copy of the letter to the superintendent of police in Lar expressing his confidence that the appeal to Tehran would produce results: "I have informed the Iranian Ministry

98 IOR/R/15/1/283: Extract from Letter Dated September 1930 from HMS *Lupin*, Henjam.

99 Superintendent Mohammad Navad Sa'adi to Ministry of Foreign Affairs, *Bahman* 23, 1312 (February 12, 1934); and Special Imperial Office to Ministry of Foreign Affairs, *Bahman* 30, 1312 (February 19, 1934), in *Gozideh-ye Asnad-e Khalij-e Fars*, Vol. 2, pp. 59–61.

100 See p. 88.

101 IOR/R/15/1/281: Translation of a letter dated *Muharram* 7, 1355 (March 30, 1936) from Shaykh Sa'id bin Maktum, Ruler of Dubai, to Iranian Minister of Foreign Affairs, Tehran.

of Foreign Affairs about Rahmatullah Ghaffari bin al-Hajj Muhammad 'Ali Lari who stealthily absconded from my town Dubai with the money of the people of my town and the people of Abu Dhabi," wrote Sa'id. He went on to say, "You will, no doubt, receive orders to use force against him."[102]

The correspondences, when discovered, earned Shaykh Sa'id a rebuke from the Political Agent in Bahrain, who warned him that the letters contravened his treaty with the British government, according to which he committed not to enter negotiations with any foreign power without the consent of the British. In regard to the absconder, he was informed that the British government would take up the case with Tehran to see what could be done about the matter.[103] Whether Shaykh Sa'id heeded the rebuke and broke his contact with Iran or found a more clandestine method of maintaining contact is a matter for conjecture, for truly clandestine communication leaves no paper trail. What can be said is that even while Dubai viewed Iran's expansionist policy and hyperactive activity in the Gulf as a threat to its interests, it preferred not to merely hide behind British protection, which came to be viewed as having limited worth; but rather, Dubai, as a state in the making, exhibited a pragmatic approach that did not rule out engaging directly with Iran in pursuit of its own interests.

Arabs, Iranians, and the Reform Movement of 1938

The demise of the pearling industry coupled with the worldwide economic depression of the 1930s proved disastrous for the pearl merchants of the Trucial States, most of whom were Sunni Arab tribesmen from the Al Bu Falasa clan. During the 1930s, new sources of revenue entered the coffers of the Trucial shaykhs in the form of rents paid by Imperial Airways for landing facilities in Sharjah in 1932 and Dubai in 1937; for oil exploration options in all the Trucial States in 1935 and 1936; and oil exploration concessions in 1937 in Dubai and Sharjah and in 1939 in Abu Dhabi. The rulers were thus possessed of a modest source of revenue that was independent of the

[102] IOR/R/15/1/281: Translation of a letter dated *Muharram* 7, 1355 (March 30, 1936) from Shaykh Sa'id bin Maktum, Ruler of Dubai, to the Superintendent of Police, Lar.

[103] IOR/R/15/1/281: Political Agent Bahrain (Loch) to Shaykh Sa'id bin Maktum, April 16, 1936.

traditional merchant elites. Moreover, the growing economic independence of the rulers was beginning to erode the delicate power-sharing arrangement between merchants and ruler that had characterized the shaykhdoms for more than a century.[104]

The depression had a less grave effect on the merchants of Iranian extraction whose fortunes were not dependent on the pearl industry. Hawala families, such as the Al Fahim family from Harmud in rural Laristan, made their livelihood in Abu Dhabi in the import and redistribution of foodstuffs and textiles. Muhammad Al Fahim describes in his memoir how his father and uncles prospered even when the pearl industry was in a slump by engaging in shipping, transporting, and trading goods between Abu Dhabi, Dubai, Lingah, and Bahrain.[105] Smuggling was a factor as well: merchants who had long-standing connections with Iran and who knew how to get around the stiff customs laws were in a position to profit.[106] During the 1930s, a tangible disparity grew up between the relative fortunes of merchants of Iranian extraction and local Arabs. Iranian merchants not only maintained a high standard of living but also enjoyed the patronage of the ruling families on account of the revenue they generated. An example is Mohammed Ra'is Rasul, an Iranian businessman who became a subject of disagreement between the British and the Al Bu Falasa opposition faction. The British wanted to deport him in 1938 on account of his frequent trafficking in arms while the tribal elders who opposed British interventions pressured Shaykh Sa'id to reverse the decision and allow him to remain in Dubai.[107] Mohammad Ra'is Rasul was an avowed Iranian nationalist who provided the Iranian government with intelligence reports about the Trucial Coast and excitedly advised it to exploit opportunities to come between the shaykhs and the British.[108] From the perspective of Shaykh Sa'id's cousins who wanted to unseat him, this was not an entirely unwelcome

104 Al-Sayegh, "Merchants' Role in a Changing Society," pp. 87–102.

105 Mohammed Al Fahim, *From Rags to Riches: A Story of Abu Dhabi* (1995; Repr., London: Centre for Arab Studies, 1996), pp. 49–53.

106 IOR/R/15/1/282: His Majesty's Chargé d'Affaires Tehran to Secretary of State for Foreign Affairs, August 9, 1928. See also Villiers, *Sons of Sinbad*, p. 297.

107 Administration Report of the Persian Gulf Residency for the Year 1938, p. 37.

108 See for example, Hajji Ra'is Hasan to Ministry of Foreign Affairs (Tehran), *Esfand* 9, 1311 (February 28, 1933), in *Gozideh-ye Asnad-e Khalij-e Fars*, Vol. 2, pp. 57–58.

scenario. They were staunchly opposed to the growth of British influence over the ruler and the way in which it curtailed tribal autonomy in local affairs, especially those that had a negative bearing on their finances.

The occasional expression of nationalism on the part of first- and second-generation Iranian immigrants to Dubai, gave the urban Arabs cause for resentment. This is illustrated in an episode that took place in April 1930 when some of the children of immigrants changed their clothes and put on Pahlavi caps and trousers.[109] According to the reports that arrived to the Political Resident, the Arab inhabitants of Dubai strongly objected to this and directed their appeal to Shaykh Sa'id personally. Sa'id responded by issuing a notice, warning that the wearing of Persian headgear was prohibited in his town and threatened to punish anyone who defied him.[110] "Anyone unwilling to obey," he warned, "should return to his home in Persia where he can wear what he likes."[111] A similar incident took place in Abu Dhabi in the fall of 1932: when the Iranian warships ordered from Italy arrived to the Persian Gulf, some of the residents of Abu Dhabi displayed Iranian flags on their houses in token of their rejoicing, until they were ordered by the Ruler of Abu Dhabi to remove their decorations immediately.[112]

For the tribal pearl merchants who suffered huge economic losses in the 1930s, the relative prosperity of the merchants of Iranian extraction who engaged in the sea trade was an ever-present reminder of their own reduced wealth and status. But the object of their indignation was the British imperial apparatus that had curtailed the privileges they believed were the natural rights of the ruling elite. Their grievances were expressed again by a second attempt to unseat Shaykh Sa'id in 1934 and a third attempt in 1938 during the course of the reform movement that gained the support of larger swathes of the population in Dubai. The reform movement of 1938, inspired by a similar movement in Kuwait and to a lesser extent the reform movement in Bahrain,

109 IOR/L/P&S/12/3792: Political Resident (Biscoe) to Minister at Tehran, May 13, 1930.
110 IOR/L/P&S/12/3792: Political Resident (Biscoe) to Minister at Tehran, April 29, 1930.
111 IOR/L/P&S/12/3792: Notice from Sa'id bin Maktum, *Shawwal* 21, 1348 (March 22, 1930).
112 IOR/R/15/2/488: Extract from Bushire Summary of News No. 11 of 1932 from the Arab States for the month of November 1932.

evinced a growing political awareness among the educated elites on the Trucial Coast.

The burning questions of income and privileges for the ruling family were highlighted in the clash that broke out in May 1938 when Shaykh Sa'id's son extended his taxi service into an area that was traditionally claimed by the brother of Shaykh Mani' bin Rashid.[113] The outbreak ended in a promise by Shaykh Sa'id to grant certain concessions to the Rashid faction, which led the internal opposition against Sa'id. These concessions included an end to the taxi monopoly. He also promised to consider giving a fixed allowance to the male members of the ruling family.[114] But soon it became clear that Sa'id did not intend to grant additional concessions, and he appealed to the British for armed intervention against his cousins.[115] The British Resident wrote to Sa'id urging him to save himself by enacting reforms, but Sa'id paid no heed, and by October fresh hostilities were again imminent. After a considerable trial of strength, Bahrain's new Political Agent, Hugh Weightman (1937–1940), conducted negotiations between the two sides and helped them reach an agreement – albeit an agreement that rendered Sa'id considerably less powerful.[116] The agreement allowed for the establishment of a formal majlis along the lines of the Kuwait model, to be composed of 15 members "elected" by the "principal people" of Dubai, which in practice turned out to be a homogenous group – namely the members of Shaykh Sa'id's opposition. Shaykh Mani' was to be the Majlis spokesperson and Shaykh Sa'id was to be the president; however, according to the agreement the president was forbidden from taking any action in any matter without the approval of the Majlis. Rents, taxes, and customs were to be considered state revenue, the expenditure of which was subject to the decisions of the Majlis. The shaykh's personal income was fixed at one-eighth of the total state revenue.

113 Intelligence Summary of the Political Agent Bahrain for the Period 16th May to 15th June 1938 in *Iran Political Diaries,* Vol. 13, pp. 111–114.

114 Intelligence Summary of the Political Agent Bahrain for the Period 16th to 30th June 1938 in *Iran Political Diaries,* Vol. 13, pp. 115–117.

115 IOR/L/P&S/12/3827: Political Resident to Shaykh Sa'id bin Maktum, October 1, 1938.

116 IOR/L/P&S/12/3827: Political Resident to the Secretary of State for India, November 8, 1938.

With its newfound authority the Dubai Majlis undertook a series of projects designed to enhance Dubai's commercial infrastructure, such as widening the roads and improving the shoreline. Shaykh Mani' portrayed the Majlis as a "reform movement" and depicted his role in it as a "national duty."[117] He was also quick to point out when Shaykh Sa'id skipped the assembly's meetings, calling into question the ruler's commitment to the people of Dubai.[118] It soon became evident that the "reformers," who were Al Bu Falasa tribesmen, viewed the Majlis as a means by which they could regain the influence and privileges that had been lost to them. This was implicit in a decision by the Majlis to allocate a fixed income from the state budget to each of its members and pensions to certain members of the ruling family. A tax for imported goods was decided upon – a measure that would mainly affect Dubai's merchants of Iranian origin, who monopolized the import trade.[119] To ensure its implementation, an Arab – a close relation of Shaykh Mani' – was appointed to replace the "Persian" director of customs.[120] The new Majlis busied itself with certain badly needed local reforms, including the reorganization of customs, provisions for law and order, and the establishment of schools in the town; however, it soon became clear that the profitable contracts were being granted to members of the Rashid faction. A British dispatch noted that "discontent began to show itself and gradually a feeling spread that for one despot there had merely been substituted a board of despotism."[121] A dispatch that went out from the Governor of Bandar Abbas to the authorities in Tehran lamented that, owing to what was described as a "coup," the Iranian merchants resident in Dubai had lost the influence they once exercised in local affairs.[122]

117 Rosemarie J. Said, "The 1938 Reform Movement in Dubai," *al-Abhath* 23, nos. 1–4 (December 1970), pp. 259 and 275.
118 IOR/L/P&S/12/3827: Agreement between the Shaykh of Dubai and Members of the Al Bu Falasa, October 20, 1938.
119 Intelligence Summary of the Political Agent Bahrain for the Period 1st to 15th November 1938 in *Iran Political Diaries,* Vol. 13, pp. 311–312.
120 Abdullah, *The United Arab Emirates*, p. 131.
121 IOR/L/P&S/12/3827: British Resident to the Secretary of State for India, April 20, 1939.
122 Ministry of the Interior to Ministry of Foreign Affairs, *Khordad* 6, 1318 (May 28, 1939) with enclosure, in *Gozideh-ye Asnad-e Khalij-e Fars*, Vol. 2, pp. 71–72.

When Sa'id saw that support for the British-imposed Majlis was lagging, he seized upon an opportunity to reverse his fortunes. On the occasion of his son's wedding, large numbers of armed tribesmen arrived in town, ostensibly to participate in the festivities, but soon, with their help, the opposition was routed and Dubai town was in Sa'id's hands. During the fighting, Mani' escaped with about a hundred men to Sharjah from whence he continued to intrigue against Shaykh Sa'id.[123] Consequently, the Majlis was stripped of its executive powers, and thenceforward its membership was regulated by Shaykh Sa'id. The opposition faction that had long troubled Sa'id was dispersed and he was left in full control of Dubai.[124]

The Trucial States on the Eve of the Second World War

The events of the interwar period had ushered in far-reaching changes for the Trucial shaykhdoms both internally and externally. Externally the shaykhdoms were affected by the rise of Iran in the regional power equation. Iran's nonrecognition of the independence of the Trucial shaykhs and its claims to sovereignty over their traditional tribal domains were challenges that fostered their unprecedented degree of reliance on British protection and an unprecedented degree of imperial intervention in the traditional tribal societies situated along the Gulf's southern perimeter. During these years, the British government enhanced its position on the Trucial Coast by means of a very heavy hand. By the end of the interwar period, Iran's reassertion of sovereignty in its southern coasts and islands had brought about the transfer of Britain's locus of control in the Gulf from the Iranian to the Arabian littoral.

British protection of the Arab shaykhdoms during the course of Iran's ascent engendered an unprecedented degree of intrusion into their internal affairs. The special relationship between the ruling shaykhs and the British government, which had formerly prospered under a considerable degree of consensus among the tribal elites, no longer enjoyed the benefit of tribal consensus. The special relationship

123 Intelligence Summary of the Political Agent Bahrain for the Period 16th to 30th March 1939, in *Iran Political Diaries,* Vol. 13, pp. 311–312.

124 IOR/L/P&S/12/3827: Political Resident to the Secretary of State for India, April 20, 1939.

persisted, not because of consensus but because of overwhelming British superiority. The ruling shaykhs' ongoing cooperation with the British government on different levels fueled severe opposition from within the ruling families and from Sunni tribal elites, whose consent and financial support had traditionally been vital to their staying power. But it was during the interwar years that the delicate power-sharing arrangement between the shaykhs and the merchants, which had characterized the shaykhdoms for more than a century, was irrevocably altered. The collapse of the pearl industry and the rise of independent sources of revenue for the rulers by means of air and oil concessions enabled the rulers to survive despite the flagging support for their personal rule from within their own families. The socio-economic and political transformations of the interwar years hampered the ability of the tribal elites to alter the policies that harmed their pocketbooks and diminished their traditional influence.

On the eve of the Second World War, the most successful merchant group in the Trucial States, from an economic perspective, was the group of Sunni merchants and traders of Iranian origin. The Hawala were the backbone of the region's long-distance trade. They were progressive, multilingual, and relatively open to Europe; whereas the Arab tribesmen, by and large, had not yet come to view trade as a desirable occupation. The transnational business links and entrepreneurial savvy of the Hawala merchants had kept their enterprises afloat while the fortunes and influence of the tribal elites were devastated by the collapse of the pearl market. By the end of the 1920s, many of the seasonal residents of Iranian extraction were pleased to establish their permanent homes in port towns such as Dubai, Sharjah, Ras al-Khaimah, and Abu Dhabi. In Dubai, large Iranian-style homes with their innovative wind towers situated along the creek bear witness to the historical events that had established Dubai as the home of Iran's largest diaspora community in the region.

Trucial Arabs' perceptions of Iran took a decisive turn for the worse during the interwar years. Encounters with expressions of Iranian nationalism and irredentism made a deep impression. The heavy-handed treatment of travelers from the Trucial Coast at the hands of zealous Iranian officials and the interference with and seizure of numerous dhows belonging to inhabitants of the shaykhdoms were episodes that became emblazoned in the memories of the rulers and inhabitants of the shaykhdoms. Iran's occupation of Hengam Island, which was claimed as a dependency of Dubai and inhabited by Arab tribesmen, was an event that would not be forgotten. On the eve of the Second World War, Iran's claims to sovereignty over Bahrain, Abu Musa, and the Tunbs, and its shadowy claims to suzerainty over the entire southern littoral, were real but remote antagonisms for which no resolution appeared on the horizon.

6 *Bahrain, Iran, and the British*

His Excellency Shaikh Hamad wishes me to draw your attention to a comparison of the conditions of his subjects residing in Persia and those of Persian nationals resident in Bahrain. Persians in Bahrain enjoy equal privileges and rights to the Shaikh's own subjects. They are allowed to have their own schools, which are notoriously hot-beds of anti-Bahrain propaganda, they occupy positions on councils, they sit on courts, they are at liberty to buy and possesses property, they are free to come and go and they are treated with justice and consideration, in fact with kindness. The lot of Baharna living in the Persian towns of Mohammerah, Qasbah etc. is very different. These people ... are deliberately oppressed by the Persian Government which makes every possible effort to force them to renounce their nationality.[1]

Charles Belgrave, advisor to Shaykh Hamad, 1932

The unique challenge that Iran posed to the British position in Bahrain during the interwar years invited a degree of imperial intervention in Bahrain such as was unprecedented in any of the Gulf shaykhdoms. When Iran reraised its claim to Bahrain and demonstrated its willingness to exploit sectarian tensions in Bahrain to the detriment of Britain's position in the Persian Gulf, the British government intervened with a strong hand to quell sectarian unrest and limit Iran's influence. The dramatic interventions of the 1920s led to the creation of a modern state administration under the aegis of the government of India. Consequently, the India Office began to consider transferring the headquarters of the Persian Gulf Residency from Bushehr to Bahrain (though the transfer was not carried out until 1946).[2] The

[1] IOR/R/15/2/486: Office of the Adviser to the Government, Bahrain (Belgrave) to Political Agent (Prior), *Jumada al-Thani* 8, 1351 (October 8, 1932).

[2] H. M. Government, Foreign Office, "Historical Summary of Events in the Persian Gulf Sheikhdoms and the Sultanate of Muscat and Oman, 1928–1953, PG 53 (London: Foreign Office, June 1953; Repr.: Archive Editions, 1987), p. 1.

discovery of oil in 1932 and the introduction of oil revenues to the state treasury in 1935 further consolidated Bahrain's position as the linchpin of British strategy in the Persian Gulf. This was prominently expressed in the transfer of Britain's naval base from the Iranian littoral to al-Jufayr, Bahrain in 1935.

Anti-British, nationalist sentiments found expression among the Iranian communities in Bahrain in the aftermath of the First World War just as anti-British sentiment grew up across the region. Some elements of the Iranian immigrant population in Bahrain voiced these sentiments by agitating for a renewal of Iranian sovereignty over the archipelago. Anti-colonial sentiment found expression also among Bahrain's tribal and Sunni elites, who opposed the imposition of reforms that curtailed their traditional status and privileges. Because British intervention in Bahrain in the interwar years was largely a product of the challenges posed by Iran, the Iranian nationals residing in Bahrain grew up as an object of resentment by the traditional ruling class. Arab elites propagated a discourse that deemphasized the traditional Sunni-Shiʿi cleavage and focused on the "Arab nation" as a focus of cohesion. Others focused on the legal status of the "natives" in contrast with that of the "foreigners." Modern political consciousness, which focused on ethnic and cultural identity as markers of belonging, was born in Manama in the midst of the tortuous Anglo-Iranian struggle over Bahrain.

Sectarian Violence and External Intervention, 1919–1925

The application of the Bahrain Order in Council in 1919 mandated the establishment of British courts to adjudicate matters concerning foreigners in order to bring the judicial proceedings in Bahrain in line with the other British courts in the Gulf.[3] The establishment of the new courts would not abolish the traditional religious and tribal courts, but it would subordinate them to the British imperial apparatus. In November, Major Dickson assumed the post of Political Agent in Bahrain (1919–1920) and he was tasked with bringing Bahrain's judicial system in line with the new dual authority scheme. But Dickson's mandate to create new courts for foreigners triggered disagreement between the British and the ruling shaykh over who was to be defined

[3] "File A/9 II Bahrain Order in Council," British Library: India Office Records and Private Papers, IOR/R/IOR/R/15/2/7, in Qatar Digital Library, www.qdl.qa/en/archive/81055/vdc_100023902657.0x000015 (accessed October 1, 2015).

as a "foreigner." Shaykh 'Isa was not willing to relinquish his authority over the Najdis, the Arab dependents of Ibn Sa'ud, and the dependents of the Ruler of Qatar who dwelled in his territory. He also objected to ending the practice of charging *khidma*, the traditional court fees that provided a source of revenue for him and his tribal allies.

The first tactic employed by Dickson was to try to work within the customary system by attempting to persuade both the ruler and the leading members of society, who counseled the ruler in his informal majlis, of the wisdom of implementing these reforms. In letters to his superiors, Dickson provided copies of his written appeals to the ruling shaykh and described the great lengths that he went to, to persuade Shaykh 'Isa and his supporters of the advantages of reorganizing the court system. He also appealed to other community leaders and close associates of the ruler, whose support could have potentially lent legitimacy to the proposed reforms. Dickson described reaching an understanding with the judge of the Sunni Shari'a court and obtaining the support of Yusuf Kanoo, a wealthy and influential Sunni merchant of Iranian origins.[4] These men promised to press his case with the ruler. Despite this, support for retaining the status quo was still stronger in Manama than support for the reforms proposed by the British Political Agent. Shaykh 'Isa's written replies to Dickson's letters were courteous and tractable, but after consultations with his tribal allies, he became determined to resist these British encroachments on his authority by whichever means were at his disposal.[5] The British decided to implement their reforms with or without his support.

On November 26, 1920, Dickson issued a public proclamation affirming that foreign subjects including Iranian nationals and subjects of Arab chiefs other than the Al Khalifa were entitled to British protection and legal jurisdiction. Over the course of the subsequent year and a half, Shaykh 'Isa played rival power centers off against each other to try to obstruct the imposition of reforms that curtailed his traditional authority. Segments of Bahrain's population coalesced into two main factions, one supporting and the other opposing British-imposed reforms. The oppositionist faction to which 'Isa belonged was led by his second son, Shaykh 'Abdullah, and was mainly

[4] "File A/9/II Bahrain Order in Council," British Library: India Office Records and Private Papers, IOR/R/IOR/R/15/2/7, in Qatar Digital Library, www.qdl.qa/en/archive/81055/vdc_100000000193.0x0002e6 (accessed September 11, 2017).

[5] IOR/R/15/1/319: Political Agent Bahrain (Dickson), Notice, *Rabi' al-Awwal* 14, 1339 (November 26, 1920).

composed of Sunni pearl merchants and nakhodas, the Dawasir tribe and the Najdis, who feared the loss of their superior status and privileges. They particularly abhorred the idea of being treated on equal terms with the Shi'a in respect to taxes and courts of justice. Support for reform was spearheaded by the Baharna (Arab Shi'a) who pleaded with the British for protection from the oppression they suffered under the Al Khalifa. The Sunni Arabs viewed the Iranians, especially Shi'i Iranians, with suspicion, supposing them to be complicit in the aims of the Baharna.[6]

In so far as it produced results, the British continued to employ tactics of bargaining and persuasion to drive forward a program of modernization in Bahrain. In July 1920, Shaykh 'Isa acquiesced in allowing the establishment of a municipal council (*majlis baladiyya*) modeled along the lines of the municipal institution established in Basra. The British gained his acquiesce in this matter by promising that his son, Shaykh 'Abdullah, could serve as its president. The municipal council was established with eight members, four chosen by 'Isa from among the peninsular Arabs and four chosen by Dickson from among the foreign communities. However, under 'Abdullah's leadership, the municipal council did not serve as an instrument of reform as the British hoped it would. Rather, Shaykh 'Abdullah used his leadership position to obstruct reforms and reinforce the long-standing supremacy of the Sunnis over the Shi'a. Moreover, he also appeared to be using his position as president of the council and leader of the anti-British opposition to supplant his older half-brother, Shaykh Hamad, as heir apparent.[7]

In January 1920, Major Dickson was replaced by Major Clive Daly as Political Agent in Bahrain (1921–1926). The Baharna saw his arrival as an opportune moment. Leading members of the Bahrani community came together and submitted a petition to Daly pleading for his sympathy and the help of the British government. They used flattery of the most stirring kind, praising Britain and its historical kings and queens for rescuing the downtrodden from their oppressors, freeing slaves and spreading justice throughout the world. The Shi'i community of Bahrain, they lamented, was "in a state of great

[6] IOR/R/15/2/131: Major Daly, Note on the Political Situation at Bahrain, November 1921.
[7] Ibid.

humiliation," subject to plunder, "public massacre," and innumerable injustices every day. What they requested was that the British government, "Chief of the Gulf," would perform its God-given duty and rescue the Shi'a from the oppression of the Al Khalifa. If Britain failed to do this, the Shi'a of Bahrain, they said, would all perish from the earth.[8]

The new Political Agent wrote to his superiors to say that when he arrived, he found Bahrain in a "constant state of unrest" due to the "tyrannical conduct" of its ruler, 'Isa bin 'Ali Al Khalifa, toward the Shi'i population.[9] His son, 'Abdullah, president of the municipal council, was also identified as a tyrant. The British government, still reluctant to interfere in Bahrain's domestic affairs, instructed Daly to use persuasion to bring about better circumstances for the oppressed Bahraini subjects. In June, Daly was successful in persuading Shaykh 'Isa to remove Shaykh 'Abdullah from the presidency of the municipal council in favor of his elder son, Shaykh Hamad. Hamad's elevation to the administration was a turning point. He derived his influence from associating with the British and proved amenable to their program of reform.[10] The anti-British faction, led by 'Abdullah, was angry about 'Abdullah's dismissal, and particularly inflamed with Daly's appointment of an Iranian immigrant as the new secretary of the municipality.

The new secretary, Muhammad Sharif Qutb al-Din Awazi,[11] was a relative newcomer, a Sunni merchant from Evaz, Iran, who arrived in Bahrain around 1915. As secretary to Shaykh Hamad, he was empowered with the combined roles of municipal governor (*hakim*

8 IOR/R/15/2/83: Political Resident (Trevor) to Foreign Secretary to the Government of India, December 30, 1921, with enclosure "Translation of a Petition Presented to the Political Resident on 21st December 1921 by a Large Deputation of Bahrain Subjects"; Major Daly, "Some Examples of Oppression of Bahrain Subjects by the Ruling Family in Bahrain," January 3, 1922.

9 IOR/R/15/2/83: Political Resident (Trevor) to Foreign Secretary to the Government of India, December 30, 1921; Major Daly, Note on the Political Situation at Bahrain, November 1921.

10 IOR/R/15/2/83: Political Agent Bahrain to Political Resident, February 7, 1922, with enclosure "Copy of a Letter Marked 'Private' Handed to the Political Agent Bahrain by Shaykh Hamad bin Easa," n.d.; Political Resident (Trevor) to Foreign Secretary to the Government of India, April 14, 1922.

11 Elsewhere rendered Ewazi, Evazi, Awazi, and Awadhi, referents to the city of Evaz in the Fars province of Iran.

balad) and chief of police (*amir*).[12] The police force that he assembled was composed almost entirely of Iranian immigrants. In the eyes of Shaykh ʿAbdullah, who still led the faction that opposed the British, Muhammad Sharif was an Iranian foreigner who colluded with the British imperialists to topple the traditional tribal order.[13]

When Shaykh ʿAbdullah was removed from office in June 1920, he began directing a harsh campaign against the municipality and its supporters, which were viewed as a Trojan horse for imperial intervention. Tensions ran high along the lines of the traditional sectarian cleavages, the urban Najdis against urban Iranians and the Sunni Arab tribes against the Shiʿi Arab peasants. The Baharna were subjected to a harsh intimidation campaign at the hands of the tribesmen, which included political murders, abduction and rape, arbitrary arrest and imprisonment, confiscation of land and property, and theft and extortion.[14] The police force headed by Muhammad Sharif was the target of several attempted ambushes and Sharif was the target of some intrigues aimed at driving a wedge between him and the British.[15] In February 1922 the Baharna began to fight back. Several members of the community attacked a tribal guard to free a prisoner, a member of the Baharna community who had been arrested and beaten. The incident grew into an uprising when the Baharna closed their shops, refused to pay taxes, and then on February 16, 1922, presented a list of demands to the ruler.[16] Their demands included the abolition of *sukhra* (forced labor); the exclusion of Shaykh ʿAbdullah from influence over court cases concerning the Shiʿa; the provision of an adequate and sanitary

[12] IOR/L/P&S/10/249: Political Resident to Secretary of State for the Colonies, August 19, 1921, with enclosure, "Bahrain Municipal Council Regulation No. 1 of 1921."

[13] IOR/R/15/1/338: Political Agent Bahrain (Daly) to Political Resident, October 17, 1923, with enclosure, "translation of a petition without date" signed by Shaykh ʿIsa and the heads of ten tribes including the Al Sada, Al Bu Falasa, Mosallam, Jalahima, Zayyani, Naʿim, Mananʿa, Al Dawasir, Al Bu ʿAli, and Bin Jawdar tribes.

[14] IOR/R/15/1/83: Political Resident (Trevor) to Foreign Secretary to the Government of India, December 30, 1921, with enclosure "Translation of a Petition Presented to the Political Resident on 21st December 1921 by a Large Deputation of Bahrain Subjects"; Major Daly, "Some Examples of Oppression of Bahrain Subjects by the Ruling Family in Bahrain," January 3, 1922.

[15] IOR/L/P&S/10/1039: Political Resident (Trevor) to Foreign Secretary to the Government of India (Bray), January 19, 1922.

[16] IOR/R/15/2/83: The Agency Bahrain to the Political Resident Bushire, February 22, 1922.

prison; the issue of court summons in lieu of arbitrary arrests; the provision of written rental contracts and enforcement of the terms within the contracts; and an end to the practice of forcing Baharna to care for livestock belonging to the Al Khalifa free of charge. There was a fear that because the British government supported the shaykh's independence, Britain would be accused of connivance with the victimization of the Baharna that was perpetrated by members of his family.[17]

Ultimately, the Foreign Office prescribed an interventionist policy in Bahrain – but the reason had less to do with humanitarian considerations than with Britain's wider, strategic goals. Intervention was deemed necessary to safeguard Britain's position in the Persian Gulf in the face of Iran's increasingly assertive policy in the region. A serious local campaign to revive Iran's claim to sovereignty over Bahrain was apparent by the summer of 1922. Calling themselves "the Iranian patriots residing in Bahrain" the Iranian immigrant labor community initiated a variety of agitations in favor of reviving Iran's claim to Bahrain including letters and visits to the *Kargozar* at Bushehr, telegrams to the authorities in Tehran, and a spate of articles that appeared in the Iranian press.[18] Meanwhile, a fresh drive was inaugurated in Iran's port towns to distribute Iranian identity documents to travelers from Bahrain.[19] The tense situation in Bahrain attracted the attention of Lord Curzon, then foreign minister, who warned the India Office of the danger that Iran could try to become involved.[20] In view of the changing strategic environment, the Foreign Office instructed the India Office to wait for the right moment and then to "take the necessary steps to exercise the strongest moral pressure on the shaykh, to be followed if necessary by forcible intervention."[21]

In Bahrain, another outbreak of violence in April 1923 – this time involving Iranian nationals – proved to be the breaking point. Bloody clashes in the market between Najdis and Iranians escalated into a series of attacks and counter attacks. The Iranians appealed directly to

[17] IOR/L/P&S/10/1039: Political Resident (Trevor) to the Foreign Secretary of the Government of India (Bray), January 27, 1923.
[18] See Chapter 3.
[19] Administration Report of the Persian Gulf Residency for the Year 1922, p. 23.
[20] IOR/L/P&S/10/1039: Foreign Office to India Office, March 18, 1922.
[21] IOR/L/P&S/10/1039: Foreign Office to India Office, March 8, 1923.

Tehran for protection and talk surfaced that Tehran was considering referring its Bahrain claim to the League of Nations.[22] The fighting broadened along sectarian lines when on May 12 members of the Dawasir tribe attacked the Bahrani village of A'ali and men from the Khalid branch of the Al Khalifa family attacked Bahrani residents of Sitra. Twelve died in these raids, dozens were wounded, and women were raped. Having already received the green light from London to intervene at the opportune moment, the British Resident in Bushehr departed for Manama on May 18, 1923. After refusing to retire voluntarily, Shaykh 'Isa was informed of Britain's decision to forcibly remove him from power and to recognize his son, Hamad, as "deputy ruler" in his place.[23]

The deposition of Shaykh 'Isa did not put down the resistance. What followed was a period of about two and a half years during which time Clive Daly, supported by Shaykh Hamad, implemented a robust program of reforms that portended the end of the traditional power and privileges of the tribes and the Sunni merchant class. In the Sunni tribal strongholds of Muharraq and al-Budayyi', the Baharna and 'Ajam were perceived together as a veritable "fifth column," an enemy from within that provoked imperial intrusions into the traditional, tribal way of life in Bahrain.[24] Among those who were most anxious about the erosion of tribal authority and privileges were the Dowasir, who threatened to quit the island en masse and emigrate with their tribesmen to the mainland. They were joined in their opposition by the Khalid branch of the Al Khalifa ruling family: Shaykh 'Isa's brother Khalid bin 'Ali Al Khalifa and his sons, 'Ali, Ibrahim, and Salman, viewed the Baharna as eager accessories in the demise of their own traditional, tribal privileges, and responded by waging a brutal campaign of intimidation against them.

The tribal partisans of Shaykh 'Isa held meetings, mostly at the home of a prominent Najdi merchant, 'Abd al-Wahhab al-Zayyani, and

[22] FO 416/72: Sir P. Loraine to the Marquess Curzon of Kedleston, April 27, 1923; Annual Report on Persia for the Year 1923, pp. 31–32; IOR/L/P&S/10/1039: Viceroy, Foreign and Political Department to Secretary of State for India, May 15, 1923.

[23] IOR/L/P&S/10/1039: Lieutenant Colonel H. G. Knox, "Report on Bahrain Reforms," May 31, 1923.

[24] IOR/R/15/1/338: Political Agent Bahrain (Daly) to Political Resident, October 17, 1923, with enclosure "translation of a petition without date" signed by Shaykh 'Isa, 'Abd al-Wahhab al-Zayyani and the heads of tribes including Al Dawasir, Al Sada, Al Bu Falasa, Al Mosallam, Al Jalahimah, Al Na'im, Al Mana'a, Al Bin 'Ali, and Bin Jowdar.

Figure 7 Shaykh ‘Isa bin ‘Ali Al Khalifa.
Source: Bahrain Ministry of Interior, https://bit.ly/39Dt3BN (accessed February 17, 2020).

Figure 8 Shaykh Hamad bin ‘Isa Al Khalifa.
Source: *The Nabhani Offering on the History of the Arabian Peninsula*, Qatar National Library, 12961, p. 203, www.qdl.qa/universal-viewer/qnlhc/12961 (accessed May 28, 2019).

entered into a “covenant” to protest against British intrusions in the internal affairs of Bahrain.[25] This “covenant” evolved into the “Bahrain National Congress,” whose self-elected representatives met together in al-Zayyani’s majlis. With encouragement from two prominent Hawala merchants, Yusuf Fakroo and Ahmad Kanoo, al-Zayyani organized a petition against British interference, which was signed by Shaykh ‘Isa and the heads of 10 Sunni tribal families.[26] That Fakroo and Kanoo did not sign it attests to the strength of tribal modes of action at that time in Bahrain.

In June 1923, Dawasir tribesmen attacked the Bahraini village of A‘ali again. Under British supervision, a criminal court was set up to try the suspects. After the ringleader was tried and sentenced, several Bahrani notables, who had encouraged their countrymen to testify against the

[25] Rashid Abdul Rahman al-Zayani, *Memories and History* (Manama: Al Ayam Press, 1999), pp. 25–64.

[26] IOR/R/15/1/338: The Agency Bahrain to the Political Resident Bushire, October 17, 1923.

perpetrators, were assassinated near the Dawasir abode of al-Budayyiʿ. The response of the British-backed administration of Shaykh Hamad was decisive. He issued an ultimatum and the entire tribe was compelled to emigrate en masse from the Bahrain archipelago. They settled in Dammam on the mainland but were permitted to return to Bahrain in 1927.[27]

The Khalid branch of the Al Khalifa, together with their *fidawiyya* (armed guards), continued the intimidation campaign, carrying out another attack on the Bahrani residents of Sitra in September 1923. Shaykh Hamad was averse to acting against his own uncle and cousins. But caught between a rock and a hard place, and desirous of holding onto his leadership position, Shaykh Hamad acquiesced to the demands of the British and convened a trial. As a result, Shaykh ʿAli bin Khalid Al Khalifa was found guilty of having led the attack and was sentenced to banishment for 10 years. His brother, Shaykh Salman bin Khalid, was banished for one year and his father, Shaykh Khalid bin ʿAli Al Khalifa, was ordered to move his residence from Sitra to al-Rifaʿ.

These punishments were not sufficient to rein them in. Seeking revenge against the Baharna who witnessed against them, they again attacked Sitra from a base on the mainland, killing several men, women, and children. Before a trial could be convened, the perpetrators, Ibrahim and Salman, fled to the mainland; they were tried in absentia and sentenced to death.[28] At the suggestion of some Hawala merchants, they traveled to Lingah to explore the possibility of lobbying Iran for protection. However, the preponderance of British authority in Iran's southern ports impeded their efforts and they departed Lingah in search of a more remote hideaway.[29] By 1927, they were quietly resettled in Bahrain with Shaykh Hamad's blessing.

Another indication that reconciliation with Iran was being viewed in some quarters as an alternative to British protection was an episode that occurred in March 1925 when Shaykh Khalifa bin Hamad traveled all the way to Tehran. Shaykh Khalifa was a member of the ruling family

27 M. G. Rumaihi, *Bahrain: Social and Political Change since the First World War* (London: Center for Middle Eastern and Islamic Studies, 1976), pp. 180–182.

28 Al-Tajir, *Bahrain: 1920–1945,* pp. 57–69; Khuri, *Tribe and State in Bahrain,* pp. 95–99.

29 Army General Staff to the Ministry of Foreign Affairs, *Borj Sowr* 29, 1303 (May 19, 1924), with attachment, in *Faslnameh-ye Motala'at-e Tarikhi* 8, no. 33 (Summer 1390/2011), pp. 238–242; Administration Report of the Persian Gulf Residency for the Year 1923, p. 68.

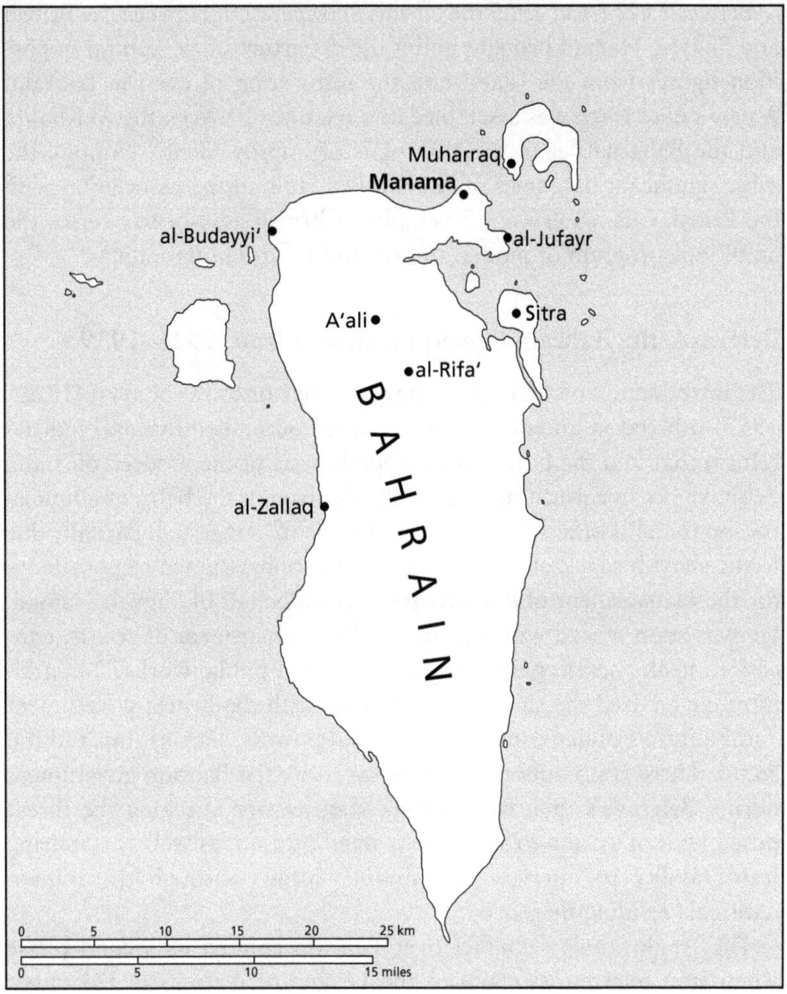

Map 3 Bahrain.

who felt marginalized by the new order that the British were creating in Bahrain. In March 1925, he arrived in Tehran and presented documents purporting to prove Iranian ownership of Bahrain and asked the Iranian government to intervene.[30] Aside from some excitement in the Iranian press, his appeals for protection came to naught.[31]

30 IOR/R/15/1/320, Political Resident (Bushire) to Minister Tehran (Loraine), June 22, 1925.

31 IOR/R/15/1/320: *Bayan-e Haghighat* (Shiraz), October 14.

Between 1924 and 1925 the effective cooperation between the British and Shaykh Hamad brought about the departure of the central opposition figures from the island and the restoration of calm in Bahrain. A new police force was assembled and relations between the Al Khalifa and the Baharna began to show signs of improvement.[32] Among the most significant outcomes of Shaykh Hamad's strong association with the British was his decision to employ a British advisor to oversee the ambitious program of modernization and reform in Bahrain.

Belgrave, the Bahrain Government, and Iran, 1926–1939

The introduction of Charles Belgrave as advisor to the Shaykh (1926–1957) ushered in an era of unprecedented administrative and judicial reform that laid the bureaucratic foundations of the modern oil state. Belgrave became much more actively involved in the Bahrain administration than his official title "financial advisor" suggested. Partially due to the shaykh's lack of initiative, Belgrave soon assumed responsibility for the management of key departments on behalf of Shaykh Hamad. He was soon tasked with the day-to-day management of courts, education, health services, land registration, and public works.[33] In addition, he advised the shaykh on relations with the British government and Bahrain's policy concerning regional powers, such as Iran and Ibn Sa'ud. There is no doubt that steps taken by the Bahrain government during Belgrave's time went a long way toward checking the threat posed by Iran's claim to sovereignty over Bahrain, as well as stymieing Iran's ability to interfere in Bahrain's affairs through the Iranian nationals residing there.

The Anglo-Iranian conflict over Bahrain entered its second phase when Iran referred its claim to the League of Nations in December 1927. Belgrave obtained a letter, signed by Shaykhs 'Isa and Hamad, which authorized the British government to defend Bahrain against the claim of Iran in the League of Nations. Going beyond that, 'Isa authorized his son, Muhammad, to accompany and assist the British delegate, should the matter come before the Assembly.[34]

[32] Al-Tajir, *Bahrain: 1920–1945*, pp. 94–99.

[33] Hassan Ali Radhi, *Judiciary and Arbitration in Bahrain: A Historical and Analytical Study* (The Hague: Klewer Law, 2003), pp. 48–49.

[34] Belgrave Diaries, March 10 and 12, 1928; IOR/R/15/1/356: Shaykh 'Isa bin 'Ali Al Khalifa to Political Agent Bahrain (countersigned by Shaykh Hamad bin 'Isa Al Khalifa), *Ramadan* 22, 1346 (March 15, 1928).

While Iran's protest to the League of Nations was a serious development for the British, it was not taken seriously by Arabs in Bahrain. In fact, when news of Iran's protest to the League reached Manama, the Political Agent reported that Reza Shah had become the brunt of some Arab jokes. He reported learning of this while having lunch with some of Bahrain's Sunni merchant elites. One of them joked that Reza Shah, who also claimed the Trucial Coast, was like the legendary King of Abyssinia (*Malik al-Habash*) who claimed the whole world and purported to bestow imperial possessions such as Cairo and Basra on his courtiers as favors in return for trifling services.[35]

While Bahrain's Arabs did not view Iran's appeal to the League of Nations as a serious threat, it was a serious development from the perspective of British policy makers in London who were fearful that an examination of the dispute by the League would give substance to Iran's claim and make Britain appear weak. This development triggered greater vigilance on the part of the Bahrain administration for any action that might have been construed as an admission of Iran's claim to Bahrain. For example, the practice of allowing travelers to land in Bahrain possessing only *ilm-o-khabar* issued by Iran's port authorities came under fresh scrutiny: *ilm-o-khabar*, which authorized "travel from one domestic port to another domestic port," could have been construed as an admission of Iranian sovereignty.[36] At Belgrave's initiative and with Shaykh Hamad's full support, measures were adopted in 1929 to restrict entry only to those who possessed a valid passport and visa issued by a British consul.[37] In his diary, Belgrave expressed a hope that the tighter regulations would "bring the Persian question to a head."[38] He was particularly pleased and amused at the first fruits of his labor. On January 5, 1929, an Iranian customs inspector arrived on board a mail steamer, announcing that he was going ashore to inspect the customs at Manama and Muharraq. He got as far as the end of the pier before he was turned away. Belgrave relates, "he was furious and went off threatening protests from his government ... a very good thing indeed."[39]

The enforcement of new passport regulations quickly become the chief cause of complaint among Iranians resident in Bahrain, who lined

[35] IOR/R/15/1/356: Political Agent Bahrain (Barrett) to Political Resident Bushire (Haworth), February 11, 1928.
[36] IOR/L/P&S/18/B396: Memorandum: Bahrain, 1908–1928, p. 8.
[37] FO 416/84: Bahrain Government Proclamation, *Rajab* 2, 1347 (December 15, 1928); Belgrave Diaries, November 7, 1928.
[38] Belgrave Diaries, November 7, 1928. [39] Ibid., December 15, 1928.

up at Belgrave's office to appeal for exceptions that would allow their friends to land. Belgrave gives an amusing account of how 'Abd al-Nabi Bushiri, Bahrain's leading Shi'i Iranian merchant, sat on the steps of his office for hours, begging for the release of his son, who was locked up after returning from Iran without a visa for Bahrain.[40]

The decision of the Bahrain government to begin issuing its own passports in 1929 was the subject of a sharp protest from Iran. Iran urgently issued instructions to its port officials to deny entry to any traveler carrying the offensive passport booklet and to reiterate that travelers from all the Arab shaykhdoms and Muscat were required to take out Iranian travel documents before entering Iran and travelers departing for the southern littoral were required to take out *ilm-o-khabar*. This soon created a situation in which travelers from the Arab shaykhdoms possessed themselves of two travel documents – one Arab and one Iranian – to avoid hassles from port officials on both sides of the Gulf.[41] For the wealthier traders, it was a not so well-kept secret that taking out Iranian travel documents could be avoided with a "gift" of a few rupees. This method enabled the Trucial shaykhs to continue their time-honored tradition of annual falcon hunting trips to Iran.[42] Reports of a rumor that circulated in Bahrain in 1929 are particularly insightful. According to the rumor, Shaykh Muhammad, the son of Shaykh 'Isa, paid out bribes and presents to the value of 500 rupees to the officials at Lingah to embark without an *ilm-o-khabar*. It was well-understood that his acceptance of an *ilm-o-khabar* (specifying travel from one Iranian port to another Iranian port) would have amounted to an admission on the part of the Al Khalifa that Bahrain was an Iranian island.[43]

Iranian schools in Bahrain became a focus of scrutiny in 1929 when Arab protests evoked a desire on the part of the shaykhs to close the

[40] Ibid., July 9, 1929.
[41] Ministry of the Interior to the Ministry of Foreign Affairs, *Azar* 13, 1307 (December 4, 1928) and Ministry of Foreign Affairs to Ministry of the Interior, *Dey* 15, 1307 (January 5, 1929), in *Gozideh-ye Asnad-e Khalij-e Fars*, Vol. 1, pp. 138–141.
[42] See for example, Ministry of the Interior to Ministry of Foreign Affairs, *Ordibehesht* 11, 1311 (May 1, 1932) and enclosures, in *Gozideh-ye Asnad-e Khalij-e Fars*, Vol. 2, pp. 50–56.
[43] IOR IOR/L/PS/12/3792: Extract from Summary of the News from the Arab States for the Month of January 1929.

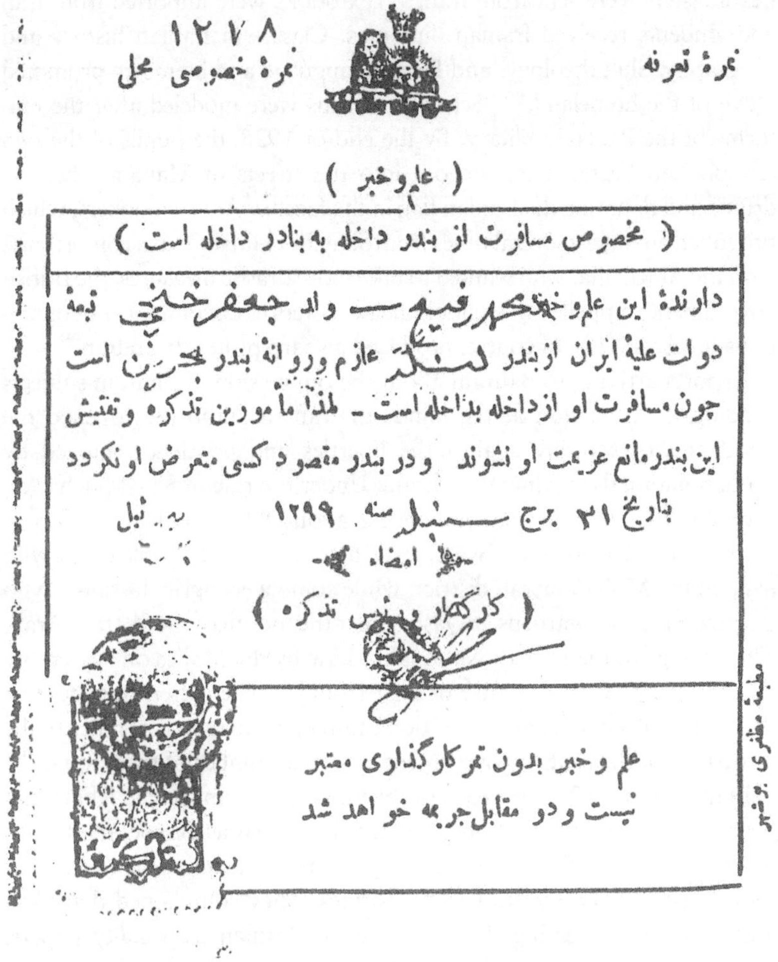

۱۲۷۸

نمرهٔ تعرفه

نمرهٔ خصوصی محلی

(علم وخبر)

(مخصوص مسافرت از بندر داخله به بنادر داخله است)

دارندهٔ این علم وخبر محمد رفیع ولد جعفر تبعهٔ

دولت علیهٔ ایران از بندر لنگه عازم وروانه بندر بحرین است

چون مسافرت او از داخله بداخله است ـ لهذا مامورین تذکره و تفتیش

این بندر مانع عزیمت او نشوند و در بندر مقصود کسی متعرض او نگردد

بتاریخ ۲۱ برج سنبله سنه ۱۲۹۹

امضاء

(کارگذار و رئیس تذکره)

علم وخبر بدون تمر کارگذاری معتبر

نیست ودو مقابل جریمه خواهد شد

مطبعهٔ مظفری بوشهر

Figure 9 An "ilm-o-khabar" travel pass issued in Iran.
Source: *Gozideh-ye Asnad-e Khalij-e Fars Jazayer-e Khalij-e Fars*, Vol. 1 (Tehran: Daftar-e Motala'at-e Siyasi va bayn al-Milali, 1372/1993), p. 29.

schools completely.[44] The two Iranian schools, Ettehad, and its offshoot, Okhovvat, had grown up as the foci of Pahlavi propaganda in Bahrain. By this time, the schools were receiving financial contributions from the Iranian government, through the educational department at Bushehr, and

[44] Ibid., January 12, 1929.

headmasters were sent from Iran.[45] Textbooks were imported from Iran and students received Iranian diplomas. Classes in Iranian history and geography, Shiʿi theology, and Persian language and literature promoted "love of the homeland."[46] School uniforms were modeled after the uniforms of the Pahlavi military. By the end of 1928, the pupils of the two schools had begun marching out into the streets of Manama, beating drums and flaunting the Iranian flag in the faces of Arab onlookers, which provoked an outcry several times from Shaykh Hamad.[47] In a compromise with the Al Khalifa, who wanted to take more drastic measures, the British government compelled the schools' headmasters to discontinue the contentious displays. This, of course, produced a sharp protest from Iran.[48]

Reports arriving to Bahrain about the oppression of Bahrain subjects residing in Khuzestan at the hands of Iranian authorities opened the floodgates of scrutiny against the liberties and privileges enjoyed by Iranian nationals residing in Bahrain. Under the rule of Shaykh Khazʿal, a community of Baharna numbering about 8,000 had grown up in Khuzestan. Most of them were petty merchants and shopkeepers who lived in the Mohammerah district, while some were agriculturalists who had acquired date gardens at Qasba, near the mouth of the Shatt al-Arab. The passage of the Iranian Nationality Law by the Majles on September 7, 1929, marked the increase of their troubles. Thereafter, they became the subject of a harsh nationalization campaign and their resistance to the intrusions of the central government landed a number of them in jail.[49]

In the end of 1929, the heads of the Baharna community in Khuzestan began making representations to Lieutenant-Colonel Biscoe, the British Resident (1929–1932), seeking his support against the treatment they received from the Iranian authorities. They complained that local authorities were forcing them to take out Iranian nationality papers; forcing them to wear Pahlavi headgear, which they found repugnant;

[45] Razavian, "Iranian Communities in the Persian Gulf," p. 350.
[46] Fuccaro, "Mapping the Transnational Community," in *Transnational Connections in the Arab Gulf*, p. 52.
[47] Bahrain Government Annual Report for the year 1348 (1929–1930), pp. 110–111, in *The Bahrain Government Annual Reports, 1924–1970*, Vol. 1 (Archive Editions, 1986). (Hereafter, references to the Bahrain Government Annual Reports that can be found in this set of eight volumes will be referred to by their year and page number.) See also Belgrave Diaries, June 15, 1927; January 31, 1928; February 1, 1928; and January 12, 1929.
[48] FO 416/84: *Shafaq-e Sorkh*, *Dey* 7, 1307 (December 27, 1928).
[49] Belgrave Diaries, October 22, 1930.

conscripting their sons into the Iranian army; and forbidding them to visit Bahrain unless they made a solemn declaration that they have accepted Iranian nationality. In reply to them, Biscoe differentiated between those who were agriculturalists and those who were traders. The traders, he said, were entitled to protection as Bahraini nationals. He advised them to accept Iranian nationality under protest and register their protest with the British vice-consulate so that the issue could be reversed after the Bahrain question was definitely settled. But the agriculturalists, he said, he was unable to help because, according to Iranian law, no foreigner was allowed to own land in Iran; they would either need to part with their property in Iran or part with their Bahraini nationality.[50]

Having failed to obtain the protection they sought from the British, in 1932 the Baharna began to address petitions to the Bahrain government. One petition read:

> We are your subjects, Baharna fugitives who fled from Mohammerah, at present residing in Basrah, on account of the oppression of the Persian Government and forcible conscription of our sons. We are your subjects and believe that you will not leave us scattered everywhere. We beseech you to free us from their tyranny, as the son always belongs to the same nationality as his father. We observe that Persians are free in Bahrain, and how is it that we, your subjects, are oppressed in their country? We request your aid to release us from their tyranny. We are anxiously awaiting a reply.[51]

The comparison drawn between the oppression of Baharna in Iran opposite the privileged status of Iranians in Bahrain was a comparison that took root in the fertile soil of growing Arab sentiment in Bahrain. Sunni and Shi'i Arabs were becoming increasingly linked in their common dislike of Iranian foreigners, whose expressions of loyalty to Iran made them seem complicit in the persecution of Bahrain subjects. Just as tensions were mounting over the treatment of Baharna in Iran, a series of lengthy articles appeared in *Ettala'at* tracing Bahrain's connection with Iran from times immemorial and purporting to conclusively prove Iran's claim to Bahrain.[52] The excitement that these articles and others generated among the Iranian immigrant communities in Bahrain was said to be irksome for Shaykh Hamad and the

[50] FO 416/89: Consul-General Bisco to Government of India Simla, May 5, 1931.
[51] IOR/R/15/2/486: Translation of a petition dated August 29, 1932 from *Baharna* residents of Persia now at Basra addressed to the adviser, Bahrain government.
[52] *Ettala'at*, August 23–25 and 27, 1932.

arrival of fresh petitions from the Baharna around that time appeared to him as a golden opportunity to retaliate against Iranian nationals residing in Bahrain.[53] Iranian nationals, he said, should no longer be appointed or elected to public bodies in Bahrain; their schools should be subject to government inspection; the wearing of Pahlavi hats should be discouraged; and measures should be implemented to prevent Iranian nationals from holding property in Bahrain.[54]

As the British government debated the wisdom of the shaykh's proposals, the Iranian authorities adopted an even more severe attitude toward the Baharna, forbidding them from traveling to Bahrain or the Shi'i shrines in Iraq unless they first made a solemn declaration that they have adopted Iranian nationality. In 1934, reports reached Bahrain of the imprisonment of the leading members of the Baharna community at Qasba, and the vicious beatings that killed one and seriously injured the others.[55]

Amidst these dire circumstances, the shaykh's request to exercise jurisdiction over Iranian nationals in Bahrain finally found favor with the British government. By 1935, new legislation was being drafted "to give the Bahrain Government some much needed satisfaction" in treating Iranians resident in Bahrain in the same way as Bahrain subjects were treated in Iran with regard to the ownership of property.[56] The transfer of jurisdiction over foreign nationals to the shaykh was carried out in 1937 by an amendment to the Order in Council.[57] What followed was a series of measures designed to bring the Iranians resident in Bahrain under the authority of the Bahrain government and end some of the abuses that had cropped up as a result of the dual authority system.

First, the promulgation of the nationality and property laws in 1937 targeted the more affluent Iranian nationals by forcing them to forfeit their Iranian nationality and become Bahrain subjects in order

[53] IOR/R/15/2/486: Office of the Adviser to the Government Bahrain (Belgrave) to Political Agent Bahrain (Prior), October 8, 1932; Bahrain Government Annual Report for the year 1351 (March 1932–February 1933), p. 393.

[54] Ibid.

[55] IOR/R/15/2/486: The Advisor to the Government of Bahrain (Belgrave) to Political Agent Bahrain, March 14, 1934.

[56] IOR/R/15/2/490: Political Resident to Government of India New Delhi, March 2, 1935.

[57] IOR/R/15/2/490: The Bahrain (Amendment) Order in Council, 1937.

to retain their immoveable property in Bahrain.[58] This brought particular pressure to bear on Iranian businessmen such as ʻAli Kazem Bushiri, the affluent contractor, who owned a large amount of commercial and residential property. His letter to the Iranian government, dated December 16, 1937, describes the tough choice he faced between accepting Bahraini citizenship or parting with his valuable properties.[59] Another regulation issued in September 1937 targeted indigents, mainly Shiʻi migrants, by allowing the Bahrain government to deport people who did not possess valid travel documents.[60] By 1938, according to a British memo, hundreds had been apprehended and 44 of them deported.[61] A proclamation issued in 1938 gave the shaykh leverage over the Iranian schools, whose nationalist propaganda was regarded as an affront to his authority, by forbidding boys of Bahraini nationality to attend without the express permission of the Bahrain government.[62]

Iranian nationals were not eager to accept Bahrain nationality. In the years immediately following the government's issue of a law requiring landowners to acquire Bahraini nationality, applications for citizenship numbered only in the dozens. Those who applied for and received nationality were primarily the wealthier traders and shop owners.[63] By 1948, the Bahrain government reported that a mere 233 immigrants and children of immigrants from Iran who had applied for and received Bahraini nationality.[64] Some Iranian merchants evaded the effects of the 1937 law by transferring their property to their children,

[58] IOR/R/15/2/490: The Bahrain Nationality Law, 1937; The Bahrain Law Regarding Ownership of Immoveable Property in Bahrain by Foreigners Regulation, 1937.

[59] ʻAli Kazem Bushiri to the Prime Minister of Iran, *Azar* 25, 1316 (December 16, 1937), in *Faslnameh-ye Motalaʼat-e Tarikhi* 8, no. 33 (Summer 1390/2011), p. 156.

[60] Ibid.

[61] IOR/R/15/2/494: Political Agent Bahrain to Political Resident (Fowle), June 14, 1938.

[62] This applied to most, if not all, children born to Iranian parents after 1929. According to a proclamation issued in 1929, foreign nationals could register their children with the agency as foreigners, but by the end of 1935, no Iranians had done so. See Political Agent Bahrain to Resident, November 24, 1935, IOR/R/15/2/490.

[63] Bahrain Government Annual Report for the Year 1358 (1939–1940), p. 39; and Annual Report for the Year 1359 (1940–1941), p. 36.

[64] IOR IOR/L/P&S/10/1104: Belgrave to Political Agent Bahrain (Pelly), March 21, 1948.

who were already Bahraini citizens (according to the 1929 proclamation, which naturalized children born on Bahrain's soil).[65] Others auctioned their property and returned to Iran.[66]

Iran and Iranian Nationals in Bahrain, 1919–1923

The Iranian nationals residing in Bahrain were not unaffected by the anti-colonial and nationalist feeling that swept the Persian Gulf in the aftermath of the First World War. But the expression of Iranian patriotism in Bahrain, to a large degree, was also a reflection of local politics on the archipelago. Local politics in the pre-oil era have been aptly described by Nelida Fuccaro as the "politics of patronage" where patron-client bonds represented the central ordering principle.[67] Viewing the political dynamics in Bahrain through that lens, an examination of Iranian nationalism in Bahrain on the eve of oil must also take into account the dynamics in and between Bahrain's networks of patronage.

Patronage networks among Iranian immigrants to Manama were organized along the lines of sectarian cleavages, the most significant of which was the cleavage between Sunni and Shi'i. The Sunni group, about one-third of the total, was composed of wealthy merchants, traders, boat builders, masons, and carpenters. Most of them were from the Lingah district that included Bastak, while some were from Khuzestan. The Shi'i group, the majority of Iranian immigrants to Bahrain, was mostly composed of petty shopkeepers, dock workers, day laborers, and itinerant peddlers from southern Iran in general and from the Bushehr district in particular. During the first World War, Muhammad Sharif Qutb al-Din Awazi came to prominence as the leading merchant of the Sunni immigrant community of Iranian (non-Hawala) origin. He embraced his status as a British-protected foreigner and eschewed efforts to drag Iran into Bahrain affairs.[68] His association with the British gave him an advantage over his rival, Mohammed

[65] IOR/R/15/2/151: Office of the Adviser to the Government, Bahrain (Belgrave) to Political Agent, *Ramadan* 1, 1357 (October 25, 1938); and Political Agent to Office of the Adviser to the Government, Bahrain (Belgrave), November 1, 1938.
[66] See for example, Bahrain Government Annual Report for the Year 1358 (1939–1940), p. 29.
[67] Fuccaro, *Histories of City and State in the Persian Gulf*, pp. 73–111.
[68] IOR/R/15/1/319: Agency Bahrain (Daly) to Political Resident, October 30, 1922; IOR/L/P&S/10/1039: Political Resident (Knox) to Secretary of State for India, May 29, 1923.

Tayyib Khunji. Among the Shi'a, 'Abd al-Nabi Bushiri enjoyed the largest urban constituency. He was rivaled by 'Abd al-Nabi Kazeruni, a merchant with a smaller following among urban Shi'i laborers.[69]

Iranian patriotism and tribal resistance to foreign intervention converged in the flood of anti-British sentiment that swept the region after the first World War.[70] The use of Bahrain's port as a stopover for an expeditionary force that would engage in military operations against the Ottomans aggravated broad swathes of the island's inhabitants.[71] The anti-British opposition faction headed by Shaykh 'Abdullah Al Khalifa spearheaded and financed anti-British press agitations.[72] Their financial support helped generate to a steady stream of articles decrying British imperialism in both the Arabic and Persian press.[73] Among those responsible for supplying anti-British articles to the Arabic and Persian press were some young, Sunni Arab academicians, Ahmad and 'Abd al-Rahman Faramarzi.

The Faramarzi brothers were born to Shaykh 'Abd al-Wahhab, the head of the large Faramarzi clan, in the area of Bastak. When the boys were infants, feuds and disturbances broke out leading to the death of several members of the clan, and in 1899, their father moved his family to Bushehr. After the introduction of harsh customs dues by the Qajar government around 1904, 'Abd al-Wahhab relocated again, this time to Bahrain. The two boys received a primary education in Bahrain and continued their studies in Bastak and al-Hasa'. After that, the two boys rejoined their father in Bahrain and were soon recruited as teachers for Ettehad, the Iranian school for boys.[74] In the closing years of the first World War, 'Abd al-Rahman took up an interest in journalism and began contributing anti-British articles to the Persian newspapers,

69 IOR/R/15/2/138: Political Agent Bahrain (Prior) to Consul-General Barrett, November 4, 1929; Advisor (Belgrave) to Political Agent Bahrain (Prior), Memorandum, November 5, 1929.

70 For an example of Sunni-Shi'i cooperation in the anti-British cause, see *'Asr-e Azadi*, October 17, 1922. The article names prominent Arab and Sunni merchants as friends of the small anti-British, Nationalist Party headed by the Shi'i merchant, 'Abd al-Nabi Kazeruni.

71 Farah, *Protection and Politics in Bahrain*, pp. 202–203.

72 Administration Report of the Persian Gulf Residency for the Year 1922, p. 51; Administration Report of the Persian Gulf Residency for the Year 1923, p. 69; see also *'Asr-e Azadi*, October 17, 1922, IOR/R/15/1/319.

73 Behbudi, *Ruzshumar-e Tarikh-e Mu'asir-e Iran*, Vol. 2, p. 740.

74 'Ali Behzadi, *Shebh-e Khaterat* (Tehran: Negarestan-e Ketab, 1375/1996), pp. 471–472.

Estakhr and *'Asr-e Azadi*, published in Shiraz, and the Arabic newspapers, *al-Ahram* and *al-Muqattam*, published in Cairo. He related that as a result of their anti-British activism, the British decided to deport him and his brother. When the brothers heard of this, in the spring of 1922, they returned to the Bushehr district by way of Qatar.[75] Stopping in Shiraz on their way to Tehran, they helped stir up a press campaign demanding the establishment of an Iranian post office in Bahrain.[76]

The Faramarzi brothers found productive careers in Tehran as civil servants, parliamentarians, and littérateurs during which time both men continued to trumpet the Bahrain cause. Ahmad found his path into the civil service by posing as an advisor to the government on Bahrain and the conditions in the south of Iran. He lobbied the government on behalf of a group of Sunni Iranian merchants who opposed British interference in Bahrain, with whom he was in constant contact.[77] Prominent Bahrain merchants of Iranian origin, such as Mohammed Amin Khonji, provided him with descriptions of the abuses that Bahrain people suffered under British imperial rule, and through him tried to promote the idea of bringing Bahrain back under Iranian authority.[78] By way of the army, he conveyed petitions to the central government on behalf of opposition figures in Bahrain. He advocated the notion that the Al Khalifa shaykhs were tired of British interference and ready to embrace Iranian overlordship; he urged the government to use all means at its disposal to attract them to the side of the Iranian government.[79] Ahmad went on to author a number of books and articles on the history and geography of the Persian Gulf and a lengthy polemic in support of Iran's claim to Bahrain.[80]

[75] Ibid. [76] IOR/R/15/1/319: *Estakhr*, July 25, 1922.

[77] Mohammed Amin Khonji to Prime Minister, *Dalv* 2, 1302 (January 22, 1924) and *Bahman* 22, 1302 (February 11, 1924), in *Faslnameh-ye Motala'at-e Tarikhi* 8, no. 33 (Summer 1390/2011), pp. 243–247.

[78] Mirza Ahmad Faramarzi to Ministry of Foreign Affairs, *Sonboleh* 4, 1342 (August 26, 1924), in *Faslnameh-ye Motala'at-e Tarikhi* 7, no. 27 (Winter 1388/2009), pp. 245–246; see also, Behbudi, *Ruzshumar-e Tarikh-e Mu'asir-e Iran*, Vol. 2, p. 739.

[79] Bayrami, "Chalesh-e Iran va Engelestan bar sar-e Hakemiyyat bar Bahreyn," pp. 127–166.

[80] See Ahmad Faramarzi's article "Naft-e Bahreyn va Negar-e Jarideh-ye Kharejeh," reproduced in 'Ali Farahmand, "Naqdi bar Tarikhi Tahrikat-e Engelis va Edde'aha-ye barkhi A'rab dar Khalij-e Fars, 1313," *Tarikh-e Ravabet-e Khareji*, nos. 24–25 (Fall/Winter 1384/2005), pp. 137–170.

In Bahrain, Iranian nationalist sentiments were soon appropriated as part of a local struggle between competing factions within the Iranian immigrant community. In July 1920, two leading Iranian merchants were appointed by Political Agent Harold Dickson as the representatives of foreign communities in the Majlis, Muhammad Sharif Awazi on behalf of the Iranian Sunnis and ʻAbd al-Nabi Bushiri on behalf of the Iranian Shiʻa. Soon after, both were also appointed to the municipal council. Their patronage by the British gave them a distinct advantage over other rival community leaders. One of those who particularly resented British interference in Bahrain was ʻAbd al-Nabi Kazeruni the patron of a small group of Shiʻi Iranian shopkeepers.[81] For him, the rise of Iranian nationalist sentiment in the region and Iran's claim to sovereignty over Bahrain were useful tools that could be employed to contest British intrusions in Bahrain, which dealt him a distinct disadvantage in relation to his competitors.

As new immigrants, there was a fair amount of cooperation between the two ʻAbd al-Nabi's, especially in the establishment of religious and educational institutions in Bahrain for the Shiʻi immigrant labor force.[82] But enmity between them apparently grew up during a land dispute that was decided by the British Political Agent in favor of Bushiri. Major Daly related that Kazeruni appealed to Muhammad Sharif to help him "down" Bushiri but the later refused.[83] The elevation of Sharif to the municipal secretariat in June 1921 and the growing cooperation between Sharif and Bushiri was viewed by ʻAbd al-Nabi Kazeruni with suspicion. Daly related that the tensions between Bushiri and Kazeruni almost came to blows in the spring of 1922, when a fracas nearly erupted between the *taʻzieh* processions of their respective factions. The disturbance was put down by the police force headed by none other than Muhammad Sharif.[84]

In his bid to challenge the leadership of Muhammad Sharif and ʻAbd al-Nabi Bushiri, which had converged under the umbrella of British protection, ʻAbd al-Nabi Kazeruni mobilized his faction, a group of about 40 men, under the title of "the Nationalist Party," and encouraged them by various means to agitate in favor of renewing Iran's

[81] See Chapter 1. [82] Sayf, *al-Ma'tam fi al-Bahrayn*, Vol. 1, pp. 109–111.
[83] IOR/R/15/1/319: The Agency Bahrain (Daly) to the Political Resident (Trevor), November 1, 1922.
[84] IOR/R/15/1/319: The Agency Bahrain (Daly) to the Political Resident (Knox), April 22, 1923.

claim to Bahrain.[85] Their apparent objective was to drag the Iranian government into Bahrain's affairs to the detriment of British influence on the archipelago. Their activities included letters and visits to the *Kargozar* at Bushehr, inspiration for a spate of articles that appeared in the Persian press, and telegrams to the authorities in Tehran.[86]

In the interest of gaining the support of the Iranian government, 'Abd al-Nabi Kazeruni and one of his loyalists, Abu Talib, a tally clerk for the Mesopotamia Persia Corporation, endeavored to forge ties with Iranian journalists, local authorities, and military men. Abu Talib was instrumental in an agitation for Bahrainis abroad to visit Iranian consulates and register themselves as Iranian citizens. He was also responsible for organizing a patriotic reception in Bahrain for Major 'Ali Asghar Khan, the commander of the Bushehr garrison, thereby gaining the attention of the Iranian Ministry of War and Ministry of Foreign Affairs.[87]

In another intrigue that took place during the summer of 1922, the two men hosted a Shirazi journalist, Mirza Ahmad Khan Jahromi, in Bahrain.[88] After hearing their accusations against Muhammad Sharif, the journalist approached Sharif and attempted to obtain extortion money in return for a pledge not to print his name in the paper. But having failed to get anything from him, the journalist returned to Shiraz and unleashed a vilification campaign against Muhammad Sharif and, to a lesser extent, against 'Abd al-Nabi Bushiri.[89] Both men were characterized as the worst kind of Anglophiles, a label that was particularly damaging in the context of the anti-British rancor in Iran. Muhammad Sharif was accused of spying for the British during the Great War.[90] He was also accused of assisting the British in

85 IOR/R/15/1/319: Political Agent Bahrain to Political Resident, March 24, 1922; Political Resident to Minister at Tehran, March 25, 1922; and Administration Report of the Persian Gulf Residency for the Year 1922, p. 53.

86 See for example, *'Asr-e Azadi*, July 30, September 21, October 17 and 25, and November 4, 1922, and *Estakhr*, July 25 and September 17, 1922, IOR/R/15/1/319.

87 IOR/R/15/1/320: The Residency to Mr. William Spence, Director, Mesopotamia Persia Corporation Limited, February 21, 1924. See also Chapter 3.

88 IOR/R/15/1/319: Political Residency (Trevor) to Foreign Secretary to the Government of India (Bray), October 17, 1922.

89 IOR/R/15/1/319: The Agency Bahrain (Daly) to Political Resident (Trevor), October 30, 1922.

90 IOR/R/15/1/319: *Estakhr*, September 17, 1922, and *'Asr-e Azadi*, September 21, and October 17 and 25, 1922.

committing myriad crimes against the poor Iranians residing in Bahrain and 'Abd al-Nabi Bushiri was named as his accomplice.[91] Among other outrages, it was said that Muhammad Sharif hauled down the Iranian flag in Bahrain, prevented the observance of Shi'i rituals, and used his position to punish Iranians just for the crime of being patriotic. Sharif was also said to be the one responsible for the illegal smuggling trade from Bahrain.[92] The articles called upon the shah, the Cabinet, and the Majles to consider the plight of the Iranians suffering in Bahrain and appoint a governor or consul to save them from the tyranny of Sharif and the British.[93]

The group of patriots attempted to enlist the support of the local authorities, including *Kargozars*, governors, and postal and customs authorities, inviting them to visit Bahrain and play a role in the reassertion of Iranian sovereignty there.[94] Certain local authorities, who heeded British warnings not to try to visit Bahrain, were implicated by name in the Shiraz press campaign.[95] They were characterized as Iranian authorities who turned a deaf ear to the poor Iranian citizens who suffered under the oppression of the British and the Iranian Anglophiles in Bahrain.[96]

The rhetoric of the patriots affirmed both their national and factional loyalties and reflected the unique character of Iranian national and anti-colonial feeling that was forged in a predominantly Arab society under British protection. A good example is a petition dated January 5, 1923, addressed to the chairman of the Majles from the "grief-stricken community" of Iranian nationals in Bahrain. It was

[91] Ibid. See also *'Asr-e Azadi*, November 4, 1922, IOR/R/15/1/319.
[92] IOR/R/15/1/319: *'Asr-e Azadi*, September 21 and October 17 and 25, 1922.
[93] Ibid.
[94] See for example, Head *Kargozar* of the Persian Gulf Ports (Bushehr) to Ministry of Foreign Affairs, *Jowza'* 14, 1301 (June 5, 1922); and *Kargozar* of Arabistan to the Ministry of Foreign Affairs, *Tir* 13, 1302 (July 23, 1923), in *Gozideh-ye Asnad-e Khalij-e Fars*, Vol. 1, pp. 36–40 and 54–57; see also Muhammad 'Asiri to the Head *Kargozar* of the Persian Gulf Ports, August 12, 1922; and a letter "from Bahrain of the Persian Gulf" to the Head of the Persian Gulf Postal Administration, December 29, 1922, in Behbudi, *Ruzshumar-e Tarikh-e Mu'asir-e Iran*, Vol. 2, pp. 289 and 583.
[95] IOR/R/15/1/319: Political Residency to Resident, HMS *Cyclamen*, March 24, 1922; Political Residency to Minister Tehran, March 26, 1922.
[96] IOR/R/15/1/319: *'Asr-e Azadi*, October 17 and November 4, 1922.

endorsed by more than 40 individuals who declared that "any time the government asks, we are proud and ready to explain why Bahrain is an integral part of Iran."[97] They pleaded with the authorities in Tehran to intervene and reverse the effects of the Order in Council, which they said placed them under British jurisdiction: "Will we be considered Iranian subjects (*ro'aya*) or foreigners?" they asked. "And if we are subjects of Iran, then is the government of Iran informed about British interference … or do [the British] intervene without the knowledge of the [Iranian] government?"[98]

The letter asserts that goods smuggled from Bahrain into Mohammerah, Bushehr, Lingah, and Bandar Abbas were costing the government 1 to 2 million tomans per year. Based on their sense of Iranian dignity and national feeling, they entreated the government to do a better job of combating the smuggling trade. (Merchants profiting from the smuggling were members of the opposing faction, namely that of Muhammad Sharif). The signatories requested that a deputy (*vakil*) should be appointed to represent their interests in Tehran and they also asked the government to send a teacher from Tehran who could teach the Iranian children in Bahrain.[99]

By the middle of 1923, the ability of the nationalist faction to appeal to the Iranian authorities was sharply curtailed as a result of acute British interventions – most notably the forced retirement of Shaykh 'Isa and the elevation of Shaykh Hamad as regent. Shaykh Hamad proved amenable to the kind of decisive measures that the British proposed for eliminating Iran's influence in Bahrain. Whereas Shaykh 'Isa had opposed the deportation of Iranian agitators, viewing them as a useful pressure tool against the British, Shaykh Hamad derived his power from his association with the British and proved favorable toward their desire to deport and exile those who agitated against the new Bahrain administration. The threat of expulsion was an effective means of containing agitation from the Iranian patriots, but also an effective means of curtailing the threat posed by the Arab opposition faction made up of Sunni and tribal elites who opposed the imposition of reforms.

[97] 'Ali Zarrin Qalam, *Sarzamin-e Bahreyn: Az Dowran-e Bastan ta Emruz* (Tehran: Ketabfurushi-ye Sirus, 1337/1958), pp. 166–170.
[98] Ibid. [99] Ibid.

Iran, Iranians, and the Rise of Arab Sentiment in Bahrain, 1923–1939

Bahrain's unique experience with Iran and Iranian nationalism during the interwar period was instrumental in the emergence of a new nationalist discourse. Tribal elites, who had been exposed to the anti-colonial struggle in India and the promotion of Arab nationalism in Cairo, readily adopted the language of Arabism as a subject of political organization in service to their struggle against unwanted foreign intrusions. Moreover, the deposition of Shaykh ʿIsa by the British proved to be a critical juncture in the rise of Arab nationalist sentiment in Bahrain.[100]

A new vocabulary, which focused on the dichotomy between the "Arab nation" and the Iranian "foreigners," emerged after the Arab-Iranian clashes that took place during the month of Ramadan in 1923. These were the clashes that were viewed by the British as the propitious moment to intervene and forcibly retire Shaykh ʿIsa. Violence erupted on May 10 as the result of a quarrel in the market between Najdis and Iranians. The *casus belli* was said to be the discovery of a stolen watch, belonging to ʿAbdullah al-Qusaybi, in the possession of an Iranian shopkeeper. Attacks and counterattacks between Najdis and Iranians left eight dead and many more wounded. Hostilities continued for several days, during which an armed party of Najdis arrived by boat and attempted to land near the Persian quarter.[101] In the midst of the fray, accusations of biased dealing surfaced against the police force, headed by Muhammad Sharif and composed of mostly Iranians; ʿAbdullah al-Qusaybi accused the police of siding with the Iranian party against his Najdi men during the riots. Shaykh Hamad agreed with al-Qusaybi and ordered the police to surrender their weapons. Al-Qusaybi continued to air his grievances against the "foreign police force," and was ordered by the British Political Agent to stay inside his office until the riots could be quelled. The violence was at last subdued by the arrival of the Resident, the removal of the instigators from the island, and the forced retirement of Shaykh ʿIsa.

[100] Jamal Zakariyya Qasim, *al-Khalij al-ʿArabi: Dirasa li-Tarikh al-Imarat al-ʿArabiyya, 1914–1945* (Cairo: Dar al-Fikr al-ʿArabi, 1973), pp. 202–242.

[101] IOR/R/15/2/127: Knox to Secretary of State for the Colonies, May 12, 1923.

In the immediate aftermath of the riots, the tribal allies of Shaykh 'Isa promoted an account of the assaults that focused on the role of Muhammad Sharif and his "Iranian police force." They submitted a letter to the Resident protesting Britain's interference in Bahrain's internal affairs. Moreover, they accused Britain of a lack of respect for the "Arab nation."[102] At the top of their list of grievances were the actions of the British government in "entrusting the municipal affairs of an Arab town to a Persian man."[103] The letter also alleged that it was "national fanaticism" that had caused the Iranians to convert a simple dispute into a bloody riot. And much to their astonishment, the British solution to the troubles caused by the "fanatical" Iranian foreigners was the forced abdication of the legitimate Ruler of Bahrain.[104]

The supporters of Shaykh 'Isa shunned the majlis convened by Shaykh Hamad, and gathered instead under the title of the "Bahrain National Congress," organized by 'Abd al-Wahhab al-Zayyani. The congress produced a petition signed by Shaykh 'Isa and 10 Sunni tribal shaykhs, demanding that authority be restored to 'Isa. 'Abd al-Wahhab al-Zayyani organized a second petition, supported by prominent Sunni pearl merchants and tribal heads, namely Ahmad bin Lahej Al-Nu'aymi and Ahmad al-Dawsari.[105] The congress appointed 12 representatives and produced another petition, which was presented to the Political Resident during his visit in the first week of November 1923. The petition demanded that Shaykh 'Isa should remain as ruler, unless out of his own free will he appointed Hamad to rule in his stead. It called for the restoration of the authority of the traditional law courts in accordance with Shari'a. And among other demands, it called for the establishment of a national parliament to look after the interests of the people of Bahrain.

These men, the leaders of the Bahrain National Congress, were viewed by Shaykh Hamad as the main threat to his regency and to

[102] IOR/R/15/1/338: Political Agent Bahrain (Daly) to Political Resident, October 17, 1923, with enclosure "translation of a petition without date" signed by Shaykh 'Isa and the heads of 10 tribes including the Sada, Al Bu Falasah, Mosallam, Jalahimah, Zayyani, Na'im, Manan'ah, Dawasir, Al Bin 'Ali, and Bin Jodar tribes.

[103] Ibid. [104] Ibid.

[105] IOR/R/15/1/338: Political Agent Bahrain (Daly) to Political Resident Bushire (Trevor), October 29, 1923.

the stability of Bahrain. When Shaykh Hamad requested help in deporting it leaders, the British government was more than willing to oblige because it viewed them as the primary obstacle to much-needed reform.[106] On November 7, 1923, the representatives of the Bahrain National Congress were invited to a meeting with the British Resident. After the meeting, two of its main leaders, 'Abd al-Wahhab al-Zayyani and Ahmad bin Lahej, were detained and then deported to India.[107] The Dawasir tribe was given an ultimatum, the result of which was the exodus of a large segment of the tribe.[108] A subsequent revenge attack on the Bahrani village of Sitra on January 7, 1924, perpetrated by Shaykh 'Isa's brother, Shaykh Khalid Al Khalifa, and his sons resulted in their trial and conviction by Shaykh Hamad Al Khalifa.[109]

By the end of 1924, relations between Sunnis and Baharna were showing signs of improvement, but disaffected tribal elites, some of whom had been punished or deported for their complicity in the violence, fought back by promoting a narrative of the events that identified the root cause of Bahrain's problems as collusion between Iranian "foreigners" and British imperialists. By the mid-1920s, Nasr al-Khayri, whose unpublished manuscript chronicled Bahrain's history up until those fateful events of Ramadan 1923, identified the Iranian immigrants as the main threat to Bahrain's traditional tribal order. This emergent emphasis on the Arab-Iranian dichotomy coalesced into a national narrative that differentiated between the legitimate national subjects of Bahrain and the foreign "other."[110] The receptivity of these ideas was also reflected in the activities of Arab schools where headmasters, with encouragement from Belgrave, adopted the practice of parading with red Arab flags, mirroring the nationalist exhibitions put on by the Iranian schoolchildren.[111]

The experience of Bahrain subjects in Pahlavi Iran was particularly instrumental in forging new bonds between Bahrain's Sunni and Shi'i

106 IOR/R/15/1/338: Political Resident Bushire (Trevor) to the Foreign and Political Department Simla, October 29, 1923.
107 IOR/R/15/1/338: Political Resident Bushire (Trevor) to the Foreign Secretary to the Government of India Delhi, November 10, 1923.
108 Rumaihi, *Bahrain*, pp. 180–182.
109 Al-Tajir, *Bahrain: 1920–1945*, pp. 667–669.
110 Nasr ibn Jawhar ibn Mubarak Al-Khayri, *Qala'id al-nahrayn fi tarikh al-Bahrayn*, ed. 'Abd al-Rahman ibn 'Abdullah al-Shuqayr (Manama: Al-Ayyam lil-Nashr, 2003 [ca. 1920s]).
111 Administration Report of the Persian Gulf Residency for the Year 1927, p. 34.

Arabs and further isolating Iranian nationals from the Arab populace. In the end of 1929, Manama was awash with talk of the oppression of Baharna at the hands of Iranian authorities in Khuzestan. These reports were punctuated with declarations of the Baharna's loyalty to their Bahraini nationality and statements to the effect that they would rather die than become Iranian subjects.[112] The Political Agent reported that these circumstances engendered a growing undercurrent of Arab feeling against all Iranian nationals. Arabs, he said, resented their privileged position and the support they received from the British government. Iranians were well represented in the municipal council of Manama, on the police force, and in the commercial court (*majlis al-tujjar*). As foreigners, they were allowed to have their own schools, acquire property, and conduct their trade without restriction. And there was a suspicion that as British protected persons, they were able to make considerable headway against subjects of the shaykh in commercial endeavors. Many Iranians owned very valuable property in Bahrain including land, buildings, gardens, and water rights. The Political Agent observed, "There was a feeling in Bahrain that they should be made to return to where they came from."[113]

In the 1930s, the popularization of the political language of Arabism was buoyed by a critical juncture in the evolution of the modern nation-state – the collapse of the pearling industry and the rise of the oil industry. Competition for scarce economic resources in the wake of the pearling collapse fashioned another field of popular contestation against the Iranian "other." The discovery of oil in 1932 and its exploitation by the Bahrain Petroleum Company (BAPCO) began to provide a source of income for hundreds of destitute pearl workers and manual laborers. Through employment in the foreign-owned oil company, the Shi'a were brought into greater contact with the Sunnis, and in some cases even placed in positions of authority over them, a factor that contributed to a growing sense of commonality between the two groups.[114]

112 IOR/R/15/2/486: Office of the Adviser to the Government, Bahrain (Belgrave) to Political Agent (Prior), October 8, 1932, with enclosures; and Office of the Adviser to the Government, Bahrain (Belgrave) to Political Agent (Loch), March 14, 1934, with enclosures.

113 IOR/R/15/2/138: Political Agent Bahrain (Prior) to Consul-General Barrett, November 4, 1929.

114 Rumaihi, *Bahrain*, p. 27.

While the arrival of the oil company eased certain communal divisions, it exacerbated others – particularly the division between Arabs and Iranians. Early skilled and semiskilled employment in the company was largely dominated by Iranians of Persian heritage. The company's employment of foreigners, especially Iranian nationals, was the subject of numerous protests from the Bahrain government and the Political Agent, who feared that the influx of Iranian labor migrants would exacerbate sectarian tensions and provoke the interference of the Iranian government. In its June 1932 transfer agreement, BAPCO had committed to restrict its employment to subjects of the shaykh as far as possible, and recruit foreign labor only if skilled labor and technical expertise could not be found among British Indian and Bahraini subjects. But despite repeated warnings, the company continued to recruit Iranians for semiskilled labor, arguing that they were unable to obtain sufficient Bahrainis to handle their requirements. From BAPCO's perspective, the employment of Iranians offered a number of advantages over the employment of British Indians and other foreign nationals: Iranians arrived to Bahrain at their own expense whereas the recruitment of Indians involved travel and relocation expenses; many Iranians came with prior experience in the oil industry, having worked for APOC; and unlike Indians, Iranians could be hired without formal contracts – making it possible to hire and fire them at will. Even though the company increased its recruitment of Indians in the latter half of the 1930s, Iranians still factored large on the labor rosters.[115]

In the 1930s, the urban neighborhoods of Manama were inundated with new arrivals from Iran. In his administrative report for the year 1937, Charles Belgrave noted that in spite of the vigilance of passport officials, "great numbers of indigent Persians have entered Bahrain, illegally, at various points on the coast."[116] Many of these people obtained work with BAPCO and filled jobs that "should be occupied by Bahrain subjects," he noted.[117] He went on to say, "the enormous

115 Seccombe and Lawless, "Foreign Worker Dependence in the Gulf, and the International Oil Companies: 1910–50," pp. 559–560.
116 Government of Bahrain, Administrative Report for the Years, 1926–1927, p. 41, in R. Jarman, ed. *The Bahrain Government Annual Reports 1924–1970*, Vol. 2 (Archive Editions, 1986).
117 Ibid.

increase in Persians, most of whom entered Bahrain without permission, is especially noticeable in Manama, where almost every other person in the bazaar and nine out of ten of the beggars appear to be Persians."[118]

New laws that imputed citizenship to the children of immigrants born on Bahraini soil and to those holding registered property (in 1929 and 1937, respectively) did little to ameliorate the popular notion that ethnic Persians, Baluchis, and other minorities born on Bahraini soil were not real Bahrainis. Their perceived foreignness was epitomized in one local man's depiction of a municipal employee as a "Persian opium smoker who is almost illiterate and cannot speak Arabic properly."[119] In response to the complaint that the oil company hired a disproportionate number of foreign laborers to the detriment of the national labor force, the Political Agent drew attention to what he called a "local misapprehension."[120] "Local people," he said, "are inclined to forget that children born in Bahrain of ... Persian parents are Bahrain subjects unless they divest themselves of Bahraini nationality."[121] He went on to say that due to greater attention to the issue of nationality, the actual number of Iranian nationals employed by the company was steadily decreasing.[122]

The company's gradual shift from dependence on Iranian skilled labor to Indian skilled labor in the latter half of the 1930s did not stem the tide of the growing sense that Bahraini jobs should be for Bahrainis.[123] Whether it was the introduction of Iranians or Indians or Iraqis to the Bahrain labor market, Arab subjects of the shaykh began to agitate for the "Bahrainization" of the labor market as a countermeasure to what they saw as the increasing "Indianization" of Bahrain. It is not therefore surprising that the leaders of the 1938 reform

[118] Ibid.
[119] IOR/R/15/1/343: Political Agent Bahrain to Political Resident, October 29, 1938, with enclosures.
[120] IOR/R/15/1/343: Political Agent Bahrain to Political Resident, December 10, 1938.
[121] Ibid.
[122] IOR/R/15/1/343: Political Agent Bahrain to Political Resident, December 10, 1938.
[123] IOR/R/15/2/490: Political Agent Bahrain to Political Resident (Fowle), June 4, 1933.

movement put an emphasis on the idea that employment and political participation in Bahrain should be for the "natives" of Bahrain.

Arabs, Iranians, and the Reform Movement of 1938

The 1938 majlis movement in Kuwait and a similar movement in Dubai that same year gave inspiration to agitations for a more representative form of government in Bahrain. The unrest that rose up in Manama in the end of 1938 can be attributed to a number of interrelated circumstances; the rise of organized youth movements drawing their inspiration from the nationalist press in Cairo, Baghdad, and Damascus; dissatisfaction with labor conditions for Bahraini nationals; dissatisfaction with an education system that failed to equip Bahrainis to compete with foreigners for skilled jobs; the activism of some individuals who harbored personal grievances against the Bahrain administration; and uncertainty surrounding the successor to ailing Shaykh Hamad.

The first sign of unrest took the form of inter-sectarian meetings between some of the prominent Sunni and Shiʿi merchants with the aim of collaboration on a number of social and political initiatives. Hajji Yusuf Fakroo, a merchant from a well-established Hawala family, was among the Sunnis who took the lead in these discussions.[124] The Sunnis were to a large extent, motivated by a desire to secure Shiʿi recognition of Shaykh Salman Al Khalifa as Hamad's heir apparent in exchange for the promise of reforms that would benefit the Shiʿi villagers. The events of 1923 had taught them that a smooth transition of power required support from the island's majority Shiʿi population.[125] The result was a petition, signed by five leading Sunni, Shiʿi, and Hindi merchants, which presented demands for reform in the police, courts, education department, and the formation of a legislative committee.[126] What was perhaps a more significant outcome of these meetings was the growing

[124] IOR/R/15/2/176: Political Agent Bahrain (Weightman) to Political Resident in Kuwait, October 13, 1938, with enclosures.
[125] IOR/R/15/2/176: Confidential Minute, Political Agent Bahrain, n.d.
[126] IOR/R/15/1/343: Translation of a Memorandum Containing Demands Submitted to His Highness Shaykh Sir Hamad by Five Merchants of Bahrain Dated *Ramadan* 19, 1357–November 12, 1938.

recognition of the need for elected representation in national bodies and a growing awareness of entitlements for the indigenous labor force.

The agitation for reform was thrust into a new phase when Hawala merchants, fluent in nationalist ideas, came together with some Sunni Arabs who harbored grievances against the Bahrain administration and especially the courts that were now dominated by Belgrave. This group included ʻAli bin Khalifa al-Fadhil, who resented his dismissal from the municipality and was later convicted of misappropriating *waqf* (religious endowment) funds; Saʻd al-Shamlan, a judge who had been debarred from appearing in court owing to malpractices; Ahmed al-Shirawi, a judge whose reputation suffered from similar malpractices; and Ibrahim ʻAbd al-Kamal, who had done nine months in jail for fraud. Resentful of a British-imposed justice system, which they viewed as unfair, they managed to stir up the semi-educated and politically aware youths of Manama and Muharraq among whom grievances against the Bahrain administration could also be found in abundance.[127]

During the second half of the 1930s, a number of social and cultural clubs had emerged that served as a focus of nationalist activity among the younger generation, particularly the semi-educated Hawala youth whose nationalist sentiments sprung from their frequent contacts with the outside world. Several of these groups, namely Shabab al-Ahrar (Free Youth) Shabab al-Umma (Islamic Youth) and al-Shabab al-Watani (National Youth) joined the agitation for reforms.[128] Their angry graffiti began to appear on the walls of Manama.[129] Rumors circulated to the effect that the British government – which came down hard on the side of reforms in 1923 – would again put its support behind the reform party; however, unbeknownst to the would-be reformers, the British government was inclined to view the status quo as better suited to its interests than the disorder proffered by the angry youth.[130]

127 Bahrain Government Administrative Report for the Year 1357 (March 1938–Februrary 1939), pp. 29–30; IOR/R/15/1/343: Political Agent Bahrain to Political Resident, November 12, 1938.

128 IOR/R/15/1/176: letters and leaflets by *Shabab al-Ahrar*, *Shabab al-Umma* and *Shabab al-Watani.*

129 IOR/R/15/1/176: Confidential Minute, Political Agent Bahrain, n.d.

130 IOR/R/15/1/343: Political Agent Bahrain to Political Resident, November 12, 1938; IOR/R/15/1/344: Political Resident to the Secretary to the Government of India, April 14, 1939.

During Ramadan, al-Shamlan, al-Shirawi and ‘Abd al-Kamal were arrested for their role in trying to stir up an agitation against Shaykh Hamad. The fourth instigator, ‘Ali bin Khalifa al-Fadhil turned to the youth who had grievances of their own – namely the low rate of pay that they received in comparison with foreign workers in the labor market. He encouraged them to stage a labor strike in the oil fields and offices of BAPCO. The youth formed a picket line and tried to prevent laborers from appearing at work, but they found it difficult to stir up their coworkers, especially the Baharna. The Baharna shunned civil disobedience, preferring instead to make their grievances known to the Bahrain administration through the intercession of their community leaders.[131] Thus, when the labor strike failed, the throng of angry young people attempted to stir up the Iranian nationals who worked as shopkeepers in the market in a clever ploy that resembled the Ramadan clashes of 1904 and 1923. After a meeting in which ‘Ali bin Khalifa al-Fadhil addressed a crowd of several hundred young people in Jum‘a Mosque, the young people stormed out into the market and made a demonstration ordering the shops to close. The police, who expected this to happen, handily brought the situation under control, and the ringleaders, second-generation Sunni and Shi‘i immigrants from Iran, were arrested.[132]

Angry protests were sent to the Bahrain administration by several of the youth organizations.[133] One of them signed by Shabab al-Umma declared “the whole nation has been experiencing various sorts of chaos in the courts, corruption in the education and schools and

131 Bahrain Government Administrative Report for the Year 1357 (March 1938–Februrary 1939), pp. 29–30; IOR/R/15/1/343: Political Agent Bahrain (Weightman) to Political Resident, November 12, 1938; IOR/R/15/1/344: Advisor to the Government of Bahrain (Belgrave) to Political Agent Bahrain, January 18, 1939, with enclosure; IOR/R/15/2/176: Translation of a petition from the people of Hedd to His Highness Shaykh Sir Hamad, received by His Highness on *Ramadan* 24, 1357; Memorandum, Advisor to the Government of Bahrain (Belgrave), *Ramadan* 29, 1357 (November 22, 1938); Memorandum, Advisor to the Government of Bahrain (Belgrave), *Shawwal* 15, 1357 (December 8, 1938).

132 Bahrain Government Administrative Report for the Year 1357 (March 1938–Februrary 1939), pp. 29–30; IOR/R/15/1/343: Political Agent Bahrain to Political Resident, November 12, 1938.

133 IOR/R/15/1/343: Petition from *Shabab al-Umma* to Political Agent Bahrain, *Ramadan* 16, 1357 (November 9, 1938) and Petition by *Shabab al-Watani* to Political Agent Bahrain, n.d.

mishandling of all the resources."[134] Their first demand was the release of the "native prisoners," the formation of a council for the education department, the formation of a council for judicial affairs to be composed of Bahrain "natives" selected by the nation, and the establishment of a committee that would see that justice is done for the laborers.[135] These demands attest to the familiarity of the youth with the discourse of national rights being promoted by the Arabic press as well as their own interest in emphasizing the "native-born" criteria of the true Bahraini national over the Arab criteria that had been promoted by the supporters of Shaykh 'Isa in the 1920s.

Efforts were made in the Bahrain government to remove the causes of unrest by implementing a series of reforms in the court system, the labor sector and the educational system. But some elements of the populist rhetoric of the national movement that was born out of the 1920s and 1930s gained steam in future decades. Cultural and sports clubs that served as vehicles for the spread of nationalist ideas burgeoned in the years following the Second World War. Expanding national education and rising literacy spread political consciousness to the urban and agricultural strata of society. Already in the 1930s the traditional politics of patronage were giving way to new forms of communal organization that focused variously on the interests of the "native" Bahrainis to the exclusion of the foreign born.

Bahrain on the Eve of the Second World War

Bahrain's unique experience with Iranian nationalism situated Bahrain at the center of the Arab-Iranian conflict in the Persian Gulf during the interwar years. The particularly virulent strain of anti-colonial, nationalist impulses manifested in Iran in the aftermath of the first World War also found expression among segments of the Iranian immigrant communities in Bahrain. One group, which depicted themselves as the authentic Iranian patriots, viewed Bahrain as an Iranian island where British pressure prevented Arab shaykhs from returning to the protective arms of Iran. Their agitations for the renewal of Iranian sovereignty over Bahrain in the thick of the sectarian fighting and bold British-sponsored reforms of the early 1920s gained the attention of the centralizing state in Tehran and helped to cast Bahrain as a vital

[134] Ibid. [135] Ibid.

component of the official nationalist discourse of the Pahlavi state. Another group – Sunni tribal elites whose traditional tribal privileges and influence were diminished by economic transformations and modernizing reforms – also attempted, albeit unsuccessfully, to use Iran's aspirations toward Bahrain as a brake pedal against the march of imperial penetration.

The challenge of Pahlavi Iran to the British position in the Persian Gulf in general and in Bahrain in particular, drew Britain into the kind of intervention in Bahrain that was unparalleled in any of the other Arab shaykhdoms. The prospect of interference by regional powers – Iran in particular – was the catalyst for the dramatic British interventions of the 1920s that laid the bureaucratic foundations of the modern nation-state. The modernization of the traditional tribal administration was further hastened by the decisive economic transformation of the 1930s. The collapse of the pearl industry after 1929 followed by the introduction of oil revenues to the ruler's coffer in 1935 weakened the traditional influence of the pearl merchants and consolidated political and economic power in the hands of the ruler. The relative stability afforded by the emergence of a modern economy and state administration made Bahrain the most attractive site for the future headquarters of the British Persian Gulf Administration. The transfer of the British air route and naval base from Iran to Bahrain, in 1932 and 1935, respectively, consolidated the position that it would occupy as the bastion of British hegemony in the Persian Gulf until their complete withdrawal in 1971.

By the time of the Second World War, the crystallization of an historic process was discernible in Bahrain whereby the old pattern of patronage politics – which had long tied the Al Khalifa family and its tribal allies to the British government – had become a focus of popular discontent. National divisions were conspicuously overtaking the importance formerly attached to religious solidarities. New ideas had been introduced, including ideas about national rights and popular representation in decision-making bodies.[136] A younger generation of activists, the majority of them the children of immigrants from Iran, composed a critique that cast British imperialism and Arab tribalism as

[136] Assem Dessouki, "Social and Political Dimensions of the Historiography of the Arab Gulf," in *Statecraft in the Middle East: Oil, Historical Memory, and Popular Culture*, eds. Eric Davis and Nicolas Gavrielides (Miami: Florida University Press, 1991), pp. 110–111.

the root of Bahrain's social ills. Traditional elites composed a polemic in which foreigners who prospered under British tutelage were the agents of colonial exploitation.[137] Intermittent calls for "Arabization" or "Bahrainization" – political goals that were by no means coterminous – divulged the new fault lines crisscrossing the social and political landscape of Bahrain.

[137] Fuccaro, *Histories of City and State in the Persian Gulf*, p. 177.

Conclusion

The dramatic events of the interwar period constituted a watershed, separating millennia of interconnectedness and interdependency in the Persian Gulf from an era of geopolitical rivalry and Arab-Iranian conflict. Indeed, these two decades heralded the dawn of economic and political modernity in the Persian Gulf subregion. This period witnessed the collapse of the Qajar dynasty, the coming to the fore of Reza Shah Pahlavi and his assumption of the nationalist mantle, the introduction of nationalist policies into the Persian Gulf, and the incorporation of the Gulf Arab shaykhdoms into the Arab nationalist awakening. Reza Shah's Iran took issue with Britain's dominant position in the Gulf and rejected its claim to protect the Arab shaykhs of the southern littoral and strove to make Iran the main security provider in the Persian Gulf waterway. Iran's ambition to gain sovereignty over the entire Persian Gulf region and regain territories of its former days was an ambition that resonated in the minds of many Iranian people. Iran's bellicose policies also made a substantial and lasting impression on the rulers and inhabitants of the Gulf Arab shaykhdoms.

The interwar period was witness to the dawn of pan-Arab ideas in the Gulf Arab shaykhdoms and these ideas were appropriated as an answer to growing Iranian nationalist agitations and British penetration. In the 1920s, nationalist newspapers from Cairo and Baghdad were making their mark on the educated and semi-educated elites in Kuwait, Manama, Dubai, and Sharjah. The recruitment of teachers from Iraq, Palestine, and Cairo contributed to the spread of pan-Islamic and pan-Arab ideas and the founding of youth movements and literary clubs. Merchant elites, who had been exposed to the anti-colonial struggle in India and the promotion of Arab nationalism in Cairo, adopted the language of Arabism as a subject of political mobilization. Emblematic of these transformative processes was the emergence of a new discourse in Bahrain that deemphasized the traditional religious and sectarian divides and focused instead on the dichotomy between the "Arab nation" and the Iranian "foreigner." By the beginning of the Second World War, the importance of national divisions in the shaykhdoms conspicuously overshadowed the importance formerly attached to sectarian and religious solidarities.

The interwar years also marked the incorporation of the Persian Gulf into the pan-Arab idea. The Iranian threat to its Arab neighbors was introduced as a rallying point for Arab unity in the nationalist press of Cairo, Damascus, and Baghdad. Illustrative of this process was an article that appeared in a December 1934 issue of *al-Muqattam*, a pro-British paper published in Cairo. Under the heading "The Issues of the Shatt al-Arab and Bahrain before the League of Nations," the author outlined four serious causes of Arab concern. These were Iran's refusal to recognize the state of Iraq; its desire to "occupy a portion of the Iraqi Shatt al-Arab"; its desire to take possession of the Island of Bahrain; and its "secret desire" to "extend its influence over the western coast of the Persian Gulf, inhabited by Arabs" who were in treaty relations with the British government. The article culminated in a warning to Iran to "deviate from this policy on account of the effect it has on the minds of all the Arabs."[1]

The application of pan-Arab ideals to the affairs of the Gulf Arab states was energetically promoted in the 1930s by some prominent Kuwaiti businessmen who resented foreign interference in the affairs of Kuwait. With the support of the Iraqi government, some wealthy merchants engaged in the Kuwait-Basra trade began to promote the idea that Kuwait should be joined to Iraq.[2] By 1934, a spirited campaign for political unification was being conducted in the Iraqi nationalist press. One gambit that was used to arouse interest in the idea of political union was the insertion of some rumors in the Cairo and Baghdad newspapers to the effect that the British government conspired to set up a "Gulf Kingdom" by extending and consolidating their control over the Arab states from Kuwait to Muscat.[3] Other articles complained of oppression that inhabitants of the shaykhdoms suffered under the existing regimes and identified British involvement as the chief impediment to the freedom and independence of the Arab people. The Arab states of the Persian Gulf were advised to look for

[1] IOR/R/15/2/486: *al-Muqattam* (Cairo), December 17, 1934.
[2] Crystal, *Oil and Politics in the Gulf*, pp. 52–53.
[3] IOR/R/15/1/505: Summary of three articles from *al-Thagr* of Basra dated January 16, February 1, and February 5, 1934, respectively.

help and freedom to the new Iraqi state. After the failure of the 1938 reform movements, a number of disaffected young men from Bahrain and Dubai joined their conationalists in Kuwait under the framework of the "Society for the Unification of the Arabian Gulf."[4] Their choice of Basra as the nerve center for the dissemination of propaganda portended Iraq's emerging ambition to be the primary agent of Arab-nationalism in the Persian Gulf region.

Iran looked on with growing alarm as Gulf unity schemes were being aired in the Arab nationalist press and radio broadcasts. What was particularly alarming, from the perspective of Iran, was the rumor that the British government was conspiring to create a federation of Gulf Arab states under its tutelage. Myriad communiqués devoted to this rumor attested to the importance attached to the Persian Gulf in Iran's strategic thinking.[5] But Iran's inability to impact on developments in the region exposed the yawning chasm between its words and deeds. Iran's failure in this regard was the subject of a particularly terse critique leveled by an Iranian diplomat in Brussels, who bluntly put the question: "Do the interests of Iran in the Persian Gulf amount to one-one hundredth of the interests of the British government which is located thousands of miles away from Iran?" How can it be, he asked, that "every person expresses interests in these waters but we who are seated right on their edge do not have the right to them!!! Today the British and tomorrow the Japanese or someone else will express interest in these waters and again we will watch."[6]

Nowadays the persistence of great power involvement in the Persian Gulf endures, changed in form but not in essence. The substitution of the American military in place of the British one in the aftermath of Britain's withdrawal in 1971 has continued to frustrate Iran's ambition for primacy in the region. Today, Iranian sea power is significantly

[4] Falah 'Abdullah Mudayris, *al-Harakat wa-l-Jama'at al-Siyasiyya fi al-Bahrayn, 1938–2002* (Beirut: Dar al-Kunuz al-Adabiyya, 2004), p. 7.

[5] Ministry of Foreign Affairs to Embassy Cairo, *Dey* 21, 1309 (January 11, 1931); Embassy Baghdad to Ministry of Foreign Affairs, *Bahman* 9, 1309 (January 29, 1931); Memorandum by the Ministry of Foreign Affairs, *Esfand* 20, 1309 (February 9, 1931); Memorandum by the Basra Consulate, *Dey* 9, 1312 (December 30, 1933), in 'Ali Farahmand, "Engelis va Parvazha-ye Iran-zedayi az Khalij-e Fars," *Tarikh-e Ravabet-e Khareji*, no. 22 (Spring 1384/2005), pp. 212–222.

[6] Minister of Iran Brussels to Ministry of Foreign Affairs, *Dey* 30, 1305 (January 21, 1927), in *Gozideh-ye Asnad-e Khalij-e Fars*, Vol. 1, pp. 297–303.

outgunned by Western naval forces, not the least of which is the American Fifth Fleet stationed in Bahrain. While the Gulf Arab monarchies and emirates view American forces in the Gulf as a guarantor of their own security, Iran views the American presence as a menace and an obstacle to its regional ambitions. The capacity of flamboyant naval exhibition to stir up national pride remains a potent tool in the hands of Iran's leaders: whereas Reza Shah showcased Iranian naval power by inviting the merchants of Bushehr and Lingah to tour Iran's new gun boats, the Islamic Republic of Iran loops video footage of missiles blasting over the ocean, submarines surfacing, fast torpedo boats practicing attacks, and helicopters deploying divers and commandoes.

Since the time of Reza Shah, Iran's regional ambitions have been a great source of anxiety and indignation for the Arab states of the Persian Gulf. In 1970, after a UN mission determined that the Bahraini populace rejected the idea of unification with Iran, Iran officially dropped its claim to the island; however, the propensity on the part of some Iranian officials to continue to characterize Bahrain as the "fourteenth province of Iran" has continued to fuel mistrust and suspicion.[7] Moreover Iran's forcible seizure of Abu Musa and the Tunbs the day after the British forces withdrew contributed to the perception among inhabitants of the Gulf that a greater role for Iran would merely amount to Iranization of the Gulf region. Arab-Iranian relations were severely worsened after the Islamic Revolution in 1979. Shi'i revolutionary ideology inserted a new dimension into the balance of power politics in the Gulf, providing some ideological tools through which Iran could attempt to destabilize the Gulf Arab regimes. The rise of violent conflict during the eight-year war between Iran and Iraq went a long way to embitter the Arab-Iranian divide that earlier state policies and nationalist movements had created. Iran's pursuit of nuclear capability and its willingness to stir up and fan the flames of sectarianism across the region has increased the reliance of the Gulf Arab rulers on an American security architecture that preserves their own family rule and regional standing.

[7] See for example, Ali Khan Ghazanfar, "GCC warns Iran against making hostile remarks," *Arab News*, February 23, 2009, www.arabnews.com/node/321272, (accessed December 17, 2018).

One of the central arguments of this book is that the basic security architecture in the Persian Gulf, which relies upon a Western power to constrain dissatisfied regional powers and preserve the existing international order, crystalized during the interwar period. The interwar period coincided with the rise of the modern state in Iran and the awakening of its ambition to regain the territorial dimensions of bygone days. The Arabian Peninsula went through rapid economic and political change. Oil was discovered in Bahrain, Kuwait, and Saudi Arabia. An airport and lodging house built at Sharjah transformed the Trucial Coast from an "inhospitable," tribal backwater to a highway between East and West. The interwar years marked an increase in the number of Europeans and Americans in all of the Arab shaykhdoms. Conversely, it was also a period in which travel between port towns in Iran and the shaykhdoms became subjected to travel and trade restrictions. Flows of people, capital, and goods previously hindered only by the impulses of nature became subjected to state regulations. Borders were closed to economic migrants and human smuggling materialized. People living in Bahrain and in the border area between Iran and Iraq were required to choose citizenship in one place or the other. Modern notions of citizenship and nationality began to vie for significance with traditional frameworks of identity, such as membership in a tribe, town, or religious community. Transnational frameworks of identity came under strain in light of political ideologies that demanded exclusionary identity frameworks. Families with multinational origins began to revise their histories to highlight aspects of "belonging" to either the Arab or Iranian "nation." People of Persian heritage who opted to maintain their long-established residences on the Arabian littoral became like "foreigners" in their own country.

The events of the interwar years accelerated the growth of Arab nationalist politics and anti-British sentiment in the Arab shaykhdoms. These currents, which have their roots in the interwar years, would multiply and reach their zenith in the era of Gamal Abdel Nasser. From the perspective of Gulf Arabs, the British government altered course during the interwar years by adopting a policy of appeasement toward Iran and intervention in their internal affairs. Britain's image in the shaykhdoms as a friendly protecting power became overshadowed by its image as a heavy-handed and self-interested imperial power. And yet, in spite of their displeasure with the standard of British protection, Iranian proclamations and provocations in the narrow waterway, coupled with domestic instability and alternative sources of revenue, compelled the Gulf Arab rulers to deepen their dependence on the British protective umbrella, much to the chagrin of their dependents. The rulers surmised that British supremacy in the Persian Gulf was the only reliable bulwark against Iranian expansionism. Thus began a new era in the Gulf Arab shaykhdoms, an era in which the rulers drew closer to the British government, even as their dependents increasingly adopted an anti-imperialist stance. The one-time legitimacy afforded to the Arab shaykhs' relationship with the British government was all but extinguished, yet the unequal power relationship deepened in spite of the displeasure of leading members of society.

In Bahrain, Kuwait, and Dubai, rival nationalisms shook the status quo. Iranian patriots staged nationalist exhibitions and campaigned for the reassertion of Iranian sovereignty over "usurped Iranian territory" in the Persian Gulf. They were joined in this agitation by some Hawala merchants, whose business activities were negatively affected by British policies. The popular inclinations toward Iran coming from some quarters provoked the British government to act decisively, to impose Westernizing and modernizing reforms in the Arab shaykhdoms as a means of hardening their position and denying Iran any foothold. In contrast to their long-established modus operandi, the British government was no longer achieving its objectives by working within the traditional tribal system, but rather it was gradually whittling it away. Arab tribesmen blamed Iranian nationalist "agitators" for drawing the British government deeper into Arab affairs and depriving them of their traditional, tribal privileges. The younger generation of Hawala activists advocated the demise of tribalism in favor of more inclusive and representative government. This group, relatively wealthy, educated, and well-traveled, promoted the notion of national "rights" for all Arabs. Their conception of political belonging was modern and based on ethnic and civic criteria rather than religious or tribal. While they depicted themselves as "indigenous Arabs" they were not perceived that way by all segments of society. There were those who emphasized the Persian and foreign manners of the Hawala – particularly the tribal and peninsular merchant families, the traditional elites who found their fortunes drained in the 1930s when the pearling market collapsed and world markets reeled under economic depression. They found that their own influence with the ruling family had been undermined by their economic hardship and as a result of British imposed reforms while some of the Hawala continued to profit from the sea-borne trade and continued to exercise leverage in political and economic affairs.

Under Reza Shah, Iranian nationalism increasingly became a state-driven ideology that cast the notions of territorial sovereignty and cultural unity as the main pillars of legitimation for the arbitrary rule of one military man. Iran had many territorial grievances, especially in the Persian Gulf, and the government embellished, amplified, and trumpeted them ceaselessly. But Iranian propaganda was deliberately ambiguous about the exact limits of Iran's territorial claims. Iran's claims to Bahrain, Abu Musa, and the Tunbs islands were frequently asserted, but the government also asserted ambiguous claims to parts of Iraq, Kuwait, Oman, and the Arabian littoral. Claiming the entire Persian Gulf seemed as much a means of challenging the legitimacy of Britain's position in the Gulf as a way of trying to improve Iran's bargaining position. Negotiations with the British government toward the aim of resolving bilateral disputes failed to produce an agreement, ostensibly because Iran was not prepared to relinquish its claim to sovereignty over Bahrain.

Iran's narrative, of the Iranian island of Bahrain groaning under the yoke of colonial oppression, pleased public opinion in Iran – at least those members of the public whose voices are on record. But at the same time, elements contravening and subverting this master narrative inevitably persisted. Local officials tasked with putting Iran's territorial claims into force by various means were confronted with glaring contradictions. Port officials who tried to enforce Iranian law regarding Bahraini travelers learned that it was the British government, not Iran, that regulated their travel. Naval officers reprimanded for planting a flag on an island claimed by Iran learned that there was a wide disparity between the territory Iran claimed and the territory it veritably possessed. Insecurity about land and borders prevented Iran from reaching a deal with the British government and accruing revenue for a long lease of facilities on Hengam Island. Paradoxically, Iran's aversion to hosting a British base on Iranian soil was the catalyst for the transfer of the base to the Arabian littoral, and the inauguration of Bahrain's role as the main host of Western military forces for decades to come.

Harsh polices that were intended to unify Iran prompted mass waves of emigration from Iran's southern coastal areas to the Arab states of the lower Gulf and the commercial strength of Iranian coastal towns declined drastically. The half-abandoned towns of the Iranian littoral featured as a subject of interest in the diary of Alan Villiers, an Australian mariner and travel writer, who sailed along the coast in 1938 as a passenger in a Kuwaiti dhow. He recalls entering into a conversation with the helmsman of his ship, Hassan, in which Hassan related the story of his own emigration from Kalat, a village on the southern coast of Iran. Hassan's story is particularly illustrative of the narratives of emigration during the time of Reza Shah. Hassan related that life in Kalat had been generally prosperous and good until the Shah of Iran began making a "monstrous attack on the precepts of Islam."[8] According to some people, he was "ruining the country." Among the complaints against him were the changes to the old customs system, a crackdown on smuggling, which Hassan described as an "ancient business," and the demand that women "must no longer go veiled or be enclosed in the harem." "Men," he said, were no longer permitted to "wear the flowing cloak and graceful turban. Instead they must free their women and wear hats."[9]

"One day," Hassan related, "the dreadful edits arrived. An emissary came from the court of the shah to tell the people of Kalat that they must no longer carry on in the ways of their fathers. They must abandon ancient ideas, emancipate their women and themselves, as the Turks had done." The emissary explained that there would be changes in the matters of taxes and customs collection and that the government was making an effort to suppress smuggling. The people of Kalat, Hassan said, "listened to the emissary in astonished silence.... But when he was gone they paid no attention to the new decrees, for they were violently opposed to such sudden changes." But when the shah heard of their disobedience, he sent soldiers to Kalat to enforce his decrees. So, the people of Kalat devised a plot. They prepared a feast for the soldiers and gave them plenty of Arak to drink. When the soldiers were thoroughly intoxicated and helpless, the townspeople, who had drunk water instead of Arak, locked them in the jail and departed. Hasan proudly said that he helped to lock the soldiers up himself. "That done," he said, "the townspeople knew they

[8] Alan Villiers, *Sons of Sinbad* (1940; Repr., New York: Scribner, 1949), pp. 294–296.
[9] Ibid.

could not remain in Kalat." So, each "man, woman and child," took everything he or she could carry and "went down to the harbor, and sailed away in the soldiers' ships." Since that day, Hassan said, Kalat has been a deserted town.[10]

Encounters and "memories" of encounters with Iran that occurred during the interwar period have had a substantial influence on the identity formation, trajectories and orientations of many leading Gulf families. Since the advent of the Saudi-led, Arab-Iranian Cold War that emerged in the aftermath of the fall of Saddam Hussein, "memories" of displacement and dispossession during the interwar period have increasingly become politicized. The proliferation of social media networks, online forums, and blogs in Arabic dedicated to "remembering" the "Arab civilization" that was uprooted from the Iranian littoral bear witness to the role of historical memory in coloring perceptions of the contemporary "other." The impassioned discussions that play out on YouTube, Twitter, and various blogs give an indication of the politicization of history and memory in the context of the Arab-Iranian and Sunni-Shi'i conflict. One need only look at the documentary videos and historic photos disseminated by the social media channel *Arab al-Sahel al-Sharqi* ("The Eastern Shore Arabs" referring to the Arabs of the Iranian coastal regions) to get a sense of how Arabs' experience with Iran is remembered and represented.[11] The "memories" usually evoke powerful emotions associated with oppression and dispossession at the hands of ascendant Iran and dovetail handily with contemporary anxieties about Iranian ambitions in the Gulf and in the region.

Histories and memories hearkening back to the interwar years also served as instruments of politics during the Bahrain uprising that began on February 14, 2011. Protests, which pitted the mostly Shi'i opposition against the Sunni Al Khalifa ruling family were initially aimed at achieving equality and greater political freedom for all the country's citizens; however, the cry for justice quickly turned into a call for revolution, and then an arena of regional rivalry, followed by external intervention and the imposition of martial law. This series of events evoked "memories" of an earlier crisis – the crisis that began with a Baharna uprising in 1922, widened in 1923 to include Iranian nationals, gained the attention of the government in Tehran, and culminated

[10] Ibid.
[11] See www.youtube.com/useIOR/R/faresoOo (accessed August 23, 2017).

in the forcible retirement of the ruler and the controversial administrative reforms of the 1920s. Cyber activists loosely affiliated with the February 14 Coalition invoked the 1922 "peaceful uprising," on blog posts, as well as YouTube, Twitter, and Facebook accounts, and disseminated digitized copies of British archival documents attesting to past traumas suffered by the Shi'a at the hands of the Al Khalifa.

Fresh state-sanctioned counternarratives of Bahrain's past were also produced. A prominent example is a special issue of the official history journal, *al-Watheeqa*, which celebrated the life and times of Shaykh 'Isa bin 'Ali Al Khalifa. According to this narrative, the "civil strife" (*fitna*) of 1923–1924 was the consequences of a British colonial policy that manipulated ethnic and religious differences in service to its "divide and rule" tactics. British imperialist policy, it argues, suppressed the embryonic Bahraini national movement born in 1923 and headed by 'Abd al-Wahhab al-Zayyani, and sowed the seeds of *fitna* between "members of the same people."[12] According to this logic, sectarianism in Bahrain is not an organic schism, but rather a residual effect of imperialist policies whose persistent shadow leaves Bahrain vulnerable to internal fragmentation and interference from outside players. Taking control of the narrative about the February 14 movement on social media became one of the regime's central objectives. For example, an army of pro-regime Twitter accounts emerged and began to intimidate the cyber oppositionists and generate fresh memes that highlighted Iran's history of subversion in Bahrain.[13] One oft-repeated (and retweeted) declaration asserted that "Iran was behind the commotion in Bahrain in 1922 [because] it incited people of Iranian origin to stir up the unrest."[14] It was drawn from an anonymous online article titled "Iranian Fingers Pollute the Political Conflict in Bahrain," which provided a hardline exposition of the Bahrain protests and also a list of all the historical instances in which Iran intervened or

[12] 'Abd al-Rahman 'Abdullah al-Najahi, "al-'Alaqat al-Siyasiyya bayn Hakim al-Bahrayn al-Shaykh 'Isa bin 'Ali Al Khalifa wa-al-Sulata al-Baritaniyya," *Al-Watheeqa*, no. 65 (August 2014), p. 52, www.icc.gov.bh/en/media-center (accessed August 18, 2018).

[13] See for example, Manama Press, Twitter Post (Arabic), December 5, 2011, https://bit.ly/2NOtca9 (accessed October 18, 2018).

[14] Manama Press, Twitter Post (Arabic), December 5, 2011, https://bit.ly/2QAzzk3.

purportedly intervened in Bahrain's affairs.[15] Another meme declared that Iran has been attempting to encroach on Bahrain since 1924 but that the Al Khalifa have thus far succeeded in guiding Bahrain to safety.[16]

Bahrain's distant past was also invoked by the Islamic Republic of Iran in service to its own bid for influence in Bahrain. A prominent example is a special issue of the state-sponsored journal *Faslnameh-ye Motala'at-e Tarikhi* (Historical Studies Quarterly) that was entirely dedicated to the topic of Bahrain in history.[17] This issue traces the history of Iran's connections to Bahrain since times immemorial, narrates the stories of the "people's uprising" that took place in Bahrain in 1922–1923, examines the evidence for Iran's claims to sovereignty over Bahrain, and analyzes how British colonial policy over the years brought about "the separation of Bahrain from Iran."[18] Coming as it did in the summer of 2011, just after Saudi and Emirati troops had crushed the mostly Shi'i uprising in Manama, this special issue was much more than an academic exercise. It represented one prong of a larger strategy on the part of Iran to highlight the sectarian imbalance in Bahrain, to pose as the patron of Bahrain's oppressed Shi'i community and in doing so, to attempt to delegitimize and destabilize the Al Khalifa monarchy. An editorial that appeared in Iran's official media is illustrative. It argued: "the regime had the chance to reform itself [since] 1922 .... This tribal dictatorship cannot be reformed."[19] Protestors, it warned, would only be subjected to more slaughter and imprisonment "until the Al Khalifa are removed from power."[20] Rhetoric such as this helped to feed the narrative of the Bahraini regime, which claimed that the February 14, 2011 uprising, was an Iranian-hatched foreign plot.[21]

[15] Middle East Online, "Iranian Fingers Pollute Political Conflict in Bahrain" (Arabic), June 22, 2011, https://bit.ly/2xiDGt0; see also, "Iran and Bahrain: How Many Explosions Do You Want to Be Convinced?" (Arabic), December 5, 2011, https://bit.ly/2QEKwkm (accessed September 17, 2018).

[16] Dr. Khalid al-Hamdani, Twitter Post, July 24, 2015, https://bit.ly/2QBYMKT.

[17] See Political Studies and Research Institute, *Faslnameh-ye Motala'at-e Tarikhi* 8, no. 33 (Summer 2011), http://mtq.iIOR/R/index.php (accessed October 21, 2018).

[18] Ibid.

[19] Mohammad Mazhari, "Bahrain Regime to Be Tougher in 2017 Realizing Its Fail," *Mehr News*, February 28, 2017, https://en.mehrnews.com/news/123914/ (accessed October 9, 2018).

[20] Ibid. [21] *Gulf News* (Dubai), March 20, 2011.

This study has shown that intense feelings of anxiety and indignation among the Gulf's Arab rulers about the intentions and regional ambitions of Iran date from the period of national awakening in Iran after the First World War and the introduction of Iranian nationalist policies to the Persian Gulf waterway, islands, and littoral. Myriad studies have traced the evolution of the Arab-Iranian conflict in the Gulf since the Second World War, but the conflict has thus to be understood within the context of its formative period. This book is an endeavor to shed light on the dynamics of the triangular relationship between Iran, Britain, and the Arab shaykhdoms during the interwar period. This period was a period of transition during which time the once integrated civilizational unit was transformed into a subregion regarded as an arena of geopolitical rivalry. This study fills a significant gap in the historical literature on the Persian Gulf, the history of Arab-Iranian relations in the Persian Gulf, and the history of Iran's role in the Gulf during the Reza Shah period. It also contributes to the historiography of the Gulf Arab states by examining their responses to the dawn of nationalism in the Persian Gulf and the increasingly sharp forms of imperialist intervention that nationalist ambitions provoked.

The most salient theme that ties this narrative together is the contest for sovereignty, primacy, and autonomy in the Persian Gulf. For the British government, the contest was against the virulent anti-colonial and nationalist feeling in Iran that posed a threat to their strategic interests the Persian Gulf. For Iran, the contest was against the British government, though it greatly impacted upon the semi-autonomous Arab shaykhdoms and their inhabitants. For the Gulf Arab rulers, the contest was against the swelling British apparatus as much as it was against the rising tide of domestic discontent that constrained their freedom of action. Domestic discontent was expressed through traditional, tribal patterns of behavior as well as through new modes of political activism fueled by modern ideas of citizenship, political "rights," and pan-Arab ideology. The transformative character of this period was exemplified by the emergence of an Arab society on the eve of the Second World War whose title openly called for the unification of the "Arabian Gulf."[22]

Another theme that is central to this story is nationalist representations of the Persian Gulf by Iran and Iranian nationals during the

[22] Mudayris, *al-Harakat wa-l-jama'at al-siyasiyya fi al-Bahrayn*, p. 7.

period of Iran's national awakening. The Persian Gulf comprised a central theme in the anti-colonial, nationalist discourse, which came to be dominated by the state during the reign of Reza Shah Pahlavi. The highly visible British presence in the Persian Gulf was a lightning rod for the vital expression of anti-British sentiment in the aftermath of the First World War. Britain's support for the semi-independent shaykhs of the Arabian littoral, like its support for the Shaykh of Mohammerah and other semi-autonomous tribal chiefs in the south of Iran, was viewed as part of its archetypal "divide and rule" strategy, designed to serve British colonial interests at the expense of Iranian sovereignty. The British presence in the Persian Gulf, like the American presence today, was an unwanted foreign intrusion in a subregion that Iran viewed as its own exclusive sphere of influence. Since the time of Reza Shah Pahlavi, Iran's ability to control naval activity in the Persian Gulf has been treated by state propaganda as a confirmation of Iran's independence and sovereignty. And yet, while promoting that logic, today's leaders in Iran are confronted with an uncomfortable contradiction – the master narrative of a Persian Gulf owned and controlled by Iran is continually challenged by visible and perceptible reminders of American superiority.

Since the time of Reza Shah, Iran's official position has been and continues to be that the Persian Gulf will be more secure when Western forces withdraw and regional states assume responsibility for Gulf security. But the Gulf Arab states suspect that such a scheme would merely be a temporary phase that would eventually lead to Iranian domination of the Gulf and the loss of their own sovereignty. Decades of Arab-Iranian rivalry, and indeed full-fledged wars, have fed and fueled these suspicions, whose origins are found in the dramatic events of the interwar period.

Appendices

APPENDIX A:

British Officials

Ministers in Tehran

Percy Cox[1]	1918–1920
Herman Norman	1920–1921
Percy Loraine	1921–1926
Robert Clive	1926–1931
Reginald Hoare[2]	1931–1935
Hughe Knatchbull-Hugessen	1935–1939

Political Residents in the Persian Gulf (Bushehr)

Cecil Hamilton Gabriel	1919 (acting)
Arthur Prescott Trevor	1919–1920 (acting)
Arnold Talbot Wilson	1920 (acting)
Arthur Prescott Trevor	November 1920–April 1923
Stuart G. Knox	April 1923 (acting)
Arthur Prescott Trevor	October 1923–April 1924
Francis Bellville Prideaux	April 1924–June 1925
Charles D. Crosthwaite	June 1925 (acting)
Francis Bellville Prideaux	October 1925–January 1927
Lionel Berkeley Holt Haworth	January 1927–November 1928
Frederick William Johnston	November 1928–April 1929
Cyril Charles Johnson Barrett	April 1929–November 1929

[1] Ministers in Tehran are formally titled Envoy Extraordinary and Minister Plenipotentiary, a rank one step lower than that of ambassador.

[2] During the greater part of the period 1933–1935, Victor Mallet served as Chargé d'Affaires in Hoare's absence.

Hugh Vincent Biscoe	November 1929–May 1932
Trenchard Craven William Fowle	July 1932–September 1939
Charles Geoffrey Prior	September 1939–October 1941

Political Agents in Bahrain

Norman N. E. Bray	December 1918–June 1919
Harold Dickson	November 1919–November 1920
Clive Daly	January 1921–September 1926
Cyril Barrett	September 1926–April 1929
Reginald Alban	April 1927–November 1929
Geoffrey Prior	April 1929–November 1932
Percy G. Loch	November 1932–April 1937
Tom Hickenbothem	April 1937–October 1937
Hugh Weightman	October 1937–October 1940

APPENDIX B:

Iranian Officials

Prime Ministers

Mirza Hasan Khan Vusuq al-Dowleh	Aug. 1918–July 1920
Hasan Pirnia Moshir al-Dowleh	July 1920–Oct. 1920
Fathollah Khan Akbar Sepahdar-e A'zam	Oct. 1920–Feb. 1921
Sayyed Zia' al-Din Tabataba'i	Feb. 1921–June 1921
Ahmad Qavam al-Saltaneh	June 1921–Jan. 1922
Hasan Pirnia Moshir al-Dowleh	Jan. 1922–June 1922
Ahmad Qavam al-Saltaneh	June 1922–Feb. 1923
Mirza Hasan Mostowfi al-Mamalek	Feb. 1923 –June 1923
Hasan Pirnia Moshir al-Dowleh	June 1923–Oct. 1923
Reza Khan Sardar-e Sepah	Oct. 1923–Dec. 1925
Mohammad 'Ali Foroughi Zoka' al-Molk	Dec. 1925–June 1926
Mirza Hasan Mostowfi al-Mamalek	June 1926–May 1927
Mehdi Qoli Khan Hedayat Mokhber al-Saltaneh	May 1927–Sep. 1933
Mohammad 'Ali Foroughi Zoka' al-Molk	Sept. 1933–Dec. 1935
Mahmud Jam Mudir al-Molk	Dec. 1935–Oct. 1939

Foreign Ministers

Firuz Mirza Firuz Nosrat al-Dowleh	July 1918–July 1920
Asadollah Moshar al-Saltaneh	July 1920–Oct 1920
Mostafa Qoli Fahim al-Dowleh	Oct 1920–Jan 1921
Kamal Hedayat*	

* Acting foreign minister

Jahangir Nazem al-Molk Mansur*	Jan. 1921–Feb. 1921
Hasan Esfandiari Mohtashem al-Dowleh	Feb. 1921–Mar. 1921
Mahmud Jam Mudir al-Molk	Mar. 1921–May 1921
Taghi Mo'azzaz al-Dowleh Nabavi	May 1921– June 1921
Hasan Esfandiari Mohtashem al-Dowleh	June 1921–Sept. 1921
Abu al-Qasem Entezam al-Molk 'Amid*	Sept. 1921–Oct. 1921
Mohammad Mosaddeq al-Saltaneh	Oct. 1921
Asadollah Moshar al-Saltaneh	Oct. 1921–Jan. 1922
Ibrahim Hakim al-Molk Hakimi	Jan. 1922–June 1922
Ahmad Qavam al-Saltaneh	June 1922–Jan. 1923
Mohammad 'Ali Foroughi Zoka' al-Molk	Feb. 1923–June 1923
Mohammad Mosaddeq al-Saltaneh	June 1923–Sept. 1923
Mohammad 'Ali Foroughi Zoka' al-Molk	Oct. 1923–Sept. 1924
Hasan Mushar al-Molk	Sep. 1924–Jan. 1926

(Teymurtash appointed court minister, November 1925)

Mirza Da'ud Khan Meftah*	Jan. 1926–July 1926
Sayyed Hasan Taqizadeh	July 1926–July 1926
'Ali Qoli Khan Ansari**	July 1926–May 1928
Mirza Fathollah Khan Pakravan*	June 1928–Dec. 1928
Abu al-Qasem Khan 'Amid*	Dec. 1928–Jan. 1929
Mohammad 'Ali Khan Farzin	Feb. 1929–May 1930
Mohammad 'Ali Foroughi	May 1930–Sept. 1933

* Acting foreign minister

** During the greater part of 1927, while Ansari was immersed in negotiations in Moscow, Mirza Fathollah Khan Pakravan served as the deputy or "acting" foreign minister (receiving his instructions from Teymurtash) and continued in that capacity officially in May 1928 when Ansari left the post.

(Fall of Teymurtash, September 1933)

Sayyed Bagher Khan Kazemi	Sept. 1933–Mar. 1936
Inayatullah Khan Sami'i	Mar. 1936–Feb. 1938
Sayyed Mostafa 'Adil*	Feb. 1938–May 1938
'Ali Soheyli	May 1938–July 1938
Mozaffar 'Alam	July 1938–Oct. 1940

* Acting foreign minister

APPENDIX C:

Al Maktum Family of Dubai

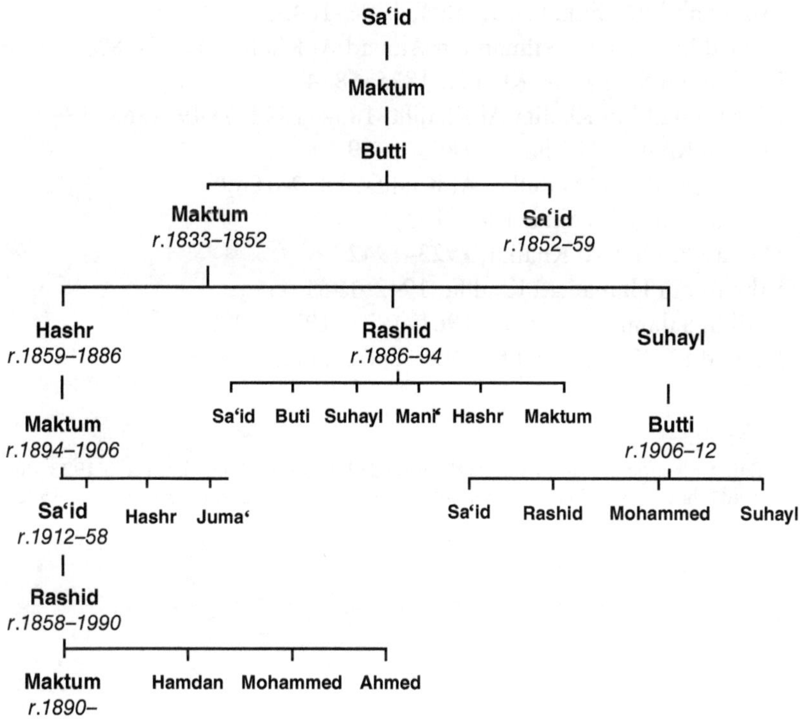

APPENDIX D:

Al Khalifa Rulers of Bahrain

Ahmad bin Muhammad bin Khalifa, 1783–1796
'Abdullah bin Ahmad Al Khalifa, 1796–1843,
ruled jointly with Salman bin Ahmad Al Khalifa, 1796–1825
Khalifa bin Salman Al Khalifa, 1825–1834
Muhammad bin Khalifa Al Khalifa, 1834–1842, 1849–1868, 1869
'Ali bin Khalifa Al Khalifa, 1868–1869
Muhammad bin 'Abdullah Al Khalifa, 1869–1869
'Isa bin 'Ali Al Khalifa, 1869–1923[1]
Hamad bin 'Isa Al Khalifa, 1923–1942
Salman bin Hamad Al Khalifa, 1942–1961
'Isa bin Salman Al Khalifa, 1961–1971, 1971–1999
Hamad bin 'Isa Al Khalifa, 1999–2002, 2002–

[1] Bahrain's official history rejects the forced abdication of Shaykh 'Isa in 1923 and holds that Shaykh Hamad became the legitimate ruler upon 'Isa's death in 1932.

Glossary

'Ajam	non-Arab, especially referring to Iranians
amniyyeh	gendarmerie; rural military police
Baharna (adj. Bahrani)	Arab Shi'a native to Bahrain, al-Hasa' and al-Qatif
Bahraini	a person from Bahrain (including Baharna)
dhow	a sailing vessel
fiddawiyya (sing. *fidawi*)	tribal guard; armed retainer
Hawala	Sunni immigrants from southern Iran to the shaykhdoms
ilm-o-khabar	a travel document
Kargozar	agent of Iran's foreign ministry
Kargozari	agency of Iran's foreign ministry
Majles	the parliament of Iran
majlis	a shaykh's informal advisory council
Majlis	a formal council having appointed or elected members
majlis baladiyya	municipal council
mudir	director; manager
nakhoda	captain of a sailing vessel
nazmiyyeh	police
sepoy	Indian soldier in British service
shaykh	tribal elder; male member of a ruling family
sukhra	forced labor
qadi	judge
ta'zieh	theatrical drama of the martyrdom of Imam Hossein
'ulama'	religious scholars
vakil	representative; deputy
waqf	religious endowment

Bibliography

Unpublished Archival Documents

India Office Records, British Library, London

IOR/R/15/1	Bushire Residency Records, 1763–1947
IOR/R/15/2	Bahrain Agency Records, 1920–1950
IOR/R/15/4	Trucial Coast Agency Records, 1937–1950
IOR/R/15/5	Kuwait Agency Records, 1899–1961
IOR/L/P&S/10	Political and Secret Department Subject Files, 1902–1931
IOR/L/P&S/12	Political and Secret Department External Collections, 1931–1949
IOR/L/P&S/18/B	Political and Secret Department Memoranda (Arabia and the Persian Gulf)
IOR/L/P&S/18/C	Memoranda on Central Asia and Persia, 1840–1947
IOR/L/P&S/20/C	Political and Secret Department Library

Cabinet Records, National Archives, Kew

CAB 23	Interwar Conclusions
CAB 24	Interwar Memoranda

Foreign Office Records, National Archives, Kew

FO 371	General Correspondence
FO 416	Persia, 1899–1957
FO 608	Peace Conference, 1919–1920

Special Collections, University of Exeter Library, Exeter

Charles D. Belgrave, Personal Diaries, 1926–1957

Historical Newspapers

al-Eslah (Kabul)
al-Thagr (Basra)
'Asr-e Azadi (Shiraz)
Bayan-e Haghighat (Shiraz)
Daily Mail (London)
Ettala'at (Tehran)
Golestan (Shiraz)
Iran-e Bastan (Tehran)
Karun (Tehran)
Majles (Tehran)
New York Times
Setareh-ye Iran (Tehran)
Shafaq-e Sorkh (Tehran)
Times of Mesopotamia (Baghdad)
al-Muqattam (Cairo)
Argus (Melbourne)
Bahr-e Fars (Shiraz)
Chahr-e Nameh (Cairo)
Estakhr (Shiraz)
Ettehad (Tehran)
Habl al-Matin (Calcutta)
Iran (Tehran)
London Gazette
Neday-e Vatan (Tehran)
Setareh'yé Djéhane (Tehran)
Setareh-ye Jehan (Tehran)
Time Magazine
Tufan (Shiraz)

Contemporary Newspapers

Arab News (Jeddah)
al-Ayam (Manama)
Gulf News (Dubai)
Kayhan (Tehran)
Mehr News (Tehran)
The Telegraph (London)

Published Archival Documents (English)

Admiralty, Naval Intelligence Division. *Iraq and the Persian Gulf.* Oxford, 1944; Repr., Archive Editions, 1987.

Aitchison, Charles Umpherson, ed. *A Collection of Treaties, Engagements and Sanads Relating to India and Neighboring Countries: Relating to Aden and the Southwestern Coast of Arabia*, Vol. 11, 5th ed. Calcutta: Government of India, 1933; Repr., Liechtenstein: Kraus-Thomson, 1973.

Bidwell, Robin Leonard, Kenneth Bourne, and Donald Cameron Watt, eds. *British Documents on Foreign Affairs – Reports and Papers from the Foreign Office Confidential Print. Part II, From the First to the Second World War, Series B, Turkey, Iran, and the Middle East, 1918–1939.* 35 vols. Frederick, MD: University Publications of America, 1985.

Blake, G., and R. Schofield, eds. *Arabian Boundaries 1853–1960.* 30 vols. Archive Editions, 1988.

Burrell, R. M., and R. Jarman, eds. *Iran Political Diaries 1881–1965.* 14 vols. Archive Editions, 1997.

Government of India, Foreign Department. *Persian Gulf Administration Reports, 1873–1957.* Calcutta, Delhi, and Simla. Repr.: Archive Editions, 1986.

H. M. Government, Cabinet Office. "Historical Summary of Events in the Territories of the Ottoman Empire, Persia and Arabia Affecting the British Position in the Persian Gulf, 1907–1928," PG 13. London: Committee of Imperial Defense, October 1928. Repr., Archive Editions, 1987.

H. M. Government, Foreign Office. "Historical Summary of Events in the Persian Gulf Sheikhdoms and the Sultanate of Muscat and Oman, 1928–1953," PG 53. London: Foreign Office, June 1953. Repr., Archive Editions, 1987.

Jarman, R. ed. *Bahrain Government Annual Reports: 1924–1970.* 8 vols. Archive Editions, 1986.

Jarman, R. ed. *Political Diaries of the Arab World: Persian Gulf 1904–1965.* 24 vols. Archive Editions, 1998.

League of Nations. *Official Journal.* 21 vols. Geneva: League of Nations, 1920–1940.

Lorimer, J. G. *Gazetteer of the Persian Gulf, Oman, and Central Arabia.* 2 vols. ed. Richard Lockington Birdwood. Calcutta: Superintendent of Government Printing, 1908–1915. Repr., Archive Editions, 1986.

Qatar Digital Library. India Office Records 1763–1951. www.qdl.qa/en (accessed October 13, 2019).

Rush, Alan, ed. *Records of Kuwait 1899–1961.* 8 vols. Archive Editions, 1989.

Tuson, Penelope, ed. *Records of Bahrain 1820–1960.* 8 vols. Archive Editions, 1993.

Tuson, Penelope, ed. *Records of the Emirates 1820–1960.* 12 vols. Archive Editions, 1990.

U.S. Department of State. *Foreign Relations of the United States: Diplomatic Papers, 1934.* Washington, DC: Government Printing Office, 1951.

Published Archival Documents (Persian)

Gozideh-ye Asnad-e Khalij-e Fars: Jazayer-e Khalij-e Fars: Vol. 1. Tehran: Daftar-e Motala'at-e Siyasi va bayn al-Milali, 1372 (1993).

Gozideh-ye Asnad-e Khalij-e Fars: Ravabet-e Iran ba Keshvarha-ye Hawzeh-ye Khalij-e Fars va Tahavvolat-e Dakheli-ye anha: Vol. 2. Tehran: Daftar-e Motala'at-e Siyasi va bayn al-Milali, 1369 (1990).

Nosrat al-Dowleh: Majmu'ah-e Moqatibat, Asnad, Khatirat, va-'Asr-e Firuz Mirza Firuz. Vol. 2, ed. Mansoureh Ettehadieh. Tehran: Ketab-e Siyamak (1990).

Ravabet-e Dowlat-e Shahanshahi ba Keshvarha-ye Howzeh-ye Mas'uliyat-e Edareh-ye Nohom-e Siyasi dar Panjah Saleh-ye Shahanshahi-ye Pahlavi: Emarat-e 'Arabi-ye Mottahedeh, Bahreyn, 'Oman, Qatar. Tehran: Edareh-ye Entesharat va Madarek (1976).

Unpublished Theses and Dissertations (English)

Almahmood, Mahmood. "The Rise and Fall of Bahrain's Merchants in the Pre-Oil Era," PhD dissertation. American University, 2013.

Balaghi, Shiva. "Nationalism and Cultural Production in Iran, 1848–1906," PhD dissertation. University of Michigan, 2008.

Butti, Obaid A. "Imperialism, Tribal Structure, and the Development of Ruling Elites: A Socio-Economic History of the Trucial States between 1892 and 1939," PhD dissertation. Georgetown University, 1992.

Moghadam, Gholam Reza. "Iran's Foreign Trade Policy and Economic Development in the Interwar Period," PhD dissertation. Stanford University, 1986.

Muller, Laleh. "Iran and the Persian Gulf in the Pahlavi Era," PhD dissertation. New York University,1997.

Razavian, Mohammad, T. "Iranian Communities of the Persian Gulf: A Geographical Analysis," PhD dissertation. University of London, 1975.

Al-Rumaihi, Mohammad Ghanim. "Social and Political Change in Bahrain since the First World War," PhD thesis. Durham University, 1973.

Books and Articles (English)

Abdullah, Muhammad Morsy. *The United Arab Emirates: A Modern History*. London: Croom Helm, 1978.

"Changes in the Economy and Political Attitudes, and the Development of Culture on the Coast of Oman between 1900 and 1940." *Arabian Studies* 2 (1975), pp. 167–178.

Abrahamian, Ervand. *Iran between Two Revolutions*. Princeton, NJ: Princeton University Press, 1982.

Adamiyat, Fereydoun. *Bahrein Islands: A Legal and Diplomatic Study of the British-Iranian Controversy*. New York: Frederick A. Praeger, 1952.

Ahmadi, Kourush. *Islands and International Politics in the Persian Gulf: Abu Musa and Tunbs in Strategic Perspective*. New York: Routledge, 2008.

Amin, Cameron Michael. "The Press and Public Diplomacy in Iran, 1820–1940." *Iranian Studies* 48, no. 2 (2015), pp. 269–287.

Atabaki, Touraj. "From Multilingual Empire to Contested Modern State," in *Iran in the 21st Century: Politics, Economics and Conflict*, eds., Homa Katouzian and Hossein Shahidi. New York: Routledge, 2008, pp. 41–62.

Atabaki, Touraj, ed. *The State and the Subaltern: Modernization, Society and the State in Turkey and Iran*. London: I.B. Tauris, 2007.

Atabaki, Touraj, and Erik J. Zürcher, eds., *Men of Order: Authoritarian Modernization under Atatürk and Reza Shah*. London: I.B. Tauris, 2004.

Banani, Amin. *The Modernization of Iran, 1821–1941*. Stanford, CA: Stanford University Press, 1961.

al-Barhana, Husain M. *The Legal Status of the Arabian Gulf States*. New York: Oceana Publications, 1968.

Behnam, Mariam. *Zelzelah: A Woman before Her Time*. Dubai: Motivate, 1994.

Belgrave, Charles Dalrymple. *Personal Column*. Beirut: Librairie du Liban, 1972.

Burrell, R. M. "Britain, Iran and the Persian Gulf: Some Aspects of the Situation in the 1920s and 1930s," in *The Arabian Peninsula*, ed. Derek Hopwood. London: George Allen and Unwin LTD, 1972, pp. 160–188.

Chehabi, H. E. "The Banning of the Veil and Its Consequences," in *The Making of Modern Iran: State and Society under Riza Shah, 1921–1941*, ed. Stephanie Cronin. New York: RoutledgeCurzon, 2003, pp. 193–210.

Cottam, Richard W. *Nationalism in Iran*. Pittsburgh: University of Pittsburgh Press, 1979.

Crawford, Harriet E. W. *Dilmun and Its Gulf Neighbors*. Cambridge: Cambridge University Press, 1998.

Cronin, Stephanie. *The Army and the Creation of the Pahlavi State in Iran, 1910–1926*. London: I.B. Tauris, 1997.

Crystal, Jill. *Oil and Politics in the Gulf: Rulers and Merchants in Kuwait and Qatar*. 1990; Repr., Cambridge: Cambridge University Press, 1995.

Curzon, George. *Persia and the Persian Question*. 2 vols. London: Longmans, Green and Co., 1892; Repr., London: Elibron Classics, 2012.

al-Dailami, Ahmed. "Purity and Confusion": The Hawala between Persians and Arabs in the Contemporary Gulf," in *The Persian Gulf in Modern Times*, ed. Lawrence G. Potter. New York: Palgrave Macmillan, 2014, 299–326.

Dann, Uriel. "British Persian Gulf Concepts in the Light of Emerging Nationalism in the Late 1920s," in *The Great Powers in the Middle*

East 1919–1939, ed. Uriel Dann. New York: Holmes and Meier, 1988, pp. 50–68.

Davies, Charles E. *The Blood Red Arab Flag: An Investigation into Qasimi Piracy, 1797–1820*. Exeter: University of Exeter Press, 1997.

Dessouki, Assem. "Social and Political Dimensions of the Historiography of the Arab Gulf," in *Statecraft in the Middle East: Oil, Historical Memory, and Popular Culture*, eds., Eric Davis and Nicolas Gavrielides. Miami: Florida University Press, 1991.

Devos, Bianca, and Christoph Werner, eds., *Culture and Cultural Politics under Reza Shah: The Pahlavi State, New Bourgeoisie and the Creation of a Modern Society in Iran*. New York: Routledge, 2014.

Dresch, Paul. *Tribes, Government and History in Yemen*. Oxford: Clarendon Press, 1989.

Dresch, Paul, and James Piscatori, eds., *Monarchies and Nations: Globalization and Identity in the Arab States of the Gulf*. London: I.B. Tauris, 2005.

Edmonds, Cecil John. *East and West of Zagros: Travel, War and Politics in Persia and Iraq 1913–1921*, ed. Yann Richard. Leiden: Brill, 2010.

Elwell-Sutton, L. P. *Persian Oil: A Study in Power Politics*. London: Lawrence and Wishart, 1955.

Al Fahim, Mohammed. *From Rags to Riches: A Story of Abu Dhabi*. 1995. Repr., London: Centre for Arab Studies, 2001.

Farah, Talal Toufic. *Protection and Politics in Bahrain, 1869–1915*. Beirut: American University of Beirut, 1985.

Fattah, Hala. *The Politics of Regional Trade in Iraq, Arabia, and the Gulf: 1745–1900*. Albany: State University of New York Press, 1997.

Ferrier, Ronald W. *The History of the British Petroleum Company*. 2 vols. Cambridge: Cambridge University Press, 1982.

Fiore, Massimiliano. *Anglo-Italian Relations in the Middle East, 1922–1940*. Farnham: Ashgate, 2012.

Floor, Willem. *The Persian Gulf: The Hula Arabs of the Shibkuh Coast of Iran*. Washington, DC: Mage, 2014.

Bandar Abbas: The Natural Trade Gateway of Southeast Iran. Washington, DC: Mage, 2011.

"The Rise and Fall of the Banu Ka'b. A Borderer State in Southern Khuzestan." *Iran* 44 (2006), pp. 277–315.

"The Iranian Navy in the Gulf during the Eighteenth Century." *Iranian Studies* 20, no. 1 (1987), pp. 31–53.

"Industrialization in Iran 1900–1941," IMEIS Occasional Paper No. 25. University of Durham, 1984.

The Rise and Fall of Bandar-e Lingah: The Distribution Center for the Arabian Coast 1750–1930. Washington, DC: Mage, 1910.

Fuccaro, Nelida. "Pearl Towns and Early Oil Cities: Migration and Integration in the Arab Coast of the Persian Gulf," in *The City in the Ottoman Empire: Migration and the Making of Urban Modernity*, eds. Ulrike Freitag, Malte Fuhrmann, Nora Lafi and Florian Riedler. London: Routledge, 2010, pp. 99–116.

Histories of City and State in the Persian Gulf: Manama since 1800. New York: Cambridge University Press, 2009.

Gellner, Ernest. *Anthropology and Politics: Revolutions in the Sacred Grove*. Cambridge, MA: Blackwell, 1995.

Ghani, Cyrus. *Iran and the Rise of Reza Shah: From Qajar Collapse to Pahlavi Power*. New York: I.B. Tauris, 2000.

Ghareeb, E., and I. al-Abed, eds., *Perspectives on the United Arab Emirates*. London: Trident Press, 1997.

Ghods, M. Reza. "Iranian Nationalism and Reza Shah." *Middle Eastern Studies* 27, no. 1 (January 1991), pp. 35–45.

Iran in the 20th Century: A Political History. Boulder, CO: Lynne Rienner, 1989.

Gilbar, Gad, G. "Demographic Developments in Late Qajar Persia, 1810–1906." *Asian and African Studies* 11, no. 2 (1976), pp. 125–156.

al-Gurg, Easa Saleh. *The Wells of Memory: An Autobiography*. London: John Murray, 1998.

Hawley, Donald. *The Trucial States*. London: Twayne Publishers, 1971.

Harrison, Paul Wilberforce. *Doctor in Arabia*. New York: The John Day Company, 1940.

Haseeb, Khair el-Din. *Arab-Iranian Relations*. Beirut: Centre for Arab Unity Studies, 1998.

Haworth, Lionel. "Persia and the Persian Gulf." *Journal of the Royal Central Asian Society* 16, no. 4 (1929), pp. 495–509.

Heard-Bey, Frauke. "The Tribal Society of the UAE and Its Traditional Economy," in *Perspectives on the United Arab Emirates*, eds. E. Ghareeb and I. al-Abed. London: Trident Press, 1997, pp. 98–116.

From Trucial States to United Arab Emirates. 2nd ed. London: Longman, 1996.

Issawi, Charles. *The Economic History of Iran: 1800–1914*. Chicago: University of Chicago Press, 1971.

Joyner, Christopher C. *The Persian Gulf War: Lessons for Strategy, Law and Diplomacy*. Westport, CT: Greenwood Press, 1990.

Kanoo, Khalid, M. *The House of Kanoo: A Century of an Arabian Family Business*. New York: Palgrave Macmillan, 1998.

Karshenas, Massoud. *Oil, State, and Industrialization in Iran*. Cambridge: Cambridge University Press, 1990.

Kashani-Sabet, Firoozeh. *Frontier Fictions: Shaping the Iranian Nation, 1804–1946*. Princeton, NJ: Princeton University Press, 1999.

Katouzian, Homa. *State and Society in Iran: The Eclipse of the Qajars and the Emergence of the Pahlavis*. London: I.B. Tauris, 2000.

"The Campaign against the Anglo-Iranian Agreement of 1919." *British Journal of Middle Eastern Studies* 25, no. 1 (May 1998), pp. 5–46.

Keddie, Nikki R. *Iran and the Muslim World: Resistance and Revolution*. New York: New York University Press, 1995.

Kelly, J. B. "The Persian Claim to Bahrain." *International Affairs* 33, the Royal Institute for International Affairs, no. 1 (January 1957), pp. 51–70.

Keynoush, Banafsheh. *Saudi Arabia and Iran: Friends or Foes?* (New York: Palgrave Macmillan, 2016).

Khadduri, Majid. "Iran's Claim to the Sovereignty of Bahrayn." *The American Journal of International Law* 45, no. 4 (Oct. 1951), pp. 631–647.

Khoury, Philip S. and Joseph Kostiner, eds., *Tribes and State Formation in the Middle East*. Los Angeles: University of California Press, 1990.

Khuri, Fuad I. *Tribe and State in Bahrain: The Transformation of Social and Political Authority in an Arab State*. Chicago: University of Chicago Press, 1980.

Kitto, John. *Uncle Oliver's Travels: Persia*. 2 vols. London: William Clowes, 1838.

Lienhardt, Peter. "The Authority of Shaykhs in the Gulf: An Essay in Nineteenth-Century History." *Arabian Studies* 2 (Middle East Center, University of Cambridge, 1975), pp. 61–75.

Lockhart, Lawrence. *The Fall of the Safavi Dynasty and the Afghan Occupation of Persia*. Cambridge: Cambridge University Press, 1958.

Majd, Mohammad Gholi. *Great Britain and Reza Shah: The Plunder of Iran, 1921–1941*. Gainesville: University Press of Florida, 2001.

Marashi, Afshin. *Nationalizing Iran: Culture, Power, and the State, 1870–1940*. Seattle: University of Washington Press, 2008.

Martin, Vanessa. *The Qajar Pact: Bargaining, Protest and the State in Nineteenth-Century Persia*. London: I.B. Tauris, 2005.

Martin, Vanessa, and Morteza Nouraei. "The Role of the Karguzar in the Foreign Relations of State and Society of Iran from the Mid-Nineteenth Century to 1921: Part 1: Diplomatic Relations." *Journal of the Royal Asiatic Society of Great Britain and Ireland* (Third Series) 15 (2005), pp. 261–277.

Matthee, Rudi. "The Portuguese Presence in the Persian Gulf: An Overview," in *Imperial Crossroads: The Great Powers and the Persian Gulf*, eds. Jeffrey Macris and Saul Kelly. Annapolis, MD: Naval Institute Press, 2012, pp. 1–12.

McFee, William. *The Law of the Sea*. Philadelphia: Lippencott, 1950.

Menashri, David. *Post-Revolutionary Politics in Iran: Religion, Society, and Power*. London: Frank Cass, 2001.

Mirfendereski, Guive. "The Ownership of the Tonb Islands: A Legal Analysis," in *Small Islands, Big Politics: The Tombs and Abu Musa in the Persian Gulf*, ed. Hooshang Amirahmadi. New York: St. Martin's Press, 1996, pp. 117–160.

Mojtahed-Zadeh, Pirouz. *Security and Territoriality in the Persian Gulf: A Maritime Political Geography*. London: RoutledgeCurzon, 2003.

"The Political Geography and History of the Island of Abu Musa." *The Iranian Journal of International Affairs* 4, nos. 3–4 (1992), pp. 485–500.

Moyse-Bartlett, H. *The Pirates of Trucial Oman*. London: McDonald, 1966.

al-Naqeeb, Khaldoun Hasan. *Society and State in the Gulf and Arab Peninsula*. London and New York: Routledge and Centre for Arab Unity Studies, 1990.

Onley, James. "Britain and the Gulf Shaikhdoms, 1820–1971: The Politics of Protection," CIRS Occasional Paper No. 4. Georgetown University in Qatar, 2009.

The Arabian Frontier of the British Raj: Merchants, Rulers, and the British in the Nineteenth Century Gulf. Oxford: Oxford University Press, 2007.

"Britain's Informal Empire in the Gulf, 1820–1971." *Journal of Social Affairs* 22, no. 87 (2005), pp. 29–45.

"Britain's Native Agents in Arabia and Persia in the Nineteenth Century." *Comparative Studies of South Asia, Africa and the Middle East* 24, no. 1 (2004), pp. 129–137.

"The Politics of Protection in the Gulf: The Arab Rulers and the British Resident in the Nineteenth Century." *New Arabian Studies* 6 (November 2004), pp. 30–92.

Onley, James, and Sulayman Khalaf. "Shaikhly Authority in the Pre-Oil Gulf: An Historical Anthropological Study." *History and Anthropology* 17, no. 3 (September 2006), pp. 189–208.

Perry, John R. "Mir Muhanna and the Dutch: Patterns of Piracy in the Persian Gulf." *Studia Iranica* 2 (1973), pp. 79–95.

Potter, Lawrence G. "Society in the Persian Gulf: Before and After Oil," CIRS Occasional Paper No. 18. Georgetown University in Qatar, 2017.

Potter, Lawrence G. ed. *The Persian Gulf in History*. New York: Palgrave Macmillan, 2009.

al-Qasimi, Sultan bin Muhammad. *Power Struggles and Trade in the Persian Gulf: 1620–1820*. Exeter: University of Exeter Press, 1999.

Rabi, Uzi. "Britain's 'Special Position' in the Gulf: Its Origins, Dynamics and Legacy." *Middle Eastern Studies* 42, no. 3 (May 2006), pp. 351–364.

Radhi, Hassan Ali. *Judiciary and Arbitration in Bahrain: A Historical and Analytical Study*. The Hague: Klewer Law, 2003.

Ramazani, Rouhollah, K. *The Foreign Policy of Iran: A Developing Nation in World Affairs, 1500–1941*. Charlottesville: University Press of Virginia, 1966.

al-Rasheed, Madawi, ed. *Transnational Connections in the Arab Gulf*. New York: Routledge, 2005.

Rezun, Miron. *The Soviet Union and Iran: Soviet Policy in Iran from the Beginnings of the Pahlavi Dynasty until the Soviet Invasion in 1941*. Leiden: Institut Universitaire de Hautes Études Internationales, 1981.

"Reza Shah's Court Minister: Teymourtash." *International Journal of Middle East Studies* 12, no. 2 (September 1980), pp. 119–137.

Rihani, Ameen Fares. *Around the Coasts of Arabia*. London: Constable, 1930.

Rumaihi, M. G. *Bahrain: Social and Political Change since the First World War*. London: Center for Middle Eastern and Islamic Studies, 1976.

Rush, Alan. *Al-Sabah: History and Genealogy of Kuwait's Ruling Family 1752–1987*. London: Ithaca Press, 1987.

Russell-Wood, A. J. R. *The Portuguese Empire, 1415–1808: A World on the Move*. Baltimore, MD: Johns Hopkins University Press, 1998.

Said, Rosemarie J. "The 1938 Reform Movement in Dubai." *al-Abhath* 23, nos. 1–4 (December 1970), pp. 247–318.

Şahin, Kaya. *Empire and Power in the Reign of Süleyman: Narrating the Sixteenth-Century Ottoman World*. Cambridge: Cambridge University Press, 2013.

al-Sayegh, Fatma. "Merchants' Role in a Changing Society: The Case of Dubai, 1900–1990." *Middle Eastern Studies* 34, no. 1 (January 1998), pp. 87–102.

Seccombe, I. J., and R. I. Lawless. "Foreign Worker Dependence in the Gulf, and the International Oil Companies: 1910–50." *International Migration Review* 20, no. 3 (Autumn 1986), pp. 548–574.

Slot, B. J. *The Origins of Kuwait*. Leiden: Brill, 1991.

Soucek, Svat. "Arabistan or Khuzistan." *Iranian Studies* 17, nos. 2/3 (Spring–Summer 1984), pp. 195–213.

Standish, John F. *Persia and the Gulf: Retrospect and Prospect*. London: Curzon, 1998.

"British Maritime Policy in the Persian Gulf." *Middle Eastern Studies* 3, no. 4 (1967), pp. 324–254.

Stanley-Price, Nicholas. "Imperial Airways and the Airfield at Sharjah, 1932–1939." *Liwa: Journal of the National Center for Documentation and Research* 3, no. 6 (December 2011), pp. 24–38.

Sykes, Sir Percy. *A History of Persia*. 2 vols. 1915; Repr., New York: RoutledgeCurzon, 2004.

al-Tajir, Mahdi Abdalla. *Bahrain: 1920–1945, Bahrain, the Shaikh and the Administration*. New York: Croom Helm, 1987.

Tapper, Richard, ed. *Tribe and State in Iran and Afghanistan*. New York: Croom Helm, 1983.

Vaziri, Mostafa. *Iran as an Imagined Nation: The Construction of National Identity*. New York: Paragon House, 1993.

Villiers, Alan. *Sons of Sinbad*. 1940; Repr., New York: Scribner, 1949.

Ward, Steven R. *Immortal: A Military History of Iran and Its Armed Forces*. Washington, DC: Georgetown University Press, 2009.

Wheeler, Julia, and Paul Thuysbaert. *Telling Tales: An Oral History of Dubai*. Dubai: Explorer, 2005.

Whigham, H. J. *The Persian Problem*. London: Isbister and Company, 1903.

Wilber, Donald. *Riza Shah Pahlavi: The Resurrection of Iran, 1878–1944*. New York: Exposition Press of Florida, 1975.

Worth, Richard. *Fleets of World War II*. Cambridge, MA: Decapo, 2001.

Wright, Denis. *The English amongst the Persians: Imperial Lives in Nineteenth Century Iran*. London: I.B. Tauris, 2001.

Zahlan, Rosemarie Said. *The Making of the Modern Gulf States*. Reading: Ithaca Press, 1998.

The Origins of the United Arab Emirates: A Political and Social History of the Trucial States. London: Macmillan Press, 1978.

Zargar, Aliasghar. "A Historical Review of British Role [*sic*] in Iran-Iraqi Dispute [*sic*] on the Shatt al-Arab Waterway." *International Journal of Political Science* (Tehran) 1, no. 2 (Summer and Fall, 2011), pp. 21–35.

al-Zayani, Rashid Abdul Rahman. *Memories and History*. Manama: Al Ayam Press, 1999.

Books and Articles (Arabic)

'Abd al-Rahim, 'Abd al-Rahim 'Abd al-Rahman. *Al-Khalij al-'Arabi: Ru'ya fi al-Waqi'al-Iqtisadi wa-l-Ijtima'i wa-l-Thaqafi: Marhalat ma qabla al-Bitrul, 1900–1930*. Cairo: Dar al-Kitab al-Jami'i, 1994.

'Abd al-Rahman 'Abdullah al-Najahi, "al-'Alaqat al-Siyasiyya bayn Hakim al-Bahrayn al-Shaykh 'Isa bin 'Ali Al Khalifa wa-al-Sulata al-Baritaniyya." *Al-Watheeqa*, no. 65 (August 2014), pp. 30–91.

'Ali Akbar Bushehri, "al-Ayam al-Bahrayniyya: al-Wajih al-Mohsin Mustafa bin 'Abd al-Latif al-'Abbasi, 1383–1307/1890–1964, *al-Ayam* (Manama), 2 *Ramadan* 1432 (August 2, 2011), www.alayam.com/News/sevendays/Islamic/5212 (accessed September 15, 2014).

'Ali Akbar Bushehri, "'Amid al-'A'ila Shaykh al-'Ajam 'Ali Kazem Bushehri," *Tarikh Mamlakat al-Bahrayn*, October 23, 2012, http://bahrain.svalu.com/1033.html (accessed February 18, 2013).

al-'Aydarus, Muhammad Hasan. *Al-Juzur al-'Arabiyya wa-l-ihtilal al-Irani namudhaj lil-'alaqat al-'Arabiyya al-Iraniyya: Dirasa Watha'iqiyya Arshifiyya.* 2 vols. Dubai: Dar al-'Aydarus lil-Kitab al-Hadith, 2002.

Tarikh al-Khalij al-'Arabi al-Hadith wa-l-Mu'asir. Cairo: 'Ayn lil-Dirasat wa-l-Buhuth al-Insaniyya wa-l-Ijtima'iyya, 1996.

al-'Azami, Walid Hamdi. *Al-Niza 'bayna Dawlat al-Imarat al-'Arabiyya wa-Iran hawla Juzur Abu Musa wa-Tunb al-Kubra wa-l-Sughra fi al-Watha'iq al-Baritaniyya, 1764–1971.* London: Dar al-Hikma, 1993.

Dashti, Muhammad Isma'il. *Shaqa'iq al-Nu'man fi Tarikh al-Khalij wa-l-Kuwayt wa-Iran wa-l-Imarat wa-l-Jazirah al-'Arabiyya wa 'Uman.* Damascus: Dar al-Mahabba, 2005.

Ibrahim, 'Abd al-'Aziz, 'Abd al-Ghani. *Al-Salam al-Baritani fi al-Khalij al-'Arabi, 1899–1947.* Riyadh: Dar al-Marikh li-l-Nashr, 1981.

Hukumat al-Hind al-Baritaniyya wa-l-Idara fi al-Khalij al-'Arabi: Dirasa Watha'iqiyya. Riyadh: Matbu'at Darat al-Malik 'Abd al-'Aziz, 1981.

Al Khalifa, Mai bint Mohammed. *Mi'at 'Am min al-Ta'lim al-Nizami fi al-Bahrayn: al-Sanawat al-Ula lil-Ta'sis.* Beruit: al-Mu'assasa al-'Arabiyya li-l-Dirasat wal-Nashr, 1999.

al-Khatiri, Hamad. *Awthaq al-Ma'ayyir fi Nasab Bani Yas wa-l-Manasir.* Abu Dhabi: Wizarat Shu'un al-Ri'asa, Markaz al-Watha'iq wa-al-Buhuth, 2007.

al-Khayri, Nasr ibn Jawhar ibn Mubarak. *Qala'id al-nahrayn fi tarikh al-Bahrayn*, ed. 'Abd al-Rahman ibn 'Abdullah al-Shuqayr. Manama: al-Ayyam lil-Nashr, 2003 [ca. 1920s].

Mudayris, Falah, 'Abdullah. *Al-Harakat wa-l-Jama'at al-Siyasiyya fi al-Bahrayn, 1938–2002.* Beruit: Dar al-Kunuz al-Adabiyya, 2004.

al-Qahtani. 'Abd al-Qadir Hammud 'Abd al-'Aziz. *Dirasat fi Tarikh al-Khalij al-'Arabi al-Hadith wa-l-Mu'asir.* Doha: al-Majlis al-Watani li-l-Thaqafa wa-l-Funun wa-l-Turath, Idarat al-Thaqafah wa-l-Funun, Qism al-Dirasat wa-l-Buhuth, 2008.

Qasim, Jamal Zakariyya. *Tarikh al-Khalij al-'Arabi al-Hadith wa-l-Mu'asir.* Madinat Nasr: Dar al-Fikr al-'Arabi, 1997.

Al-Khalij al-'Arabi: Dirasa li-Tarikh al-Imarat al-'Arabiyya, 1914–1945. Cairo: Dar al-Fikr al-'Arabi, 1973.

al-Rihani, Amin Faris. *Rihalat fi al-Bilad al-'Arabiyya Muzayyanat bi-Rusum wa-Hara'it wa-Fihrist A'lam.* Beruit: Dar al-Rihani li-l-Tiba'at wa-l-Nasr, 1968.

Sayf, 'Abdullah. *al-Ma'tam fi al-Bahrayn.* 2 vols. Manama: al-Matba'a al-Sharqiyya, 1995.

al-Wahidi, Husayn ibn 'Ali. *Tarikh Linjah: al-Lu'lu'a al-'Arabiyya 'ala al-Sahil al-Sharqi li-l-Khalij.* Dar al-Umma li-l-Nashr wa-l-Tawzi', 1985.

al-Wasmi, Khalid Nasr. *Tarikh al-Khalij al-'Arabi fi al-'Asr al-Hadith wa-l-Mu'asir: Dirasa 'an al-Tanafus al-Urubbi fi al-Khalij al-'Arabi wa-l-'Alaqat al-Urubbiyya al-'Umaniyya.* Kuwait: Dar Qirtas li-l-Nashr, 2006.

Books and Articles (Persian)

Bayandor, Gholam 'Ali. *Khalij-e Fars.* Khorramshahr, 1317 (1938); Repr.: Bonyad-e Mowufat-e Doktor Mahmud Afshar, 1388 (2009).

Bayrami, Samaneh. "Chalesh-e Iran va Engelestan bar sar-e Hakemiyyat bar Bahreyn." *Faslnameh-ye Motala'at-e Tarikhi* 8, no. 33 (Summer 1390/2011), pp. 128–165.

Behbudi, Hedayatollah, ed. *Ruzshumar-e Tarikh-e Mu'asir-e Iran.* 2 vols. Tehran: Mu'assaseh-ye Motala'at va Pezhuheshha-ye Siyasi, 1385–1388 (2006–2010).

Behzadi, 'Ali. *Shebh-e Khaterat.* Tehran: Negarestan-e Ketab, 1375 (1996).

Farahmand, 'Ali. "Engelis va Parvazha-ye Iran-zedayi az Khalij-e Fars." *Tarikh-e Ravabet-e Khareji*, no. 22 (Spring 1384/2005), pp. 160–231.

"Naqdi bar Tarikhi Tahrikat-e Engelis va Edde'aha-ye barkhi 'Arab dar Khalij-e Fars, 1313." *Tarikh-e Ravabet-e Khareji*, no. 24, 25 (Fall/Winter 1384/2005), pp. 137–170.

Faramarzi, Ahmad. *Jazireh-ye Khark.* Tehran: Ibn Sina, 1347 (1968).

Karim Khan-e Zand va Khalij-e Fars. Tehran: Chap Davar, 1346 (1967).

Rah-ahan-e Orupa va Khalij-e Fars. Tehran: Ibn Sina, 1346 (1967).

Janab, Mohammad 'Ali. *Khalij-e Fars, Nofuz-e Biganagan va Ruydadha-ye Siyasi, 1875–1900.* Tehran: Pezhuheshgah-e 'Ulum-e Insani, 2536 (1977).

Jalalpur, Shohreh, and Shiva Jalalpur. "Engelestan va Jodayi-ye Bahreyn az Iran."*Faslnameh-ye Motala'at-e Tarikhi* 8, no. 33 (Summer 1390/2011), pp. 195–208.

Khosravi, Abuzar, and 'Ali Akbar Mardani. "Este'amar-e Engelis va Jodayi-ye Bahreyn az Iran."*Faslnameh-ye Motala'at-e Tarikhi* 8, no. 33 (Summer 1390/2011), pp. 168–193.

Logha'i, Azita. "Bahreyn dar Matbu'at-e Mashrutah (1322–1325)"*Faslnameh-ye Motala'at-e Tarikhi* 8, no. 33 (Summer 1390/2011), pp. 79–89.

Makki, Hossein. *Tarikh-e Bist Saleh-ye Iran.* 8 vols. Tehran: Sepehr, 1357 (1978).

Malikzad, 'Ali. *Ketab-e Joghrafiya-ye Tabi'i va Tarikh-e Siyasi-ye Khalij-e Fars.* Tehran, 1333 (1954).

Mojtahed-Zadeh, Pirouz. *Joghrafiya-ye Tarikhi-ye Khalij-e Fars: Nam-e Khalij-e Fars dar Tul-e Tarikh.* Tehran: Sayeh-e Rawshan, 1383 (2004).

Sheykh-neshenha-ye Khalij-e Fars. Tehran: Motala'at Matbu'at-e 'Ata'i 1349 (1970).

Nash'at, Sadeq. *Tarikh-e Siyasi-ye Khalij-e Fars*. Tehran: Kanun-e Ketab, 1344 (1965).

Qajar, Mohammad 'Ali Bahmani. "Naqsh-e Niru-ye Daryayi va Bayandor dar Ekhraj-e Engelisha az Hengam va Basa'idu." *Faslnameh-ye Motala'at-e Tarikhi* 7, no. 27 (Winter 1388/2009), pp. 71–111.

Tamamiyat-e Arzi-ye Iran: Sayri dar Tarikh-e Marzha-ye Iran. Tehran: Mu'assasah-ye Motala'at va Pezhuheshha-ye Siyasi, 1390 (2001).

Qalam, 'Ali Zarrin. *Sarzamin-e Bahreyn: Az Dowran-e Bastan ta Emruz*. Tehran: Ketabfurushi-ye Sirus, 1337 (1958).

Rumi, Cyrus. *Shenasnameh-ye Matbu'at-e Fars: Az Aghaz ta Emruz*. Shiraz: Entesharat-e Navid, 1323 (2009).

Sadid al-Saltaneh, Mohammad 'Ali. *Tarikh-e Masqat va 'Uman, Bahreyn va Qatar va Ravabet-e anha ba Iran*. Tehran: Dunya-ye Ketab, 1370 (1991).

Bandar 'Abbas va Khalij-e Fars. Tehran: Dunya-ye Ketab, 1363 (1984).

Soleimani, Karim and Michael VahidiRad. "Muzakarat-e naft-e Iran va Engelis va Tajdid-e Nazar dar Qarardad Darsi dar Dowreh-ye Riza Shah." *Tarikh-e Iran* 64, no. 5 (Spring 1389/2010), pp. 82–100.

Valdani, Asghar Ja'fari. *Negahi Tarikhi bih Jazayer-e Irani-ye Tunb va Abu Musa*. Tehran: Entesharat-e Vezarat-e Umur-e Kharejeh, 1376 (1997).

Zamani, Mohsen Ganjbakhsh. "Piruzi-ye Iran bar Engelis dar Nabard-e Basa'idu."*Tarikh-e Ravabet-e Khareji*, no. 22 (Spring 1384/2005), pp. 237–276.

Index

Lightning Source UK Ltd.
Milton Keynes UK
UKHW020402020622
403867UK00009B/90

9 781108 733410